THE JEW IN THE MEDIEVAL WORLD

Saml F. Roth

1989

THE JEW IN THE MEDIEVAL WORLD

A Source Book: 315-1791

Jacob R. Marcus

A TEMPLE BOOK

ATHENEUM, NEW YORK, 1983

To Nettie

The original publication of this book was made possible by
The National Federation of Temple Sisterhoods

Published by Atheneum
Reprinted by arrangement with
The Jewish Publication Society of America
Copyright 1938 by Union of American Hebrew Congregations
All rights reserved
Library of Congress catalog card number 60-8666
ISBN 0-689-70133-0
Manufactured by Halliday Lithograph Corporation,
West Hanover and Plympton, Massachusetts
Published in Canada by McClelland and Stewart, Ltd.
First Atheneum Printing August 1969
Second Printing January 1972
Third Printing September 1972
Fourth Printing February 1973
Fifth Printing February 1974
Sixth Printing November 1975
Seventh Printing September 1977
Eighth Printing September 1978
Ninth Printing November 1979
Tenth Printing March 1981
Eleventh Printing August 1983

Table of Contents

Contents

SECTION III
JEWRY AND THE INDIVIDUAL JEW
A. JEWISH SELF-GOVERNMENT

Contents · ix

B. Jewish Sects, Mystics, and Messiahs

C. JEWISH NOTABLES

Contents

D. The Inner Life of the Jew

Preface

THIS source book attempts to reflect the life of the medieval Jew as seen through the eyes of contemporaries. The documents and historical narratives given here have been selected with the view of allowing the actors and witnesses of events—that is, the historical facts—to speak for themselves.

The author of this work has not set out with any conscious, apologetic motive. His sole interest is to give in translation material which will reflect conditions as they actually were. Anti-Jewish legislation, narratives, and memoirs are printed here without any attempt to "edit" them: they are reproduced as written because they portray faithfully the anti-Jewish sentiment which was so characteristic of a large group of non-Jews at the time of their composition. When, however, there is a fear that the unsuspecting reader might accept as authentic history naive and fabulous stories of ritual murder, host desecrations, and the like, the necessary notes for clarification have been added.

Just what centuries ought to be included in the concept "medieval Jewry" is not easy to determine. The medieval age in general history is not altogether synchronous with the medieval age in Jewish history. The medieval epoch in Jewish life is much more extensive at both ends. It may be said to begin about 315 when Constantine the Great, under the influence of Christian religious totalitarianism, began to enact against the Jews disabling laws which ultimately reduced them to the status of second-class citizens. Throughout the centuries that followed, the Jew enjoyed (or suffered under) a type of legislation, voluntarily chosen or imposed by the state, which differed from the legislation for the dominant Christian or Moslem masses.

The Jews were never more than a tolerated group even when accorded exceptionally favorable privileges, and they were nearly always cordially disliked. Thus, in general, it is safe to say that large patches of the medieval period were characterized by political and social disabilities. Not all the disabilities were necessarily destructive —if they had been the Jews would not have survived.

The medieval age comes to an end for Western Jewry with the proclamation of political and civil emancipation in France in September, 1791. The rise of the democratic state meant the abrogation of special class and group legislation and the promulgation of one organic statute under which all inhabitants of a state were to live. With the rise of the democratic state, religion or "race" was no bar to citizenship; there was one law for all people.

This process of emancipation began in France in 1791 and accordingly in our sources we have not gone beyond the eighteenth century. One might argue that this terminus is arbitrary, that the majority of the Jews lived in Eastern Europe and that medieval legislation and life prevailed there till after the World War. That is true, but our plea is that we have decided to stop at the first real manifestation of the modern age, and that there is nothing typical of nineteenth century Russian czaristic medievalism that is not already described in the sources from 315 to 1791.

It might also be argued with some justice that even in Central Europe, medievalism is still continuous as reflected in the legislation of the National Socialist regime in Germany. However, it has not yet been determined whether the changes in Germany are to be permanent or whether they are merely episodic; whether they are merely atavistic, the last resurgent effort of a dying medievalism, or whether they are the precursors of some new and different world order. The fact is that the great western world powers that have been associated with liberalism, democracy, and "modernism" still maintain themselves and have definitely ended the exceptional status of the Jews. For the present at least we prefer to end the medieval age with 1791.

This work is an attempt at a source book of Jewish *history*. It makes no attempt to treat of *literature* as such. Yet, inasmuch as all sources of Jewish origin are, by a liberal definition, literature *per se*, there is practically no phase of Jewish literature that is not reflected in this book. A brief turning of the pages will disclose historical narratives, codes, legal opinions, martyrologies, memoirs, polemics, epitaphs, advertisements, folk-tales, ethical and pedagogical writings, book prefaces and colophons, commentaries, communal statutes, and the like.

The problem of what to select has been difficult. There have been other source books and anthologies before this—most of them in German and in Hebrew—and the writer has found them helpful and has been grateful for their guidance. With very few exceptions, however, their interests have been almost exclusively literary. Their reliability, too, may be questioned by virtue of the fact that they frequently overlook the primary sources and quote instead secondary or tertiary sources. Many of these older source books were apologetic in motivation, lacked adequate introductions and notes, and were not so organized in their arrangement of the material as to give a systematic concept of medieval life and legislation. Documents of purely historical import are seldom found.

The difficulties of selection become more obvious when it is realized that there are at least fifteen centuries of medieval Jewish life, that in this work alone sources are translated from over a dozen languages and dialects, and that the lands treated extend from the Dutch Colony of New Amsterdam (New York) to the borders of China.

Accordingly, the principles that have motivated the selections have been those of importance, interest, clarity, and diversification. It has been attempted, within the compass of a fair-sized volume, to omit nothing of prime importance. We are not sure that we have always succeeded. Nothing is said, for instance, of Rabbenu Gershom, one of the great figures of early central European Jewish life. But this is due to the fact that our sources often fail us and that we have only scattered references and doubtful texts relating to great men and important events: material that cannot be used in a source book.

On the other hand there is no dearth of stories, and very interesting ones, too, dealing with the persecutions of the Jew. Here we have an embarrassment of riches. No attempt, therefore, has been made to exhaust the material dealing with the persecutions and expulsions of the Jews of England, France, Austria, Portugal, Lithuania, etc. No attempt has been made to exhaust the records of the crusades. We wish to emphasize: a source book is not a martyrology. We have selected only those accounts of brutal mistreatment and expulsion which are of prime importance, typical, and, we hope, interesting in some degree.

We have at times preferred the account of a witness or of a contemporary to that of the chief agent. In our opinion the reasoned, cautious account by Joseph Ha-Kohen of the activities of Reubeni, the sixteenth century Messianic adventurer, is superior, in its compactness and objectivity, to the diary of Reubeni himself. We have found the anonymous description of the Spanish expulsion in 1492 by a contemporary Italian Jew more informative than the dry, matter-of-fact official decree of expulsion.

It will be noticed that there is a preponderance of material dealing with the later Jewish Middle Ages, the sixteenth through the eighteenth centuries, and particularly with the central European area. The reason for this stress on the last few centuries is that many sources for the earlier centuries have been lost or destroyed; the invention

of printing in the fifteen century, however, has served to increase
and to preserve our records, and the spirit of individualism and
classicism that came in with the Renaissance has tended to stimulate
the writing of historical narratives and personal memoirs. The emphasis on German Jewish materials is for two reasons. In the first
place Germany is one of the few countries with a continuous stream
of Jewish history since at least the tenth century. The second and
more important reason is that general and Jewish historical science
reached its highest development in nineteenth century Germany in
a vast library of primary sources and explanatory literature. There
is a wealth of Jewish historical materials in the German lands and
we have accordingly availed ourselves of them liberally, as long as
they were fairly typical of Jewish life.

The material we have selected is divided into three main sections.
A glance through the Table of Contents will at once reveal the
character of its organization. The first section deals with the relation of the State to the Jew and reflects the civil and political status
of the Jew in the medieval world. The second section treats of the
profound influence exerted by the Church—both Catholic and
Protestant—on Jewish life and well-being. It is obvious that this
"separation" of Church and State is bound to be arbitrary. For
instance, the anti-Jewish legislation of the Visigothic kings is as
much ecclesiastical as it is regal; the attitude of the Mayence archbishop during the Crusade of 1096 is as much political as it is clerical,
for the archbishop was both the civil and the religious head of the
city. Within the topical divisions, the materials are presented in
chronological sequence.

The third and final section is devoted to a study of the Jew "at
home." This general section is composed of a series of four sub-
divisions which treat of the life of the Jew in its various aspects.
The first subdivision, "Jewish Self-Government," attempts through
codes, communal statutes, and the like to give some idea of the
autonomy which medieval Jewry enjoyed in all parts of Europe
till the dawn of emancipation. The second group of sources, "Jewish
Sects, Mystics, and Messiahs," describes the various schisms and
heresies throughout the ages, and particularly the pseudo-Messiahs
who have played so important a part in rousing the nationalist and
political hopes of the unhappy masses. The third group, "Jewish
Notables," is a collection of materials throwing light on the achieve-
ments or struggles of a group of men—and some women, too—
notable for the part they have played in Jewish life. The final group,
"The Inner Life of the Jew," is an effort to portray the Jew in

almost every type of social, cultural, political, and economic activity.

No attempt has been made to devote a special section to Jewish economic life as such. Business contracts, receipts, inventories, and the like, though important, are as a rule equally boring. Yet no effort has been spared to select materials which will adequately reflect the economic interests and problems of the medieval Jew. It is no exaggeration to say that practically every selection in this book throws some light on the business life of the Jew so that even he who runs may read. A glance at the caption "Economic Life" in the Index will show the wealth of material on this subject.

One of the basic problems of a source book such as this is to insure clarity and understanding, no mean task, for the medieval world was in many of its institutions and its ideals totally different from ours. The average reader—and this includes the Jew as well as the non-Jew—has a double problem when he undertakes to understand or penetrate within the ambit of a cultural epoch that was both medieval and Jewish. To illuminate the obscurities the author has prefaced each item with a detailed introduction. In addition many notes have been inserted within the text in the hope of resolving difficulties. Phrases or sentences in parentheses ( ) are by the original writer of the source; materials in square brackets [ ] are insertions by the editor. It is hoped that they will not prove disconcerting.

The author has attempted, as far as it was possible for him, to make his translations from the original sources and from the best editions. Wherever translations already existed, these have been employed unless incorrect or too paraphrastic. Occasionally, too, even though translations have been adopted that were based on earlier texts, the author has checked and corrected the translations to accord with later, more critical editions. In his own translations the author has leaned to the side of literalness with the hope of thus giving the reader some concept of the medieval idiom.

No unjustified liberties have been taken with the original texts. Obvious errors have, of course, been corrected; recurrent pious phrases and honorific titles such as "of blessed memory" and "rabbi" have frequently been omitted. The punctuation and paragraphing have been supplemented and modernized, and archaic spellings have at times been changed. The spellings and transliterations from the Hebrew have been adopted, with exceptions, from the *Jewish Encyclopedia*. Arabic and other Oriental transliterations follow, in large part, the *Encyclopaedia of Islam*. Diacritical marks have been omitted. The attempt has been made to secure uniformity in spell-

ing, not always as easy as it may seem. A rather prominent American
Jewish merchant of the colonial period, whom we mention, is known
as Isaac Elizer, Eliezur, and Elizur, and all three spellings are authenticated. Manasseh ben Israel is a common spelling of the name
of the famous Dutch Jewish scholar and publicist, but he himself
signs his name: Menasseh. Biblical quotations as a rule are cited from
the translation of the Jewish Publication Society.

It would defeat the purpose of this book to translate completely,
for example, Frederick the Great's general-patent for Prussian Jewry
('1750'), a ponderous charter of about fifteen thousand words. Many
documents, therefore, because of their size are quoted in extract
only. All omissions are indicated by four dots (. . . .). Detailed
references to the sources may be found at the back of the book.
No attempt has been made to list the monographs or literature consulted for use in the introductions and notes. The relevant literature
is known to the research historian; others are probably not interested
in such detail.

There now remains to the author the pleasant task of expressing
his appreciation to all who have helped in the preparation of this
work. A page of acknowledgments to those publishers and authors
who have graciously permitted the use of their translations is appended.

To the Librarians of the Hebrew Union College, the University
of Cincinnati, the Jewish Theological Seminary, and the Jewish
Division of the New York Public Library, the writer expresses his
thanks for their unfailing courtesy in supplying him with the many
works he found it necessary to consult. Dr. William Rosenau of
Baltimore has been kind enough to read the manuscript and to give
the author the benefit of his suggestions. Dr. Jacob Menkes of New
York has been most helpful, especially in matters touching on the
history of the Polish Jews. Thanks are also due to Dr. Emanuel
Gamoran, Educational Director of the Commission on Jewish Education, for his valued advice and constant interest in the preparation
of this work.

My dear teacher and colleague, Dr. Jacob Z. Lauterbach, Professor Emeritus of Talmud and Rabbinics at the Hebrew Union College, has been most gracious in always putting at my service his
great knowledge of rabbinic literature and his fine critical mind;
Dr. Sol B. Finesinger, Professor of Talmud at the Hebrew Union
College, has given most generously of his time in checking much of
my work. To both of these men, my dear friends, who have been
most helpful I wish to express my sincerest thanks.

Finally the author wishes to express his deepest gratitude to Mr. Samuel Sandmel whose work in the correction of the manuscript and whose loyal assistance in every possible way made him an invaluable companion in the preparation of this work. I also wish to express my gratitude to Morton A. Bauman for the personal interest he has manifested in the preparation of the typescript.

Jacob R. Marcus

Cincinnati, Ohio
October, 1937

A NOTE ON THE

Bibliographies

THE purpose of the bibliographies which follow almost every item is to refer the reader to standard textbooks and to suggest literature and additional sources for the more advanced students. No attempt has been made to supply a bibliographical apparatus for the scholar or the research worker. A historian trained in Jewish history does not need such an apparatus. The historian, however, who has no Jewish background but is interested in furthering his knowledge of Jewish history is advised to consult the *Jewish Encyclopedia*, the *Jüdisches Lexikon*, and the *Encyclopaedia Judaica*. Such a historian will also find useful Cecil Roth's systematic bibliography on "The Jews in the Middle Ages," in the *Cambridge Medieval History*, VII, 937–947. For the later Jewish Middle Ages the student's attention is directed to Jacob R. Marcus' *Brief Introduction to the Bibliography of Modern Jewish History*, Hebrew Union College, 1935 (mimeographed), which covers the period from 1650 to 1935.

Because this source-book is not intended primarily for research men, no foreign literature has been given in spite of the fact that many, if not most, of the basic monographs in the field of Jewish history are in German, Hebrew, French, etc.

Three textbooks are constantly referred to: I. Elbogen, *History of the Jews* (Elbogen); C. Roth, *A Bird's-Eye View of Jewish History* (Roth); and A. L. Sachar, *A History of the Jews* (Sachar). Elbogen's *History* is a brief but sound work by the eminent Jewish historian. Roth's *Bird's-Eye View* attempts to cover the entire range of Hebrew and Jewish history in less than 400 pages; the book is readable, sound, but almost too brief in spots. Sachar's book is popular, but well-rounded and well-proportioned, and probably the most useful one-volume work for the average reader.

Among the readings for advanced students three works are constantly cited: H. Graetz, *History of the Jews*, 6 vols. (Graetz); H. Graetz, *Popular History of the Jews*, 5 vols., translated by A. B. Rhine (Graetz-Rhine); and M. L. Margolis and A. Marx, *A History of the Jewish People* (Margolis and Marx).

Graetz's *History of the Jews* is the standard general Jewish history. It is an abbreviated translation made from an early German edition. Though somewhat antiquated and frequently biased, it will always remain the classic work, distinguished by scholarship of a high calibre.

Graetz's *Popular History of the Jews* is a summary of the material in the larger *History of the Jews*. It was translated by A. B. Rhine and augmented with material on the East European Jews not found in the original Graetz works. In this respect the *Popular History of the Jews* is superior to the *History of the Jews*.

The Margolis and Marx *History of the Jewish People* is the best one-volume history of the Jews in any language. It is really an encyclopedic reference work, painstakingly accurate, and always useful.

Works and source-materials which do not concern themselves directly with Jewish history are rarely quoted. Students who wish information about this literature are referred to *A Guide to Historical Literature,* by Allison, Fay, Shearer, and Shipman, and to similar European works.

ABBREVIATIONS

d.	died
JE	*Jewish Encyclopedia*
JQR	*Jewish Quarterly Review*
MGWJ	*Monatschrift für Geschichte und Wissenschaft des Judentums*
N.S.	new series
O.S.	old series
REJ	*Revue des études juives*
ZGJD	*Zeitschrift für die Geschichte der Juden in Deutschland*

SECTION I
The State and the Jew

1.

Jews and the Later Roman Law
315–531

THE Middle Ages, for the Jew at least, begin with the advent to power of Constantine the Great (306–337). He was the first Roman emperor to issue laws which radically limited the rights of Jews as citizens of the Roman Empire, a privilege conferred upon them by Caracalla in 212. As Christianity grew in power in the Roman Empire it influenced the emperors to limit further the civil and political rights of the Jews. Most of the imperial laws that deal with the Jews since the days of Constantine are found in the Latin *Codex Theodosianus* (438) and in the Latin and Greek code of Justinian (534). Both of these monumental works are therefore very important, for they enable us to trace the history of the progressive deterioration of Jewish rights.

The real significance of Roman law for the Jew and his history is that it exerted a profound influence on subsequent Christian and even Moslem legislation. The second-class status of citizenship of the Jew, as crystallized in the Justinian code, was thus entrenched in the medieval world, and under the influence of the Church the disabilities imposed upon him received religious sanction and relegated him even to lower levels.

In our first selection—laws of Constantine the Great—Judaism is denied the opportunity of remaining a missionary religion because of the prohibition to make proselytes.

The laws of Constantius (337–361), the second selection, forbid intermarriage between Jewish men and Christian women. A generation later, in 388, all marriages between Jews and Christians were forbidden. Constantius also did away with the right of Jews to possess slaves. This prohibition to trade in and to keep slaves at a time when slave labor was common was not merely an attempt to arrest conversion to Judaism; it was also a blow at the economic life of the Jew. It put him at a disadvantage with his Christian competitor to whom this economic privilege was assured.

The third selection, a law of Theodosius II (408–450), prohibits Jews from holding any advantageous office of honor in the Roman state. They were compelled, however, to assume those public of-

3

fices which entailed huge financial losses and almost certain ruin, and they were not even granted the hope of an ultimate exemption. This *Novella* (New Law) *III* of Theodosius II also makes a direct attack on the Jewish religion by reenacting a law which forbade the building of new Jewish synagogues. This prohibition was known a generation before this. It was reenacted now, probably to pacify the aroused Christian mob in the Eastern Empire which desired to crush the religious spirit of the Jews who were massing at Jerusalem and confidently looking forward to the coming of a Messianic redeemer in 440. This disability, later taken over by some Moslem states, was reenunciated by the Church which sought to arrest the progress of Judaism, its old rival.

A Latin law of Justinian (527–565), the final selection, does not allow a Jew to bear witness in court against an orthodox Christian. Thus as early as the sixth century the Jews were already laboring under social, economic, civil, political, and religious disabilities.

I. Laws of Constantine the Great, October 18, 315—CONCERNING JEWS, HEAVEN-WORSHIPPERS,* AND SAMARITANS

❧We wish to make it known to the Jews and their elders and their patriarchs that if, after the enactment of this law, any one of them dares to attack with stones or some other manifestation of anger another who has fled their dangerous sect and attached himself to the worship of God [Christianity], he must speedily be given to the flames and burnt together with all his accomplices.

Moreover, if any one of the population should join their abominable sect and attend their meetings, he will bear with them the deserved penalties.

II. Laws of Constantius, August 13, 339—CONCERNING JEWS, HEAVEN-WORSHIPPERS, AND SAMARITANS

❧This pertains to women, who live in our weaving factories and whom Jews, in their foulness, take in marriage. It is decreed that these women are to be restored to the weaving factories. [Marriages between Jews and Christian women of the imperial weaving factory are to be dissolved.]

This prohibition [of intermarriage] is to be preserved for the future lest the Jews induce Christian women to share their shame-

---

* Heaven-Worshippers were a sect closely allied to Judaism.

ful lives. If they do this they will subject themselves to a sentence of death. [The Jewish husbands are to be punished with death.]

A JEW SHALL NOT POSSESS A CHRISTIAN SLAVE

If any one among the Jews has purchased a slave of another sect or nation, that slave shall at once be appropriated for the imperial treasury.

If, indeed, he shall have circumcised the slave whom he has purchased, he will not only be fined for the damage done to that slave but he will also receive capital punishment.

If, indeed, a Jew does not hesitate to purchase slaves—those who are members of the faith that is worthy of respect [Christianity]—then all these slaves who are found in his possession shall at once be removed. No delay shall be occasioned, but he is to be deprived of the possession of those men who are Christians.

III. *A Law of Theodosius II, January 31, 439*—NOVELLA III: CONCERNING JEWS, SAMARITANS, HERETICS, AND PAGANS

⟨Wherefore, although according to an old saying [of the Greek Hippocrates, the "father" of medicine] "no cure is to be applied in desperate sicknesses," nevertheless, in order that these dangerous sects which are unmindful of our times may not spread into life the more freely, in indiscriminate disorder as it were, we ordain by this law to be valid for all time:

No Jew—or no Samaritan who subscribes to neither [the Jewish nor the Christian] religion—shall obtain offices and dignities; to none shall the administration of city service be permitted; nor shall any one exercise the office of a defender [that is, overseer] of the city. Indeed, we believe it sinful that the enemies of the heavenly majesty and of the Roman laws should become the executors of our laws—the administration of which they have slyly obtained—and that they, fortified by the authority of the acquired rank, should have the power to judge or decide as they wish against Christians, yes, frequently even over bishops of our holy religion themselves, and thus, as it were, insult our faith.

Moreover, for the same reason, we forbid that any synagogue shall rise as a new building. [Fewer synagogues meant less chance of Christians becoming Jews.] However, the propping up of old synagogues which are now threatened with imminent ruin is permitted. To these things we add that he who misleads a slave or a freeman against his will or by punishable advice, from the service of the Christian religion to that of an abominable sect and ritual, is to be punished by loss of property and life. [That is, the Jew who converts any one to Judaism loses life and property.]

On the one hand, whoever has built a synagogue must realize that he has worked to the advantage of the Catholic church [which will confiscate the building]; on the other hand, whoever has already secured the badge of office shall not hold the dignities he has acquired. On the contrary, he who worms himself into office must remain, as before, in the lowest rank even though he will have already earned an honorary office. And as for him who begins the building of a synagogue and is not moved by the desire of repairing it, he shall be punished by a fine of fifty pounds gold for his daring. Moreover, if he will have prevailed with his evil teachings over the faith of another, he shall see his wealth confiscated and himself soon subjected to a death sentence.

And since it behooves the imperial majesty to consider everything with such foresight that the general welfare does not suffer in the least, we ordain that the tax-paying officeholders of all towns as well as the provincial civil servants—who are obligated to employ their wealth and to make public gifts as part of their burdensome and diverse official and military duties—shall remain in their own classes, no matter what sect they belong to. Let it not appear as if we have accorded the benefit of exemption to those men, detestable in their insolent maneuvering, whom we wish to condemn by the authority of this law. [Jews have to accept financially ruinous public offices without hope of exemption.]

This further limitation is to be observed, namely, that these public servants from these above mentioned sects shall never, as far as private affairs are concerned, carry out judicial sentences, nor be wardens of the jail. This is done in order that Christians, as it sometimes happens, may not be hidden away and suffer a double imprisonment through the hatred of the guards. [Imprisonment is bad enough without having a Jewish jailer.] And furthermore it may be doubted that they have been justly imprisoned.

IV. *A Law of Justinian, July 28, 531*—CONCERNING HERETICS AND
      MANICHAEANS AND SAMARITANS

ℭSince many judges, in deciding cases, have addressed us in need of our decision, asking that they be informed what ought to be done with witnesses who are heretics, whether their testimony ought to be received or rejected, we therefore ordain that no heretic, nor even they who cherish the Jewish superstition, may offer testimony against orthodox Christians who are engaged in litigation, whether one or the other of the parties is an orthodox Christian. [But a Jew may offer testimony on behalf of an orthodox Christian against some one who is not orthodox.]

BIBLIOGRAPHY

REFERENCES TO TEXTBOOKS

Elbogen, pp. 14–18; Roth, pp. 140–148.
Golub, J. S., *Medieval Jewish History*, Sec. I; Sec. III, "The Christian Church."

READINGS FOR ADVANCED STUDENTS

Graetz, II, pp. 559–574, 611–626; III, pp. 10–23; Graetz-Rhine, II, pp. 402–411, 425–437, 458–479; Margolis and Marx, pp. 228–230, 265, 297.
Abbott, G. F., *Israel in Europe*, pp. 41–61. A rather popular work by a publicist.
Milman, H. H., *The History of the Jews*, II, Book xx. Though Milman had no first hand knowledge of Jewish sources, he was at home in the medieval Latin historical literature.
Parkes, J., *The Conflict of the Church and the Synagogue*. The best book in English on the relation of the Christian Church to the Jew in the early Middle Ages.
JE, "Constantine I"; "Diaspora"; "Disabilities"; "Justinian."

ADDITIONAL SOURCE MATERIALS IN ENGLISH

Scott, S. P., *The Civil Code*, XII, pp. 75ff.; XVII, pp. 170, 255.

2.

Julian and the Jews
361–363

CHRISTIANITY was for the first time tolerated by the Roman Emperors in 311. The only serious attempt made to hinder its progress after this time was by the Emperor Julian (361–363) who had left the Christian fold. Although apparently in favor of freedom of religion, he was in reality unjust to the Christians but rather partial to the Jews. In a famous Greek letter to the Jews, (selection one below), he abolished the special taxes paid to the Roman government and sought also to stop the payment of a tax paid by Jews for the support of the Jewish patriarchate in Palestine. In this same letter he also encouraged the rebuilding of Jerusalem and, we may assume, of the Jewish Temple. Had this attempt been successful it would have meant the reestablishment of the Jewish state with its sacrifices, priests, and more important, its Sanhedrin or Senate.

The second selection describes the work of the actual building of the Temple. It is very probable that it was not so much an earthquake, as Church historians say, but the death of Julian in 363 and the coming into power again of a Christian emperor that finally put an end to this project. (Some modern historians believe—without sufficient ground, in our opinion—that the work on the Temple was never even begun, and look upon the account as a fable.) The story of this attempted rebuilding of the Temple is found in the *Ecclesiastical History* written in Greek by Salamanius Hermias Sozomenus about 443–450. Sozomen was a native Palestinian and claimed to have his knowledge from eye-witnesses. He was a conservative Christian without sympathy for the Jews or for Julian.

1. *Julian Proposes to Rebuild Jerusalem, 362–363*—TO THE COMMUNITY OF THE JEWS

❡In times past, by far the most burdensome thing in the yoke of your slavery has been the fact that you were subjected to unauthorized ordinances and had to contribute an untold amount of money to the accounts of the treasury. [Ever since Vespasian, about 72 C.E., the Jews had been paying the Romans special Jewish taxes, like the *Fiscus Judaicus.*] Of this I used to see many instances with my own eyes, and I have learned of more, by finding the records which are preserved against you. Moreover, when a tax was about to be levied on you again I prevented it, and compelled the impiety of such obloquy to cease here; and I threw into the fire the records against you that were stored in my desks; so that it is no longer possible for anyone to aim at you such a reproach of impiety. My brother [cousin] Constantius of honored memory [in whose reign, 337–361, severe laws were enacted against the Jews] was not so much responsible for these wrongs of yours as were the men who used to frequent his table, barbarians in mind, godless in soul. These I seized with my own hands and put them to death by thrusting them into the pit, that not even any memory of their destruction might still linger amongst us.

And since I wish that you should prosper yet more, I have admonished my brother Iulus [Hillel II, d. 365], your most venerable patriarch, that the levy which is said to exist among you [the taxes paid by world Jewry for support of the Palestinian patriarchate] should be prohibited, and that no one is any longer to have the power to oppress the masses of your people by such exactions; so that everywhere, during my reign, you may have security of mind, and in the enjoyment of peace may offer more fervid prayers for my reign to the Most High God, the Creator, who has deigned to crown me with his own immaculate right hand. For it is natural that men who are distracted by any anxiety should be hampered in spirit, and should not have so much confidence in raising their hands to pray; but that those who are in all respects free from care should rejoice with their whole hearts and offer their suppliant prayers on behalf of my imperial office to Mighty God, even to Him who is able to direct my reign to the noblest ends, according to my purpose.

This you ought to do, in order that, when I have successfully concluded the war with Persia, I may rebuild by my own efforts the sacred city of Jerusalem [closed to the Jews since Hadrian, 135 C.E.], which for so many years you have longed to see inhabited, and may bring settlers there, and, together with you, may glorify the Most High God therein.

II. *The Failure To Rebuild the Temple, 363*

❲Though the emperor hated and oppressed the Christians, he manifested benevolence and humanity towards the Jews. He wrote to

the Jewish patriarchs and leaders, as well as to the people, requesting
them to pray for him, and for the prosperity of the empire. In
taking this step he was not actuated, I am convinced, by any respect
for their religion; for he was aware that it is, so to speak, the mother
of the Christian religion, and he knew that both religions rest
upon the authority of the [biblical] patriarchs and the prophets;
but he thought to grieve the Christians by favoring the Jews, who
are their most inveterate enemies. But perhaps he also calculated
upon persuading the Jews to embrace paganism and sacrifices; for
they were only acquainted with the mere letter of Scripture, and
could not, like the Christians and a few of the wisest among the
Hebrews, discern the hidden meaning [the allegorical meaning,
through which the Christians could prove the validity of Christianity from the Old Testament].

Events proved that this was his real motive; for he sent for some
of the chiefs of the race and exhorted them to return to the observance of the laws of Moses and the customs of their fathers. On
their replying that because the Temple in Jerusalem was overturned,
it was neither lawful nor ancestral to do this in another place than
the metropolis out of which they had been cast, he gave them public
money, commanded them to rebuild the Temple, and to practice
the cult similar to that of their ancestors, by sacrificing after the
ancient way. [Sacrifice was permitted by Jewish law only in Jerusalem.] The Jews entered upon the undertaking, without reflecting
that, according to the prediction of the holy prophets, it could not
be accomplished. They sought for the most skillful artisans, collected
materials, cleared the ground, and entered so earnestly upon the
task, that even the women carried heaps of earth, and brought their
necklaces and other female ornaments towards defraying the expense.

The emperor, the other pagans, and all the Jews, regarded every
other undertaking as secondary in importance to this. Although the
pagans were not well-disposed towards the Jews, yet they assisted
them in this enterprise, because they reckoned upon its ultimate
success, and hoped by this means to falsify the prophecies of Christ.
[Since Jesus in the New Testament had prophesied the destruction
of the Temple, its rebuilding would make of him a false prophet.]
Besides this motive, the Jews themselves [relying on the sympathy
of Julian] were impelled by the consideration that the time had
arrived for rebuilding their Temple.

When they had removed the ruins of the former building, they
dug up the ground and cleared away its foundation; it is said that

on the following day when they were about to lay the first foundation, a great earthquake occurred, and by the violent agitation of
the earth, stones were thrown up from the depths, by which those
of the Jews who were engaged in the work were wounded, as likewise those who were merely looking on. The houses and public
porticos, near the site of the Temple, in which they had diverted
themselves, were suddenly thrown down; many were caught
thereby, some perished immediately, others were found half dead
and mutilated of hands or legs, others were injured in other parts
of the body.

When God caused the earthquake to cease, the workmen who
survived again returned to their task, partly because such was the
edict of the emperor, and partly because they were themselves
interested in the undertaking. Men often, in endeavoring to gratify
their own passions, seek what is injurious to them, reject what would
be truly advantageous, and are deluded by the idea that nothing is
really useful except what is agreeable to them. When once led
astray by this error, they are no longer able to act in a manner
conducive to their own interests, or to take warning by the calamities
which are visited upon them. [The Church Father here records his
belief that the Temple could not be rebuilt.]

The Jews, I believe, were just in this state; for, instead of regarding this unexpected earthquake as a manifest indication that God
was opposed to the reerection of their Temple, they proceeded to
recommence the work. But all parties relate that they had scarcely
returned to the undertaking, when fire burst suddenly from the
foundations of the Temple, and consumed several of the workmen.
[J. M. Campbell in the *Scottish Review*, 1900, believed that an ex-
plosion of oil put an end to the work. This sounds fanciful.]

This fact is fearlessly stated, and believed by all; the only discrepancy in the narrative is that some maintain that flame burst from
the interior of the Temple, as the workmen were striving to force
an entrance, while others say that the fire proceeded directly from
the earth. In whichever way the phenomenon might have occurred,
it is equally wonderful.

A more tangible and still more extraordinary miracle ensued;
suddenly the sign of the cross appeared spontaneously on the garments of the persons engaged in the undertaking. These crosses
looked like stars, and appeared the work of art. Many were hence
led to confess that Christ is God, and that the rebuilding of the
Temple was not pleasing to Him; others presented themselves in the
church, were initiated, and besought Christ, with hymns and sup-

plications, to pardon their transgression. If any one does not feel disposed to believe my narrative, let him go and be convinced by those who heard the facts I have related from the eye-witnesses of them, for they are still alive. Let him inquire, also, of the Jews and pagans who left the work in an incomplete state, or who, to speak more accurately, were unable to commence it.

BIBLIOGRAPHY

REFERENCES TO TEXTBOOKS

Elbogen, pp. 14–18; Roth, pp. 140–148.
Golub, J. S., *Medieval Jewish History*, Sec. I; Sec. III, "The Christian Church."

READINGS FOR ADVANCED STUDENTS

Graetz, II, pp. 595–603.
Adler, M., "The Emperor Julian and the Jews," *JQR*, O. S., V (1893), pp. 591–651.
JE, "Julian the Apostate."

ADDITIONAL SOURCE MATERIALS IN ENGLISH

The Ecclesiastical History of Socrates Scholasticus, Book III, chapter XX, in *A Select Library of Nicene and Post-Nicene Fathers of the Christian Church*, Second Series, II, contains an earlier account of the rebuilding of the Temple.

3.

Islam and the Jews
600–1772

THE Pact of Omar is the body of limitations and privileges entered into by treaty between conquering Moslems and conquered non-Mohammedans. We have no special treaty of this sort with the Jews, but we must assume that all conquered peoples, including the Jews, had to subscribe to it. Thus the laws cited below and directed against churches apply to synagogues too. The Pact was probably originated about 637 by Omar I after the conquest of Christian Syria and Palestine. By accretions from established practices and precedents, the Pact was extended; yet despite these additions the whole Pact was ascribed to Omar. There are many variants of the text and scholars deny that the text as it now stands could have come from the pen of Omar I; it is generally assumed that its present form dates from about the ninth century.

The Pact of Omar has served to govern the relations between the Moslems and "the people of the book," such as Jews, Christians, and the like, down to the present day.

In addition to the conditions of the Pact listed below, the Jews, like the Christians, paid a head-tax in return for protection, and for exemption from military service. Jews and Christians were also forbidden to hold government office. This Pact, like much medieval legislation, was honored more in the breach than in the observance. In general, though, the Pact increased in stringency with the centuries and is still in force in such lands as Yemen.

In 1772 a Moslem scholar in Cairo was asked how Jews and Christians should be treated. The answer is found in the second selection, issued four years before the American Declaration of Independence. This answer is not law, but only the opinion of a conservative Moslem. The Pact and the opinion are both in Arabic.

1. Pact of Omar, The Ninth Century (?)

⟪In the name of God, the Merciful, the Compassionate!

This is a writing to Omar from the Christians of such and such a city. When you [Moslems] marched against us [Christians], we

13

a condition or requirement

asked of you protection for ourselves, our posterity, our possessions, and our co-religionists; and we made this stipulation with you, that we will not erect in our city or the suburbs any new monastery, church, cell or hermitage; that we will not repair any of such buildings that may fall into ruins, or renew those that may be situated in the Moslem quarters of the town; that we will not refuse the Moslems entry into our churches either by night or by day; that we will open the gates wide to passengers and travellers; that we will receive any Moslem traveller into our houses and give him food and lodging for three nights; that we will not harbor any spy in our churches or houses, or conceal any enemy of the Moslems. [At least six of these laws were taken over from earlier Christian laws against infidels.]

That we will not teach our children the Koran [some nationalist Arabs feared the infidels would ridicule the Koran; others did not want infidels even to learn the language]; that we will not make a show of the Christian religion nor invite any one to embrace it; that we will not prevent any of our kinsmen from embracing Islam, if they so desire. That we will honor the Moslems and rise up in our assemblies when they wish to take their seats; that we will not imitate them in our dress, either in the cap, turban, sandals, or parting of the hair; that we will not make use of their expressions of speech, nor adopt their surnames [infidels must not use greetings and special phrases employed only by Moslems]; that we will not ride on saddles, or gird on swords, or take to ourselves arms or wear them, or engrave Arabic inscriptions on our rings; that we will not sell wine [forbidden to Moslems]; that we will shave the front of our heads; that we will keep to our own style of dress, wherever we may be; that we will wear girdles round our waists [infidels wore leather or cord girdles; Moslems, cloth and silk].

That we will not display the cross upon our churches or display our crosses or our sacred books in the streets of the Moslems, or in their market-places; that we will strike the clappers in our churches lightly [wooden rattles or bells summoned the people to church or synagogue]; that we will not recite our services in a loud voice when a Moslem is present; that we will not carry palm-branches [on Palm Sunday] or our images in procession in the streets; that at the burial of our dead we will not chant loudly or carry lighted candles in the streets of the Moslems or their market-places; that we will not take any slaves that have already been in the possession of Moslems, nor spy into their houses; and that we will not strike any Moslem.

All this we promise to observe, on behalf of ourselves and our co-religionists, and receive protection from you in exchange; and if we violate any of the conditions of this agreement, then we forfeit your protection and you are at liberty to treat us as enemies and rebels.

II. *The Status of Jews and Christians in Moslem Lands, 1772—*
QUESTION

⟪What do you say, O scholars of Islam, shining luminaries who dispel the darkness (may God lengthen your days!)? What do you say of the innovations introduced by the cursed unbelievers [Jewish and Christian] into Cairo, into the city of al-Muizz [founder of Cairo, 969] which by its splendor in legal and philosophic studies sparkles in the first rank of Moslem cities?

What is your opinion concerning these deplorable innovations which are, moreover, contrary to the Pact of Omar which prescribed the expulsion of the unbelievers from Moslem territory? [This is exaggerated. Omar exiled the infidels only from Arabia.]

Among other changes they have put themselves on a footing of equality with the chiefs, scholars, and nobles, wearing, like them, costly garments of cloth of India, expensive silk and cashmere fabrics, and they imitate them even in the cut of these very garments.

In addition, whether through necessity or otherwise, they ride on saddles which are of the same type as those of chiefs, scholars, and officers, with servants at their right, at their left, and behind them, scattering and pushing back Moslems for whom they thus block the streets.

They carry small batons in their hands just like the chiefs. They buy Moslem slaves, the offspring of negro, Abyssinian, and even white slaves; this has become so common and so frequent among them that they no longer consider this offensive. They even buy slaves publicly, just like the Moslems.

They have become the owners of houses and build new ones of a solidity, durability, and height possessed by neither the houses nor mosques of the Moslems themselves. This state of affairs is spreading and is extending beyond all proportions. They contribute for the extension of their churches and convents; they seek to raise them higher and to give them a strength and a durability which even the mosques and the monasteries themselves do not have.

Christian foreigners, foes who solicit our tolerance, settle in the country for more than a year without submitting themselves thereby to taxation and without renewing their treaties of protection. The women of the tolerated non-Moslem natives liken themselves to our women in that they deck themselves in a garment of black silk and cover their faces with a veil of white muslin with the result that in the streets they are treated with the consideration due only to respectable Moslem women.

Ought one to allow these things to the unbelievers, to the enemies of the faith? Ought one to allow them to dwell among believers under such conditions? Or, indeed, is it not the duty of every Moslem prince and of every magistrate to ask the scholars of the holy law to express their legal opinion, and to call for the advice of wise and enlightened men in order to put an end to these revolting innovations and to these reprehensible acts? Ought one not compel the unbelievers to stick to their pact [of Omar]; ought one not keep them in servitude and prevent them from going beyond the bounds and the limits of their tolerated status in order that there may result from this the greatest glory of God, of His Prophet, and of all Moslems, and likewise of that which is said in the Koran?

Be good enough to give us a precise answer, one based on authentic traditions.

THE ANSWER OF THE SHAIKH HASAN AL KAFRAWI, THE SHAFIITE *

《Praise be to God, the guide of the right way!

The decision given by the Shaikh ar-Ramli [a great Cairo legal authority, d. 1596], by the Shaikh al-Islam [the Moslem religious authority in Constantinople], and by the learned scholars whose decrees can hardly be written down here, may be worded as follows: "It is forbidden to the tolerated peoples living on Moslem territory to clothe themselves in the same manner as the chiefs, the scholars, and the nobles. They should not be allowed to clothe themselves in costly fabrics which have been cut in the modes which are forbidden to them, in order that they may not offend the sensibilities of poor Moslems and in order that their faith in their religion should not be shaken by this. [Poor Moslems may regret their faith when they see how well-dressed the Christians and Jews are.]

"They should not be permitted to employ mounts like the Moslems. They must use neither saddles, nor iron-stirrups, in order to be distinguished from the true believers. They must under no circumstance ride horses because of the noble character of this animal. The Most-High has said [Koran 8:62]: 'And through powerful

* Professor of canon law in Cairo, d. 1788.

squadrons [of horses] through which you will strike terror into your own and God's enemies.' [A verse of the Koran makes a good support for a law. Verses may even be torn out of their context.]

"They should not be permitted to take Moslems into their service because God has glorified the people of Islam. He has given them His aid and has given them a guarantee by these words [Koran 3:140]: 'Surely God will never give preeminence to unbelievers over the true believers.' Now this is just what is happening today, for their servants are Moslems taken from among men of a mature age or from those who are still young. This is one of the greatest scandals to which the guardians of authority must put an end. It is wrong to greet them even with a simple 'how-do-you-do'; to serve them, even for wages, at the baths or in what relates to their riding animals; and it is forbidden to accept anything from their hand, for that would be an act of debasement by the faithful. They are forbidden while going through the streets to ape the manners of the Moslems, and still less those of the emirs of the religion. They shall only walk single-file, and in narrow lanes they must withdraw even more into the most cramped part of the road. degradation

"One may read that which follows in Bukhari and Muslim [religious authorities of the ninth century]: 'Jews and Christians shall never begin a greeting; if you encounter one of them on the road, push him into the narrowest and tightest spot.' The absence of every mark of consideration toward them is obligatory for us; we ought never to give them the place of honor in an assembly when a Moslem is present. This is in order to humble them and to honor the true believers. They should under no circumstances acquire Moslem slaves, white or black. Therefore they should get rid of the slaves which they now have for they have no right to own them. If one of their slaves who was formerly an infidel, becomes a Moslem, he shall be removed from them, and his master, willingly or unwillingly, shall be compelled to sell him and to accept the price for him.

"It is no longer permitted them to put themselves, with respect to their houses, on an equal footing with the dwellings of their Moslem neighbors, and still less to build their buildings higher. If they are of the same height, or higher, it is incumbent upon us to pull them down to a size a little less than the houses of the true believers. This conforms to the word of the Prophet: 'Islam rules, and nothing shall raise itself above it.' This is also in order to hinder them from knowing where our weak spots are and in order to make a distinction between their dwellings and ours.

"They are forbidden to build new churches, chapels, or monasteries in any Moslem land. We should destroy everything that is of new construction in every place, such as Cairo, for instance, founded under the Moslem religion, for it is said in a tradition of Omar: 'No church shall be built in Islam.' They shall no longer be permitted to repair the parts of these [post-Islamic] buildings which are in ruins. However, the old buildings [of pre-Islamic times] which are found in a land whose population had embraced Islam need not be destroyed. They shall not, however, be enlarged by means of repairs or otherwise. In case the tolerated peoples [Jews, Christians, etc.] act contrary to these provisions we will be obliged to destroy everything that has been added to the original size of the building. [Only pre-Islamic churches and synagogues may be repaired; new ones must be torn down.]

"Entrance into Moslem territory by infidels of foreign lands under the pact guaranteeing protection to the tolerated peoples is permitted only for the time necessary to settle their business affairs. If they exceed this period, their safe-conduct having expired, they will be put to death or be subject to the payment of the head-tax. [Jews and Christians of foreign lands must pay a special head-tax if they wish to remain permanently in Moslem lands.] As to those with whom the ruler may have signed treaties, and with whom he, for whatever motive, may have granted a temporary truce, they form only the smallest fraction. But they, too, must not pass the fixed limit of more than four months [without paying the tax], particularly if this occurs at a time when Islam is prosperous and flourishing. The Most-High has said [Koran 2:234]: 'They should wait four-months,' and he has again said [47:37]: 'Do not show any cowardice, and do not at all invite the unbelievers to a peace when you have the upper-hand and may God be with you.'

"Their men and women are ordered to wear garments different from those of the Moslems in order to be distinguished from them. They are forbidden to exhibit anything which might scandalize us, as, for instance, their fermented liquors, and if they do not conceal these from us, we are obliged to pour them into the street."

This which precedes is only a part of that which has been written on this subject, and if we should wish to mention it all here it would take too long. But this brief recital will be sufficient for those men whose intelligence God has enlightened, to whom he has given the breath of life, and whose inner thoughts he has sanctified. Now let us beg the Sovereign Master of the world to extend His justice over humanity universally, in order that they may direct all their efforts toward raising with firmness the banner of the religion.

In a tradition of the sincere and faithful [Calif Abu Bekr, 632–634] it is likewise said: "The abolition of a sacrilegious innovation is preferable to the permanent operation of the law." In another tradition it is also said: "One hour of justice is worth more than sixty years of ritual." The verses of the Koran and the traditions are very numerous on this subject, and they are known by all the faithful. God has cursed the former nations because they have not condemned scandalous things; and He has said [Koran 5:82]: "They [the children of Israel] seek not at all to turn one another from the bad actions which they have committed. O how detestable were their actions. But He has punished these men because of their obstinate conduct." The Most-High has also said [Koran 9:113]: "Those who bid what is right and forbid what is wrong, who observe the divine precepts, will be rewarded. Announce these glad tidings to the Moslems."

May the Most High God admit us to the number of this company and may He lead us in the paths of His favor. Certainly God is powerful in everything; He is full of mercy to His servants; He sees all.

Written by the humble Hasan al Kafrawi, the Shafiite.

1772.

BIBLIOGRAPHY

REFERENCES TO TEXTBOOKS

Elbogen, pp. 47–48; Roth, pp. 149–151; Sachar, pp. 155–161.

READINGS FOR ADVANCED STUDENTS

Graetz, III, pp. 53–89; Graetz-Rhine, II, pp. 488–513; Margolis and Marx, pp. 248–254.

Gottheil, R. J. H., "Dhimmis and Moslems in Egypt," *Old Testament and Semitic Studies in Memory of William Rainey Harper*, II, pp. 351–414.

Torrey, C. C., *The Jewish Foundation of Islam*. A scholarly critique of the Jewish influence on early Islam.

Wismar, A. L., *A Study in Tolerance as Practiced by Muhammad and His Immediate Successors*. A good study.

Encyclopaedia of Religion and Ethics, "Persecution (Muhammadan)"; "Toleration (Muhammadan)."

JE, "Disabilities"; "Islam"; "Omar I."

ADDITIONAL SOURCE MATERIALS IN ENGLISH

Tritton, A. S., *The Caliphs and Their Non-Muslim Subjects. A Critical Study of the Covenant of 'Umar*. Chap. i, "The Covenant of 'Umar."

4.

The Jews of Spain and the Visigothic Code
654–681

THE Visigothic Code, originally in Latin, includes the laws of a number of Catholic kings who ruled Spain from 586 to 711. Reccared (586–601), the first Visigothic king to become a Catholic, was also the first king to pursue an active anti-Jewish policy. Some of his successors in the seventh century went farther and allowed the Jews only the alternatives of baptism or exile. Many Jews thus became unwilling converts and secretly practiced Judaism. These were the "Judaizing Christians." In order to stamp out this secret Judaism some kings resorted to most drastic punishments. These actions were prompted both by religious bigotry and the desire for a standardized Catholicism of all citizens. In addition the prospect of gain through confiscation of Jewish property probably lured some of them. Fortunately for the Jews this legislation was not always carried into effect, for the royal authority met with opposition in many parts of Spain.

The first document reproduced below from this famous Latin code is a sort of declaration of faith presented by the Judaizing Christians of Toledo to King Recceswinth (649–672). The second, issued by King Erwig (680–687), offers those Jews, who had for some reason or other not yet become Catholics, the alternatives of expulsion or baptism. Though the Visigothic state was overthrown by the Arabs in 711, this seventh century code continued to influence Catholic Spain all through the Middle Ages. The Spanish Inquisition of the 15th century shows traces of this influence.

I. MEMORIAL OF THE JEWS PRESENTED TO THE KING, 654

℃To our most pious and noble lord and master, King Recceswinth: We, Jews of the city of Toledo, who have hereto attached our signatures or seals, call your attention to the fact that formerly we were compelled to present a memorial to King Chintila, of holy memory, by which we bound ourselves to uphold the Catholic faith, as, in like manner, we do now. [Under Chintila, 637, the secret-Jews had promised to be good Christians.]

But, whereas the perfidy born of our obstinacy and the antipathy resulting from our ancestral errors influenced us to such an extent that we did not then truly believe in our Lord Jesus Christ and did not sincerely embrace the Catholic faith, therefore now, freely and voluntarily, we promise Your Majesty for ourselves, our wives, and our children, by this, our memorial, that henceforth we will observe no Jewish customs or rites whatever, and will not associate, or have any intercourse with any unbaptized Jews. [The secret-Jews offered this petition to protect themselves from punishment of expulsion. The actual text was probably dictated by a priest.]

Nor will we marry any person related to us by blood, within the sixth degree, which union has been declared to be incestuous and wicked. [Catholic law then objected to the marriage even of distant cousins.] Nor will we, or our children, or any of our posterity, at any time hereafter, contract marriage outside our sect [Christianity]; and both sexes shall hereafter be united in marriage according to Christian rites. We will not practice the operation of circumcision. We will not celebrate the Passover, Sabbath, and other festival days, as enjoined by the Jewish ritual. We will not make any distinction in food, according to our ancient usages. We will not observe, in any way, ceremonies prescribed by the abominable practices and habits of the Hebrews.

But, with sincere faith, grateful hearts, and perfect devotion, we believe that Christ is the son of the living God, as declared by ecclesiastical and evangelical tradition; and we hereby acknowledge Him to be such, and venerate Him accordingly. Moreover, all the ceremonies enjoined by the Christian religion—whether said ceremonies relate to festivals, or to marriage and food—we will truly and exactly observe; and we will maintain the same with sincerity, without any objection or opposition thereto; and without any subterfuge on our part, by means of which we might hereafter deny our acts, return to what has been prohibited, or not completely fulfill all that we have promised.

With regard to the flesh of animals which we consider unclean, if we should be unable to eat the same on account of our ancient prejudices, nevertheless, when it is cooked along with other food, we hereby promise to partake of the latter with no manifestation of disgust or horror. [They cannot, however, promise to eat pork except when cooked with other foods.]

And if, at any time, we should be found to have transgressed, and to have violated any of the promises hereinbefore specified; or should presume to act contrary to the doctrines of the Christian faith; or if we should, in word or deed, neglect to fulfill the obligations to which we have bound ourselves, as being acceptable to the Catholic religion; we hereby swear by the Father, Son and Holy Spirit, who form one God in the Trinity, that, in case a single transgressor should be found among our people, he shall be burned, or stoned to death, either by ourselves, or by our sons. And should Your Majesty graciously grant such culprit his life, he shall at once be deprived of his freedom, so that Your Majesty may deliver him to be forever a slave to anyone whom Your Majesty may select; and Your Majesty shall have full authority to make whatever disposition of him and his property as may seem expedient; not only on account of the power attached to your royal office, but also by the authority granted by this our memorial. Made in the name of God, at Toledo, on the Kalends of March, in the sixth year of Your Majesty's happy reign [March 1, 654].

II. JEWS SHALL NOT REMOVE THEMSELVES OR THEIR CHILDREN OR SLAVES FROM THE BLESSING OF BAPTISM, 681

⟨Since truth itself [Matthew 7:7] teaches us to seek, to investigate, to knock [at the door of heaven and it will be opened], admonishing us that [Matthew 11:12] "ardent men inherit the kingdom of heaven," there is no doubt that he falls short of the reward of divine favor who does not exert himself to gain that favor. [Christians must make every effort to convert Jews.]

Therefore, if any Jew—of those, naturally, who are as yet not baptized or who have postponed their own or their children's baptism—should prevent his slaves from being baptized in the presence of the priest, or should withhold himself and his family from baptism, or if any one of them should exceed the duration of one year after the promulgation of this law without being baptized, the transgressor of these [conditions], whoever he may be, shall have his head shaved, receive a hundred lashes, and pay the required penalty of exile. His property shall pass over into the power of the king; it shall remain perpetually in the possession of him to whom the king wishes to bestow it, inasmuch as the stubborn life [of the Jew] shows him to be incorrigible.

BIBLIOGRAPHY

REFERENCES TO TEXTBOOKS

Golub, J. S., *Medieval Jewish History*, Sec. III, "Spain."

READINGS FOR ADVANCED STUDENTS

Graetz, III, pp. 41–52, 101–110; Graetz-Rhine, II, pp. 479–487; III, pp. 14–20; Margolis and Marx, pp. 303–307.

Katz, S., *The Jews in the Visigothic and Frankish Kingdoms of Spain and Gaul* (Mediaeval Academy monograph no. 12). The best presentation of the subject in English.

Milman, H. H., *The History of the Jews*, II, Book xxii, pp. 250–263.

Ziegler, A. K., *Church and State in Visigothic Spain*. A detailed study of the relation of the State to the Church. The Jewish problem is treated on pp. 186–199. The author holds the State, not the Church, responsible, primarily, for mistreatment of the Jews.

JE, "Spain."

ADDITIONAL SOURCE MATERIALS IN ENGLISH

Lindo, E. H., *The History of the Jews of Spain and Portugal*. This work contains translations and a discussion of many of the laws concerning Jews enacted during the Visigothic period.

Scott, S. P., *The Visigothic Code*. Contains practically all the laws of the period touching the Jews.

The Expulsion of the Jews from France
1182

THE Jews had already been settled in France for over a thousand years when Philip Augustus came to power in 1179. This brilliant but unscrupulous ruler, then about fifteen years of age, needed money and help to strengthen his hold on the throne and to fight the powerful feudal barons. He gained these objectives, in part, by confiscating Jewish wealth; thus he secured not only money but also the goodwill of the Church and of the Christian debtors. That he himself actually believed that Jews committed ritual murders is difficult to determine. It is sufficient to say that, in taking drastic action against his Jewish subjects, he had recourse to such accusations.

Four months after taking over the reigns of government he imprisoned all the Jews in his lands and released them only after a heavy ransom had been paid (1180). The next year (1181) he annulled all loans made to Christians by Jews, taking instead a comfortable twenty per cent for himself. A year later (1182) he confiscated all the lands and buildings of the Jews and drove them out of the lands governed by himself directly. It is difficult to determine if his decree affected the Jews in the baronial lands.

Several years later (1198) Philip Augustus readmitted the Jews and carefully regulated their banking business so as to reserve large profits to himself through a variety of taxes and duties. He made of this taxation a lucrative income for himself.

The following account describes the events leading up to the expulsion in 1182. It is taken from the *Gesta Philippi Augusti*, a contemporary Latin history by the monk Rigord who first began this chronicle about 1186. Rigord, who was rather naive, tells his story from the point of view of a devoted son of the Church. He died some time after 1205.

⟨[Philip Augustus had often heard] that the Jews who dwelt in Paris were wont every year on Easter day, or during the sacred week of our Lord's Passion, to go down secretly into underground vaults and kill a Christian as a sort of sacrifice in contempt of the

Christian religion. For a long time they had persisted in this wickedness, inspired by the devil, and in Philip's father's time, many of
them had been seized and burned with fire. St. Richard, whose body
rests in the church of the Holy Innocents-in-the-Fields in Paris, was
thus put to death and crucified by the Jews, and through martyrdom
went in blessedness to God. [Louis VII, then king, held the Jews
guiltless in this death.] Wherefore many miracles have been wrought
by the hand of God through the prayers and intercessions of St.
Richard, to the glory of God, as we have heard.

And because the most Christian King Philip inquired diligently,
and came to know full well these and many other iniquities of the
Jews in his forefathers' days, therefore he burned with zeal, and
in the same year in which he was invested at Rheims with the holy
governance of the kingdom of the French, upon a Sabbath, the
sixteenth of February [1180], by his command, the Jews throughout
all France were seized in their synagogues and then bespoiled of
their gold and silver and garments, as the Jews themselves had
spoiled the Egyptians at their exodus from Egypt. This was a
harbinger of their expulsion, which by God's will soon followed. . . .

At this time [1180–1181] a great multitude of Jews had been
dwelling in France for a long time past, for they had flocked thither
from divers parts of the world, because peace abode among the
French, and liberality; for the Jews had heard how the kings of the
French were prompt to act against their enemies, and were very
merciful toward their subjects. And therefore their elders and men
wise in the law of Moses, who were called by the Jews *didascali*
[teachers], made resolve to come to Paris.

When they had made a long sojourn there, they grew so rich that
they claimed as their own almost half of the whole city, and had
Christians in their houses as menservants and maidservants, who
were open backsliders from the faith of Jesus Christ, and *judaized*
with the Jews. And this was contrary to the decree of God and the
law of the Church. And whereas the Lord had said by the mouth
of Moses in Deuteronomy [23:20–21], "Thou shalt not lend upon
usury to thy brother," but "to a stranger," the Jews in their
wickedness understood by "stranger" every Christian, and they
took from the Christians their money at usury. And so heavily
burdened in this wise were citizens and soldiers and peasants in the
suburbs, and in the various towns and villages, that many of them
were constrained to part with their possessions. Others were bound
under oath in houses of the Jews in Paris, held as if captives in prison.
[Germanic law permitted a creditor to hold a debtor prisoner.]

The most Christian King Philip heard of these things, and compassion was stirred within him. He took counsel with a certain hermit, Bernard by name, a holy and religious man, who at that time dwelt in the forest of Vincennes, and asked him what he should do. By his advice the King released all Christians of his kingdom from their debts to the Jews, and kept a fifth part of the whole amount for himself.

Finally came the culmination of their wickedness. Certain ecclesiastical vessels consecrated to God—the chalices and crosses of gold and silver bearing the image of our Lord Jesus Christ crucified —had been pledged to the Jews by way of security when the need of the churches was pressing. These they used so vilely, in their impiety and scorn of the Christian religion, that from the cups in which the body and blood of our Lord Jesus Christ was consecrated they gave their children cakes soaked in wine. . . .

In the year of our Lord's Incarnation 1182, in the month of April, which is called by the Jews Nisan, an edict went forth from the most serene king, Philip Augustus, that all the Jews of his kingdom should be prepared to go forth by the coming feast of St. John the Baptist [June 24]. And then the King gave them leave to sell each his movable goods before the time fixed, that is, the feast of St. John the Baptist. But their real estate, that is, houses, fields, vineyards, barns, winepresses, and such like, he reserved for himself and his successors, the kings of the French. [Some of this wealth may have been used to build the Louvre.]

When the faithless Jews heard this edict some of them were born again of water and the Holy Spirit and converted to the Lord, remaining steadfast in the faith of our Lord Jesus Christ. To them the King, out of regard for the Christian religion, restored all their possessions in their entirety, and gave them perpetual liberty.

Others were blinded by their ancient error and persisted in their perfidy; and they sought to win with gifts and golden promises the great of the land—counts, barons, archbishops, bishops—that through their influence and advice, and through the promise of infinite wealth, they might turn the King's mind from his firm intention. [The lords appealed to were the political enemies of the king.] But the merciful and compassionate God, who does not forsake those who put their hope in Him and who doth humble those who glory in their strength . . . so fortified the illustrious King that he could not be moved by prayers nor promises of temporal things. . . .

The infidel Jews, perceiving that the great of the land, through whom they had been accustomed easily to bend the King's predecessors to their will, had suffered repulse, and astonished and stupefied by the strength of mind of Philip the King and his constancy in the Lord, exclaimed with a certain admiration: *"Shema Israel!"* [that is, "Here O Israel"] and prepared to sell all their household goods. The time was now at hand when the King had ordered them to leave France altogether, and it could not be in any way prolonged. Then did the Jews sell all their movable possessions in great haste, while their landed property reverted to the crown. Thus the Jews, having sold their goods and taken the price for the expenses of their journey, departed with their wives and children and all their households in the aforesaid year of the Lord 1182.

BIBLIOGRAPHY

READINGS FOR ADVANCED STUDENTS

Graetz, III, pp. 400–407; Graetz-Rhine, III, pp. 241–245; Margolis and Marx, pp. 367–370.

Milman, H. H., *The History of the Jews*, II, Book xxiv, pp. 315–318.

JE, "France."

ADDITIONAL SOURCE MATERIALS IN ENGLISH

Grayzel, S., *The Church and the Jews in the XIIIth Century*. Contains the Latin texts and translations of many documents dealing with the status of the Jews in France in the time of Philip Augustus. See Index under "Philip, King of France, II (Augustus)."

"Jews, Crusades, and Usury, Paris XIIth and XIIIth centuries," *History Reference Council Bulletin*, nos. 95–96. The *Bulletins* of the History Reference Council, 14 Kirkland Place, Cambridge, Mass., are useful for source materials.

6.

The Charter of the Jews of the
Duchy of Austria
July 1, 1244

INASMUCH as the Jews, during the Middle Ages, were looked upon as a distinct racial and religious group who could not and should not be subject to the same laws as Christians, they were given special charters by which they were governed. The most famous of these is that granted by Frederick the Belligerent in July, 1244 to the Jews of his duchy of Austria. This document is important because it was soon adopted, with some changes, by most East European countries to which the masses of Jews finally drifted: Hungary, Bohemia, Poland, Silesia, and Lithuania. This charter—a very favorable one—was issued to encourage money-lending among the Austrian Jews and probably also to attract moneyed Jews to migrate to this outlying German state which was in need of ready credit. Every effort is therefore made in this Latin constitution to grant the Jews ample opportunity to sell their wares and, above all, to lend money. They were given adequate protection: they were subject to the direct jurisdiction of the Duke who guaranteed them safety of life and limb. The right of the Jews to govern themselves in communal and religious matters was not specified by the Duke, but this was taken for granted. We may assume, indeed, that the Jews of Austria enjoyed extensive political autonomy under this pact.

ⓒFrederick, by the grace of God Duke of Austria and Styria and lord of Carniola, offers greetings at all times to all who will read this letter in the future. Inasmuch as we desire that men of all classes dwelling in our land should share our favor and good will, we do therefore decree that these laws, devised for all Jews found in the land of Austria, shall be observed by them without violation.

1.   We decree, therefore, first, that in cases involving money, or immovable property, or a criminal complaint touching the person or property of a Jew, no Christian shall be admitted as a witness against a Jew unless there is a Jewish witness together with the Christian. [The Jewish witness was a guarantee of fair play.]

II.   Likewise, if a Christian should bring suit against a Jew, asserting that he had pawned his pledges with him and the Jew should deny this, and then if the Christian should not wish to accord any belief in the mere statement of the Jew, the Jew may prove his contention by taking an oath upon an object equivalent in value to that which was brought to him, and shall then go forth free. [Moneylending on pledges was the leading Jewish business at this time.]

III.   Likewise, if a Christian has deposited a pledge with a Jew, stating that he had left it with the Jew for a smaller sum than the Jew admits, the Jew shall then take an oath upon the pledge pawned with him, and the Christian must not refuse to pay the amount that the Jew has proved through his oath.

IV.   Likewise, if a Jew says that he returned the Christian's pledge as a loan to the Christian, without, however, the presence of witnesses, and if the Christian deny this, then the Christian is able to clear himself in this matter through the oath of himself alone.

V.   Likewise, a Jew is allowed to receive all things as pledges which may be pawned with him—no matter what they are called—without making any investigation about them, except bloody and wet clothes which he shall under no circumstances accept. [Such garments presuppose murder and theft.]

VI.   Likewise, if a Christian charges that the pledge which a Jew has, was taken from him by theft or robbery, the Jew must swear on that pledge that when he received it he did not know that it had been removed by theft or robbery. In this oath the amount for which the pledge was pawned to him shall also be included. Then, inasmuch as the Jew has brought his proof, the Christian shall pay him the capital and the interest that has accrued in the meantime. [Then the Christian takes back his property.]

VII.   Likewise, if a Jew, through the accident of fire or through theft or violence, should lose his [own] goods, together with the pledges pawned with him, and this is established, yet the Christian who has pledged something with him nevertheless brings suit against him, the Jew may free himself merely by his own oath. [The Jew loses the money advanced and the Christian, his pledge.]

VIII.   Likewise, if the Jews engage in quarreling or actually fight among themselves, the judge of our city shall claim no jurisdiction over them; only the Duke alone or the chief official of his land shall exercise jurisdiction. If, however, the accusation touches the person, this case shall be reserved for the Duke alone for judgment. [Important criminal cases are to be decided not by the Jewish court, but by the Duke.]

IX.   Likewise, if a Christian should inflict any sort of a wound upon a Jew, the accused shall pay to the Duke twelve marks of gold which are to be turned in to the treasury. He must also pay, to the person who has been injured, twelve marks of silver and the expenses incurred for the medicine needed in his cure.

X.   Likewise, if a Christian should kill a Jew he shall be punished with the proper sentence, death, and all his movable and immovable property shall pass into the power of the Duke.

XI.   Likewise, if a Christian strikes a Jew, without, however, having spilt his blood, he shall pay to the Duke four marks of gold, and to the man he struck four marks of silver. If he has no money, he shall offer satisfaction for the crime committed by the loss of his hand.

XII.   Likewise, wherever a Jew shall pass through our territory no one shall offer any hindrance to him or molest or trouble him. [The Jew is to pay no road-fees in all Austrian lands.] If, however, he should be carrying any goods or other things for which he must pay duty at all custom offices, he shall pay only the prescribed duty which a citizen of that town, in which the Jew is then dwelling, pays.

XIII.   Likewise, if the Jews, as is their custom, should transport any of their dead either from city to city, or from province to province, or from one Austrian land into another, we do not wish anything to be demanded of them by our customs officers. [Heavy road-fees were often imposed on Jewish corpses in transit.] If, however, a customs officer should extort anything, then he is to be punished for *praedatio mortui*, which means, in common language, robbery of the dead.

XIV.   Likewise, if a Christian, moved by insolence, shall break into or devastate the cemetery of the Jews, he shall die, as the court determines, and all his property, whatever it may be, shall be forfeited to the treasury of the Duke.

xv.   Likewise, if any one wickedly throw something at the synagogues of the Jews we order that he pay two talents to the judge of the Jews. [This judge was a Christian who looked after the interests of the Jews.]

xvi.   Likewise, if a Jew be condemned by his judge to a money penalty, which is called *wandel* ("fine"), he shall pay only twelve dinars to him.

xvii.   Likewise, if a Jew is summoned to court by order of his judge, but does not come the first or second time, he must pay the judge four dinars for each time. If he does not come at the third summons he shall pay thirty-six dinars to the judge mentioned. [Fines were a source of income to the judge.]

xviii.   Likewise, if a Jew has wounded another Jew he may not refuse to pay a penalty of two talents, which is called *wandel*, to his judge.

xix.   Likewise, we decree that no Jew shall take an oath on the Torah unless he has been summoned to our [the Duke's] presence. [This happened only in important cases.]

xx.   Likewise, if a Jew was secretly murdered, and if through the testimony it cannot be determined by his friends who murdered him, yet if after an investigation has been made the Jews begin to suspect some one, we are willing to supply the Jews with a champion against this suspect. [The champion fought the suspect and God gave victory to the right.]

xxi.   Likewise, if a Christian raises his hand in violence against a Jewess, we order that the hand of that person be cut off.

xxii.   Likewise, the [Christian] judge of the Jews shall bring no case that has arisen among the Jews before his court, unless he be invited due to a complaint. [Civil suits between Jews were settled by the Jews themselves.]

xxiii.   Likewise, if a Christian has redeemed his pledge from a

Jew but has not paid the interest, the interest due shall become compounded if it is not paid within a month.

xxiv.   Likewise, we do not wish any one to seek quarters in a Jewish house. [Forced entertainment of officials was considered a burden.]

xxv.   Likewise, if a Jew has lent money to a magnate of the country on his possessions or on a note and proves this documentarily, we will assign the pledged possessions to the Jew and defend them for him against violence. [In this way Jews acquired estates, which they farmed.]

xxvi.   Likewise, if any man or woman should kidnap a Jewish child we wish that he be punished as a thief [by death].

xxvii.   Likewise, if a Jew has held in his possession, for a year, a pledge received from a Christian, and if the value of the pledge does not exceed the money lent together with the interest, the Jew may show the pledge to his judge and shall then have the right to sell it. If any pledge shall remain for a "year and a day" [really, a year, six weeks, and three days] with a Jew, he shall not have to account for it afterwards to any one.

xxviii.   Likewise, whatever Christian shall take his pledge away from a Jew by force or shall exercise violence in the Jew's home shall be severely punished as a plunderer of our treasury. [The Duke felt that the wealth of the Jews practically belonged to him.]

xxix.   Likewise, one shall in no place proceed in judgment against a Jew except in front of his synagogues, saving ourselves who have the power to summon them to our presence. [Court was held for the Jews in the yards in front of their synagogues.]

xxx.   Likewise, we decree that Jews shall indeed receive only eight dinars a week interest on the talent. . . . [This was 173.33 per cent annual interest. Such a high rate was not unusual because of the insecurity of the times.]

> *Given at Starkenberg, in the year of the incarnation of the Lord, 1244, on the first of July.*

BIBLIOGRAPHY

REFERENCES TO TEXTBOOKS

Elbogen, pp. 67–77; Roth, pp. 195–197.

READINGS FOR ADVANCED STUDENTS

Graetz, III, pp. 567–569; Graetz-Rhine, III, pp. 338–340; Margolis and Marx, pp. 376–378.

Dubnow, S. M., *History of the Jews in Russia and Poland,* I, pp. 43–54. A discussion of the Boleslav and Casimir charters, variations of the 1244 Austrian charter.

Grunwald, M., *Vienna* (Jewish Communities Series), pp. 1ff.

Kisch, G., "Research in Medieval Legal History of the Jews," in *Proceedings of the American Academy for Jewish Research,* VI (1934–1935), and "The Jewry-Law of the Medieval German Law-Books," in *Proceedings,* VII (1935–1936). Both of these essays throw great light on the relation of the Jew and the Jewish community to the medieval state.

JE, "Austria"; "Kammerknechtschaft."

ADDITIONAL SOURCE MATERIALS IN ENGLISH

"The Bishop of Speyer Gives the Jews of His City a Charter, 1084," O. J. Thatcher and E. H. McNeal, *A Source Book for Mediaeval History,* pp. 577–578.

"The Privilege of Frederick I for the Jews, 1157," Thatcher and McNeal, pp. 573–577. This is a confirmation of the charter granted the Jews of Worms, Germany, about 1090, by Emperor Henry IV. It is the opinion of some scholars that both the Speyer and Worms charters are based on a ninth century Carolingian formula-prototype. The charter of 1244 is very probably a development of these early charters.

Jacobs, J., *The Jews of Angevin England, Documents and Records, etc.,* is a very useful source book for the period in England. It also contains, p. 134 and p. 212, charters granted Jews by Richard the Lion-Hearted and his brother, John Lackland.

Radin, M., "A Charter of Privileges of the Jews in Ancona of the Year 1535," *JQR,* N.S., IV (1913–1914), particularly pp. 240ff.

7.

Medieval Spanish Law and the Jews
Las siete partidas
Spain, 1265

L*AS siete partidas*, the Seven-Part Code, is one of the most remarkable law codes of medieval times. The code, written in the Castilian vernacular, was compiled about 1265, under the supervision of Alfonso X, the Wise (1252–1284), of Castile. Its laws, however, did not go into effect until 1348, and then only with certain reservations. From Castile they spread to all of Spain and thence into the Spanish possessions in the Philippines, Porto Rico, Florida, and Louisiana. The sources of this code are largely Visigothic, later Roman, and Church law, all of which were hostile to the Jew. This hostility did not, however, deter the Castilian state from protecting scrupulously the Jewish religion as well as the person and property of the Jews. The Jews and Moors, national minorities, were too numerous and too important to be mistreated as yet by the new Castilian state.

TITLE XXIV

CONCERNING THE JEWS

℮ Jews are a people, who, although they do not believe in the religion of Our Lord Jesus Christ, yet, the great Christian sovereigns have always permitted them to live among them. . . .

LAW I. WHAT THE WORD JEW MEANS, AND WHENCE THIS TERM IS DERIVED

A party who believes in, and adheres to the law of Moses is called a Jew, according to the strict signification of the term, as well as one who is circumcised, and observes the other precepts commanded by his religion. This name is derived from the tribe of Judah which was nobler and more powerful than the others, and, also possessed another advantage, because the king of the Jews had to be selected from that tribe, and its members always received the first wounds in battle. The reason that the church, emperors, kings and princes, permitted the Jews to dwell among them and with Christians, is

34

because they always lived, as it were, in captivity, as it was constantly [a token] in the minds of men that they were descended from those who crucified Our Lord Jesus Christ.

LAW II. IN WHAT WAY JEWS SHOULD PASS THEIR LIVES AMONG CHRISTIANS; WHAT THINGS THEY SHOULD NOT MAKE USE OF OR PRACTICE, ACCORDING TO OUR RELIGION; AND WHAT PENALTY THOSE DESERVE WHO ACT CONTRARY TO ITS ORDINANCES

Jews should pass their lives among Christians quietly and without disorder, practicing their own religious rites, and not speaking ill of the faith of Our Lord Jesus Christ, which Christians acknowledge. Moreover, a Jew should be very careful to avoid preaching to, or converting any Christian, to the end that he may become a Jew, by exalting his own belief and disparaging ours. Whoever violates this law shall be put to death and lose all his property. And because we have heard it said that in some places Jews celebrated, and still celebrate Good Friday, which commemorates the Passion of Our Lord Jesus Christ, by way of contempt: stealing children and fastening them to crosses, and making images of wax and crucifying them, when they cannot obtain children; we order that, hereafter, if in any part of our dominions anything like this is done, and can be proved, all persons who were present when the act was committed shall be seized, arrested and brought before the king; and after the king ascertains that they are guilty, he shall cause them to be put to death in a disgraceful manner, no matter how many there may be. [Christians already believed that Jews kidnapped and killed Christian children for religious purposes.]

We also forbid any Jew to dare to leave his house or his quarter on Good Friday, but they must all remain shut up until Saturday morning; and if they violate this regulation, we decree that they shall not be entitled to reparation for any injury or dishonor inflicted upon them by Christians. [Christians were prone to commit violence on Good Friday, the anniversary of the crucifixion of Jesus.]

LAW III. NO JEW CAN HOLD ANY OFFICE OR EMPLOYMENT BY WHICH HE MAY BE ABLE TO OPPRESS CHRISTIANS

Jews were formerly highly honored, and enjoyed privileges above all other races, for they alone were called the People of God. But for the reason that they disowned Him who had honored them and given them privileges; and instead of showing Him reverence humiliated Him, by shamefully putting Him to death on the cross; it was proper and just that, on account of the great crime and wickedness which they committed, they should forfeit the honors and privileges which they enjoyed; and therefore from the day when they crucified Our Lord Jesus Christ they never had either king or priests among themselves, as they formerly did. The emperors, who in former times were lords of all the world, considered it fitting and right that, on account of the treason which they committed in killing their lord, they should lose all said honors and privileges, so that no Jew could ever afterwards hold an honorable position, or a public office by means of which he might, in any way, oppress a Christian. [Nevertheless Alfonso entrusted his body and purse to Jewish physicians and financiers.]

LAW IV. HOW JEWS CAN HAVE A SYNAGOGUE AMONG CHRISTIANS

A synagogue is a place where the Jews pray, and a new building of this kind cannot be erected in any part of our dominions, except by our order. Where, however, those which formerly existed there are torn down, they can be built in the same spot where they originally stood; but they cannot be made any larger or raised to any greater height, or be painted. A synagogue constructed in any other manner shall be lost by the Jews, and shall belong to the principal church of the locality where it is built. And for the reason that a synagogue is a place where the name of God is praised, we forbid any Christian to deface it, or remove anything from it, or take anything out of it by force; except where some malefactor takes refuge there; for they have a right to remove him by force in order to bring him before the judge. Moreover, we forbid Christians to put any animal into a synagogue, or loiter in it, or place any hindrance in the way of the Jews while they are there performing their devotions according to their religion. [But Moors were not allowed to have mosques. Jews were not at the bottom of the social scale.]

LAW V. NO COMPULSION SHALL BE BROUGHT TO BEAR UPON THE JEWS ON
SATURDAY, AND WHAT JEWS CAN BE SUBJECT TO COMPULSION

Saturday is the day on which Jews perform their devotions, and remain quiet in their lodgings, and do not make contracts or transact any business; and for the reason that they are obliged by their religion to keep it, no one should on that day summon them or bring them into court. Wherefore we order that no judge shall employ force or any constraint upon Jews on Saturday, in order to bring them into court on account of their debts; or arrest them; or cause them any other annoyance; for the remaining days of the week are sufficient for the purpose of employing compulsion against them, and for making demands for things which can be demanded of them, according to law. Jews are not bound to obey a summons served upon them on that day; and, moreover, we decree that any decision rendered against them on Saturday shall not be valid; but if a Jew should wound, kill, rob, steal, or commit any other offense like these for which he can be punished in person and property, then the judge can arrest him on Saturday.

We also decree that all claims that Christians have against Jews, and Jews against Christians, shall be decided and determined by our judges in the district where they reside, and not by their old men. [Jewish courts have no jurisdiction if one of the parties is a Christian.] And as we forbid Christians to bring Jews into court or annoy them on Saturday; so we also decree that Jews, neither in person, nor by their attorneys, shall have the right to bring Christians into court, or annoy them on this day. And in addition to this, we forbid any Christian, on his own responsibility, to arrest or wrong any Jew either in his person or property, but where he has any complaint against him he must bring it before our judges; and if anyone should be so bold as to use violence against the Jews, or rob them of anything, he shall return them double the value of the same.

LAW VI. JEWS WHO BECOME CHRISTIANS SHALL NOT BE SUBJECT TO
    COMPULSION; WHAT ADVANTAGE A JEW HAS WHO BECOMES A
    CHRISTIAN; AND WHAT PENALTY OTHER JEWS DESERVE WHO DO
    HIM HARM

No force or compulsion shall be employed in any way against a Jew to induce him to become a Christian; but Christians should convert him to the faith of Our Lord Jesus Christ by means of the texts of the Holy Scriptures, and by kind words, for no one can love or appreciate a service which is done him by compulsion. We also decree that if any Jew or Jewess should voluntarily desire to become a Christian, the other Jews shall not interfere with this in any way, and if they stone, wound, or kill any such person, because he wishes to become a Christian, or after he has been baptized, and this can be proved; we order that all the murderers, or the abettors of said murder or attack, shall be burned. [This law was first issued by Constantine the Great in 315.] But where the party was not killed, but wounded, or dishonored; we order the judges of the neighborhood where this took place shall compel those guilty of the attack, or who caused the dishonor, to make amends to him for the same; and also that they be punished for the offence which they committed, as they think they deserve; and we also order that, after any Jews become Christians, all persons in our dominions shall honor them; and that no one shall dare to reproach them or their descendants, by way of insult, with having been Jews; and that they shall possess all their property, sharing the same with their brothers, and inheriting it from their fathers and mothers and other relatives, just as if they were Jews; and that they can hold all offices and dignities which other Christians can do.

LAW VII. WHAT PENALTY A CHRISTIAN DESERVES WHO BECOMES A JEW

Where a Christian is so unfortunate as to become a Jew, we order that he shall be put to death just as if he had become a heretic; and we decree that his property shall be disposed of in the same way that we stated should be done with that of heretics.

LAW VIII. NO CHRISTIAN, MAN OR WOMAN, SHALL LIVE WITH A JEW

We forbid any Jew to keep Christian men or women in his house, to be served by them; although he may have them to cultivate and take care of his lands, or protect him on the way when he is compelled to go to some dangerous place. Moreover, we forbid any Christian man or woman to invite a Jew or a Jewess, or to accept an invitation from them, to eat or drink together, or to drink any wine made by their hands. [Jewish law also forbade the use of Christian-made wine.] We also order that no Jews shall dare to bathe in company with Christians, and that no Christian shall take any medicine or cathartic made by a Jew; but he can take it by the advice of some intelligent person, only where it is made by a Christian, who knows and is familiar with its ingredients. [Alfonso probably had a Jewish physician the very time he issued this law.]

LAW IX. WHAT PENALTY A JEW DESERVES WHO HAS INTERCOURSE WITH A CHRISTIAN WOMAN

Jews who live with Christian women are guilty of great insolence and boldness, for which reason we decree that all Jews who, hereafter, may be convicted of having done such a thing shall be put to death. For if Christians who commit adultery with married women deserve death on that account, much more do Jews who have sexual intercourse with Christian women, who are spiritually the wives of Our Lord Jesus Christ because of the faith and the baptism which they receive in His name; nor do we consider it proper that a Christian woman who commits an offense of this kind shall escape without punishment. Wherefore we order that, whether she be a virgin, a married woman, a widow, or a common prostitute who gives herself to all men, she shall suffer the same penalty which we mentioned in the last law in the Title concerning the Moors, to which a Christian woman is liable who has carnal intercourse with a Moor [i.e., confiscation of property, scourging, or death].

LAW X. WHAT PENALTY JEWS DESERVE WHO HOLD CHRISTIANS AS SLAVES

A Jew shall not purchase, or keep as a slave, a Christian man or woman, and if anyone violates this law the Christian shall be restored to freedom and shall not pay any portion of the price given for him, although the Jew may not have been aware when he bought him, that he was a Christian; but if he knew that he was such when he purchased him, and makes use of him afterwards as a slave, he shall be put to death for doing so. Moreover, we forbid any Jew to convert a captive to his religion, even though said captive may be a Moor, or belong to some other barbarous race. If anyone violates this law we order that the said slave who has become a Jew shall be set at liberty, and removed from the control of the party to whom he or she belonged. If any Moors who are the captives of Jews become Christians, they shall at once be freed, as is explained in the Fourth Partida of this book, in the Title concerning Liberty, in the laws which treat of this subject [but Christians, including the Church, were allowed to own Christian slaves].

LAW XI. JEWS SHALL BEAR CERTAIN MARKS IN ORDER THAT THEY MAY BE KNOWN

Many crimes and outrageous things occur between Christians and Jews because they live together in cities, and dress alike; and in order to avoid the offenses and evils which take place for this reason, we deem it proper, and we order that all Jews, male and female, living in our dominions shall bear some distinguishing mark upon their heads so that people may plainly recognize a Jew, or a Jewess; and any Jew who does not bear such a mark, shall pay for each time he is found without it ten maravedis of gold; and if he has not the means to do this he shall receive ten lashes for his offense. [This is an attempt to put into effect the "Jew-Badge" law of Pope Innocent III, 1215.]

BIBLIOGRAPHY

READINGS FOR ADVANCED STUDENTS

Graetz, III, pp. 592–596, 615–617; Graetz-Rhine, III, pp. 349–353; Margolis and Marx, pp. 419–429.
Lindo, E. H., *The History of the Jews of Spain and Portugal*, pp. 78–91.

ADDITIONAL SOURCE MATERIALS IN ENGLISH

Scott, S. P., *Las siete partidas*, an English translation of the code. This contains the complete body of laws dealing with the Jews, of which the above is but an excerpt.
Lindo, E. H., *The History of the Jews of Spain and Portugal*, Chap. x. Contains translations of sections of *Las siete partidas*.

8.

St. Louis and the Jews
France, before 1270

LOUIS IX (1226–1270), grandson of Philip Augustus and King of France, was an ideal medieval king: he was chivalrous, religious, ascetic, and hostile to Jews. In spite of the fact that this opposition worked to his own disadvantage he opposed the money-lending activity of his Jewish subjects; he sanctioned laws against them, and eventually even ordered their expulsion. It is to be questioned, however, if the edict of expulsion was actually carried out.

The saintly Louis was very eager to convert the Jews and to this end encouraged disputations between the Synagogue and the Church. It was hoped at these theological tournaments to convert some Jews, or at least put them to shame and thus convince irresolute Christians of the truth of Christianity and of the vileness of Judaism.

Jean, Sire de Joinville (1224–1318), an intimate friend of Louis, has, in his old French history of St. Louis, preserved for us an anecdote which throws a great deal of light on the King's attitude toward the Jews.

⟨He [Saint Louis] told me that there was once a great disputation between clergy and Jews at the monastery of Cluny. And there was at Cluny a poor knight to whom the abbot gave bread at that place for the love of God; and this knight asked the abbot to suffer him to speak the first words, and they suffered him, not without doubt. So he rose, and leant upon his crutch, and asked that they should bring to him the greatest clerk [clergyman] and most learned master among the Jews; and they did so. Then he asked the Jew a question, which was this: "Master," said the knight, "I ask you if you believe that the Virgin Mary, who bore God in her body and in her arms, was a virgin mother, and is the mother of God?"

And the Jew [probably Nathan or Joseph Official, famous controversialists] replied that of all this he believed nothing. Then the knight answered that the Jew had acted like a fool when—neither believing in her, nor loving her—he had yet entered into her monastery and house. "And verily," said the knight, "you shall pay for it!" Whereupon he lifted his crutch and smote the Jew near the ear, and beat him to the earth. Then the Jews turned to flight, and bore away their master, sore wounded. And so ended the disputation.

The abbot came to the knight and told him he had committed a deed of very great folly. But the knight replied that the abbot committed a deed of greater folly in gathering people together for such a disputation; for there were a great many good Christians there who, before the disputation came to an end, would have gone away misbelievers through not fully understanding the Jews. "And I tell you," said the king, "that no one, unless he be a very learned clerk, should dispute with them; but a layman, when he hears the Christian law mis-said, should not defend the Christian law, unless it be with his sword, and with that he should pierce the mis-sayer in the midriff, so far as the sword will enter."

BIBLIOGRAPHY

READINGS FOR ADVANCED STUDENTS

Williams, A. L., *Adversus Judaeos: a Bird's-Eye View of Christian Apologiae until the Renaissance*. The most complete study of Church anti-Jewish polemics.
JE, "Disputations."

ADDITIONAL SOURCE MATERIALS IN ENGLISH

Grayzel, S., *The Church and the Jews in the XIIIth Century*. See Index under "Louis IX" for texts and translations of documents dealing with the status of Jews in France in the time of Louis IX.

9.

The Black Death and the Jews
1348-1349

IN 1348 there appeared in Europe a devastating plague which is reported to have killed off ultimately twenty-five million people. By the fall of that year the rumor was current that these deaths were due to an international conspiracy of Jewry to poison Christendom. It was reported that the leaders in the Jewish metropolis of Toledo had initiated the plot and that one of the chief conspirators was a Rabbi Peyret who had his headquarters in Chambéry, Savoy, whence he dispatched his poisoners to France, Switzerland, and Italy.

By authority of Amadeus VI, Count of Savoy, a number of the Jews who lived on the shores of Lake Geneva, having been arrested and put to the torture, naturally confessed anything their inquisitors suggested. These Jews, under torture, incriminated others. Records of their confessions were sent from one town to another in Switzerland and down the Rhine River into Germany, and as a result, thousands of Jews, in at least two hundred towns and hamlets, were butchered and burnt. The sheer loss of numbers, the disappearance of their wealth, and the growing hatred of the Christians brought German Jewry to a catastrophic downfall. It now began to decline and did not again play an important part in German life till the seventeenth century.

The first account that follows is a translation from the Latin of a confession made under torture by Agimet, a Jew, who was arrested at Châtel, on Lake Geneva. It is typical of the confessions extorted and forwarded to other towns.

The second account describes the Black Death in general and treats specifically of the destruction of the Jewish community in Strasbourg. In this city the authorities, who attempted to save the Jews, were overthrown by a fear-stricken mob led by the butchers' and tanners' guilds and by the nobles who were determined to do away with the Jews who were their economic competitors and to whom they were indebted for loans. Thus in this city, at least, it was not merely religious bigotry and fear of the plague, but economic resentment that fired the craftsmen and the nobles to their work of extermination. Those people of Strasbourg, who had thus

43

far escaped the plague and who thought that by killing off the Jews they would insure themselves against it in the future, were doomed to disappointment, for the pest soon struck the city and, it is said, took a toll of sixteen thousand lives.

The confession of Agimet is found in the Appendix to Johann S. Schilter's 1698 edition of the Middle High German chronicle of the Strasbourg historian, Jacob von Königshofen (1346–1420). The second selection is taken from the body of Königshofen's history. This account merits credence, not only because Königshofen was an archivist and lived close to the events of which he writes, but also because he incorporated considerable material from his Strasbourg predecessor, the historian F. Closener, who was probably an eye-witness of the tragedy. The third selection is an epitaph of an otherwise unknown Jew who died a victim of the plague in 1349. Obviously, Jews, too, were not spared by this dread disease. The epitaph in the original Hebrew is in poetical form.

1. *The Confession of Agimet of Geneva, Châtel, October 10, 1348*

⟨The year of our Lord 1348.

On Friday, the 10th of the month of October, at Châtel, in the castle thereof, there occurred the judicial inquiry which was made by order of the court of the illustrious Prince, our lord, Amadeus, Count of Savoy, and his subjects against the Jews of both sexes who were there imprisoned, each one separately. [Jews were sometimes imprisoned separately to prevent suicide.] This was done after public rumor had become current and a strong clamor had arisen—because of the poison put by them into the wells, springs, and other things which the Christians use—demanding that they die, that they are able to be found guilty and, therefore, that they should be punished. Hence this their confession made in the presence of a great many trustworthy persons.

Agimet the Jew, who lived at Geneva and was arrested at Châtel, was there put to the torture a little and then he was released from it. And after a long time, having been subjected again to torture a little, he confessed in the presence of a great many trustworthy persons, who are later mentioned. To begin with it is clear that at the Lent just passed Pultus Clesis de Ranz had sent this very Jew to Venice to buy silks and other things for him. When this came to the notice of Rabbi Peyret, a Jew of Chambéry who was a teacher of their law, he sent for this Agimet, for whom he had searched, and when he had come before him he said: "We have been informed that you are going to Venice to buy silk and other wares. Here I am giving you a little package of half a span in size which contains some prepared poison and venom in a thin, sewed leather-bag. Distribute it among the wells, cisterns, and springs about Venice and the other places to which you go, in order to poison the people who use the water of the aforesaid wells that will have been poisoned by you, namely, the wells in which the poison will have been placed."

Agimet took this package full of poison and carried it with him to Venice, and when he came there he threw and scattered a portion of it into the well or cistern of fresh water which was there near the German House, in order to poison the people who use the water of that cistern. And he says that this is the only cistern of sweet water in the city. He also says that the mentioned Rabbi Peyret promised to give him whatever he wanted for his troubles in this business. Of his own accord Agimet confessed further that after this had been done he left at once in order that he should not be captured by the citizens or others, and that he went personally to Calabria and Apulia and threw the above mentioned poison into many wells. He confesses also that he put some of this same poison in the well of the streets of the city of Ballet.

He confesses further that he put some of this poison into the public fountain of the city of Toulouse and in the wells that are near the [Mediterranean] sea. Asked if at the time that he scattered the venom and poisoned the wells, above mentioned, any people had died, he said that he did not know inasmuch as he had left everyone of the above mentioned places in a hurry. Asked if any of the Jews of those places were guilty in the above mentioned matter, he answered that he did not know. And now by all that which is contained in the five books of Moses and the scroll of the Jews, he declared that this was true, and that he was in no wise lying, no matter what might happen to him. [This Jew does not seem to know that the books of Moses and the scroll of the Jews are identical!]

II. *The Cremation of Strasbourg Jewry St. Valentine's Day, February 14, 1349*—ABOUT THE GREAT PLAGUE AND THE BURNING OF THE JEWS

⦅In the year 1349 there occurred the greatest epidemic that ever happened. Death went from one end of the earth to the other, on that side and this side of the sea, and it was greater among the Saracens than among the Christians. In some lands everyone died so that no one was left. Ships were also found on the sea laden with wares; the crew had all died and no one guided the ship. The Bishop of Marseilles and priests and monks and more than half of all the people there died with them. In other kingdoms and cities so many people perished that it would be horrible to describe. The pope at Avignon stopped all sessions of court, locked himself in a room, allowed no one to approach him and had a fire burning before him all the time. [This last was probably intended as some sort of disinfectant.] And from what this epidemic came, all wise teachers and physicians could only say that it was God's will. And as the plague was now here, so was it in other places, and lasted more than a whole year. This epidemic also came to Strasbourg in the summer of the above mentioned year, and it is estimated that about sixteen thousand people died.

In the matter of this plague the Jews throughout the world were reviled and accused in all lands of having caused it through the poison which they are said to have put into the water and the wells—that is what they were accused of—and for this reason the Jews were burnt all the way from the Mediterranean into Germany, but not in Avignon, for the pope protected them there.

Nevertheless they tortured a number of Jews in Berne and Zofingen [Switzerland] who then admitted that they had put poison into many wells, and they also found the poison in the wells. Thereupon they burnt the Jews in many towns and wrote of this affair to Strasbourg, Freiburg, and Basel in order that they too should burn their Jews. But the leaders in these three cities in whose hands the government lay did not believe that anything ought to be done to the Jews. However in Basel the citizens marched to the city-hall and compelled the council to take an oath that they would burn the Jews, and that they would allow no Jew to enter the city for the next two hundred years. Thereupon the Jews were arrested in all these places and a conference was arranged to meet at Benfeld [Alsace, February 8, 1349]. The Bishop of Strasbourg [Berthold II], all the feudal lords of Alsace, and representatives of the three above mentioned cities came there. The deputies of the city of Strasbourg were asked what they were going to do with their Jews. They answered and said that they knew no evil of them. Then they asked the Strasbourgers why they had closed the wells and put away the buckets, and there was a great indignation and clamor against the deputies from Strasbourg. So finally the Bishop and the lords and the Imperial Cities agreed to do away with the Jews. The result was that they were burnt in many cities, and wherever they were expelled they were caught by the peasants and stabbed to death or drowned. . . .

[The town-council of Strasbourg which wanted to save the Jews was deposed on the 9th–10th of February, and the new council gave in to the mob, who then arrested the Jews on Friday, the 13th.]

THE JEWS ARE BURNT

On Saturday—that was St. Valentine's Day—they burnt the Jews on a wooden platform in their cemetery. There were about two thousand people of them. Those who wanted to baptize themselves were spared. [Some say that about a thousand accepted baptism.] Many small children were taken out of the fire and baptized against the will of their fathers and mothers. And everything that was owed to the Jews was cancelled, and the Jews had to surrender all pledges and notes that they had taken for debts. The council, however, took the cash that the Jews possessed and divided it among the working-men proportionately. The money was indeed the thing that killed the Jews. If they had been poor and if the feudal lords had not been in debt to them, they would not have been burnt. After this wealth was divided among the artisans some gave their share to the Cathedral or to the Church on the advice of their confessors.

Thus were the Jews burnt at Strasbourg, and in the same year in all the cities of the Rhine, whether Free Cities or Imperial Cities or cities belonging to the lords. In some towns they burnt the Jews after a trial, in others, without a trial. In some cities the Jews themselves set fire to their houses and cremated themselves.

THE JEWS RETURN TO STRASBOURG

It was decided in Strasbourg that no Jew should enter the city for a hundred years, but before twenty years had passed, the council and magistrates agreed that they ought to admit the Jews again into the city for twenty years. And so the Jews came back again to Strasbourg in the year 1368 after the birth of our Lord.

III. *The Epitaph of Asher aben Turiel, Toledo, Spain, 1349*

> This stone is a memorial
> That a later generation may know

That 'neath it lies hidden a pleasant bud,
A cherished child.
Perfect in knowledge,
A reader of the Bible,
A student of the Mishnah and Gemara.
Had learned from his father
What his father learned from his teachers:
The statutes of God and his laws.
Though only fifteen years in age,
He was like a man of eighty in knowledge.
More blessed than all sons: Asher—may he
    rest in Paradise—
The son of Joseph ben Turiel—may God com-
    fort him,
He died of the plague, in the month of Tam-
    muz, in the year 109 [June or July, 1349].
But a few days before his death
He established his home;
But yesternight the joyous voice of the bride
    and groom
Was turned to the voice of wailing.
[Apparently he had just been married.]
And the father is left, sad and aching.
May the God of heaven
Grant him comfort.
And send another child
To restore his soul.

BIBLIOGRAPHY

REFERENCES TO TEXTBOOKS

Elbogen, pp. 108–109; Roth, pp. 213ff.; Sachar, pp. 200–203.

READINGS FOR ADVANCED STUDENTS

Graetz, IV, pp. 100–135; Graetz-Rhine, IV, pp. 35–54; Margolis and Marx,
    pp. 402–412.
Nohl, J., The Black Death, pp. 181–196.
JE, "Black Death"; "Strasburg."

ADDITIONAL SOURCE MATERIALS IN ENGLISH

Nohl, J., The Black Death, pp. 196–202. Contains further correspondence on
    the seizure of Jews who were accused of responsibility for the plague.

10.

An Oath Taken by Jews
Frankfort on the Main, about 1392

IN MATTERS requiring an oath before the civil authorities the medieval Jew did not employ the same formula as the Christian or Moslem. The reason is obvious: the state was Christian or Moslem, and no Jew could or would swear after the Christian or Moslem manner. In a Christian land this would have meant a recognition of Jesus or the Trinity. Such an oath would not have been binding on the Jew and hence was never imposed. For the convenience of the Jew, therefore, an oath "according to the Jewish custom" (*more judaico*) was instituted. One of the oldest surviving authentic oaths of this type was promulgated by the Byzantine emperor, Constantine VII (912–959), but in all probability this type is still older. This Byzantine formula, which is probably based on a Hebrew or Aramaic original, was employed, with considerable variations, in most European lands during the Middle Ages.

In the course of time, as prejudice against the Jew grew, the belief became widespread among Christians that Jews would not hesitate to perjure themselves in Christian courts. To counteract this presumed tendency, the various cities and states, particularly in Germany and France, began to make the oaths more formidable and more shocking both in language and in accompanying ceremonial, hoping thereby to frighten the Jews into telling the truth. It was but a step from intimidation to humiliation and to mild torture: Jews had to wear crowns of thorns on their necks and around their knees, and long thorn branches were pulled between their legs while the oath was being administered (France, eleventh century).

The manner of administering the oath varied in different localities. In spite of the emancipation of the late eighteenth and early nineteenth centuries, the oath, "according to the Jewish custom," persisted in France till 1846, in Prussia till 1869, in Roumania till 1912. It is needless to say that Jews have always resented this type of oath, especially because of the presumption implicit in it that the Jew is a perjurer.

The following formula, originally in Middle High German, was used in Frankfort on the Main about 1392. However, there were other oaths imposed on Jews in Frankfort on the Main at this time—

and in other cities and states, too,—that were milder and more digni-
fied. A special oath for Jews was still used in the police-courts of
Frankfort as late as 1847. (See *JE*, "Oath more judaico.")

THIS IS INDEED AN OATH FOR JEWS, HOW THEY SHALL TAKE AN OATH

⟨The Jew shall stand on a sow's skin and the five books of Master
Moses shall lie before him, and his right hand up to the wrist shall
lie on the book and he shall repeat after him who administers the
oath of the Jews:

Regarding such property of which the man accuses you, you
know nothing of it nor do you have it. You never had it in your
possession, you do not have it in any of your chests, you have not
buried it in the earth, nor locked it with locks, so help you God
who created heaven and earth, valley and hill, woods, trees, and
grass, and so help you the law which God himself created and
wrote with His own hand and gave Moses on Sinai's mount. And
so help you the five books of Moses that you may nevermore enjoy
a bite without soiling yourself all over as did the King of Babylon.

And may that sulphur and pitch flow down upon your neck that
flowed over Sodom and Gomorrah, and the same pitch that flowed
over Babylon flow over you, but two hundred times more, and may
the earth envelope and swallow you up as it did Dathan and Abiram.
And may your dust never join other dust, and your earth never join
other earth in the bosom of Master Abraham if what you say is not
true and right. [This refers either to a decent burial or to resurrection.] And so help you Adonai you have sworn the truth.

If not, may you become as leprous as Naaman and Gehazi, and
may the calamity strike you that the Israelite people escaped as they
journeyed forth from Egypt's land. And may a bleeding and a
flowing come forth from you and never cease, as your people wished
upon themselves when they condemned God, Jesus Christ, among
themselves, and tortured Him and said [Matthew 27:25]: "His
blood be upon us and our children." It is true, so help you God who
appeared to Moses in a burning bush which yet remained uncon-
sumed. It is true by the oath that you have sworn, by the soul which
you bring on the Day of Judgment before the Court, [before the
God of] Abraham, Isaac, and Jacob. It is true, so help you God and
the oath you have sworn [Amen].

11.

The Expulsion from Spain
1492

IN THE spring of 1492, shortly after the Moors were driven out of Granada, Ferdinand and Isabella of Spain expelled all the Jews from their lands and thus, by a stroke of the pen, put an end to the largest and most distinguished Jewish settlement in Europe. The expulsion of this intelligent, cultured, and industrious class was prompted only in part by the greed of the king and the intensified nationalism of the people who had just brought the crusade against the Moslem Moors to a glorious close. The real motive was the religious zeal of the Church, the Queen, and the masses. The official reason given for driving out the Jews was that they encouraged the Marranos to persist in their Jewishness and thus would not allow them to become good Christians.

The following account gives a detailed and accurate picture of the expulsion and its immediate consequences for Spanish Jewry. It was written in Hebrew by an Italian Jew in April or May, 1495.

⟪And in the year 5252 [1492], in the days of King Ferdinand, the Lord visited the remnant of his people a second time [the first Spanish visitation was in 1391], and exiled them. After the King had captured the city of Granada from the Moors, and it had surrendered to him on the 7th [2d] of January of the year just mentioned, he ordered the expulsion of all the Jews in all parts of his kingdom—in the kingdoms of Castile, Catalonia, Aragon, Galicia, Majorca, Minorca, the Basque provinces, the islands of Sardinia and Sicily, and the kingdom of Valencia. Even before that the Queen had expelled them from the kingdom of Andalusia [1483].

The King gave them three months' time in which to leave. It was announced in public in every city on the first of May, which happened to be the 19th day of the *Omer*, and the term ended on the day before the 9th of Ab. [The forty-nine days between the second of Passover and *Shabuot* are called *Omer* days. The actual decree of expulsion was signed March 31 and announced the first of May, the 19th day of the *Omer*. The Jews were to leave during May, June, and July and be out of the country by August 1, the 8th of Ab.]

About their number there is no agreement, but, after many inquiries, I found that the most generally accepted estimate is 50,000 families, or, as others say, 53,000. [This would be about 250,000 persons. Other estimates run from 100,000 to 800,000.] They had houses, fields, vineyards, and cattle, and most of them were artisans. At that time there existed many [Talmudic] academies in Spain, and at the head of the greatest of them were Rabbi Isaac Aboab in Guadalajara [probably the greatest Spanish rabbi of his day], Rabbi Isaac Veçudó in Leon, and Rabbi Jacob Habib in Salamanca [later author of a famous collection of the non-legal parts of the Talmud, the *En Yaakob*]. In the last named city there was a great expert in mathematics, and whenever there was any doubt on mathematical questions in the Christian academy of that city they referred them to him. His name was Abraham Zacuto. [This famous astronomer encouraged the expedition of Vasco da Gama.] . . .

In the course of the three months' respite granted them they endeavoured to effect an arrangement permitting them to stay on in the country, and they felt confident of success. Their representatives were the rabbi, Don Abraham Seneor, the leader of the Spanish congregations, who was attended by a retinue on thirty mules, and Rabbi Meïr Melamed, who was secretary to the King, and Don Isaac Abravanel [1437–1508], who had fled to Castile from the King of Portugal, and then occupied an equally prominent position at the Spanish royal court. He, too, was later expelled, went to Naples, and was highly esteemed by the King of Naples. The aforementioned great rabbi, Rabbi Isaac of Leon, used to call this Don Abraham Seneor: "*Soné Or*" ["Hater of Light," a Hebrew pun on *Seneor*], because he was a heretic, and the end proved that he was right, as he was converted to Christianity at the age of eighty, he and all his family, and Rabbi Meïr Melamed with him. [Seneor and his son-in-law, Meïr, were converted June 15, 1492; Ferdinand and Isabella were among the sponsors.] Don Abraham had arranged the nuptials between the King and the Queen. The Queen was the heiress to the throne, and the King one of the Spanish nobility. On account of this, Don Abraham was appointed leader of the Jews, but not with their consent.

The agreement permitting them to remain in the country on the payment of a large sum of money was almost completed when it was frustrated by the interference of a prior who was called the Prior of Santa Cruz. [Legend relates that Torquemada, Prior of the convent of Santa Cruz, thundered, with crucifix aloft, to the King and Queen: "Judas Iscariot sold his master for thirty pieces of silver. Your Highness would sell him anew for thirty thousand. Here he is, take him, and barter him away."] Then the Queen gave an answer to the representatives of the Jews, similar to the saying of King Solomon [Proverbs 21:1]: "The king's heart is in the hand of the Lord, as the rivers of water. God turneth it withersoever He will." She said furthermore: "Do you believe that this comes upon you from us? The Lord hath put this thing into the heart of the king." [Isabella says it is God's will that the Jews be expelled.]

Then they saw that there was evil determined against them by the King, and they gave up the hope of remaining. But the time had become short, and they had to hasten their exodus from Spain. They sold their houses, their landed estates, and their cattle for very small prices, to save themselves. The King did not allow them to carry silver and gold out of his country, so that they were compelled to exchange their silver and gold for merchandise of cloths and skins and other things. [Ever since 1480 Jews and Gentiles were forbidden to export precious metal, the source of a nation's wealth.]

One hundred and twenty thousand of them went to Portugal, according to a compact which a prominent man, Don Vidal bar Benveniste del Cavalleria, had made with the King of Portugal, and they paid one ducat for every soul, and the fourth part of all the merchandise they had carried thither; and he allowed them to stay in his country six months. This King acted much worse toward them than the King of Spain, and after the six months had elapsed he made slaves of all those that remained in his country, and banished seven hundred children to a remote island to settle it, and all of them died. Some say that there were double as many. Upon them the Scriptural word was fulfilled [Deuteronomy 28:32]: "Thy sons and thy daughters shall be given unto another people, etc." [All Spanish Jews, who were still in Portugal in 1493, were enslaved by King John (1481–1495). The children were sent to the isle of St. Thomas, off the coast of Africa.] He also ordered the congregation of Lisbon, his capital, not to raise their voice in their prayers, that the Lord might not hear their complaining about the violence that was done unto them.

Many of the exiled Spaniards went to Mohammedan countries, to Fez, Tlemçen, and the Berber provinces, under the King of Tunis. [These North African lands are across the Mediterranean from Spain.] On account of their large numbers the Moors did not allow them into their cities, and many of them died in the fields from hunger, thirst, and lack of everything. The lions and bears, which are numerous in this country, killed some of them while they lay starving outside of the cities. A Jew in the kingdom of Tlemçen, named Abraham, the viceroy who ruled the kingdom, made part of them come to this kingdom, and he spent a large amount of money to help them. The Jews of Northern Africa were very charitable toward them. A part of those who went to Northern Africa, as they found no rest and no place that would receive them, returned to Spain, and became converts, and through them the prophecy of Jeremiah was fulfilled [Lamentations 1:13]: "He hath spread a net for my feet, he hath turned me back." For, originally, they had all fled for the sake of the unity of God; only a very few had become converts throughout all the boundaries of Spain; they did not spare their fortunes; yea, parents escaped without having regard to their children.

When the edict of expulsion became known in the other countries, vessels came from Genoa to the Spanish harbors to carry away the Jews. The crews of these vessels, too, acted maliciously and meanly toward the Jews, robbed them, and delivered some of them to the famous pirate of that time who was called the Corsair of Genoa. To those who escaped and arrived at Genoa the people of the city showed themselves merciless, and oppressed and robbed them, and the cruelty of their wicked hearts went so far that they took the infants from the mothers' breasts.

Many ships with Jews, especially from Sicily, went to the city of Naples on the coast. The King of this country was friendly to the Jews, received them all, and was merciful towards them, and he helped them with money. The Jews that were at Naples supplied them with food as much as they could, and sent around to the other parts of Italy to collect money to sustain them. The Marranos in this city lent them money on pledges without interest; even the Dominican Brotherhood acted mercifully toward them. [The Dominican monks were normally bitterly opposed to Jews.] On account of their very large number, all this was not enough. Some of them died by famine, others sold their children to Christians to sustain their life. Finally, a plague broke out among them, spread to Naples, and very many of them died, so that the living wearied of burying the dead.

Part of the exiled Spaniards went over sea to Turkey. Some of them were thrown into the sea and drowned, but those who arrived there the King of Turkey received kindly, as they were artisans. He lent them money and settled many of them on an island, and gave them fields and estates. [The Turks needed smiths and makers of munitions for the war against Christian Europe.]

A few of the exiles were dispersed in the countries of Italy, in the city of Ferrara, in the [papal] countries of Romagna, the March, and Patrimonium, and in Rome. . . .

He who said unto His world, Enough, may He also say Enough unto our sufferings, and may He look down upon our impotence. May He turn again, and have compassion upon us, and hasten our salvation. Thus may it be Thy will!

BIBLIOGRAPHY

REFERENCES TO TEXTBOOKS

Elbogen, pp. 80–86; Roth, pp. 218–232; Sachar, pp. 204–220.

READINGS FOR ADVANCED STUDENTS

Graetz, IV, pp. 334–356; Graetz-Rhine, IV, pp. 207–244; Margolis and Marx, pp. 440–476.

Abbott, G. F., *Israel in Europe*, pp. 141–166.

Milman, H. H., *The History of the Jews*, II, Book xxvi.

Prescott, W. H., *History of the Reign of Ferdinand and Isabella the Catholic*, II, Part I, Chap. xvii: "Expulsion of the Jews from Spain." An interesting, scholarly presentation.

JE, "Spain."

ADDITIONAL SOURCE MATERIALS IN ENGLISH

Halper, B., *Post-Biblical Hebrew Literature*, "The Advantages of a Republic over a Monarchy," II, pp. 221–224. A brief discussion on political science by Isaac Abravanel.

Lindo, E. H., *The History of the Jews of Spain and Portugal*, pp. 277–280 contains the decree of expulsion. Comments on the expulsion by Isaac Abravanel, financial adviser to Isabella, may be found on p. 284. Another contemporary account occurs on p. 285.

Marx, A., "The Expulsion of the Jews from Spain," *JQR*, O. S., XX (1908), pp. 240ff.; *JQR*, N. S., II (1911–1912), pp. 257–258. This is the complete account of which source No. 11 is an extract.

12.

The Massacre of the New Christians of Lisbon
April, 1506

IN 1497 all the Jews of Portugal were compelled by the King to become Christians, yet these "New Christians" continued in secret to practice the Jewish faith. The Christian masses, fired by religious fanaticism, frightened by plague, and enraged by the economic competition—now unrestricted—of these secret-Jews, attacked them whenever they could. The worst outbreak occurred in 1506 when about two thousand were literally butchered and cremated. This unhappy incident so affected King Emmanuel (1495–1521) that he permitted these pseudo-Christians to leave the country, if they wished, and to take their property with them.

The following account of the massacre is taken from the Latin work of Geronymo Osorio (1506–1580), a Catholic prelate of Portugal who wrote the story of the reign of Emmanuel. This history by the Catholic bishop is distinguished by a spirit of broad tolerance and humanity.

℃About the same time [a time of drought and plague and of high prices] there happened a great tumult at Lisbon, raised by the fury and madness of the rabble; in this almost all the Jews, who, as we before observed, had been converted to Christianity, were cruelly massacred.

The affair was as follows: The greatest part of the citizens had left the town because of the plague, and many French, Belgian, and German ships had arrived there at this time. On the 19th of April [Sunday afternoon about 3 o'clock] many of those who remained in the city went to St. Dominic's church to attend divine service. On the left side of this church is Jesus Chapel, much frequented by people at their devotion. Above the altar is placed a representation of Jesus on the cross, and the hole, representing the wound in our Savior's side, had a glass cover. When many people had fixed their eyes and attention on that wound, a lucid brightness shone from it. On this appearance many said it was a miracle and that the divinity testified his presence by a wonderful sign.

Some one of the Jews, who not long before had taken upon him the profession of Christianity, with a loud voice denied it to be a miracle, adding that it was very unlikely that a piece of dry wood should show forth a miracle. [A German Catholic who was also in the church said he saw nothing unusual.] Many indeed doubted of the truth thereof; yet considering the time, place, and congregation, it was highly imprudent for any one, especially a Jew, to endeavor to convince people of a mistake, when they were firmly persuaded the thing was true. The populace, naturally headstrong, inconsiderate, and apt to be struck with anything that appears marvelous, upon hearing that a Jew derogated from the credit of the miracle, began to make an uproar. They called him a perfidious, wicked betrayer of religion and an outrageous and malicious enemy of Christ, and declared him worthy of torture and death.

Nay, their fury arose at last to such a degree, that falling on this unhappy wretch, they dragged him by his hair into the market-place before the church, where they tore him to pieces, and making a fire, threw his body into it. [The mob was excited also because the King had that very day freed some New Christians arrested for celebrating the Passover.] All the common people flocked to this tumult, and a certain monk made a speech too well adapted to their humor at the time. In this he excited them with great vehemence to revenge the impiety of the Jew. The mob too apt of their own accord to be outrageous, by this means became the more transported with fury. Two other [Dominican] monks, at the same time holding forth a crucifix, loudly excited the people to slaughter, at every other word calling out: "Heresy, heresy! Avenge the heresy, and extinguish the wicked race!" [The Dominican friars warred against the New Christians as heretics and wanted to introduce the Inquisition into Portugal.]

The French and German [sailors] quickly came ashore, and having joined the Portuguese, they committed great havoc. This cruel massacre was begun by five hundred, who were at last joined by several others. Transported with madness and boiling with rage, they fell upon the wretched Jews, of whom they killed great numbers, and threw many half alive into the flames. By this time several fires were kindled near the place where the first offender had been burnt, for the canaille about the streets with eagerness and alacrity had brought fuel from all parts, that nothing might be wanting to execute this horrible design. [German sailors bought more fuel when the supply ran low.] The shrieks and outcries of the women, together with the piteous supplications of the men, might, one would think, have softened the most savage hearts into pity; but the actors in this horrid scene were so divested of humanity that they spared neither sex nor age, but wreaked their fury on all without distinction; so that above five hundred Jews were either killed or burnt that day.

The news of this massacre having reached the country, next day [Monday, the 20th of April] above a thousand men from the villages flocked into the city and joined the murderers, and the slaughter was renewed. The Jews, being under the greatest terror, concealed themselves in their houses; but the blood-thirsty rabble broke open the doors, rushed in upon them, and butchered men, women, and children in a most barbarous manner; they dashed the infants against the walls, and, dragging all out of doors by the feet, threw them into the fire, some quite dead, and others yet breathing life.

Such an insensibility overwhelmed this wretched people that they were scarce able to lament their ruin or deplore their misery; nay, those who lay concealed, though they beheld their parents or children dragged away to torture and death, durst not even utter a mournful groan, for fear of being discovered. In short they became so stupefied with terror that there was little difference betwixt the living and the dead. Their houses were plundered, and the bloody rioters carried off great quantities of gold and silver and several other things of value. The French put their booty aboard their ships, and had it not been for the desire of plunder, many more would have been murdered that day. [The mob did go out of its way to plunder and butcher the hated tax collector Mascarenhas.] Several of the Jews, both young and old, fled to the altars for refuge, and taking hold of crosses and the images of saints, in a most suppliant manner implored the divine protection; but the fury of this abandoned rabble proceeded to such a length that without any regard to religion, they broke into the churches, and dragging the Jews from thence, either cruelly butchered or threw them alive into the fire.

Several who had any resemblance of this people in their looks were in great danger and some were actually killed on that suspicion, and others received many wounds and blows on the same account. [Even non-Jews were murdered.] Some persons took this opportunity to vent their malice upon those against whom they had a pique by asserting they were Jews, and before the falsity could be confuted, satiated their revenge by their blood. The magistrates had not spirit to oppose the fury of the multitude; however, many worthy persons preserved, with the greatest fidelity, such of the Jews as fled to them for shelter and concealed them in places of safety. Yet above a thousand were massacred this day.

The third day [Tuesday, the 21st of April] those inhuman barbarians returned again to the slaughter; but they scarcely found any to murder, for most of the Jews who survived had either saved themselves by flight or lay safely concealed; yet some slaughter was committed. On these three days above two thousand of the Jewish race were murdered. In the evening Ayres de Sylva [chief justice] and Alvaro de Castro [governor of the civil court], men of the first distinction, who presided in the courts of judicature, came with guards into the city; their arrival put a stop to the fury of the mob. The French and Germans repaired to their ships with a considerable booty and set sail with all possible expedition.

Emmanuel, having got account of this massacre, immediately dispatched Diogo de Almeida and Diogo Lobo to Lisbon with full power to punish the perpetrators of this horrid villainy. Many now suffered for their madness and cruelty. The monks who had stirred up the people to slaughter, being first in a solemn manner degraded from the priestly office and dignity, were afterwards strangled and burnt. Those who appeared remiss in restraining the popular fury were partly stripped of their honors, and partly fined; and the city was deprived of several privileges. [Many rioters were hanged.]

BIBLIOGRAPHY

REFERENCES TO TEXTBOOKS

Elbogen, pp. 80–86; Roth, pp. 218–232; Sachar, pp. 204–220.

READINGS FOR ADVANCED STUDENTS

Graetz, IV, pp. 357–421; Margolis and Marx, pp. 473–476.

Baron, S. W., *A Social and Religious History of the Jews*, II, pp. 58ff. This three volume history by Baron is a valuable handbook for every student of Jewish life in the medieval period.

Braunstein, B., *The Chuetas of Majorca. Conversos and the Inquisition of Majorca.* (Columbia University Oriental Series, Vol. XXVIII.) This work throws much light on the life of crypto-Jews.

Herculano, A., *History of the Origin and Establishment of the Inquisition in Portugal*, translated by J. C. Branner, pp. 262ff. A standard work.

Lindo, E. H., *The History of the Jews of Spain and Portugal*, pp. 351ff.

JE, "Lisbon"; "Portugal."

ADDITIONAL SOURCE MATERIALS IN ENGLISH

Gibbs, J., *The History of the Portuguese During the Reign of Emmanuel*, London, 1752, is a translation of *De rebus Emmanuelis* of Osorio and is the source for this chapter. Osorio's account of the forcible conversion of the Jews of Portugal may also be found in E. H. Lindo's *The History of the Jews of Spain and Portugal*, pp. 325–329. Lindo also quotes briefly, p. 330, from Samuel Usque's *Consolation for the Tribulations of Israel* which describes the sufferings of the Jews in Portugal during this period.

Inquisition and Judaism, The, A Sermon addressed to Jewish Martyrs on the Occasion of an Auto da Fe at Lisbon, 1705. By the Archbishop of Cranganor; also A Reply to the Sermon, by Carlos Vero (David Nieto). Translated by Moses Mocatta. Philadelphia, 1860. This sermon, preached to sixty-six penitents on the square of the Rocio in Lisbon by Archbishop Diogo da Anunciação, is ninety-three pages long. Rabbi David Nieto's reply was published in London in 1723 or 1724.

13.

The Cairo Purim
1524

PURIM commemorates the deliverance of the Persian Jews from the hands of the notorious Haman who had determined to massacre them all. Similarly, individuals and Jewish communities celebrate those specific days on which they, too, were saved from some local enemy. Cairo still observes the 28th of Adar, the anniversary of its deliverance from the rapacious Ahmed Shaitan, who in 1524 had declared himself Sultan of Egypt and under threat of death had imposed an enormous tribute on the Cairo Jewish community. The Hebrew account of this deliverance which follows closely the style and the structure of the Book of Esther, is still read in the Cairo synagogue on this special Purim. The author of this Purim *Megillah* or scroll is said to be Samuel Sirillo, one of the rabbis of Cairo during those trying days. As a matter of fact, in one paragraph the author, whoever he is, lapses into the first person.

¶And it came to pass in the days of King Sulaiman (this is King Sulaiman who reigned in Turkey [1520–1566], and the Levant, and Greece, and in many military camps), that in those days, when King Sulaiman sat on the throne of his kingdom, which was in Constantinople, the great city, he considered all the provinces of his kingdom, and he sent to each province a chief to judge its people in righteousness and equity.

After these things, King Sulaiman promoted one of his chiefs, whose name was Ahmed Shaitan, and he placed his seat above all the chiefs that were with him. [The Hebrew text puns by calling him not "Shaitan," but "Satan."] And he sent him to be a ruler over the land of Egypt [1523], and he commanded him saying: "Egypt have I given to thee, and in it shalt thou dwell, and according to thy word shall all my people be ruled; only in the throne will I be greater than thou. Only be thou strong and very courageous to judge in righteousness, and to discard unjust gain, and the coinage shalt thou issue in my name."

And Ahmed Shaitan came into the land of Egypt, and he went up to the citadel, and dwelt there. And he began to oppress, and to

61

exact money, and he did that which was evil in the sight of the Holy One. And the taxes increased in his days, and Ahmed Shaitan forsook the command of the King, and gathered together much substance; and his spirit was not satisfied, neither was his eye satisfied, for he was a man of very great greed. And his soul was greatly lifted up, and he determined to rebel against the King. . . . [He was disgruntled because he had not been made the Grand Vizier of the Ottoman Empire.] On that day, at the time when Ahmed Shaitan went up into the citadel, his whole force made him King over them. And at the time when they made him King over them, they proclaimed in the streets of Cairo, and in all the neighboring cities, that Ahmed Shaitan was made King [early in 1524].

And it came to pass, when he had been made king, that he laid a tax upon all the inhabitants of Egypt, for he wanted to take away all their money. And Ahmed Shaitan's force came and said unto him: "Thou knowest, O our lord the King, what thy servants have done unto thee, and that we have made thee King in Egypt. And now, if thy servants have found favor in thine eyes, and if it please the King, let a decree be given to destroy, to kill, and to cause to perish, all Jews, both young and old, little children and women, and to take the spoils of them for a prey, and to take vengeance of them, for they are our enemies and adversaries."

And Ahmed Shaitan said unto them: "The Jews are given unto you, and do unto them as is pleasing in your eyes." [Possibly Ahmed was embittered because Abraham de Castro, the mint-master, a Jew, had fled to tell Sulaiman of Ahmed's treason.]

And it came to pass when the Jews heard this thing, that they made a very grievous mourning, and they cried with a loud and bitter cry. And they proclaimed a fast, and they wept, and they put earth upon their heads, and they put on sackcloth, from the least amongst them even unto the greatest, and the land mourned, and all the inhabitants thereof languished. And they continued fasting and crying every day until their weeping rose up to heaven. The couriers went out, being hastened by the commandment of Ahmed Shaitan, and the decree was given in the quarter of the Jews, and all the Jews were perplexed.

And it came to pass, when the force of Ahmed Shaitan heard the commandment of their King, that there assembled themselves together of them and of the people of the land about two thousand men. And they came upon the city securely, and they plundered all that belonged to them, and they took much spoil. And it was so that every one who found a Jew sought to kill him, and they killed five

Jews. [Ahmed's mercenaries were intent on plunder rather than on murder.] And the Jews fled, running in haste to save their lives, for they said: "We be all dead men." And a great cry arose in Cairo, and one Jew died from great fear. And the outcry of the children of Israel rose up to the Holy One to heaven, and He remembered His covenant which He had made with Abraham, and Isaac, and Jacob.

There was a certain Jew in the citadel of the city [Abraham Alkurkumani, a finance officer of Ahmed Shaitan], and God sent him to be my helper and deliverer, and the supporter of my right hand. And it was so that when the Jews were crying, the matter was reported to one of Ahmed Shaitan's chiefs [Alkurkumani], and he stood up before him, for he was an officer of his. And he said unto him: "If I have found favor in thy sight, O King, and if it please the King, let the Jews alone. For what is their transgression, and what is their sin, that thou shouldst deliver them into the hand of those who seek to do them evil. And if it be pleasing to the King, let their silver and their gold be given into the treasuries of the King; I will be surety for it, at my hands thou mayest require it." And Ahmed Shaitan said to the officer: "Go and do as thou desirest, and do to the whole people as is good in thine eyes, for thou hast found favor in my sight." [Alkurkumani thus prevented a general sack of the Jewish quarter.]

And the officer came and proclaimed in the quarter of the Jews: "Thus said the King, 'Let no man stretch out his hand against the Jews.'" And the officer said to the Jews: "Peace shall be upon you; fear not, for the King has given orders concerning you." And it came to pass when the force of Ahmed Shaitan had plundered the Jews, that they took all the spoil, and carried it into the house of [Alkurkumani, the treasurer,] one of the chiefs.

After these things, Ahmed Shaitan desired of the Jews a hundred and fifty thousand great gold pieces, and he also said: "If ye bring them not quickly, I shall kill you with the sword." [Ahmed needed money to fight Sulaiman.] And when the Jews heard this evil thing, they mourned and could not answer him, for they were terrified before him. And it came to pass, when the children of Israel saw that the hand of the Holy One had touched them, that they threw earth upon their heads and blew the trumpet, and they convoked an assembly, and every one returned from his evil way, and they cried unto the Holy One with a loud voice and with weeping. And whilst they were weeping and making supplication before the Almighty, some men from amongst them went up, and fell down to the ground before Ahmed Shaitan, but he listened not to them. And Ahmed

Shaitan imposed a tax upon the land, and upon the people of Egypt, and upon the merchants, and he said unto them: "Bring unto me silver and gold without number." [He oppressed Moslems, too.]

And Ahmed Shaitan took from the Jews of Cairo much money, and they were being seized by the hand of their enemies to smite them very sorely. And when the tribulation and the evil decree pressed heavily upon them, some of the Jews hid themselves; and the command was given to all the people of Cairo that they should hang every Jew who should hide himself, on the door of his house. And every day the task-masters stretched out their hands against the Jews to smite them very sorely. And certain men of Ahmed Shaitan's force came, and seized the Jews, to take from them their silver and their gold and everything that belonged to them. And they cried to the Holy One in their trouble, and that He may save them out of their distresses. And they made supplication before the Holy One with a loud voice, and the Holy One heard their groaning, and there was not a house in Cairo in which there was not weeping, and lamentation, and sobbing.

And on the nineteenth day of the month Adar [February 23, 1524], Ahmed Shaitan sought to destroy all the Jews that were in Cairo, both young and old, little children and women, and to take the spoil of them for a prey. And on the eighteenth day of the month Adar [i.e., the previous day], the Jews assembled themselves to stand for their life in prayer and supplication, and great crying, and in fasting and weeping; and sackcloth and ashes were spread under many. [The Jews with their children held special services led by the Rabbi Samuel Sirillo.] And the cry of the children of Israel went up to the Holy One, and He heard their groaning, and He remembered His covenant with them. And God saw their works, and their fasting, and their sackcloth, and He did not despise their humiliation, and He sent them help suddenly, and He saved them from the hands of their enemies and of those who sought their hurt.

In that night [February 22] our cry went up before God, and our prayers were written in the book of remembrances, and they were read before the [Divine] King. And He said: "I have surely seen the affliction of My people which are in Egypt, and have heard their cry by reason of their task-masters, for I know their sorrows."

On that day [February 22] was a council held by the chiefs who remained of King Sulaiman's force, and who had been addressing Ahmed Shaitan with a double heart. And they agreed to seize Ahmed Shaitan. . . .

And [on the very day on which the Jews were to be massacred]

King Sulaiman's force pursued the force of Ahmed Shaitan [February 23], and they overtook them, as they were coming out of the city, [to which they had fled], and they destroyed the city, and they plundered it, and burnt a part of it with fire. Now the Jews who were in the city they plundered, but did not kill one of them.

And on the twenty-eighth day of the month Adar [March 3], King Sulaiman's force pursued Ahmed Shaitan, and they overtook him, and seized him, and cut off his head. And King Sulaiman's force brought Ahmed Shaitan's head fixed upon a spear, and they hung it up on the gate of Zuwailah [where executions took place] before the eyes of all the people. And it came to pass when King Sulaiman's force entered Cairo, carrying with them the head of Ahmed Shaitan, that the people of Cairo rejoiced with a great rejoicing.

And the Jews saw the salvation of the Holy One, and the wonders which were done to them, as in the days of Haman the Agagite, who had sought to destroy, to kill, and to cause to perish all Jews, both young and old, little children and women, and to take the spoil of them for a prey—for as the Amalekite [Haman] had counseled, thus counseled also Ahmed Shaitan to do. But the Holy One brought their counsel to nought, and caused their thoughts to perish, and their violent dealing came down upon their own pates. The Jews were assembled, and agreed to fast on the twenty-seventh of the month Adar, and to make the twenty-eighth day a feast and rejoicing, and for sending portions one to another and gifts to the poor, because the Holy One had done to them marvels and wonderful things, and had helped them out of the hands of those who had sought their life. The Jews, therefore, who dwell in Cairo ordained and took upon them, and upon their children, and upon all who join themselves to them, to fast on the twenty-seventh day of the month Adar, and to read this scroll on the twenty-eighth day of it, and to make it a day of feasting and rejoicing.

BIBLIOGRAPHY

READINGS FOR ADVANCED STUDENTS

Graetz, IV, pp. 392–396; Graetz-Rhine, IV, pp. 252–255.
JE, "Ahmed-Pasha"; "Castro, Abraham de"; "Purims, Special."

ADDITIONAL SOURCE MATERIALS IN ENGLISH

Margoliouth, G., "Megillath Missraim, or the Scroll of the Egyptian Purim," JQR, O. S., VIII (1895–1896), pp. 281–288. Source No. 13 is an excerpt of Margoliouth's translation.

14.

A Petition for the Readmission
of the Jews to England
November 13, 1655

IN 1290 the Jews had been expelled from England, and it was only in the sixteenth century, after the expulsion from Spain and Portugal, that individual Marranos settled secretly in London as Spanish and Portuguese Catholics. Oliver Cromwell, in the next century, was anxious to further the settlement of wealthy Jews in England and in the colonies, in order to enlarge the commercial and colonial power of the Commonwealth. To this end he encouraged Menasseh ben Israel (1604–1657), a brilliant Amsterdam rabbi of Portuguese origin, to come to London to negotiate for the readmission of the Jews. Ever since 1649 this scholarly rabbi, whose reputation extended all over Christendom, had been interested in the return of Jewry to the British Isles, particularly as a place of refuge for the Polish Jews fleeing from the Cossacks and for the Spanish and Portuguese Marranos fleeing from the Inquisition.

On November 13, 1655 Menasseh's petition, in French, asking for the unconditional readmission of the Jews, was presented to the Council. This petition, given below, was not granted; Menasseh ben Israel's hope of opening England to the mass migration of persecuted Jews was a failure. The Puritan love for the biblical Hebrews apparently did not extend to the Jews, their descendants; the voices of religious liberty and political tolerance were drowned out by the clamor of Puritanical prejudice and commercial rivalry. Menasseh returned to Holland, a broken man.

However, the Marranos who were already in the land were, through the connivance of the ambitious Cromwell, allowed to remain as Jews. This was the beginning of the Jewish resettlement in present day England.

❮These are the boons and the favors which I, Menasseh ben Israel, in the name of my Hebrew nation, beseech of your most serene Highness, and may God prosper you and give you much success in all your undertakings. Such is the wish and desire of your humble servant.

66

I.   The first thing which I ask of your Highness is that our Hebrew nation be received and admitted into this mighty republic under the protection and care of your Highness like the citizens themselves, and for greater security in the future I entreat your Highness, if it is agreeable to you, to order all your commanders and generals to defend us on all occasions. [Only a few months back a harmless Jewish beggar had been mobbed in London.]

II.   That it please your Highness to allow us public synagogues, not only in England, but also in all other conquered places which are under the power of your Highness, and to allow us to exercise our religion in all details as we should. [The Jews were anxious for rights especially in Jamaica, conquered by the English in May, 1655.]

III.   That we should be allowed to have a plot or cemetery outside the city for burying our dead without being molested by anyone.

IV.   That it be allowed us to trade freely in all sorts of merchandise just like every one else.

V.   That (in order that those who come in shall do so for the benefit of the citizens and live without doing harm or causing trouble to any one) your most serene Highness should appoint a person of prominence to inform himself of those who enter and to receive their passports. He should be informed of those who arrive and should oblige them to take an oath to be faithful to your Highness in this country.

VI.   And in order that the justices of the peace should not at all be bothered with litigation and quarrels which may arise among those of our nation, we ask that your most serene Highness grant the liberty to the rabbi of associating with himself two Jewish clergymen in order to adjust and to judge all the disputes at law in conformity with the Mosaic code, with the privilege, nevertheless, of appealing a sentence to the civil judges. The sum to which the party will have been condemned must first be deposited, however [before the appeal from the Jewish court to the state courts is made].

VII.   That if, peradventure, there should be any laws against our Jewish nation, then first and before all things they should be revoked so that by this means it should be possible for us to live with greater security, under the safeguard and protection of your most serene

Highness. [There were many anti-Jewish laws dating from 1066 to 1290.]

If your most serene Highness grants us these things we will always be most attached to you and under obligations to pray to God for the prosperity of your Highness and of your illustrious and most sage Council. May it be His will to grant much success to all the undertakings of your most serene Highness. Amen.

BIBLIOGRAPHY

REFERENCES TO TEXTBOOKS

Elbogen, pp. 127–128; Roth, pp. 300–303; Sachar, pp. 229–231.

READINGS FOR ADVANCED STUDENTS

Graetz, V, pp. 18–50; Graetz-Rhine, V, pp. 97–118; Margolis and Marx, pp. 489–493.

Henriques, H. S. Q., *The Jews and the English Law*. A fine study. Written from the point of view of a lawyer rather than a historian.

Hyamson, A. M., *A History of the Jews in England*, 2nd ed., 1928. Useful for background.

Milman, H. H., *The History of the Jews*, II, pp. 434–437.

Roth, C., *A Life of Menasseh ben Israel*. The best life of Menasseh. There is also an excellent bibliography appended.

JE, "Cromwell, Oliver"; "England"; "Manasseh ben Israel."

ADDITIONAL SOURCE MATERIALS IN ENGLISH

Wolf, L., *Menasseh ben Israel's Mission to Oliver Cromwell*. This standard work contains the important writings of Menasseh, touching the readmission of the Jews to England, and also a detailed and scholarly introduction.

A facsimile of a Jewish petition to Oliver Cromwell in 1656 may be found in Bevan and Singer, *The Legacy of Israel*, between pp. 406 and 407. The text of this 1656 petition is also reprinted and discussed on pp. xxix–xxxi.

15.

The Settlement of the Jews
in North America
1654–1655

THE first settlement of Jews in a group in North America was in what is today New York City. Early in September, 1654, twenty-three refugees arrived there on the French frigate, *St. Charles.* They had probably come from Dutch Brazil which had just been recaptured by the Portuguese. Although most of the newcomers were of Spanish or Portuguese origin, they were Dutch subjects.

That very month Peter Stuyvesant, the governor of the colony, dispatched to the West India Company a letter, dated September 22, 1654, expressing the desire of the Dutch colonists to expel these Jews. This letter is the first selection reprinted below.

The second selection, dated January, 1655, is a petition by the Portuguese Jews of Amsterdam, Holland, requesting that the Dutch colonies in America be opened to Jewish trade and settlement. The granting of this petition by the West India Company prevented Stuyvesant from expelling the newly-arrived refugees. The third selection, dated April 26, 1655, is the answer of the West India Company to Stuyvesant's letter of September 22, 1654, and orders him to tolerate Jews in Manhattan.

The fourth selection is a description of the Jews in New York City in 1748 from the pen of Peter Kalm, a Swedish traveler. Jews were a novelty to him for there were very few Jews in Sweden at this time. This account was written originally in Swedish, the first three documents, in Dutch.

1. *Stuyvesant's Attempt to Expel the Jews, September 22, 1654—* JEWS: EXTRACT FROM A CERTAIN LETTER FROM DIRECTOR PETER STUYVESANT TO THE AMSTERDAM CHAMBER [OF DIRECTORS], DATED MANHATTAN, SEPTEMBER 22, 1654

The Jews who have arrived would nearly all like to remain here, but learning that they (with their customary usury and deceitful trading with the Christians) were very repugnant to the inferior magistrates, as also to the people having the most affection for you;

69

the Deaconry [which takes care of the poor] also fearing that owing to their present indigence [due to the fact that they had been captured and robbed by pirates] they might become a charge in the coming winter, we have, for the benefit of this weak and newly developing place and the land in general, deemed it useful to require them in a friendly way to depart; praying also most seriously in this connection, for ourselves as also for the general community of your worships, that the deceitful race—such hateful enemies and blasphemers of the name of Christ—be not allowed further to infect and trouble this new colony, to the detraction of your worships and the dissatisfaction of your worships' most affectionate subjects.

11. *Amsterdam Jewry's Successful Intercession for the Manhattan Immigrants, January, 1655—1655*, JANUARY PETITION OF THE JEWISH NATION

⟪To the Honorable Lords, Directors of the Chartered West India Company, Chamber of the City of Amsterdam

The merchants of the [Jewish] Portuguese nation residing in this City [of Amsterdam] respectfully remonstrate to your Honors that it has come to their knowledge that your Honors raise obstacles to

Granted [February 15, 1655] that they may reside and traffic, provided they shall not become a charge upon the Deaconry or the Company.

the giving of permits or passports to the Portuguese Jews to travel and to go to reside in New Netherland, which if persisted in will result to the great disadvantage of the Jewish nation. It can also be of no advantage to the general Company but rather damaging.

There are many of the nation who have lost their possessions at Pernambuco and have arrived from there in great poverty, and part of them have been dispersed here and there. [Pernambuco, the stronghold of Dutch Brazil, was captured by the Portuguese, January, 1654.] So that your petitioners had to expend large sums of money for their necessaries of life, and through lack of opportunity all cannot remain here [in Holland] to live. And as they cannot go to Spain or Portugal because of the Inquisition, a great part of the aforesaid people must in time be obliged to depart for other territories of their High Mightinesses the States-General [the national Dutch legislature] and their Companies, in order there, through their labor and efforts, to be able to exist under the protection of the administrators of your Honorable Directors, observing and obeying your Honors' orders and commands. [The West India

Company owned the young Dutch colony of New Netherland.]

It is well known to your Honors that the Jewish nation in Brazil have at all times been faithful and have striven to guard and maintain that place, risking for that purpose their possessions and their blood. [The Jews distinguished themselves in the defense of Pernambuco, remaining there until its fall in 1654.]

Yonder land is extensive and spacious. The more loyal people that go to live there, the better it is in regard to the population of the country as in regard to the payment of various excises and taxes which may be imposed there, and in regard to the increase of trade, and also to the importation of all the necessaries that may be sent there.

Your Honors should also consider that the Honorable Lords, the Burgomasters of the City and the Honorable High Illustrious Mighty Lords, the States-General, have in political matters always protected and considered the Jewish nation as upon the same footing as all the inhabitants and burghers. Also it is conditioned in the treaty of perpetual peace with the King of Spain [the treaty of Münster, 1648] that the Jewish nation shall also enjoy the same liberty as all other inhabitants of these lands.

Your Honors should also please consider that many of the Jewish nation are principal shareholders in the [West India] Company. They having always striven their best for the Company, and many of their nation have lost immense and great capital in its shares and obligations. [The Company lost heavily through the capture of Brazil by the Portuguese.]

The Company has by a general resolution consented that those who wish to populate the Colony shall enjoy certain districts of land gratis. Why should now certain subjects of this State not be allowed to travel thither and live there? The French consent that the Portuguese Jews may traffic and live in Martinique, [Saint] Christopher, and others of their territories, whither also some have gone from here, as your Honors know. The English also consent at the present time that the Portuguese and Jewish nation may go from London and settle at Barbados, whither also some have gone. [Martinique, Saint Christopher, and Barbados are in the West Indies.]

As foreign nations consent that the Jewish nation may go to live and trade in their territories, how can your Honors forbid the same and refuse transportation to this Portuguese nation who reside here and have been settled here well on to about sixty years, many also being born here and confirmed burghers, and this to a land that needs people for its increase? [Jewish "New Christians" from Portugal had settled in Holland as early as 1593.]

Therefore the petitioners request, for the reasons given above (as also others which they omit to avoid prolixity), that your Honors be pleased not to exclude but to grant the Jewish nation passage to and residence in that country; otherwise this would result in a great prejudice to their reputation. Also that by an Apostille [marginal notation] and Act the Jewish nation be permitted, together with other inhabitants, to travel, live, and traffic there, and with them enjoy liberty on condition of contributing like others, etc. Which doing, etc. [The "apostille" is found in the margin on page 70.]

III. *The Answer of the West India Company to Stuyvesant, April 26, 1655*

Honorable, Prudent, Pious, Dear, Faithful [Stuyvesant]. . . .

We would have liked to effectuate and fulfill your wishes and request that the new territories should no more be allowed to be infected by people of the Jewish nation, for we foresee therefrom the same difficulties which you fear. But after having further weighed and considered the matter, we observe that this would be somewhat unreasonable and unfair, especially because of the considerable loss sustained by this nation, with others, in the taking of Brazil, as also because of the large amount of capital which they still have invested in the shares of this company. Therefore after many deliberations we have finally decided and resolved to apostille [to note in the margin] upon a certain petition presented by said Portuguese Jews [January, 1655] that these people may travel and trade to and in New Netherland and live and remain there, provided the poor among them shall not become a burden to the company or to the community [in the future poor Jews would not be supported by the Manhattan churches], but be supported by their own nation. You will now govern yourself accordingly. . . .

THE DIRECTORS OF THE W[EST]. I[NDIA]. Co.
Department of Amsterdam.

Amsterdam
26th of April, 1655.

IV. *The Jews of New York City, November 2, 1748*

*November the 2d. Besides the different sects of Christians, there are many Jews settled in New York, who possess great privileges.

They have a synagogue and houses, and great country-seats of their own property, and are allowed to keep shops in town. They have likewise several ships, which they freight and send out with their own goods. In fine, they enjoy all the privileges common to the other inhabitants of this town and province.

During my residence at New York, this time, and in the next two years, I was frequently in company with Jews. I was informed, among other things, that these people never boiled any meat for themselves on Saturday, but that they always did it the day before; and that in winter they kept a fire [going continuously] during the whole Saturday [for kindling fire anew on the Sabbath is prohibited by Jewish law]. They commonly eat no pork; yet I have been told by several men of credit, that many of them (especially among the young Jews) when traveling, did not make the least difficulty about eating this, or any other meat that was put before them; even though they were in company with Christians.

I was in their synagogue last evening for the first time, and this day at noon I visited it again, and each time I was put into a particular seat, which was set apart for strangers or Christians. [This synagogue, Shearith Israel, was then on Mill (South William) Street.] A young rabbi [Benjamin Pereira] read the divine service, which was partly in Hebrew, and partly in the rabbinical dialect [Aramaic]. Both men and women were dressed entirely in the English fashion; the former had all of them their hats on, and did not once take them off during service. The galleries, I observed, were appropriated to the ladies, while the men sat below. During prayers, the men spread a white cloth [the praying shawl: the *talit*] over their heads, which perhaps is to represent sackcloth. But I observed that the wealthier sort of people had a much richer sort of cloth than the poorer ones. Many of the men had Hebrew books, in which they sang and read alternately. The Rabbi stood in the middle of the synagogue, and read with his face turned towards the east; he spoke, however, so fast, as to make it almost impossible for any one to understand what he said.

BIBLIOGRAPHY

REFERENCES TO TEXTBOOKS

Roth, pp. 355ff.; Sachar, pp. 362–367.
Levinger, L. J., *A History of the Jews in the United States*, pp. 59–71.

READINGS FOR ADVANCED STUDENTS

Margolis and Marx, pp. 603–607.
Friedenberg, A. M., "The Jews of America, 1654–1787," *American Jewish Year Book*, XXVIII (1926–1927).
Friedman, L. M., *Early American Jews*, Chap. iv, "The First Coming of the Jews to New York"; Chap. v, "The Petition of Jacques de la Motthe."
Lebeson, A. L., *Jewish Pioneers in America: 1492–1848*, Chap. iv, "Peter Stuyvesant Meets 'the Obstinate and Immovable Jews.'"
Oppenheim, S., "The Early History of the Jews in New York, 1654–1664," in *Publications of the American Jewish Historical Society*, XVIII (1909). The best study of the first Jewish settlement in New York.
JE, "America"; "Levy, Asser"; "New York"; "United States."

16.

The Readmission of the Jews into Brandenburg
May 21, 1671

WHEN Frederick William the Hohenzollern (1640–1688) became Margrave of Brandenburg there were no permanent Jewish settlements in that state or in Berlin, its capital. The Jews had been expelled from that city in the preceding century. In the meantime the Thirty Years' War (1618–1648) had intervened to devastate large parts of Central Europe. Frederick William, the Great Elector, was eager to attract colonists who would increase the population, pay taxes, stimulate commerce, and create wealth. Though a pious Christian and ambitious to convert the Jews he was, nevertheless, tolerant. He did not hesitate, therefore, to encourage Polish Jews (in 1650) to travel about and carry on trade in his lands. Finally, in a more formal fashion, he invited into Brandenburg a number of the wealthy Jews who had been expelled from Catholic Vienna on February 28, 1670. The great Jewish community of present day Berlin developed as a result of this invitation. The moneys which the Elector acquired through the taxation of the Jews gave him the means, in part, which enabled him to free himself from the control of the privileged estates and thus to build up a modern, centralized, bureaucratic state.

The following decree, originally in German, lays down the conditions under which Jews resettled in Brandenburg. The conditions of resettlement are borrowed largely from the general charter granted May 1, 1650 to Halberstadt Jewry, at that time one of the important Jewish communities in the Hohenzollern domains.

AN EDICT CONCERNING THE FIFTY FAMILIES OF PROTECTED-JEWS WHO
 ARE TO BE ADMITTED BUT WHO ARE NOT, HOWEVER, TO HAVE
 A SYNAGOGUE

⟪We, Frederick William, by God's grace Margrave of Brandenburg, Chancellor and Elector of the Holy Roman Empire etc., hereby avow publicly and do graciously inform everyone whom it may concern that for special reasons and upon the most humble request of Hirshel Lazarus, Benedict Veit, and Abraham Ries, Jews [of Vienna], and moved particularly by the desire to further business in general, we have been influenced to take and receive graciously into our land of Electoral and March Brandenburg, under our special protection, a few Jewish families, namely, fifty of them, that have left other places. We do this on the following conditions, by virtue of the power vested in us.

1. We admit into our above mentioned land of Electoral and March Brandenburg and also into our Duchy of Krossen and the included areas the above mentioned fifty families. The names, numbers of persons, and locations where each one has settled must be made known to us immediately in a correct and detailed statement. The conditions of their admission are that the right shall be given them to settle in those places and towns where it is most suitable for them, and there to rent, buy, or build rooms, entire houses, dwelling places, or accommodations for themselves. It is to be understood, however, that those which they secure through purchase may be bought back again, and that which they build must be also returned to Christians even after the passing of a certain number of years. [This type of sale, common in Poland, was called *Wyderkauff*.] They are, however, to be reimbursed for their expenses.

2. These Jewish families shall be permitted to carry on their business activities in accordance with our edicts in this entire land of our Electoral and March Brandenburg, the Duchy of Krossen, and the places included therein. We allow them explicitly to have public shops and booths, to sell and to retail cloth and similar wares by the piece or by the yard, and to keep large and small weights which must not deviate in the least from the town-scales or the large scales used by the city authorities. The Jews must not practice any deception with their weights in buying or selling. We permit them to trade in new and old clothes, to slaughter meat in their own homes, and to sell that part of the slaughtered animal which they do not require for their own use or which their laws do not allow them to eat [i.e., the hind quarter]. And finally they are allowed to seek their livelihood everywhere—in places where they live, and in other spots too. They are specifically permitted to earn their livelihood by dealing in wool and groceries, just like the other inhabitants of these territories, and they are also allowed to sell their goods at the fairs and markets.

3.   Just as we have drawn their attention above to our [Branden-burg] edicts, even so shall they continue to carry on their business according to the imperial statutes which have been decreed for Jews. [Brandenburg, though independent, was in theory subject to the laws of the Holy Roman Empire.] They shall accordingly withhold themselves, as far as possible, from all forbidden business, particularly stolen goods. In matters of business they must not molest unfairly the inhabitants of these lands or any one else, nor deliberately defraud them of anything nor harm them, nor practice usury with their moneys, but be satisfied with that rate of interest which we permit the Jews of Halberstadt. And likewise in the matter of stolen goods they are to be treated just like the Halberstadt Jews.

[The general charter for the Jews of Halberstadt (May 1, 1650), among other conditions, permits about three percent interest per week on small sums. If Jews have unwittingly lent money on stolen goods they must, if three months have not yet passed, sur-render the pledge to the rightful owner who will reimburse the pawnbroker for the amount he has lent on the pledge. The slaughter of meat ritually was also allowed. A rescript of August 10, 1661 specifically permitted the Halberstadt Jews to conduct a Jewish school, much to the disgust of the Christian merchants and artisans.]

4.   They are to pay, without any fraud, the tolls, the tax on commodities, and the "war levy" [in money or grain] just as our other subjects. Because they are settled here in the country they are, however, exempt at our tollhouses from the body-tax [*Leibzoll*] which all other Jews who travel through have to pay. However, other Jews who do not belong here shall not pass through under this pretext. Moreover each family must pay eight Reichsthalers annually as protection-money, and whenever a member of a family marries he must pay a gold gulden, without any deduction, just like the Halberstadt Jews. Concerning the other taxes of the country they must arrive at a fair agreement with the authorities of every town. If they will not be able to do this with mutual fairness, they may report to us accordingly, and we will take the necessary measures.

5.   Although we have taken the afore-mentioned fifty families under our special protection, nevertheless they shall not refuse in civil cases to be subject to and to expect justice from each town's chief magistrate. This task is specifically assigned to him and he is not to call in the other members of the town council. However, if

any one has a complaint to make against any of the Jews, it must always be submitted in writing. In so far as criminal cases occur among them, these must be brought directly to us. The authorities of each town will accordingly bear this, particularly, in mind.

6.   Although they are not permitted to have a synagogue they are allowed to arrange an assembly in their houses where they may offer their prayers and perform their ceremonies, without, however, offering any offense to the Christians. They must particularly refrain from all abuse and blasphemy, under the threat of heavy penalties. [The Halberstadters, for instance, said (1656) that the Jews abused Jesus daily in their "cursed synagogues."] They are also herewith allowed to have a ritual slaughterer as well as a schoolteacher for the instruction of their children. The privileges of these are to be the same as those laid down in the law dealing with Halberstadt Jewry.

7.   Moreover they should everywhere evidence and show themselves to be decent, peaceful, and considerate, and must take particular care that they do not carry any good coins out of the country and bring worthless ones back in. They must not dispose of their gold and silver coins in other places but must sell them, as is proper, to our mints. [Gold and silver were then considered the chief sources of a nation's wealth.] In the event that any one should bring our stolen silver to them for sale, or should they otherwise learn where some is to be found, they are expected to report not only the silver but also the persons, and in the meantime to seize the one who may offer it to them for sale.

8.   The officials of every town in this our Electoral March of Brandenburg, Duchy of Krossen, and the included territories, where some of the Jews of the already mentioned fifty families want to settle, are herewith graciously and earnestly commanded to accept this privileged Jewry willingly and gladly; to evidence to them all furtherance and good will in accommodating them; and, in our name, to let them have all proper protection and even [the right] to appeal to us ourselves. They are also to treat them fairly in the negotiations which they carry on with them about their staying and about the taxes of the land; to allow no one to affront them or molest them; to treat them as their other citizens and inhabitants; and to treat them well in accordance with the content of this, our Letter of Protection. They are particularly enjoined to assign them at once

for a fair payment, a place for the burial of their dead. [A cemetery was bought in Berlin as early as 1672.]

9.   If the now oft-mentioned Jewry will act in accordance with that above which has been laid upon them and has been promised by them, then we most graciously promise them our most benign protection and defense in these our territories from this time forth for twenty years, and, after this termination, the continuation thereof by us and our heirs, as we see fit. Failing this, we reserve for ourselves the right, after proper consideration, to recall our protection even before the twenty years have passed.

10.   Should the tumult of war—God forbid—rise in our land during these twenty years, the oft-mentioned Jewry, like our other subjects, shall not be forbidden to take refuge in our fortresses with their families, but shall be admitted and tolerated there.

Accordingly we command all our subjects and followers without regard to station and dignity, that from this day forth, for the whole twenty years, they allow the oft-mentioned Jewry to pass about freely and safely everywhere in our entire Electorate and the lands mentioned with it; that they be allowed to visit the public fairs, business centers, and trading towns; and that they be permitted to sell all their wares publicly and to pursue respectable trade and unforbidden business free and unhampered as opportunity presents itself. No one shall lay violent hands upon them. Furthermore, every magistrate and official of the courts shall aid them, at their request, in that to which they are entitled; shall accord them, like others, the right of civic hospitality; and shall not treat them in any other way, if they would avoid our high disfavor—to say nothing of a penalty of fifty golden gulden and even more, according to circumstances.

In witness whereof this patent and Letter of Protection has been signed by our own hand and confirmed by our gracious seal. Potsdam, the 21st of May, 1671.

FREDERICK WILLIAM.

BIBLIOGRAPHY

READINGS FOR ADVANCED STUDENTS

Graetz, V, pp. 169–174; Graetz-Rhine, V, pp. 184–188; Margolis and Marx, pp. 589–591.
JE, "Berlin"; "Germany."

17.

Rhode Island Refuses to Naturalize Aaron Lopez
March, 1762

IN spite of the fact that the Parliamentary Act of 1740 allowed Jews to become citizens in the colonies after seven years' residence, certain states declined to grant this privilege to individual Jews.

Selection one below, taken from the *Itineraries* of the Reverend Ezra Stiles, President of Yale College after 1778, records the decision of the Superior Court of Rhode Island which refused to naturalize Aaron Lopez and Isaac Elizer. This refusal is surprising in view of the fact that other Jews had been naturalized in Rhode Island before this, and Lopez's character was above reproach. It should not be forgotten, however, that at this time Lopez was only a small merchant and not the great merchant prince and skipper who by 1775 owned or shared in over thirty vessels.

It is probable that Lopez was anxious to secure citizenship in order the more easily to carry on trade with other English colonies. Elizer was soon naturalized in New York (1763) and Lopez in Massachusetts, October 15, 1762; for their benefit the test phrase, "upon the true faith of a Christian," in the oath of naturalization, was stricken. It is strange that the more liberal Rhode Island rejected Lopez's petition and that the more conservative Massachusetts accepted it. Lopez, apparently, was the first Jew to be naturalized in the Bay State.

Selection two, also taken from the *Itineraries* of Ezra Stiles, makes clear that this Christian Hebraist and friend of the Jews could not, as late as 1762, conceive of the Jews as part of the American people.

Selection three, taken from *The Literary Diary of Ezra Stiles etc.*, describes the character of Lopez and expresses the poignant sorrow of Stiles that Lopez, the Jew, did not die a Christian.

1. *Why the Court Refused To Naturalize Aaron Lopez, 1762—*
SUPERIOR COURT RHODE ISLAND, NEWPORT, SS. MARCH TERM 1762

℀The petition of Messrs. Aaron Lopez and Isaac Elizer, persons professing the Jewish religion, praying that they may be naturalized on an act of Parliament made in the 13th year of his Majesty's reign George the Second, having been duly considered, and also the act of Parliament therein referred to, this court are unanimously of opinion that the said act of Parliament was wisely designed for increasing the number of inhabitants in the plantations; but this colony being already so full of people that many of his Majesty's good subjects born within the same have removed and settled in Nova Scotia and other places; [the petition] cannot come within the intention of the said act. [This act of 1740 permitted Jews in the colonies to be naturalized.]

Further, by the charter granted to this colony, it appears that the full and quiet enjoyment of the Christian religion and a desire of propagating the same were the principal views with which the colony was settled; and by a law made and passed in the year 1663, no person who does not profess the Christian religion can be admitted free of this colony. [This proviso is not found in the original charter of 1663, but was added about 1699.] This court therefore unanimously dismiss the said petition as absolutely inconsistent with the first principle upon which the colony was founded and [inconsistent with] a law now of the same in full force.

11. *Ezra Stiles Believes that the Jews Will Never Become Citizens, March 18, 1762*

❝There are about fifteen families of Jews in Newport. Some of the principal of them last year made application to the Superior Court to be naturalized [according to the act of Parliament of 1740]. The Court declined or deferred acting. The Jews then applied to the General Assembly [State Legislature], which referred it to the Superior Court again as their business to determine, which Superior Court at Newport, March term 1762, gave their judgment and determination upon the petition of Aaron Lopez and Isaac Elizer copied two leaves back.

It was remarkable that before this term there had been three trials for felony of which two were capital, all guilty by jury. And on the eleventh day of March, 1762 sentence was pronounced upon the criminals successively brought to the bar; first upon John Sherman, a noted thief and burglar, for burglary, sentenced to be hanged; secondly upon Fortune, an abandoned negro who set fire to the warehouses at End Long Wharf 19th February which did damage £5000 sterling and endangered the conflagration of the town, sentenced to be hanged; thirdly upon —— Lawton for perjury in swearing to an account which he had falsely forged against another, sentenced to the pillory, etc.

And then the Jews were called up to hear their almost equally mortifying sentence and judgment which dismissed their petition for naturalization. Whether this was designedly or accidental in proceeding upon the business of Court I don't learn. But this I remark that Providence seems to make everything to work for mortification to the Jews, and to prevent their incorporating into any nation; that thus they may continue a distinct people. Tho' the Naturalization Act passed the Parliament a few years ago, yet it produced such a national disgust towards the Hebrews, that the Jews themselves joined in petition to Parliament to repeal that act, and it was thereupon repealed for Britain. [This is the "Jew Bill" of 1753 granting Jews citizenship in England. It was repealed, 1754.] And tho' it [the act of Parliament of 1740] was continued by way of permission in the plantations, upon seven years residence, yet the tumult at New York in procuring the taking place of their naturalization there, and the opposition it has met with in Rhode Island, forbodes that the Jews will never become incorporated with the people of America, any more than in Europe, Asia, and Africa.

March 18, 1762.

III. *The Character of Aaron Lopez, 1782*

⟨On 28th May [1782] died that amiable, benevolent, most hospitable, and very respectable gentleman, Mr. Aaron Lopez, merchant, who retiring from Newport, Rhode Island in these times resided from 1775 to his death at Leicester in Massachusetts. [It is more probable that Lopez left in the winter of 1776 when the British took Newport.] He was a Jew by nation, came from Spain or Portugal about 1754 [more correctly 1752], and settled at Rhode Island. He was a merchant of the first eminence; for honor and extent of commerce probably surpassed by no merchant in America. He did business with the greatest ease and clearness—always carried about with him a sweetness of behavior, a calm urbanity, an agreeable and unaffected politeness of manners. Without a single enemy and the most universally beloved by an extensive acquaintance of any man I ever knew. His beneficence to his family connexions, to his nation, and to all the world is almost without a parallel.

He was my intimate friend and acquaintance! Oh! how often have I wished that sincere pious and candid mind could have perceived the evidences of Christianity, perceived the truth as it is in

Jesus Christ, known that Jesus was the Messiah predicted by Moses and the prophets! The most amiable and excellent characters of a Lopez, of a Menasseh ben Israel [famous Amsterdam rabbi, d. 1657], of a Socrates, and a Gangenelli [Pope Clement XIV, statesman and scholar, d. 1774], would almost persuade us to hope that their excellency was infused by Heaven, and that the virtuous and good of all nations and religions, notwithstanding their delusions, may be brought together in Paradise on the Christian system, finding grace with the all benevolent and adorable Emmanuel [Jesus] who with his expiring breath and in his deepest agonies, prayed for those who knew not what they did [Luke 23:34].

Mr. Lopez was journeying with his wife and some of his family on a visit to Newport, and within five miles of Providence at Scott's Pond as he was watering his horse, the horse plunged beyond his depth with the sulky, when Mr. Lopez leaped into the water; and though his servant attempted to save him he was lost. His corpse was carried to Newport and there interred in the Jew burying ground there—the demonstration of universal sorrow attended the funeral.

BIBLIOGRAPHY

REFERENCES TO TEXTBOOKS

Levinger, L. J., *A History of the Jews in the United States*, pp. 72–84.

READINGS FOR ADVANCED STUDENTS

Friedman, L. M., *Early American Jews*, Chap. i, "Jewish Residents in Massachusetts before 1800."

Gutstein, M. A., *The Story of the Jews of Newport*. See "Lopez, Aaron" in Index.

Lebeson, A. L., *Jewish Pioneers in America: 1492–1848*, Chap. vi, "Newport—The Common Receptacle . . . of Jerusalem."

Straus, O. S., *Roger Williams, the Pioneer of Religious Liberty. Dictionary of American Biography*, "Lopez, Aaron."

JE, "Newport."

ADDITIONAL SOURCE MATERIALS IN ENGLISH

Jastrow, M., "References to Jews in the Diary of Ezra Stiles," *Publications of the American Jewish Historical Society*, X (1902), pp. 5–36.

18.

The Charter Decreed by Frederick II
for the Jews of Prussia
April 17, 1750

ON the 17th of April, 1750, Frederick the Great of Prussia (1740–1786) issued a general-patent applying to the Jews of his lands. This charter, a reworking of the basic patent of 1730 issued by his father Frederick William I (1713–1740), is a curious combination of medieval and modern elements. It is modern in the sense that the Jew is thought to be no longer a ward of the king, but instead a subject of the state—albeit second-class. The former Jewish autonomy is broken down, and the Jew is brought closer to the state economically, politically, and culturally. The charter is medieval, however, in the sense that it is filled with a spirit of distrust of and contempt for the Jew, limiting him almost exclusively to commerce and industry. Because of the protest of the Jews against its reactionary character, the charter was not promulgated till 1756.

The economic limitations imposed upon the Jews are prompted not merely by personal dislike, nor by the desire to give the Christian subjects preference over the Jewish, but also by the known policy of Frederick of forcing Jews to cease dealing in raw materials and to create new German industries. Petty trading was therefore frowned upon, but manufacturing was given every encouragement. However, viewed from the aspect of the right to engage in all forms of trade and to live anywhere—of freedom of trade and of residence —this charter is a decided change for the worse when compared to the Great Elector's edict of May 21, 1671.

The novel phase of the charter is the division of the Jews into classes according to their economic value to the state. Outside of a handful of "general-privileged" Jews who had all economic and residential rights and were not bound by this patent, the Jews were divided into "Regular Protected-Jews," and "Special Protected-Jews." The "Regular Protected-Jews" had limited rights of residence and occupation which they could transmit to the oldest child only; the "Specials" could not transfer their rights even to a single child. Jewish communal officials, the younger children of the "Regulars," all children of the "Specials," and all domestic servants were only "tolerated."

This German patent, in force in part till 1850, breathes such a spirit of inhumanity that Mirabeau, the French liberal, referred to it as "a law worthy of a cannibal."

REVISED GENERAL–PATENT AND REGULATIONS OF APRIL 17, 1750 FOR JEWRY OF THE KINGDOM OF PRUSSIA, ELECTORAL AND MARCH BRANDENBURG, THE DUCHIES AND PRINCIPALITIES OF MAGDE-BURG, CLEVES, FARTHER-POMERANIA, KROSSEN, HALBERSTADT, MINDEN, CAMIN, AND MÖRS, AS WELL AS THE COUNTIES AND TERRITORIES OF MARK, RAVENSBERG, HOHENSTEIN, TECKLEN-BURG, LINGEN, LAUENBURG, AND BÜTAU—EXPLANATION OF THE CAUSES FOR THE FURTHER REGULATION OF JEWRY:

❰We, Frederick, by God's grace, King of Prussia, Margrave of Brandenburg, Chancellor and Electoral Prince of the Holy Roman Empire, sovereign and supreme Duke of Silesia etc., etc., etc.,

Make known and order to be made known: We have noticed in our kingdom of Prussia. . . .and particularly also in this capital [Berlin] various faults and abuses among the licensed and tolerated Jews, and have particularly observed that the rampant increase of these abuses has caused enormous damage and hardship, not only to the public, particularly to the Christian inhabitants and merchants, but also to Jewry itself. For this reason and because of the sur-reptitious entry of unlicensed Jews: foreigners [non-Prussians] and those who are all but without any country, many complaints and difficulties have arisen.

We, however, out of a feeling of most gracious paternal provision wish to establish and maintain, as far as possible, the livelihood and trades of each and every loyal subject under our protection, Christians as well as Jews, in a continually good and flourishing state.

For this reason we have found it necessary to make such provi-sion that this, our most gracious purpose, may be attained, so that a proportion may be maintained between Christian and Jewish busi-ness opportunities and trades, and especially that neither [Jew or Christian] be injured through a prohibited expansion of Jewish business activity. For this purpose we have again made an exact in-vestigation of the condition, in our kingdom and in the other above mentioned imperial lands, of all Jewry, of their families, their means of subsistence, and their business activity. We have considered cer-tain feasible proposals which have as their basis justice, fairness, and common safety, and have also deemed them useful for the attain-ment of our ultimate object and the attendant welfare of all in-

habitants of the country who live by means of business activity.
As a result of these proposals we wish to prepare and to put into
effect a special regulation and constitution for all Jewry. Therefore
we establish, regulate, and order, herewith and by virtue of this,
that:

I. THE FORMER [THE 1730] GENERAL-PATENT AND REGULATIONS FOR
      JEWRY ARE TO BE PUBLISHED AND ADJUSTED ACCORDING TO
      PRESENT CONDITIONS. . . .

II. NO OTHER JEWS ARE TO BE TOLERATED EXCEPT THOSE NAMED IN THE
      LISTS THAT ARE ATTACHED TO THE END OF THESE REGULATIONS.
      . . . [THESE LISTS WERE APPENDED IN THE ORIGINAL.]

III. LIST OF THE TOLERATED COMMUNAL JEWISH OFFICIALS IN BERLIN:

The following list of communal officials for the capital here in Berlin
has been fixed:

1. One rabbi or a vice-rabbi.
2. Four assistant-judges.
3. A chief and assistant cantor with his basses and his sopranos.
   These latter must not be married.
4. Four criers, one of whom must report daily to the police
   office the arrival of foreign Jews. [These criers, or
   "knockers," used to call people to services at dawn by
   "knocking" on their doors.]
5. Two employees in the synagogal-school.
6. Six grave diggers who also do other work for the Jewish
   community.
7. One cemetery guard.
8. Three slaughterers.
9. Three butchers.
10. One secretary of the meat-market and his supervisor.
11. Three bakers and one restaurant-keeper.
12. A communal scribe.
13. Two doorkeepers and one assistant. [The doorkeepers at
    the city gates examined the papers of immigrant Jews.]
14. Two hospital attendants.
15. One physician.
16. One male and one female bath attendant.
17. A fattener of fowl and cattle.

18. Eight attendants for the sick.
19. Two Hebrew printers.
20. Two teachers for girls. Both must be married.

These and no more shall be appointed by the elders of the Jews with the approval, however, of the War and Domains Office. [There was a War and Domains Office in every province in charge of taxes and finances.] But, as far as possible, native impoverished Jews are to be prepared for, and installed in, these positions. . . .

For the instruction of the Jewish girls two married communal schoolteachers are allowed in Berlin, Königsberg, Halberstadt, Halle, and Frankfort on the Oder, also in Stargard in Pomerania. If in other cities there are more than ten Jewish families, then one married schoolteacher is permitted; in the rest of the towns, however, none at all is permitted. . . .

IV. EVERY MONTH THE JEWISH ELDERS MUST SEND IN TO THE WAR AND DOMAINS OFFICE A LIST OF ANY CHANGES THAT HAVE OCCURRED IN THE JEWISH COMMUNITY. . . . [THESE LISTS WERE NECESSARY FOR TAX AND POLICE PURPOSES.]

V. PRINCIPLES THAT ARE TO BE OBSERVED IN THE SETTLEMENT OF JEWS

The following principles respecting the settlement of Jews shall be established and observed in the future. . . .

A distinction is to be made between Regular Protected-Jews and Special Protected-Jews who are merely tolerated during their life time. . . . [Mendelssohn was raised from a "tolerated" to a Special Protected-Jew in 1763. He never became a Regular Protected-Jew.]

Only those are to be considered Regular Protected-Jews who have the right to settle a child. . . .

The above mentioned Special Protected-Jews, however, are not authorized to settle a child [in business] nor are they to marry off a child by virtue of their privilege. . . .

In accordance with our most graciously issued cabinet-order of May 23, 1749, the fixed number of Jewish families at present is not to be exceeded except by our royal command. . . .

The Regular Protected-Jews, however, are allowed by virtue of their Letter of Protection to settle one child, a son or daughter, during their life time, but once they have made their decision they will not be authorized to change it in the future. This child may marry if it can first establish its identity legally. . . .

[Jewish second-born sons who have the legally required fortune, and an ability to establish shops and factories—and do establish and promote such factories as are not yet in the country or not sufficiently numerous—may under these conditions, settle in the country like the first-born son. They are also authorized to ask for the Letter of Protection of Regular Protected-Jews. (Circular letter of November 11, 1763. The heavy cost of the Seven Years' War induced Frederick II to grant second-born sons Letters of Protection.)]

Foreign [non-Prussian] Jews are not allowed to settle in our lands at all. However, if one should really have a fortune of ten thousand Reichsthalers and bring the same into the country and furnish authentic evidence of the fact, then we are to be asked about this and concerning the fees he is to pay. . . .

In order that in the future all fraud, cheating, and secret and forbidden increase of the number of families may be more carefully avoided, no Jew shall be allowed to marry, nor will he receive permission to settle, in any manner, nor will he be believed, until a careful investigation has been made by the War and Domains Offices together with the aid of the Treasury. . . . [There were also special heavy taxes imposed on Jews when marrying.]

Male and female servants and other domestics, however, are not allowed to marry. Should they attempt to do this they are not to be tolerated any longer. . . .

The children of [all] licensed Jews, whose fathers have died or have become impoverished, or are in such a condition that they, the children, have no right of "settlement," or do not possess the required fortune, are to be tolerated, even as are the widows of such people. However, when they come of age, they shall in no wise dare, under penalty of expulsion, to set up a business for themselves but they must either work for other licensed Jews, or go away and seek to be accepted somewhere else. They may, indeed, prepare themselves so that they take the place of Jewish communal officials who leave. Thus it will not be necessary to accept so many foreigners for this purpose.

VI. THE ESTABLISHED METHOD OF COLLECTION IS TO BE RETAINED WITH RESPECT TO THE COLLECTION OF THE PROTECTION-TAX AND OTHER PUBLIC TAXES. . . .

VII. NO PROTECTED-JEW CAN STAY AWAY FROM HOME FOR MORE THAN A YEAR WITHOUT AUTHORIZATION; OTHERWISE HIS PLACE WILL BE GIVEN TO ANOTHER. . . .

VIII. THE JEWS MUST PAY THEIR TAXES QUARTERLY AND ALL THE JEWS
  ARE RESPONSIBLE AS A BODY FOR THE PAYMENT OF THE
  TAXES. . . .

IX. WHAT IS TO BE DONE WITH IMPOVERISHED JEWS OR THOSE FACING
  BANKRUPTCY. . . .

X. WHAT ACTION IS TO BE TAKEN WHEN A JEW DELIBERATELY BECOMES
  BANKRUPT. . . .

XI. THE JEWS MUST NOT PURSUE ANY MANUAL TRADE. . . .

We herewith establish, regulate, and order earnestly that in the
future no Jew shall presume to engage in any manual trade, nor
venture upon any except seal-engraving, [art] painting, the grinding
of optical glasses, diamonds, and jewels, gold and silver embroidery,
fine cloth needlework, the collecting of gold dust by a sieving
process, and other similar trades in which vocational associations and
privileged guilds are not found. Particularly are they enjoined not
to brew beer nor to distill spirits. However, they are allowed to
undertake the distilling of spirits for the nobility, government officials, and others, with the understanding that only licensed Jews
and their sons are to be taken for this task. . . . However, those
Jews who have received or may receive special concessions for the
establishment of particular types of factories or for the sale of
goods of Christian manufacturers are to be protected in the future
as in the past. [Frederick the Great and his father, as "protection-
ists," were anxious to promote Prussian industries.]

XII. JEWS ARE FORBIDDEN THE SMELTING OF GOLD AND SILVER. . . .

XIII. THE SLAUGHTER OF MEAT FOR THEIR OWN CONSUMPTION IS PER-
  MITTED THE JEWS IF THEY KILL THE ANIMALS IN CHRISTIAN
  SLAUGHTERHOUSES. . . . [BUT THEY CANNOT SELL MEAT TO
  NON-JEWS NOR DEAL IN DOMESTIC CATTLE.]

XIV. THE JEWS IN BERLIN ARE NOT ALLOWED TO HAVE DEALINGS IN RAW
  WOOL OR WOOLEN YARNS OR TO MANUFACTURE WOOLEN
  GOODS. . . . [THEY WERE ALLOWED, HOWEVER, TO SELL THE
  DOMESTIC FINISHED PRODUCT.]

XV. JEWS ARE FURTHER ALLOWED TO SELL ONE ANOTHER BEER AND
  SPIRITS. . . . WITH THE EXCEPTION OF KOSHER WINES THEY ARE

NOT ALLOWED TO DO ANY BUSINESS IN WINES. . . . [JEWS MUST NOT, HOWEVER, SELL STRONG DRINK TO NON-JEWS.]

XVI. JEWS ARE NOT ALLOWED TO DEAL IN RAW CATTLE-AND-HORSE HIDES, PLAIN OR DYED LEATHERS, AND FOREIGN WOOLEN WARES EXCEPT THOSE WHICH ARE SPECIFICALLY PERMITTED IN THE FOLLOWING [PARAGRAPH XVIII]. . . . [CHEAP RAW MATERIALS WERE TO BE RESERVED FOR PRUSSIAN MANUFACTURERS.]

XVII. UNDER SPECIAL CONDITIONS THEY MAY SELL CHOICE GROCERIES AND SPICES TO OTHER JEWS. . . . THE JEWS ARE FORBIDDEN TO TRADE IN RAW TOBACCO, TO MANUFACTURE TOBACCO, AND TO CARRY A LINE OF [STAPLE] GROCERIES. . . .

XVIII. PRECISELY THE KINDS OF GOODS WITH WHICH THE PROTECTED-JEWS ARE ALLOWED TO DO BUSINESS

In order that all Jews under our protection may be informed and instructed precisely in the business opportunities and trades allowed them, they are allowed to trade and to do business with the following, namely:

With gold-cloth, silver-cloth, fine fabrics and ribbons, native and foreign embroidered goods, domestic gold and silver laces manufactured in the Berlin Royal Gold and Silver Factory, neck bands of lace, Spanish lace, gold and silver thread and purl; likewise with jewels, broken gold and silver, ingots, all sorts of old pocket-watches, and similar things. Furthermore they are permitted to deal in money-exchange and pledges, money-brokerage, and the buying and selling of houses and estates for other people. They are also permitted to do business in all sorts of Brabant, Dutch, Silesian, and Electoral-Saxonian fine cloth and silk textiles, in laces, muslin, and all-white domestic coarse calico linings, domestic linen, white linen thread, and tablecloths of linen and half-linen. They are also specially allowed to deal with domestic silk goods, also with foreign and native undyed, dressed leather, and with domestic velvet. [Moses Mendelssohn worked for a domestic silk goods firm.] They are also allowed to deal in all sorts of all-wool and half-wool goods and cotton goods —by whatever name they may be called—manufactured here in this country, as well as with cotton and chintz goods made in our lands.

Furthermore they are permitted to deal in horses, in undressed calf and sheep hides, feathers, wigs, hair, also camel and horsehair, tallow, wax, and honey, Polish wares [pelts, potash, hemp, etc.], undressed and unfinished pelts, but not finished furriers' wares in those cities where furriers live, unless they can without hesitation give the name of the furriers from whom they bought the finished product for further sale. [Jews must not compete with the craft-guilds, such as the furriers.] They are also allowed to trade in tea, coffee, chocolate, and foreign and domestic manufactured snuff and smoking tobacco. They are also free to trade, exchange, and do business in all sorts of old clothes, old or used furniture, house and kitchen utensils; to sum up, with everything which is not generally and specifically forbidden in the above paragraphs, even though it is neither specified or mentioned in this special paragraph. But all this is permitted them only in their own homes and in those shops and booths that have been regularly assigned them.

However, with respect to foreign and domestic Jewish trade in our Kingdom of Prussia, the special constitution that has been made there will remain in force, inasmuch as the Polish and Russian business there is still dependent on both Christian and Jewish commerce. . . . [These business laws do not apply to Prussia proper which was then surrounded on three sides by Poland.]

XIX. THE JEWS MUST NOT TRADE IN ANYTHING HEREIN FORBIDDEN THEM, UNDER THREAT OF CONFISCATION OF THEIR WARES. . . . THEY MAY NOT PEDDLE IN CITIES EXCEPT AT THE TIME OF THE FAIRS. . . .

XX. NO FOREIGN [NON-PRUSSIAN] JEWS AND JEWISH BOYS SHALL DO BUSINESS IN BERLIN. OUTSIDE OF EXCEPTIONAL CASES HEREIN SPECIFIED, THOSE WHO REMAIN OVER TWENTY-FOUR HOURS IN BERLIN MUST PAY ONE SPECIE-DUCAT TO THE POTSDAM ORPHAN HOME. . . .

Now it has been noticed that many Jews and Jewish boys from other cities and provinces that are subject to us have tarried in Berlin, year in and year out, and almost daily, constantly coming and going, and, as it were, relieving one another. Through private and public trading they have done tremendous damage, not only to the entire public, but particularly to the entire Christian and authorized Jewish trade, and have at the same time deceived and duped our treasuries through all sorts of fraud and malicious practices. Therefore, we establish, regulate, and order herewith and by virtue of this, that except for the local fairs no Jew who does not belong to Berlin—whether he is otherwise licensed or non-licensed within our land—

shall be allowed to come into the city with any wares except broken
gold and silver. Also no foreign [non-Prussian] Jew, male or female,
shall be allowed in except at the time of the fairs. . . .

XXI. ALL FOREIGN [NON-PRUSSIAN] JEWS WHO DO NOT ARRIVE WITH
THE POST-CARRIAGE OR THEIR OWN VEHICLES MAY ENTER INTO
AND LEAVE BERLIN BY ONLY TWO GATES. WHAT IS TO BE DONE
IN THIS MATTER IN OTHER LARGE CITIES. . . . [POOR JEWS WERE
NOT WANTED AND WERE WATCHED.]

XXII. WHAT IS TO BE DONE WITH JEWISH BEGGARS

It has already been decreed many times that Jewish beggars are nowhere to be allowed to cross our borders. We not only repeat this,
but order that in the event any such Jewish beggars nevertheless
reach our capital surreptitiously, they shall be brought at once to
the Poor-Jews Home at the Prenzlau Gate. [This "Home" was a
combined poorhouse and hospital.] There they are to be given alms
and on the following day evicted through the gate without being
allowed to enter into the city. . . .

[The following ordinance was promulgated by the sovereign
German County of Lippe-Detmold on October 23, 1770:

All foreign beggars, collectors, [German] Jewish peddlers, Polish
Jews, jugglers, bear-trainers, and tramps are forbidden access to this
country under penalty of a prison sentence. All gypsies caught will
be hanged and shot.]

XXIII. HOW THE FOREIGN [NON-PRUSSIAN] JEWS ENGAGED IN BUSINESS
ARE TO BE TREATED BY THE EXCISE OFFICE DURING THE FAIRS IN
BERLIN. . . . [THEY MUST PAY A TAX ON GOODS SOLD.]

XXIV. THE JEWS ARE ALLOWED TO LEND OUT MONEY ON PROPER PLEDGES

Inasmuch as the money-business is a particular source of Jewish
support, Jews are therefore allowed to lend money on pledges now
as in the past. They must not, however, accept pledges from any
non-commissioned officer or soldier, or buy anything where they
are not sufficiently assured that this is their lawful property and no
part of their soldiers' equipment. And in every case they must demand a note from the company commander with respect to these
things. Furthermore, the Jews must be very sure in all pawning and
selling that the pledges were not stolen, or secretly removed and

then pledged, either by young folks from their parents, or by unfaithful servants from their employers. On each occasion, therefore, the pawnbrokers must make enquiries from the parents or the employers.

Furthermore, those Jews, their wives, or employees must not only surrender such pledges to the owner without compensation, but in case that they knew that the pledge was stolen or secretly removed, and shall be legally convicted of this, then, in accordance with the edict of January 15, 1747, the possessors of such pledges shall be regarded just like those who have wittingly purchased stolen goods. Such a pawnbroker shall lose all rights of protection, not only for himself, but also for his children if some of them have already been settled in business, for their Letters of Protection shall be annulled, and he and his family shall be removed from the country. Furthermore, no one else is to be settled in the vacancy created by that family, and, besides this, the transgressor is to be compelled to pay the full worth of the stolen or illegally received things to the lawful owner, who, if necessary, will take an oath as to their value.

If the offender cannot pay this because his Letter of Protection has been cancelled and his family already expelled, then the entire Jewry of the town is officially to be held responsible for the payment in cash—and without any protest—to the robbed owner of the value of the stolen or illegally received things. For this reason the Jews must watch one another and pay attention carefully when they find any of their people on the wrong road and immediately report such a person to the proper authorities. Jewry, therefore, and particularly the elders are required to anticipate any annoyance and damage by ridding the country of those receivers of stolen goods and the other rascally crew among them whenever they discover them. And when they submit their information they will be given all assistance. . . .

XXV. HOW PROPER PLEDGES ARE TO BE REDEEMED AND SOLD. . . . [UN-
REDEEMED PLEDGES MAY BE SOLD AFTER A YEAR.]

XXVI. THEY MUST KEEP A CORRECT PLEDGE-BOOK. . . .

XXVII. INTEREST WHICH THE JEWS ARE AUTHORIZED TO TAKE

When a Jew lends money on bills of exchange he is, according to the edict of December 24, 1725, and until further decree, still authorized to take twelve percent interest if the bill of exchange is to run for twelve months or less. If it concerns a capital of one hundred Reichsthalers and over, which is to draw interest for more than a year, he must not take more than eight per cent interest, under threat of loss of the capital and all interest. . . .

If a Jew lends money on pledges or mortgages up to one hundred Reichsthalers, he is likewise not allowed to take more than eight per cent interest under threat of the same penalty.

If, however, a Jew lends out money in small sums on pledges, and the amount loaned on the pledge is less than ten thalers, he may take a pfennig on the thaler as interest every week. . . . [This is 17⅓ per cent interest a year, normal for the times.]

In all these cases the common law holds good that no Jew may take interest from accrued interest, or add such interest to the capital, under threat of the loss of the old capital. . . .

XXVIII. IN THE FUTURE THE JEWS SHALL NOT BUY HOUSES OF THEIR OWN. THE FORTY HOUSES OWNED BY JEWS IN BERLIN SHALL NOT BE INCREASED IN NUMBER. . . . IN OTHER CITIES WHERE THERE ARE FIVE JEWISH FAMILIES ONLY ONE OF THEM MAY BUY A HOUSE. . . .

After investigation has been made and an order has been received from those in charge of the royal finances, Jews, in those places where they are tolerated, will be allowed to build on desolate and virgin areas. . . .

However, the Jews are nowhere allowed to buy and possess estates. [Jews cannot become farmers.]

XXIX. WITH RESPECT TO THE ELECTION OF THE ELDERS AND THE RABBI, THE CONSTITUTION AND ORGANIZATION THAT HAS BEEN IN EFFECT TILL NOW WILL BE MAINTAINED. . . .

XXX. THE JEWS ARE TO BE PROTECTED IN THEIR RELIGION, CEREMONIES, AND SYNAGOGUE, AND THAT WHICH IS RELATED TO IT

We have everywhere most graciously and firmly protected all these Jewish families in their religion and in their Jewish customs and ceremonies which they have practiced till now. We also herewith confirm anew the [right to possess the] synagogues which they have built in Berlin, Königsberg, Halberstadt, Halle, and Frankfort on the Oder, as well as the schools in the other provinces, the cemeteries, and the small houses belonging to the synagogues and the cemeteries. This, however, on the condition that they must always refrain, under penalty of death and complete expulsion of the entire Jewry from Berlin and our other cities, from such abuses as the Jewish prayer which begins *Alenu* etc., as has already been emphatically decreed in detail in the edicts of 1703 and 1716. [Christians believed that this daily prayer, which denounced idolatry, was an attack on them.] They must refrain likewise from other prayers of the same type, and also from all improper excesses in their festivals, particularly during the so-called Haman or Purim festival [when they hang Haman in effigy].

Various Jews here have ventured, in an arbitrary manner, to hold assemblies and private prayer-meetings, gathering together many other Jews, old and young in their houses. This, however, runs counter to our previous decrees and the public welfare, and as such is very objectionable to the [Jewish] community also, and is very detrimental to the religious meetings in the synagogue.

Therefore, we apply again the decrees of the 2nd of February, 1745, which were issued for Berlin in this matter: that such private assemblies for prayers are to be stopped, and are to be allowed to no one, except him whom we specifically permit. Moreover, there are not to be more than two such prayer-meetings in Spandau Street, and one in Jews' Street, for old and sickly people and children, because such people can hardly go to the synagogue in the winter time. [The Prussian state regulated even the religion and morals of its subjects.]

These prayer-meetings may be held from Michaelmas [September 29] till Easter in certain houses designated by the Jewish elders. These prayer-meetings are to be conducted in such a manner that, on the one hand, none but worn-out, old and sickly Jews and children under twelve years of age, together with one or two school-teachers, shall assemble there; on the other hand, that no other religious service, ceremonies, and activities be engaged in except those which are absolutely necessary in prayer. And at the same time that which is usually collected in the synagogue for the poor Jews and otherwise may be contributed here also. The assembly is to be held at all times in a house back from the street, or in such a place where the neighbors and the public in general will not be inconvenienced by too much clamor.

If in spite of this any one be found in the future who, in an arbitrary manner and contrary to this decree, holds such prayer-meetings with others assembled, he shall be subject to a fine of ten Reichsthalers. He shall not be spared in any wise by the elders but shall be reported immediately to the city authorities.

XXXI. HOW THE PROTECTED-JEWS ARE TO CONDUCT THEMSELVES IN RE-
    LIGIOUS AND CHURCH MATTERS. . . .

Quarrels that occur actually in the synagogue because of Jewish
ceremonies and synagogal customs are to be discussed and settled
by the rabbi or vice-rabbi and the elders. According to circumstances they themselves may fine the offenders with a moderate
money penalty. However they shall not proceed against any one
with the ban and money fines that amount to more than five Reichsthalers, without the previous knowledge of the city authorities; such
penalties shall not be imposed on any one by the rabbi alone nor
even with the elders. [The elders were sometimes despotic.]
    He shall not presumptuously undertake to make any real decision
and settlement of a case in matters of secular law, for the rabbi and
the elders have no right to real jurisdiction. On the contrary, matters
of law must be referred to the proper court of justice. However,
in matters in which Jews have to do with Jews and which come
within the province of their rites, such as Jewish marriage-contracts
and their validity in bankruptcy, determination of the heir in cases
of succession to estates, which can only be settled by them through
their Mosaic laws, we concede, for the present, some sort of legal
jurisdiction to the rabbis and their learned assistant-judges. This also
applies to other judicial acts such as wills, inventories, and appointment of guardians. The Jewish jurisdiction, however, is only in the
form of arbitration. When the litigants are not satisfied with a decision they always have the privilege of referring their case back to
the ordinary judges as a simple judicial case without respect to the
statute of limitations. And the rabbis and the assistant-judges are
herewith responsible when they do not proceed legally in matters
of inventories, divisions of estates, and appointment of guardians. . . .

XXXII. COURTS TO WHICH THE PROTECTED-JEWS HAVE RECOURSE IN CIVIL
    AND CRIMINAL CASES. . . . CONCERNING THE ADMISSION OF
    JEWS, THEIR MARRIAGES, AND THE DRAWING UP OF THEIR LET-
    TERS OF PROTECTION, ETC. . . .

XXXIII. CONCERNING THE OBSERVANCE OF THIS GENERAL-PATENT FOR THE
    JEWS

In order that this general-patent for the Jews shall be contravened
as little as possible, the War and Domains Offices of their respective
Departments and the local commissaries (the tax-councils) shall

watch Jewry very carefully in the cities of the provinces and see to it that the said general-patent is everywhere exactly followed. They are particularly to see that the fixed number of families, communal officials, and Jewish-owned homes in every town is not increased, that no one is admitted without our royal concession, and least of all that no unlicensed Jew be tolerated. For this reason nothing is to be undertaken or conceded by the magistrates on their own authority; nor shall any Jew be permitted to live in the rural districts or in open towns where there is no excise office. . . . [Jews were allowed only in the larger towns.]

FINAL INJUNCTION FOR THE RIGHT OBSERVANCE OF THESE GENERAL REG-
ULATIONS FOR THE JEWS. . . .

So done and given at Berlin, the 17th of April, 1750.

FREDERICK.

BIBLIOGRAPHY

REFERENCES TO TEXTBOOKS

Sachar, pp. 273ff.

READINGS FOR ADVANCED STUDENTS

Deutsch, G., *Jew and Gentile*, Chap. v, "The Humor and Tragedy of 'Jew Taxes.' "
Freimann, A., and F. Kracauer, *Frankfort* (Jewish Community Series), pp. 129–146. A picture of Frankfort Jewry in the eighteenth century.
Grunwald, M., *Vienna* (Jewish Community Series), pp. 167ff.
Lowenthal, M., *The Jews of Germany*, pp. 197ff.
JE, "Frederick II"; "Schutzjude."

SECTION II

The Church and the Jew

19.

The Council of Elvira
about 300

THE Council of Elvira was probably the first national church council in Spain, and very probably one of the first in any land, to legislate concerning the Jews. It is obvious that at this council Christianity, not yet tolerated by the pagan Roman government, is on the defensive and is afraid of Jewish religious influence. These decrees, originally in Latin, are important, not because of their immediate influence on the Christians, then a minority in Spain, but because they foreshadow the attitude of other later church councils toward the Jews. Elvira was near Granada in southern Spain.

CANON XVI. CHRISTIAN GIRLS MAY NOT BE MARRIED TO INFIDELS

❡The daughters of Catholics shall not be given in marriage to heretics [Christians who do not follow the orthodox Catholic faith], unless these shall submit themselves to the Catholic church; the same is also decreed of Jews. . . .since there can be no communion of one that believeth, with an infidel. And if parents transgress this command, they shall be excommunicated for five years. [Christianity, still weak, opposed intermarriage to protect itself.]

CANON XLIX. JEWS MAY NOT BLESS THE CROPS OF CHRISTIANS

❡Landholders are to be admonished not to suffer the fruits, which they receive from God with the giving of thanks, to be blessed by the Jews, lest our benediction be rendered invalid and unprofitable. If any one shall venture to do so after this interdiction, let him be altogether ejected from the Church. [Some farmers evidently valued the blessing of the Jews more than that of their own Christian priests.]

CANON L. CONCERNING CHRISTIANS WHO EAT WITH JEWS

❡If any person, whether clerical or one of the faithful, shall take food with the Jews, he is to abstain from our communion, that he may learn to amend. [The Christians probably feared that social relations with Jews would lead Christians to Judaism.]

CANON LXXVIII. CONCERNING MARRIED CHRISTIAN MEN WHO HAVE RE-
LATIONS WITH A JEWESS OR AN INFIDEL

⟨If any one of the faithful, having a wife, shall commit adultery with a Jewess, or a pagan, he is to be cut off from our communion.

BIBLIOGRAPHY

REFERENCES TO TEXTBOOKS

Golub, J. S., *Medieval Jewish History*, Sec. III, "The Christian Church."

20.

Christianity Objects to the Sabbath and to the Jewish Dating of Easter
about 189–about 381

THE first Christians were Jews and, naturally, observed the Sabbath and the Jewish holidays, including the Passover, which for them was the anniversary of the death and resurrection of Jesus. The first selection below describes the attempts—at first unsuccessful—to induce the Christians of Asia Minor during the second century to cease celebrating the holiday we now know as Easter on the same day as the Jewish Passover, namely, the fourteenth of Nisan. It is not improbable that one of the reasons for this prohibition was the desire to encourage a religious and social cleavage between Christians and Jews, out of fear of Jewish religious influence. This selection is taken from the *Ecclesiastical History* written in Greek about 324 by the scholarly Eusebius (d. about 340), Bishop of Caesarea in Palestine. This history is, on the whole, a reliable source.

The second selection, taken from Eusebius' *Life of Constantine*, written in Greek between 337 and 340, is an extract of a letter on this problem of the paschal celebration written by Constantine the Great to the churches, after the first international church council which had met at Nicaea in Asia Minor in 325. By this time Christians in the Near East no longer observed the Passover on the *same* day as the Jews. They did, however, guide themselves by the Jewish calendar in that they observed Easter on the first Sunday after the beginning of the Jewish Passover.

In general there was confusion among the Christians in the observance of Easter. The Council of Nicaea decided, as the selection intimates, that the Christian Passover, that is, Easter, was to fall on a Sunday, and that it was not to coincide with the Jewish Passover or be determined in date by it.

This decision ultimately prevailed in the Roman Catholic world; today, Easter falls on the first Sunday which occurs after the first full moon after the twenty-first of March.

Although the first Christians observed the Sabbath they also began at a very early date to worship on Sunday, the day on which, as they believed, Jesus rose from the dead. It was not until 321 that

Constantine—the first emperor to encourage Christianity—declared Sunday a legal holiday, at least for city-dwellers. Constantine was probably motivated by the desire not only to please his Christian followers, but also to give all the peoples of his empire, the pagans too, a fixed day of rest. This law of 321, however, did not specifically prohibit Christians from resting and worshipping on the Jewish Sabbath also, and we know that many did. At a council in Laodicea in Phrygia in Asia Minor, held sometime between 343 and 381, the Church made this further step by forbidding Christians to rest on the Sabbath and by ordering them to honor Sunday. It is indicative, though, of Jewish influence that this very Council of Laodicea did tolerate a special Christian religious service for the Sabbath. It was not until 789, in the days of Charlemagne, that the Christian Sunday actually took over the characteristics of the Jewish Sabbath completely and became not merely a day of worship but also a day of rest.

The Latin Constantinian decree just described, selection three below, is found in the Justinian Code; the Laodicean decree, selection four, is found in the Greek canons of that church council.

1. *Easter and Passover Are Observed on the Same Day in Asia Minor,
    about 189*

《At that time [about 189] no small controversy arose because all the dioceses of Asia thought it right, as though by more ancient tradition, to observe for the feast of the Savior's passover the fourteenth day of the moon, on which the Jews had been commanded to kill the lamb. Thus it was necessary to finish the fast on that day, whatever day of the week it might be. [The Christians of Asia Minor would end their fast in memory of Jesus' suffering on the eve of the Jewish Passover. Then they would sit down to a *seder* recalling the last supper of Jesus.]

Yet it was not the custom to celebrate in this manner in the churches throughout the rest of the world, for from apostolic tradition they kept the custom which still exists that it is not right to finish the fast on any day save that of the resurrection of our Savior [Easter Sunday].

Many meetings and conferences with bishops were held on this point, and all unanimously formulated in their letters the doctrine of the church for those in every country that the mystery of the Lord's resurrection from the dead [Easter] could be celebrated on no day save Sunday, and that on that day alone we should celebrate the end of the paschal fast. [Nevertheless many Christians of Asia Minor still continued to observe Easter on the same day as Passover.]

II. *The Council of Nicaea Changes the Date of Easter, 325*

℧ Constantinus Augustus to the Churches. . . .

At this meeting [at Nicaea] the question concerning the most holy day of Easter was discussed, and it was resolved by the united judgment of all present, that this feast ought to be kept by all and in every place on one and the same day [Sunday]. For what can be more becoming or honorable to us than that this feast from which we date our hopes of immortality, should be observed unfailingly by all alike, according to one ascertained order and arrangement? [The resurrection of Jesus confirms the Christians in their expectation of immortality.]

And first of all, it appeared an unworthy thing that in the celebration of this most holy feast we should follow the practice of the Jews, who have impiously defiled their hands with enormous sin, and are, therefore, deservedly afflicted with blindness of soul. For we have it in our power, if we abandon their custom, to prolong the due observance of this ordinance to future ages, by a truer order, which we have preserved from the very day of the Passion until the present time. [Ever since the day of the Passion, or suffering of Jesus, the Christians had a traditional date for Easter independent of the Jewish dating of Passover. This contention of the Council of Nicaea is very probably incorrect. It is far more probable that the early Christians determined their date for the celebration of the resurrection of Jesus by the date of the Jewish Passover.]

Let us then have nothing in common with the detestable Jewish crowd; for we have received from our Savior a different way. A course at once legitimate and honorable lies open to our most holy religion. Beloved brethren, let us with one consent adopt this course, and withdraw ourselves from all participation in their baseness. For their boast is absurd indeed, that it is not in our power without instruction from them to observe these things. . . .

In fine, that I may express my meaning in as few words as possible, it has been determined by the common judgment of all, that the most holy feast of Easter should be kept on one and the same day [Sunday]. For on the one hand a discrepancy of opinion on so sacred a question is unbecoming, and on the other it is surely best to act on a decision which is free from strange folly and error. . . .

God preserve you, beloved brethren!

III. *Constantine Declares Sunday a Legal Holiday, March 7, 321—*
CONCERNING HOLIDAYS

⟨All judges and common people of the city and workers in all the crafts are to rest on the holy Sunday. Those who live in the country, however, shall take care of the culture of the fields freely and without restraint, since it frequently happens that the work on the grain in the furrows and the vines in the ditches cannot well be put off to another day, lest the benefit granted by a divine Providence be lost in an inopportune moment.

IV. *The Council of Laodicea Forbids Christians To Observe the Sabbath, between 343 and 381—*CANON 29

⟨The Christians must not judaize and sit idle on the Sabbath, but ought to work on that day. They must honor the Lord's Day [Sunday] in whatever way they can by resting, inasmuch as they are Christians. But if they persist in being Jews they ought to be anathema to Christ.

BIBLIOGRAPHY

READINGS FOR ADVANCED STUDENTS

Parkes, J., *The Conflict of the Church and the Synagogue,* see "Easter" and "Passover" in Index.
Catholic Encyclopedia, "Easter"; "Sunday."
Encyclopaedia of Religion and Ethics, "Sunday."
JE, "Easter"; "Sabbath and Sunday."

ADDITIONAL SOURCE MATERIALS IN ENGLISH

Eusebius, in his *Life of Constantine,* Book III, Chaps. xvii–xx, gives the complete letter of Constantine of which only part has been cited above.
Socrates Scholasticus, in his *Ecclesiastical History,* Book V, Chap. xxii, in *A Select Library of Nicene and Post-Nicene Fathers of the Christian Church,* Second Series, Vol. II, discusses the change in date of the Easter celebration so as not to coincide with the date of Passover. In the same volume of the *Nicene Fathers,* Sozomenus, in his *Ecclesiastical History,* also treats of this problem: Book I, Chap. xvi; Book VII, Chap. xviii.

21.

St. Ambrose and the Jews
388

AMBROSE (d. 397), Bishop of Milan, was one of the most notable of the Christian Fathers. A man of education and culture, his great courage and energy were never more evident than when defending the interests of the Christian church.

About the year 388 a bishop in Mesopotamia had encouraged the burning down of a synagogue in the town of Callinicum, a not uncommon occurrence. The Emperor Theodosius the Great (379–395) ordered him to rebuild it. Ambrose protested against this order in a letter to the Emperor, with whom he had great influence. However, when the letter did not have the desired effect he appealed in person to the ruler, and successfully, when he came to services.

The first selection below is an extract from Ambrose's letter to the Emperor. The second selection is an extract from Ambrose's letter to his sister in which he tells her of his successful appeal. Both letters were written in Latin in the year 388.

Nevertheless, five years later (393) Theodosius issued an order to the Count of the East to punish any Christian who attacked and destroyed synagogues.

I. AMBROSE, BISHOP, TO THE MOST CLEMENT PRINCE, AND BLESSED EMPEROR, THEODOSIUS THE AUGUSTUS. . . .

❡A report was made by the military Count of the East that a synagogue [in Callinicum, Mesopotamia] had been burnt [about August 1, 388] and that this was done by the authority of the Bishop. You gave command that the others should be punished and the synagogue be rebuilt by the Bishop himself. I do not urge that the Bishop's account [of this riot] ought to have been waited for; for priests are the calmers of disturbances and anxious for peace, except when they, too, are moved by some offense against God or insult to the Church. Let us suppose that that Bishop was too eager in the matter of burning the synagogue and too timid at the judgment-seat; are you not afraid, O Emperor, that he may comply with your sentence; do you not fear that he may fail in his faith? [If the Bishop rebuilds the synagogue he will be remiss in his duty as a Christian.] . . .

But let it be granted that no one will cite the Bishop to the performance of this task [the rebuilding of the synagogue], for I have
requested your clemency; and although I have not yet read that
this edict is revoked, let us notwithstanding assume that it is revoked.
What if others more timid—because they shrink from death—offer
that the synagogue be restored at their cost; or that the Count, having
found this previously determined, himself orders it to be rebuilt
out of the funds of Christians? . . . Shall the Jews write this inscription on the front of their synagogue: "The temple of impiety,
erected from the plunder of Christians"? [The result would be a
Jewish place of worship built of Christian funds.]

But perhaps the cause of discipline moves you, O Emperor. Which,
then, is of greater importance, the show of discipline or the cause
of religion? It is needful that censure should yield to religion. [The
Christian religion takes precedence over the law.] . . .

There is, then, no adequate cause for such a commotion, that the
people should be so severely punished for the burning of a building;
and much less since it is the burning of a synagogue, a home of
unbelief, a house of impiety, a receptacle of folly, which God himself has condemned. . . .

And certainly, if I were pleading according to the law of nations,
I could tell how many of the Church's basilicas [churches] the Jews
burnt in the time of the Emperor Julian: two at Damascus, one of
which is scarcely now repaired, and this at the cost of the Church,
not of the Synagogue; the other basilica still is a rough mass of
shapeless ruins. Basilicas were burnt at Gaza, Ascalon, Beirut, and in
almost every place in those parts, and no one demanded punishment.
And at Alexandria a basilica, which alone surpassed all the rest, was
burnt by pagans and Jews. The Church was not avenged; shall the
Synagogue be so? . . . . [Ambrose says, in excuse, that the Jews
destroyed churches during the reign of Julian the Apostate, 361–
363. This accusation is not confirmed in other contemporary Christian sources.]

The buildings of our churches were burnt by the Jews, and nothing was restored, nothing was asked back, nothing demanded. Now,
what could the Synagogue have possessed in a far distant town,
when the whole of what there is there is not much; there is nothing
of value and no abundance. And what then could the scheming
Jews lose by the fire? These are artifices of the Jews who wish to
calumniate us, that because of their complaints an extraordinary
military inquiry may be ordered. . . .

Will you give this triumph over the Church of God to the Jews? this victory over Christ's people? this exultation, O Emperor, to the unbelievers? this rejoicing to the Synagogue, this sorrow to the Church? The people of the Jews will set this solemnity amongst their feast-days and will doubtless number it amongst those on which they triumphed either over the Amorites or the Canaanites, or were delivered from the hand of Pharaoh, King of Egypt, or of Nebuchadnezzar, King of Babylon. They will add this solemnity, in memory of their having triumphed over the people of Christ. . . .

On this point I pledge myself to our God for you, do not fear your oath. Is it possible that that should displease God which is amended for His honor? You need not alter anything in that letter, whether it be sent or is not yet sent. Order another to be written, which shall be full of faith, full of piety. For you it is possible to change for the better; for me it is not possible to hide the truth. . . . [Theodosius is asked to recall the order to rebuild the synagogue.]

II. THE BROTHER TO HIS SISTER *

CYou were good enough to write me word that your holiness was still anxious, because I had written that I was anxious; so that I am surprised that you did not receive the letter in which I wrote word that satisfaction had not been granted me [as yet]. For when it was reported that a synagogue of the Jews and a conventicle of the Valentinians [Gnostic heretics] had been burnt by Christians, by the authority of the Bishop, an order was made, while I was at Aquileia [near Triest], that the synagogue should be rebuilt and the monks who had burnt the Valentinian building punished. Then, since I gained little by frequent endeavors, I wrote and sent a letter to the Emperor; and when he went to church I delivered this discourse. . . . [The substance of the sermon was: if you don't take care of the Christians, God won't take care of you.]

When I came down from the pulpit, he said to me: "You spoke about me." I replied: "I dealt with matters intended for your benefit." Then he said: "I had indeed decided too harshly about the repairing of the synagogue by the Bishop, but that has been rectified. The monks commit many crimes." Then Timasius, the general of the cavalry and infantry, began to be over-vehement against the monks, and I answered him: "I deal with the Emperor as is fitting, because I know that he has the fear of God; but with you, who speak so roughly, one must deal otherwise."

* Marcellina, a nun, a sister of Ambrose.

Then, after standing for some time, I said to the Emperor: "Let me offer for you without anxiety; set my mind at ease." [Ambrose will not perform the "sacrifice," the mass, till the edict is rescinded.] As he continued sitting and nodded but did not give an open promise, and I remained standing, he said that he would amend the edict. I went on at once to say that he must end the whole investigation lest the Count should use the opportunity of the investigation to do some injury to the Christians. He promised that it should be so. I said to him: "I act on your promise," and repeated: "I act on your promise." "Act," he said, "on my promise." And so I went to the altar. I would not have gone unless he had given me a complete promise. And indeed so great was the grace attending the offering [the mass], that I myself felt that that favor [rescinding the order] was very acceptable to our God, and that the divine presence was not wanting. And so everything was done as I wished.

BIBLIOGRAPHY

READINGS FOR ADVANCED STUDENTS

Graetz, II, pp. 612ff.
Parkes, J., *The Conflict of the Church and the Synagogue*. See "Ambrose" in Index.
JE, "Ambrose."

ADDITIONAL SOURCE MATERIALS IN ENGLISH

"The Letters of St. Ambrose" in *A Select Library of Nicene and Post-Nicene Fathers of the Christian Church*, Second Series, X, pp. 440ff., contains the full texts of the letters quoted above in abstract.

22.

Pope Gregory the Great and the Jews
590–604

GREGORY THE GREAT (590–604) is important in Jewish history because his attitude toward the Jew finally became the official policy of the Catholic church. This policy is an attempt to crystallize the status of the Jew as it had evolved under the Christian Roman emperors of the fourth, fifth, and sixth centuries. It is most clearly expressed in the very last paragraph of the letter to Fantinus quoted below.

The first of the Latin letters given below shows Gregory's distaste for forced baptisms, although he himself was most eager to bring the Jews over to Christianity.

The second letter describes the great Pope's efforts to do justice to the Jews of Palermo, in Sicily. The bishop there, Victor, had seized and occupied a synagogue, and when he saw that Gregory objected, he quickly consecrated it as a church, making its return to Jewry impossible. Gregory attempted to correct this injustice by restoring to the Jews the value of the buildings and by instituting a search for the contents that had been carried off. The reason for this attitude of Gregory was a desire to adhere closely to the principles of the Roman law which already defined the privileges and the disabilities of the Jews. He himself did nothing, however, to improve their legal condition.

I. *June 591*—GREGORY TO VIRGILIUS, BISHOP OF ARLES, AND THEODORUS, BISHOP OF MARSEILLES, IN GAUL

℧Though the opportunity of a suitable time and suitable persons for writing to your Fraternity [a term of respect] and duly returning your salutation has failed me so far, the result has been that I can now at one and the same time acquit myself of what is due to love and fraternal relationship, and also touch on the complaint of certain persons which has reached us, with respect to the way in which the souls of the erring should be saved.

Very many, though indeed of the Jewish religion, resident in this province [Rome], and from time to time traveling for various matters of business to the regions of Marseilles, have apprized us that many of the Jews settled in those parts have been brought to the font of baptism more by force than by preaching. Now I consider the intention in such cases to be worthy of praise, and allow that it proceeds from the love of our Lord. But I fear lest this same intention, unless adequate justification from [a verse of] Holy Scripture accompany it, should either have no profitable effect; or there will ensue further (God forbid) the loss of the very souls which we wish to save.

For, when any one is brought to the font of baptism, not by the sweetness of preaching but by compulsion, he returns to his former superstition, and dies the worse from having been born again.

Let, therefore, your Fraternity stir up such men by frequent preaching, to the end that through the sweetness of their teacher they may desire the more to change their old life. For so our purpose is rightly accomplished, and the mind of the convert returns not again to his former vomit. Wherefore discourse must be addressed to them, such as may burn up the thorns of error in them, and illuminate what is dark in them by preaching, so that your Fraternity may through your frequent admonition receive a reward for them, and lead them, so far as God may grant it, to the regeneration of a new life. [Though Gregory was ready to force pagans into Christianity, he believed Jews should be converted only by preaching and example.]

II. *October 598*—GREGORY TO FANTINUS, DEFENSOR * OF PALERMO

¶A little time ago [in June] we wrote to Victor, our brother and fellow-bishop, that—inasmuch as certain of the Jews have complained in a petition presented to us that synagogues with their guest-chambers [for the poor and ailing], situated in the city of Palermo, had been unreasonably taken possession of by him—he should keep aloof from the consecration of them [as churches] until it could be ascertained whether this thing had actually been done, lest perchance injury should appear to have been alleged by the Jews of their own [ill] will. And, indeed, having regard to his priestly office, we could not easily believe that our aforesaid brother [Victor] had done anything unsuitably.

But, we found from the report of Salarius, our notary [a papal agent], who was afterwards there, that there had been no reasonable

* Papal administrator.

cause for taking possession of those synagogues, and that they had been unadvisedly and rashly consecrated. [When Bishop Victor found out that the Pope wanted him to restore the synagogues he hastily consecrated them.] We therefore enjoin thy Experience [Excellency] (since what has been once consecrated cannot any more be restored to the Jews) that it be thy care to see that our aforesaid brother and fellow-bishop pay the price at which our sons, the glorious Venantius the Patrician and Urbicus the Abbot, may value the synagogues themselves with the guest-chambers that are under them or annexed to their walls, and the gardens thereto adjoining. Thus what he has caused to be taken possession of may belong to the Church, and they [the Jews] may in no wise be oppressed or suffer any injustice. [Gregory orders that the Jews be compensated for their losses.]

Moreover, let books or ornaments that have been carried off be in like manner sought for. And, if any have been openly taken away, we desire them also to be restored without any question. For, as there ought to be no license for them to do anything in their synagogues beyond what is decreed by law, so neither damage nor any cost ought to be brought upon them contrary to justice and equity, as we have ourselves already written. [Gregory here refers to his letter of June, 598, to Victor, Bishop of Palermo: "Just as one ought not to grant any freedom to the Jews in their synagogues beyond that permitted by law, so should the Jews in no way suffer in those things already conceded to them." This dictum was frequently repeated in the bulls of later popes.]

BIBLIOGRAPHY

REFERENCES TO TEXTBOOKS

Elbogen, pp. 62ff.; Roth, pp. 145ff.

READINGS FOR ADVANCED STUDENTS

Graetz, III, pp. 24ff.; Margolis and Marx, pp. 297–299.
Katz, S., "Pope Gregory the Great and the Jews," *JQR*, N. S., XXIV (1933–1934), pp. 113–136.
Parkes, J., *The Conflict of the Church and the Synagogue*, pp. 210–221.
JE, "Gregory I, the Great."

ADDITIONAL SOURCE MATERIALS IN ENGLISH

For further light on the attitude of Gregory to the Jews consult the "Selected Epistles of Gregory the Great," in *A Select Library of Nicene and Post-*

Nicene Fathers of the Christian Church, Second Series, XII–XIII. See Index under "Jews."

For an understanding of Jewish life in France in the sixth century, as seen through the eyes of a distinguished churchman, see E. Brehaut's translation of Gregory of Tours' *History of the Franks*. See the Index under "Jews"; "Priscus."

23.

The Crusaders in Mayence
May 27, 1096

IN the year 1095 the Catholic Church, aroused by the Moslem encroachments in Palestine, proclaimed a crusade against the Saracens to recover Jerusalem and the Holy Sepulcher. The following year, in the spring of 1096, bands of zealous crusaders led by monks and soldiers set out for the Holy Land. Many of the crusaders were pious; but there can be no question that many also were runaway serfs, ambitious business men, adventurers, and criminals. As they passed through Germany on their way to Jerusalem this motley crew killed thousands of "infidel" Jews in the larger cities such as Speyer, Worms, Mayence, and Cologne.

In May, 1096 a band of crusaders led by Emico, a German noble, forced its way into the city of Mayence and finally into the archiepiscopal palace where the Jews had taken refuge. The slaughter and suicide of the Jews in this palace with all the attendant horror and hysteria are graphically described in the following two selections taken from a Hebrew historical account by Solomon bar Samson—of whom we know very little—who wrote about 1140.

I.

It was on the third of Siwan. . . . at noon [Tuesday, May 27], that Emico the wicked, the enemy of the Jews, came with his whole army against the city gate, and the citizens opened it up for him. [Emico, a German noble, led a band of plundering German and French crusaders.] Then the enemies of the Lord said to each other: "Look! They have opened up the gate for us. Now let us avenge the blood of 'the hanged one' [Jesus]."

The children of the holy covenant who were there, martyrs who feared the Most High, although they saw the great multitude, an army numerous as the sand on the shore of the sea, still clung to their Creator. Then young and old donned their armor and girded on their weapons, and at their head was Rabbi Kalonymus ben Meshullam, the chief of the community. Yet because of the many troubles and the fasts which they had observed they had no strength to stand up against the enemy. [They had fasted to avert the impending evils.] Then came gangs and bands, sweeping through like a flood, until Mayence was filled from end to end.

The foe Emico proclaimed in the hearing of the community that the enemy be driven from the city and be put to flight. Panic was great in the town. Each Jew in the inner court of the bishop girded on his weapons, and all moved towards the palace gate to fight the crusaders and the citizens. They fought each other up to the very gate, but the sins of the Jews brought it about that the enemy overcame them and took the gate.

The hand of the Lord was heavy against His people. All the Gentiles were gathered together against the Jews in the courtyard to blot out their name, and the strength of our people weakened when they saw the wicked Edomites overpowering them. [The Edomites were the traditional foes of the Jews; here, Christians are meant.] The bishop's men, who had promised to help them, were the very first to flee, thus delivering the Jews into the hands of the enemy. They were indeed a poor support; even the bishop himself fled from his church for it was thought to kill him also because he had spoken good things of the Jews. . . . [Archbishop Ruthard had been paid to remain and defend the Jews. He was later accused of having received some of the plunder taken from them.]

When the children of the holy covenant saw that the heavenly decree of death had been issued and that the enemy had conquered them and had entered the courtyard, then all of them—old men and young, virgins and children, servants and maids—cried out together to their Father in heaven and, weeping for themselves and for their lives, accepted as just the sentence of God. One to another they said: "Let us be strong and let us bear the yoke of the holy religion, for only in this world can the enemy kill us—and the easiest of the four deaths is by the sword. But we, our souls in paradise, shall continue to live eternally, in the great shining reflection [of the divine glory]." [In Jewish law the four death penalties were: stoning, burning, beheading, strangulation.]

With a whole heart and with a willing soul they then spoke: "After all it is not right to criticize the acts of God—blessed be He and blessed be His name—who has given to us His Torah and a command to put ourselves to death, to kill ourselves for the unity of His holy name. Happy are we if we do His will. Happy is anyone who is killed or slaughtered, who dies for the unity of His name, so that he is ready to enter the World to Come, to dwell in the heavenly camp with the righteous—with Rabbi Akiba and his companions, the pillars of the universe, who were killed for His name's sake. [The Romans martyred Akiba during the Bar Kokba revolt, about 135 C. E.] Not only this; but he exchanges the world of darkness for the world of light, the world of trouble for the world of joy, and the world that passes away for the world that lasts for all eternity." Then all of them, to a man, cried out with a loud voice: "Now we must delay no longer for the enemy are already upon us. Let us hasten and offer ourselves as a sacrifice to the Lord. Let him who has a knife examine it that it not be nicked, and let him come and slaughter us for the sanctification of the Only One, the Everlasting, and then let him cut his own throat or plunge the knife into his own body." [A nick in the slaughterer's knife would make it ritually unfit.]

As soon as the enemy came into the courtyard they found some of the very pious there with our brilliant master, Isaac ben Moses. He stretched out his neck, and his head they cut off first. The others, wrapped in their fringed praying-shawls, sat by themselves in the courtyard, eager to do the will of their Creator. They did not care to flee into the chamber to save themselves for this temporal life, but out of love they received upon themselves the sentence of God. The enemy showered stones and arrows upon them, but they did not care to flee; and [Esther 9:5] "with the stroke of the sword, and with slaughter, and destruction" the foe killed all of those whom they found there. When those in the chambers saw the deed of these righteous ones, how the enemy had already come upon them, they then cried out, all of them: "There is nothing better than for us to offer our lives as a sacrifice." [The outnumbered Jews had no chance to win: Emico is reported to have had about 12,000 men.]

The women there girded their loins with strength and slew their sons and their daughters and then themselves. Many men, too, plucked up courage and killed their wives, their sons, their infants. The tender and delicate mother slaughtered the babe she had played with; all of them, men and women arose and slaughtered one another. The maidens and the young brides and grooms looked out of the windows and in a loud voice cried: "Look and see, O our God, what we do for the sanctification of Thy great name in order not to exchange you for a hanged and crucified one. . . ."

Thus were the precious children of Zion, the Jews of Mayence, tried with ten trials like Abraham, our father, and like Hananiah, Mishael, and Azariah [who were thrown into a fiery furnace, Daniel 3:21]. They tied their sons as Abraham tied Isaac his son, and they received upon themselves with a willing soul the yoke of the fear of God, the King of the Kings of Kings, the Holy One, blessed be

He, rather than deny and exchange the religion of our King for
[Isaiah 14:19] "an abhorred offshoot [Jesus]. . . ." [Christians and
Jews of those days often spoke contemptuously of each other's
religion.] They stretched out their necks to the slaughter and they
delivered their pure souls to their Father in heaven. Righteous and
pious women bared their throats to each other, offering to be sacrificed for the unity of the Name. A father turning to his son or
brother, a brother to his sister, a woman to her son or daughter, a
neighbor to a neighbor or a friend, a groom to a bride, a fiancé to a
fiancée, would kill and would be killed, and blood touched blood.
The blood of the men mingled with their wives', the blood of the
fathers with their children's, the blood of the brothers with their
sisters', the blood of the teachers with their disciples', the blood of
the grooms with their brides', the blood of the leaders with their
cantors', the blood of the judges with their scribes', and the blood of
infants and sucklings with their mothers'. For the unity of the
honored and awe-inspiring Name were they killed and slaughtered.

The ears of him who hears these things will tingle, for who has
ever heard anything like this? Inquire now and look about, was there
ever such an abundant sacrifice as this since the days of the primeval
Adam? Were there ever eleven hundred offerings on one day, each
one of them like the sacrifice of Isaac, the son of Abraham?

For the sake of Isaac who was ready to be sacrificed on Mount
Moriah, the world shook, as it is said [Isaiah 33:7]: "Behold their
valiant ones cry without; [the angels of peace weep bitterly]" and
[Jeremiah 4:28] "the heavens grow dark." Yet see what these martyrs
did! Why did the heavens not grow dark and the stars not withdraw
their brightness? Why did not the moon and the sun grow dark in
their heavens when on one day, on the third of Siwan, on a Tuesday,
eleven hundred souls were killed and slaughtered, among them so
many infants and sucklings who had not transgressed nor sinned, so
many poor, innocent souls?

Wilt Thou, despite this, still restrain Thyself, O Lord? For Thy
sake it was that these numberless souls were killed. Avenge quickly
the blood of Thy servants which was spilt in our days and in our
sight. Amen.

11. Rachel and Her Children

❡Now I shall recount and tell of the most unusual deeds that were
done on that day [May 27, 1096) by these righteous ones. . . . Who
has ever seen anything like this? Who has ever heard of a deed like

that which was performed by this righteous and pious woman, the young Rachel, the daughter of Rabbi Isaac ben Asher, the wife of Rabbi Judah? For she said to her friends: "I have four children. Do not spare even them, lest the Christians come, take them alive, and bring them up in their false religion. Through them, too, sanctify the name of the Holy God."

So one of her companions came and picked up a knife to slaughter her son. But when the mother of the children saw the knife, she let out a loud and bitter lament and she beat her face and breast, crying: "Where are Thy mercies, O God?" In the bitterness of her soul she said to her friend: "Do not slay Isaac in the presence of his brother Aaron lest Aaron see his brother's death and run away." The woman then took the lad Isaac, who was small and very pretty, and she slaughtered him while the mother spread out her sleeves to receive the blood, catching it in her garment instead of a basin. When the child Aaron saw that his brother Isaac was slain, he screamed again and again: "Mother, mother, do not butcher me," and ran and hid under a chest.

She had two daughters also who still lived at home, Bella and Matrona, beautiful young girls, the children of her husband Rabbi Judah. The girls took the knife and sharpened it themselves that it should not be nicked. Then the woman bared their necks and sacrificed them to the Lord God of Hosts who has commanded us not to change His pure religion but to be perfect with Him, as it is written [Deuteronomy 18:13]: "Perfect shall you be with the Lord your God."

When this righteous woman had made an end of sacrificing her three children to their Creator, she then raised her voice and called out to her son Aaron: "Aaron, where are you? You also I will not spare nor will I have any mercy." Then she dragged him out by his foot from under the chest where he had hidden himself, and she sacrificed him before God, the high and exalted. She put her children next to her body, two on each side, covering them with her two sleeves, and there they lay struggling in the agony of death. When the enemy seized the room they found her sitting and wailing over them. "Show us the money that is under your sleeves," they said to her. But when it was the slaughtered children they saw, they struck her and killed her, upon her children, and her spirit flew away and her soul found peace at last. To her applied the Biblical verse [Hosea 10:14]: "The mother was dashed in pieces with her children." . . .

When the father saw the death of his four beautiful, lovely

children, he cried aloud, weeping and wailing, and threw himself upon the sword in his hand so that his bowels came out, and he wallowed in blood on the road together with the dying who were convulsed, rolling in their life's blood. The enemy killed all those who were left in the room and then stripped them naked; [Lamentations 1:11] "See, O Lord, and behold, how abject I am become." Then the crusaders began to give thanks in the name of "the hanged one" because they had done what they wanted with all those in the room of the bishop so that not a soul escaped. [The crusaders now held a thanksgiving service in the archbishop's palace where the massacre took place.]

BIBLIOGRAPHY

REFERENCES TO TEXTBOOKS
Elbogen, pp. 102ff.; Roth, pp. 180–188; Sachar, pp. 186–192.

READINGS FOR ADVANCED STUDENTS
Graetz, III, pp. 297–310; Graetz-Rhine, III, pp. 166–229; Margolis and Marx, pp. 356–373.

Abbott, G. F., *Israel in Europe*, pp. 83–104.

The Chronicles of Rabbi Joseph ben Joshua ben Meir, the Sephardi, tr. by Bialloblotzky, contains materials on the Crusades which this sixteenth century Jewish historian drew from older and contemporary sources: I, pp. 29ff.

Lowenthal, M., *The Jews of Germany*, pp. 36ff.

Milman, H. H., *The History of the Jews*, II, Book xxiv.

Zunz, L., *The Sufferings of the Jews during the Middle Ages*. This short work chronicles the major (and many of the minor) persecutions of the Jews throughout the Middle Ages in many lands. This survey was written to explain and to justify the bitterness that characterizes many medieval Jewish liturgical writings.

JE, "Crusades, The"; "Mayence."

ADDITIONAL SOURCE MATERIALS IN ENGLISH

Halper, B., *Post-Biblical Hebrew Literature*, "The Crusaders Massacre the Jews at Meurs," II, pp. 235–239. This is a description of a massacre during the first Crusade, 1096, by the same Joseph ben Joshua.

Ludwig Lewisohn in *The Island Within*, pp. 327–339, reproduces a Jewish chronicle of the first crusade. Although his translation is made from a rather bold reconstruction of a German translation of the original Hebrew chronicle, it is still close enough to the original to give a good picture of some aspects of the crusade as it affected the Jews.

24.

The Accusation of the Ritual Murder of St. William of Norwich

1144

MEDIEVAL Christians (and some modern ones, too) believed that Christian children were seized and tortured to death by the Jews during the Passover season. This myth appears in a complete form for the first time in *The Life and Miracles of St. William of Norwich*, a Latin work written about 1173 by Thomas of Monmouth, a contemporary of the events which he relates. The story of the ritual murder of the boy William in 1144 is virtually the first of a long series of such accusations, a series that has not yet come to an end. The significance of these accusations is that by such descriptions of the Jew they have served throughout the ages to create an anti-Jewish mentality. Generations have believed that no Christian child was safe in Jewish hands. Hundreds of Jews have been imprisoned, killed, or burnt alive on this charge. The Papacy has frequently denounced this charge, yet it is equally true that in numerous instances the accusation of ritual murder was not made except with the vigorous support of the local Church authorities.

The author, Thomas of Monmouth, a monk in the Norwich Benedictine monastery, was an exceedingly credulous person. Dr. Jessopp of Norwich, one of the editors of Thomas' work, believes that our monkish author belongs to the class of those who are "deceivers and being deceived."

In the specific case of William of Norwich, the evidence, critically sifted, leads one to believe that he actually existed and that his body was found after he had died a violent death. Everything beyond this, however, is in the realm of speculation.

HOW WILLIAM WAS WONT TO RESORT TO THE JEWS, AND HAVING BEEN CHID BY HIS OWN PEOPLE FOR SO DOING, HOW HE WITHDREW HIMSELF FROM THEM

ℂWhen therefore he was flourishing in this blessed boyhood of his, and had attained to his eighth year [about 1140], he was entrusted to the skinners [furriers] to be taught their craft. Gifted with a teachable disposition and bringing industry to bear upon it, in a short time he far surpassed lads of his own age in the craft aforesaid, and he equalled some who had been his teachers. So leaving the country, drawn by a divine urge he betook himself to the city and lodged with a very famous master of that craft, and some time passed away. He was seldom in the country, but was occupied in the city and sedulously gave himself to the practice of his craft, and thus reached his twelfth year [1144].

Now, while he was staying in Norwich, the Jews who were settled there and required their cloaks or their robes or other garments (whether pledged to them, or their own property) to be repaired, preferred him before all other skinners. For they esteemed him to be especially fit for their work, either because they had learnt that he was guileless and skilful, or, because attracted to him by their avarice, they thought they could bargain with him for a lower price. Or, as I rather believe, because by the ordering of divine providence he had been predestined to martyrdom from the beginning of time, and gradually step by step was drawn on, and chosen to be made a mock of and to be put to death by the Jews, in scorn of the Lord's Passion, as one of little foresight, and so the more fit for them. [William is to be put to death to mock the crucifixion.]

For I have learnt from certain Jews, who were afterwards converted to the Christian faith, how that at that time they had planned to do this very thing with some Christian, and in order to carry out their malignant purpose, at the beginning of Lent they had made choice of the boy William, being twelve years of age and a boy of unusual innocence.

So it came to pass that when the holy boy, ignorant of the treachery that had been planned, had frequent dealings with the Jews, he was taken to task by Godwin the priest, who had the boy's aunt as his wife, and by a certain Wulward with whom he lodged, and he was prohibited from going in and out among them any more. But the Jews, annoyed at the thwarting of their designs, tried with all their might to patch up a new scheme of wickedness, and all the more vehemently as the day for carrying out the crime they had determined upon drew near, and the victim, which they had thought they had already secured, had slipped out of their wicked hands.

Accordingly, collecting all the cunning of their crafty plots, they found—I am not sure whether he was a Christian or a Jew—a man who was a most treacherous fellow and just the fitting person for carrying out their execrable crime, and with all haste—for their Passover was coming on in three days—they sent him to find out and bring back with him the victim which, as I said before, had slipped out of their hands.

HOW HE WAS SEDUCED BY THE JEWS' MESSENGER

At the dawn of day, on the Monday [March 20, 1144] after Palm Sunday, that detestable messenger of the Jews set out to execute the business that was committed to him, and at last the boy William, after being searched for with very great care, was found. When he was found, he got round him with cunning wordy tricks, and so deceived him with his lying promises. . . .

HOW ON HIS GOING TO THE JEWS HE WAS TAKEN, MOCKED, AND SLAIN. . . .

Then the boy, like an innocent lamb, was led to the slaughter. He was treated kindly by the Jews at first, and, ignorant of what was being prepared for him, he was kept till the morrow. But on the next day [Tuesday, March 21], which in that year was the Passover for them, after the singing of the hymns appointed for the day in the synagogue, the chiefs of the Jews. . . . suddenly seized hold of the boy William as he was having his dinner and in no fear of any treachery, and illtreated him in various horrible ways. For while some of them held him behind, others opened his mouth and introduced an instrument of torture which is called a teazle [a wooden gag], and, fixing it by straps through both jaws to the back of his neck, they fastened it with a knot as tightly as it could be drawn.

After that, taking a short piece of rope of about the thickness of one's little finger and tying three knots in it at certain distances marked out, they bound round that innocent head with it from the forehead to the back, forcing the middle knot into his forehead and the two others into his temples, the two ends of the rope being most tightly stretched at the back of his head and fastened in a very tight knot. The ends of the rope were then passed round his neck and carried round his throat under his chin, and there they finished off this dreadful engine of torture in a fifth knot.

But not even yet could the cruelty of the torturers be satisfied without adding even more severe pains. Having shaved his head, they stabbed it with countless thorn-points, and made the blood come horribly from the wounds they made. [Jesus had worn a crown of thorns before his death.] And so cruel were they and so eager to inflict pain that it was difficult to say whether they were more cruel or more ingenious in their tortures. For their skill in torturing kept up the strength of their cruelty and ministered arms thereto.

And thus, while these enemies of the Christian name were rioting in the spirit of malignity around the boy, some of those present adjudged him to be fixed to a cross in mockery of the Lord's Passion, as though they would say: "Even as we condemned the Christ to a shameful death, so let us also condemn the Christian, so that, uniting the Lord and his servant in a like punishment, we may retort upon themselves the pain of that reproach which they impute to us."

Conspiring, therefore, to accomplish the crime of this great and detestable malice, they next laid their blood-stained hands upon the innocent victim, and having lifted him from the ground and fastened him upon the cross, they vied with one another in their efforts to make an end of him.

And we, after enquiring into the matter very diligently, did both find the house, and discovered some most certain marks in it of what had been done there. [This was supposed to be the house of a rich Jew, Eleazar, who was later murdered by order of his debtor, Sir Simon de Novers.] For report goes that there was there instead of a cross a post set up between two other posts, and a beam stretched across the midmost post and attached to the other on either side. And as we afterwards discovered, from the marks of the wounds and of the bands, the right hand and foot had been tightly bound and fastened with cords, but the left hand and foot were pierced with two nails. Now the deed was done in this way, lest it should be discovered, from the presence of nail-marks in both hands and both feet, that the murderers were Jews and not Christians, if eventually the body were found. [Both hands and feet were not nailed lest it look like a crucifixion.]

But while in doing these things they were adding pang to pang and wound to wound, and yet were not able to satisfy their heartless cruelty and their inborn hatred of the Christian name, lo! after all these many and great tortures, they inflicted a frightful wound in his left side, reaching even to his inmost heart, and, as though to make an end of all, they extinguished his mortal life so far as it was in their power. [Jesus was similarly pierced by a lance while nailed to the cross. The chronicler here imitates the Apostle John's narrative.] And since many streams of blood were running down from all parts of his body, then, to stop the blood and to wash and close the wounds, they poured boiling water over him.

Thus then the glorious boy and martyr of Christ, William, dying the death of time in reproach of the Lord's death, but crowned with the blood of a glorious martyrdom, entered into the kingdom of glory on high to live for ever. Whose soul rejoiceth blissfully in heaven among the bright hosts of the saints, and whose body by the

omnipotence of the divine mercy worketh miracles upon earth. . . .
[St. William after his death worked many miracles that brought
streams of people to his shrine.]

As a proof of the truth and credibility of the matter we now
adduce something which we have heard from the lips of Theobald,
who was once a Jew, and afterwards a monk. He verily told us that
in the ancient writings of his fathers it was written that the Jews,
without the shedding of human blood, could neither obtain their
freedom, nor could they ever return to their fatherland. [There is
no such statement in Jewish law or literature.] Hence it was laid
down by them in ancient times that every year they must sacrifice
a Christian in some part of the world to the Most High God in scorn
and contempt of Christ, that so they might avenge their sufferings
on Him; inasmuch as it was because of Christ's death that they had
been shut out from their own country, and were in exile as slaves
in a foreign land. [The Jews rejected Jesus and were as a result
punished by exile from Palestine. Angry, they took revenge by
secretly crucifying Christian children—thus Theobald. This libel
is reminiscent of Apion, an Alexandrian writer of the first century.]
Wherefore the chief men and Rabbis of the Jews who dwell in
Spain assemble together at Narbonne, where the Royal seed [resides],
and where they are held in the highest estimation, and they cast
lots for all the countries which the Jews inhabit; and whatever
country the lot falls upon, its metropolis has to carry out the same
method with the other towns and cities, and the place whose lot
is drawn has to fulfill the duty imposed by authority. [Lots are cast
in Narbonne, France, where Jews had a "king" to decide which city
was to seize the Christian victim.]
Now in that year in which we know that William, God's glorious
martyr, was slain, it happened that the lot fell upon the Norwich
Jews, and all the synagogues in England signified, by letter or by
message, their consent that the wickedness should be carried out at
Norwich. "I was," said he, "at that time at Cambridge, a Jew among
Jews, and the commission of the crime was no secret to me. But in
process of time, as I became acquainted with the glorious display of
miracles which the divine power carried out through the merits of
the blessed martyr William, I became much afraid, and following the
dictates of my conscience, I forsook Judaism, and turned to the
Christian faith."
These words—observe, the words of a converted Jew—we reckon
to be all the truer, in that we received them as uttered by one who

was a converted enemy, and also had been privy to the secrets of our enemies.

BIBLIOGRAPHY

REFERENCES TO TEXTBOOKS

Elbogen, pp. 102ff.; Roth, pp. 183ff.

READINGS FOR ADVANCED STUDENTS

Graetz, III, pp. 378–381; Graetz-Rhine, III, pp. 226–229.

Grayzel, S., *The Church and the Jews in the XIIIth Century*, pp. 79–80.

Strack, H. L., *The Jew and Human Sacrifice*. The standard work on the relation of human blood to Jewish ritual.

JE, "Blois"; "Blood accusation."

ADDITIONAL SOURCE MATERIALS IN ENGLISH

Child, F. J., *The English and Scottish Popular Ballads*, III (1890), pp. 233–254; IV (1892), pp. 497–498; V (1898), p. 241. Here is a series of ballads dealing with Hugh of Lincoln who was reported to have been crucified by the Jews of England in 1255. The widespread influence of this ballad may be gauged from the fact that the compiler quotes twenty-one versions in his notes, some of which were collected as sung in the United States.

Grayzel, S., *The Church and the Jews in the XIIIth Century*, contains, pp. 263–271, 275, papal statements on the ritual murder accusation.

Halper, B., *Post-Biblical Hebrew Literature*, "A Jew Is Accused of Murdering a Christian, but His Innocence Is Proved," II, pp. 225–229. This account by the ibn Vergas, sixteenth century Jewish historians, is probably fiction, but is important for its typical Jewish reaction to the ritual murder accusation.

Jacobs, J., *The Jews of Angevin England*, pp. 19ff., contains two other brief accounts of the "martyrdom" of William of Norwich; one is a contemporary account; the other dates from the fifteenth century.

Jessop, A., and M. R. James, *The Life and Miracles of St. William of Norwich by Thomas of Monmouth*. This work contains the complete text and translation of the St. William legend.

Roth, C., *The Ritual Murder Libel and the Jew: The Report by Cardinal Lorenzo Ganganelli*. Dr. Roth has translated here the refutation of the ritual murder libel by Ganganelli, later Pope Clement XIV. The bull of Innocent IV against the ritual murder accusation is also included. There is also a good introduction.

Tager, A. B., *The Decay of Czarism: the Beiliss Trial*, describes a modern ritual murder trial and its background in modern Russia.

25.

The Ritual Murder Accusation at Blois
May, 1171

IN 1171 the Jews of Blois, France, were accused of having crucified a Christian child during the Passover holydays and of having thrown the corpse into the Loire. This is the first time that the accusation of ritual murder was made in continental Europe. It is difficult to account for its occurrence just at this time unless it is a reverberation of the William of Norwich tale of a generation before. The accusation that Jews require Christian blood for their Passover ritual has been made against the Jews from that time on down to the present day in practically all lands and has cost the lives of hundreds of innocent Jewish men, women, and children.

The following account of the burning of over thirty men and women at Blois is taken from *A Book of Historical Records,* a Hebrew historical work of Ephraim ben Jacob (1132—about 1200), a German Jewish Talmudist and poet of note.

❡What shall we say before God? What shall we speak? How can we justify ourselves? God must have found out our iniquity.

In the year 4931 [1171], evil appeared in France, too, and great destruction in the city of Blois, in which at that time there lived about forty Jews. It happened on that evil day, Thursday, toward evening, that the terror came upon us. A Jew [Isaac bar Eleazar] rode up to water his horse; a common soldier—may he be blotted out of the book of life—was also there watering the horse of his master. The Jew bore on his chest an untanned hide, but one of the corners had become loose and was sticking out of his coat. When, in the gloom, the soldier's horse saw the white side of the hide, it was frightened and sprang back, and it could not be brought to water.

The Christian servant hastened back to his master and said: "Hear, my lord, what a certain Jew did. As I rode behind him toward the river in order to give your horses a drink, I saw him throw a little Christian child, whom the Jews have killed, into the water. When I saw this, I was horrified and hastened back quickly for fear he might kill me too. Even the horse under me was so frightened by the splash of the water when he threw the child in that it would not drink." The soldier knew that his master would rejoice at the fall of the Jews, because he hated a certain Jewess, influential in the city. He as much as put the following words into his master's mouth: "Now I can wreak my vengeance on that person, on that woman Pulcelina."

The next morning the master rode to the ruler of the city, to the cruel Theobald, son of Theobald—may his unrighteousness and bitter, evil curses fall upon his head. He was a ruler that listened to falsehood, for his servants were wicked. [Theobald V was Count of Blois, 1152–1191. He was called "the Good."]

When he heard this he became enraged and had all the Jews of Blois seized and thrown into prison. But Dame Pulcelina encouraged them all, for she trusted in the affection of the ruler who up to now had been very attached to her. However, his cruel wife, a Jezebel, swayed him, for she also hated Dame Pulcelina. [Theobald's wife was Alix, the daughter of King Louis VII of France.] All the Jews had been put into iron chains except Pulcelina, but the servants of the ruler who watched her would not allow her to speak to him at all, for fear she might get him to change his mind.

The ruler was revolving in his mind all sorts of plans to condemn the Jews, but he did not know how. He had no evidence against them until a priest appeared—may he be destroyed and may his memory be uprooted from the land of the living—who said to the ruler: "Come, I'll advise you how you can condemn them. Command that the servant who saw the Jew throw the child into the river be brought here, and let him be tested by the ordeal in a tank of water to discover if he has told the truth."

The ruler commanded and they brought him, took off his clothes, and put him into a tank filled with holy water to see what would happen. If he floated, his words were true; if he sank, he had lied. Such are the laws of the Christians who judge by ordeals—bad laws and customs by which one cannot live! The Christians arranged it in accordance with their wish so that the servant floated, and they took him out and thus they declared the wicked innocent and the righteous guilty. [In this ordeal the normal procedure appears to have been reversed. Generally the innocent sank and the guilty floated.]

The ruler had started negotiations for a money settlement before the coming of the priest who incited the ruler not to accept any ransom for the dead child. [In the Middle Ages many crimes could be expiated legally through a money payment.] He had sent a Jew to the Jews [of the other communities] and had asked how much they would give him. The Jews consulted with their Christian friends and also with the Jews in the dungeon, and these latter advised offering only one hundred pounds and in addition their uncollected debts amounting to the sum of one hundred eighty pounds. [The Jews objected to paying high ransoms lest the Christians should find it profitable to imprison Jews.]

In the meantime the priest arrived on the scene, and from this time on the ruler paid no attention to the Jews and did not listen to them, but only to the instruction of the priest. In the day of wrath money could not help them. At the wicked ruler's command they were taken and put into a wooden house around which were placed thornbushes and faggots. As they were led forth they were told: "Save your lives. Leave your religion and turn to us." They mistreated them, beat them, and tortured them, hoping that they would exchange their glorious religion for something worthless, but they refused. Rather did they encourage each other and say to one another: "Persist in the religion of the Almighty!" [A Christian historian of that time says that some did convert.]

At the command of the oppressor they then took the two [Jewish] priests, the pious Rabbi Jehiel, the son of Rabbi David Ha-Kohen, and the just Rabbi Jekutiel Ha-Kohen, the son of Rabbi Judah, and tied them to a single stake in the house where they were to be burned. They were both men of valor, disciples of Rabbi Samuel and Rabbi Jacob [the grandsons of Rashi]. They also tied the hands of Rabbi Judah, the son of Aaron, and then set fire to the faggots. The fire spread to the cords on their hands so that they snapped, and all three came out and spoke to the servants of the oppressor: "The fire has no power over us. Why should we not go free?" [Since these three had withstood the ordeal by fire, they asked to be freed.] The enemy answered: "By our lives! You shall not get out." They kept on struggling to get out but they were pushed back into the house. They came out again and seized hold of a Christian to drag him along with them back onto the pyre. When they were right at the fire the Christians pulled themselves together, rescued the Christian from their hands, killed them with their swords, and then threw them into the fire. Nevertheless they were not burnt, neither they nor all those thirty-one persons. Only their souls were released by the fire; their bodies remained intact. When the Christians saw it they were amazed and said to one another: "Truly these are saints."

A certain Jew by the name of Rabbi Baruch, the son of David, a priest, was there and saw all this at that time with his own eyes. He lived in the territory of that ruler and had come there to arrange terms for the Jews of Blois, but, because of our sins, he had no success. However, a settlement was made by him for one thousand pounds to save the other Jews of that accursed ruler. He also saved the scrolls of the Torah and the rest of their books. This happened in the year 4931 on Wednesday, the 20th of the month of Siwan [May 26, 1171]. This day ought to be established as a fast day like the Fast of Gedaliah. [The assassination of Gedaliah, who was governor of Judah after the destruction of the Temple in 586 B.C.E., is still observed on the 3rd of Tishri.] All these facts were written down by the Jews of Orleans—a city close by that of the martyrs— and made known to the teacher, our master Rabbi Jacob [ben Rabbi Meir, Rashi's grandson, the greatest French rabbi of his day. He died in the third week after the Blois burning].

It was also reported in that letter that as the flames mounted high the martyrs began to sing in unison a melody that began softly but ended with a full voice. The Christian people came and asked us: "What kind of a song is this for we have never heard such a sweet melody?" We knew it well for it was the song: "It is incumbent upon us to praise the Lord of all." [This prayer, the *Alenu*, or Adoration, now recited daily, was then a New Year's prayer with a special melody.]

O daughters of Israel, weep for the thirty-one souls that were burnt for the sanctification of the Name, and let your brothers, the entire house of Israel, bewail the burning.

Because of our sins these men were not even given a Jewish burial but were left at the bottom of the hill on the very spot where they had been burnt. It was only later the Jews came and buried their bones. There were about thirty-two holy souls who offered themselves as a sacrifice to their Creator; and God smelled the sweet savor, for him whom He has chosen does He cause to come nigh unto Him. [The number of those burnt varies in different sources. One source lists a new-born babe.]

Of their own free will all the communities of France, England, and the Rhineland observed Wednesday, the 20th of Siwan, 4931, as a day of mourning and fasting. This was also the command of our great teacher Jacob, the son of Rabbi Meir, who wrote letters to them informing them that it was proper to fix this day as a fast for all our people, and that it must be greater even than the Fast of Gedaliah ben Ahikam; it was to be like the Day of Atonement [a twenty-four hour fast].

26.

The York Riots
England, March 16–17, 1190

THE religious zeal of the English people was fired by the Third Crusade (1189–1192) in which their king, Richard the Lion-Hearted (1189–1199), played a leading part. The coronation of Richard in September, 1189 was the occasion for a mob attack on London Jewry, and from the capital city the mob spirit spread slowly north in February-March, 1190 till it reached the ancient city of York. Here the gullible and bigoted lower estates were utilized by a band of unscrupulous nobles to wipe out the Jewish community to whom the nobles were heavily indebted. The plot succeeded, the community was destroyed, and, for the time being at least, the nobles were free of their creditors.

The following account, because of its richness of detail and because it is typical, is particularly valuable for a study of the medieval technique of wiping out a Jewish community. It is part of the *History of English Affairs* written in Latin by the monk William of Newburgh (1136–about 1201). William, who was canon of the Augustine priory at Newburgh in Yorkshire, describes conditions which he must have known at first hand, and he wrote this work, at the latest, within ten years after the events had transpired. It was the decided opinion of this monk, who is a faithful historian and viewed events from a lofty moral height, that greed for booty was the real motive of the riots in York.

⟪The zeal of the Christians against the Jews in England . . . . broke out fiercely. [Fanaticism was aroused by the Third Crusade, now beginning.] It was not indeed sincere, that is, solely for the sake of the faith, but in rivalry for the luck of others or from envy of their good fortune. Bold and greedy men thought that they were doing an act pleasing to God, while they robbed or destroyed rebels against Christ and carried out the work of their own cupidity with savage joy and without any, or only the slightest, scruple of conscience—God's justice, indeed, by no means approving such deeds but cunningly ordaining that in this way the insolence of that perfidious people might be checked and their blaspheming tongues curbed. . . . [The perfidy of the Jews lay in rejecting Jesus.]

131

The men of York were restrained neither by fear of the hot-tempered King [Richard I] nor the vigor of the laws, nor by feelings of humanity, from satiating their fury with the total ruin of their perfidious fellow-citizens and from rooting out the whole race in their city. And as this was a very remarkable occurrence, it ought to be transmitted to posterity at greater length. . . .

When the King had established himself across the sea [Richard the Lion-Hearted was back in France, December, 1189, preparing his crusade], many of the province of York plotted against the Jews, not being able to suffer their opulence, when they themselves were in need, and, without any scruple of Christian conscience, thirsting for the blood of infidels from greed for booty. The leaders of this daring plan were some of the nobles [such as the Percy family] indebted to the impious usurers in large sums. Some of these, having given up their estates to them [the Jews] for the money they had received, were now oppressed by great want; some, bound by their own sureties, were pressed by the exactions of the Treasury to satisfy the royal usurers. [The state helped the Jews collect their debts and took a large part for itself.]

Some, too, of those who had taken the cross and were on the point of starting for Jerusalem, were more easily induced to defray the expenses of the journey undertaken for the Lord's sake out of the booty taken from the Lord's enemies, especially as they had little fear of being questioned for the deed when they had started on their journey.

One stormy night no small part of the city became on fire either by chance or, as is believed, by arson perpetrated by the conspirators, so that the citizens were occupied with their own houses in fear of the fire spreading. There was nothing, therefore, in the way of the robbers, and an armed band of the conspirators, with great violence and tools prepared for the purpose, burst into the house of the before-mentioned Benedict, who had miserably died at London as was mentioned above. [This wealthy Jew of York was beaten and forced by a mob in London to become a Christian, 1189. He died on his way back home.] There his widow and children with many others dwelt; all of those who were in it were slain and the roof put on fire. [Some of Benedict's sons, however, were living in 1191–1192.]

And while the fire gloomily increased in strength, the robbers seized their booty and left the burning house, and by help of the darkness retired unobserved and heavy laden. The Jews, and especially their leader Joce, in consternation at this misdeed, having begged the assistance of the Warden of the royal castle, carried into it huge weights of their monies equal to royal treasures, and took more vigilant guard of the rest at their houses.

But after a few days these nocturnal thieves returned with greater confidence and boldness and many joined them; they boldly besieged Joce's house which rivalled a noble citadel in the scale and stoutness of its construction. [Jews were among the first in England to build private houses of stone.] At length they captured and pillaged it, and then set it on fire after having removed by sword or fire all those whom an unlucky chance had kept in it. For Joce a little before had wisely anticipated this mischance and had removed with his wife and children into the castle, and the rest of the Jews did the same, only a few remaining outside as victims.

When the robbers had departed with so great a reward of their daring, a promiscuous mob rushed up at break of day and tore to pieces the furniture which remained from the spoilers and the fire. Then at length those who had personally held the Jews in hatred, no longer having any fear of public rigor, began to rage against them openly and with abundant license. No longer content with their substance, they gave to all found outside the castle the option of sacred baptism or the extreme penalty. Thereupon some were baptized and feignedly joined Christianity to escape death. But those who refused to accept the sacrament of life, even as a matter of pretense, were butchered without mercy.

While all this was happening the multitude who had escaped into the castle seemed to be in safety. But the Warden of the castle, having gone out on some business, when he wished to return was not readmitted by the trembling multitude, uncertain in whom to trust and fearing that perchance his fidelity to them was tottering, and that being bribed he was about to give up to their enemies those whom he should protect. But he immediately went to the sheriff of the county [John Marshal] who happened to be at York with a large body of the county soldiers, and complained to him that the Jews had cheated him out of the castle entrusted to him. The sheriff became indignant and raged against the Jews. The leaders of the conspiracy fanned his fury, alleging that the timid precaution of those poor wretches was an insolent seizure of the royal castle and would cause injury to our lord, the King. And when many declared that such traitors were to be got at by some means or another, and the royal castle taken out of their hands, the sheriff ordered the people to be summoned and the castle to be besieged.

The irrevocable word went forth, the zeal of the Christian folk was inflamed, immense masses of armed men both from the town and the country were clustered round the citadel. Then the sheriff, struck with regret at his order, tried in vain to recall it and wished to prohibit the siege of the castle. But he could by no influence of reason or authority keep back their inflamed minds from carrying out what they had begun. It is true the nobles of the city and the more weighty citizens, fearing the danger of a royal movement, cautiously declined such a great transgression. But the whole of the work-people and all the youth of the town and a large number of the country folk, together with soldiers not a few, came with such alacrity and joined in the cruel business as if each man was seeking his own gain. And there were not lacking many clergymen, among whom a certain hermit seemed more vehement than the rest. . . .

Accordingly the Jews were besieged in the royal tower [probably Clifford's Tower, the ruins of which may still be seen], and the besieged lacked a sufficient supply of provisions, and would have been quickly starved out by hunger even if no one attacked them from without. But they did not have either a sufficient stock of arms for their own safety or for repelling the enemy. Naturally they held back the threatening enemy with stones taken from the inner wall. The tower was stoutly besieged for several days, and at length the machines which had been prepared for the purpose were brought into position. . . .

When the machines were thus moved into position, the taking of the tower became certain, and it was no longer doubtful that the fatal hour was nearing for the besieged. On the following night the besiegers were quiet, rejoicing in the certainty of their approaching victory. But the Jews were brave, and braced up by their very despair, had little rest, discussing what they should do in such an extremity. . . .

[At the advice of their rabbi, the noted Yomtob of Joigny, many killed themselves, after first setting fire to the tower. Those who were left offered to convert, but were mercilessly slaughtered by the aroused mob.]

The look of things in the city was at that time horrid and nauseous, and round the citadel were lying scattered the corpses of so many unfortunates still unburied. But when the slaughter was over, the conspirators immediately went to the Cathedral and caused the terrified guardians, with violent threats, to hand over the records of the debts placed there by which the Christians were oppressed by the royal Jewish usurers. Thereupon they destroyed these records of profane avarice in the middle of the church with the sacred fires to release both themselves and many others. Which being done, those of the conspirators who had taken the cross went on their proposed journey before any inquest; but the rest remained in the country in fear of an inquiry. Such were the things that happened at York at the time of the Lord's Passion, that is, the day before Palm Sunday. . . . [The massacre occurred Friday night and Saturday morning, March 16–17, 1190.]

The deeds done at York were soon carried across the sea to the prince who had guaranteed peace and security to the Jews in his kingdom after the rising at London. [After a mob had killed many Jews in London in September, 1189, Richard issued writs guaranteeing security to the Jews.] He is indignant and in a rage both for the insult to his royal majesty and for the great loss to the treasury, for to the treasury belonged whatever the Jews, who are known to be the royal usurers, seem to possess in the way of goods. Soon giving a mandate to [William of Longchamp, d. 1197,] the Bishop of Ely, the Royal Chancellor and Regent of the Kingdom, that such a great deed of audacity should be punished with a suitable revenge, the said Bishop, a man of fierce mind and eager for glory, came to the city of York about Ascension day [May 3, 1190] with an army, and began an inquiry to the great fear of the burgesses. But the chief and best known actors of the deeds done, leaving everything they had in the country, fled before his face to Scotland. But as the citizens, persistently declared that the deeds for which they were incurring his displeasure had not been done with their wish or counsel or aid, and that with slender resources they could not prevent the unbridled attack of an undisciplined mob, at length the Chancellor, having imposed a pecuniary mulct on each according to the income of his fortune, received satisfaction for not punishing them more severely. [The citizens of York are fined for not keeping the peace.]

But the promiscuous and numberless mob, whose untrained zeal had been the principal cause of the deed, could not be summoned or brought to justice. And so the Chancellor, removing him [the sheriff] who had had the administration of the county, went off without shedding blood since he could not carry out the King's command more efficaciously. Nor has anyone been brought to punishment for that slaughter of the Jews up to this day.

BIBLIOGRAPHY

READINGS FOR ADVANCED STUDENTS

Graetz, III, pp. 409–416; Graetz-Rhine, III, pp. 245–249; Margolis and Marx, pp. 384–391.

Hyamson, A. M., *A History of the Jews in England*, 1928, Chap. v, "The Massacre at York."

Milman, H. H., *The History of the Jews*, II, Book xxv.

JE, "York."

ADDITIONAL SOURCE MATERIALS IN ENGLISH

Jacobs, J., *The Jews of Angevin England*, p. 112. The author translates some of the materials of contemporary historians who report on the massacres in England at this time. See also p. 77, which records a debt of Richard de Malbys, one of the ringleaders of the York riot. See also pp. 392-396 for Isaac of York.

27.

Innocent and the Jews

1215

UNDER Innocent III (1198–1216) the Papacy reached the height of its ecclesiastical and political power. This great churchman sought to determine the destinies of all Christendom and, of course, of the comparatively small number of Jews who lived in its midst. Like his papal predecessors he had no intention of destroying Jewry, but he did insist that they, as a merely tolerated "subject" group, were to be granted no special privileges beyond those conceded to them by the earlier Church authorities. The anti-Jewish laws enacted by the Christianized Roman Empire and the Church were to be observed scrupulously so that the repression of the Jew might serve as a horrible example to those vacillating Christians who might be tempted to succumb to the religious influence of this or any other infidel group. He initiated no really new legislation: he merely expanded or sought to enforce older decrees. The general tendency of his legislation, especially in the matter of dress, was to segregate the Jew socially even more than he had been in the past. The expulsions of the Jews from Western Europe in the course of the next three centuries were the direct result of this social isolation which Innocent put into effect. His pontificate thus marks the beginning of a period of social and political decline for the Jew, particularly throughout Western and Central Europe.

The following selections, originally in Latin, are decrees of the Fourth Lateran Council, an international conference of Catholics that met at the call of the Pope in November, 1215 in the Lateran church in Rome.

I. CONCERNING THE INTEREST TAKEN BY JEWS

❲The more the Christian religion is restrained in the exaction of interest so much more does the knavery of the Jews in this matter increase, so that in a short time they exhaust the wealth of Christians. Wishing therefore to provide for Christians in this matter lest they be burdened excessively by the Jews, we ordain through synodal decree that if they hereafter extort heavy and unrestrained interest, no matter what the pretext be, Christians shall be withdrawn from association with them until the Jews give adequate satisfaction for their unmitigated oppression. Also the Christians shall be compelled, if necessary, through Church punishment from which an appeal will be disregarded, to abstain from business relations with the Jews.

[Innocent, in the preceding paragraph, threatens the Jews with a social and economic boycott if the interest they exact is excessive, and if they refuse to pay back some of the money they have thus received. Those Christians who persist in associating with Jews who exact a high rate of interest will be excommunicated.]

Moreover, we command the princes that they should not be hostile to the Christians because of this, but should rather seek to restrain the Jews from so great an oppression.

[The Christian princes, to whom the Jews were a lucrative source of revenue, encouraged the Jews in their money-lending and supported them with the authority of the state. The princes would resent the interference of the Church.]

And under threat of the same penalty we decree that Jews should be compelled to make good the tithes and dues owed to the churches which the churches have been accustomed to receive from the houses and other possessions of the Christians before they came into the possession of the Jews, regardless of the circumstances, so that the Church be preserved against loss.

[As early as 1068 the Church, at Gerona, Spain, sought to compel the Jews to pay to it a tithe on the produce of Jewish lands which had once been in Christian possession.]

II. THAT JEWS SHOULD BE DISTINGUISHED FROM CHRISTIANS IN DRESS

⟨In some provinces a difference in dress distinguishes the Jews or Saracens from the Christians, but in certain others such a confusion has grown up that they cannot be distinguished by any difference. Thus it happens at times that through error Christians have relations with the women of Jews or Saracens, and Jews or Saracens with Christian women. Therefore, that they may not, under pretext of error of this sort, excuse themselves in the future for the excesses of such prohibited intercourse, we decree that such Jews and Saracens of both sexes in every Christian province and at all times shall be marked off in the eyes of the public from other peoples through the character of their dress. Particularly, since it may be read in the writings of Moses [Numbers 15:37-41] that this very law has been enjoined upon them.

[In Aragon and parts of France, some Jews, even before this time, wore a distinctive dress, and in the Moslem lands they had been compelled to wear a garb of their own for centuries. Innocent's demand that Jews be easily distinguished shows that Jews in his day were different from Gentiles neither in speech nor in dress. Innocent's reason for insistence on separating Jews from Gentiles was that separation prevented intermarriage and the consequent losses to the Christian religion. The result of this law was that a number of states legislated that the Jews wear the "badge of shame."]

Moreover, during the last three days before Easter and especially on Good Friday, they shall not go forth in public at all, for the reason that some of them on these very days, as we hear, do not blush to go forth better dressed and are not afraid to mock the Christians who maintain the memory of the most holy Passion by wearing signs of mourning.

This, however, we forbid most severely, that any one should presume at all to break forth in insult to the Redeemer. And since we ought not to ignore any insult to Him who blotted out our disgraceful deeds, we command that such impudent fellows be checked by the secular princes by imposing on them proper punishment so that they shall not at all presume to blaspheme Him who was crucified for us.

[As early as 538 the Church, at the Third Council of Orléans, ordered that the Jews stay indoors on the Easter holidays. Innocent demands that Jews who go about well dressed during the days before Easter be punished, for to dress well on the anniversary of the suffering and the crucifixion of Jesus is an insult to Christians.]

III. THAT JEWS NOT BE APPOINTED TO PUBLIC OFFICES

⟨Since it would be altogether too absurd that a blasphemer of Christ should exercise authority over Christians, we, in this chapter, renew, because of the boldness of transgressors, what the Toledo Council has prudently decreed in this matter. We forbid that Jews be preferred for public offices since by pretext of some sort they manifest as much hostility to Christians as possible. If, moreover, any one should thus turn over an office to them, after due warning he shall be checked by a severe punishment, as is fit, by the provincial council which we command to meet every year. Indeed, the association of Christians with such a Jewish official in commercial and other matters shall not be allowed until whatever he has gotten from Christians through the office is transferred to the use of poor Christians, as the diocesan bishop shall carefully direct. And he shall be dismissed in disgrace from the office which he has impiously assumed. We extend the application of this law also to pagans.

[Ever since Theodosius II in 439, the Council of Clermont in 535, and the Third Council of Toledo in 589, Jews were not allowed to hold offices which permitted them to impose penalties on Christians. Innocent decrees that Christians who give offices to Jews are to be punished by church councils, and that the Jewish official is to be boycotted till he surrenders all he has made in his office. Then he is to be dismissed. This law, originally in the Theodosian code, remained on the statute books of Poland till March, 1931.]

IV. CONVERTS TO THE FAITH FROM AMONG THE JEWS MUST NOT OBSERVE THE OLD CUSTOMS OF THE JEWS

℄Some converted Jews, as we understand, who came voluntarily to the waters of Holy Baptism, have not altogether sloughed off the old man in order to put on the new man more perfectly. Since they retain remnants of their earlier rites they confound the majesty of the Christian religion through such a mixture. Since, moreover, it is written [Ecclesiasticus 2:12]: "Woe unto the man that goeth on the earth two ways," and since one ought not to put on a garment woven of both linen and wool [Leviticus 19:19], we therefore ordain that such persons must be restrained in every way by the prelates of the churches from the observance of their old religious rites. For in the observance of Christianity it is necessary that a healthy compulsion should preserve these Jews whom free will has carried to the Christian religion. It is a lesser evil not to know the way of the Lord than to go back, after it has been acknowledged.

[As early as 633 the Fourth Council of Toledo objected to the backsliding of Jewish converts to Christianity. Innocent warns converts against retaining their Jewish customs. Even as they are not allowed to mix their yarns, even so they are not allowed to mix their religions. He ends by saying that, inasmuch as they have come to Christianity voluntarily, they have no excuse for retaining their old habits, and they are to be forced to drop them.]

V. THE EXPEDITION TO RECOVER THE HOLY LAND. . . .

℄If any of those setting out thither [for the Holy Land] are bound by oath to pay interest, we command that their creditors shall be compelled by the same means [ecclesiastical censure] to release them from their oaths and to desist from the exaction of interest. But if any creditor shall compel them to pay interest, we order that he shall be forced, by a similar chastisement, to pay it back.

We command that the Jews, however, shall be compelled by the secular power to remit interest; and until they remit it all faithful

Christians shall, under penalty of excommunication, refrain from every species of intercourse with them. For those, moreover, who are unable at present to pay their debts to the Jews, the secular princes shall provide by a useful delay, so that after they [the crusaders] begin their journey they shall suffer no inconvenience from interest, until their death or return is known with certainty. The Jews shall be compelled, after deducting the necessary expenses, to count the income which they receive in the meantime from the mortgaged property toward the payment of the principal; since a favor of this kind, which defers the payment and does not cancel the debt, does not seem to cause much loss. Moreover let the prelates of the Church who are proven to be negligent in doing justice to the crusaders and their families, understand that they shall be severely punished.

[Innocent, who was anxious to recover the Holy Land, thought it wrong that crusaders should pay interest on debts to Jew or Gentile and therefore ordered that the interest already taken from crusaders be returned. He decreed further that crusaders without means need not pay the principal on their debts to their Jewish creditors until they returned from their crusade. This was a moratorium. And finally the net income of the mortgaged property held by Jews must be applied to the reduction of the principal of the debt.]

BIBLIOGRAPHY

REFERENCES TO TEXTBOOKS

Roth, pp. 197ff.; Sachar, pp. 192ff.

READINGS FOR ADVANCED STUDENTS

Graetz, III, pp. 494–513; Graetz-Rhine, III, pp. 293ff.; Margolis and Marx, pp. 374–375.

Abrahams, I., *Jewish Life in the Middle Ages*, 1932, Chap. xvi, "The Jewish Badge."

Philipson, D., *Old European Jewries*, Chap. iii, "The Ghetto in Church Legislation."

JE, "Badge"; "Church Councils"; "Innocent III"; "Popes."

ADDITIONAL SOURCE MATERIALS IN ENGLISH

Grayzel, S., *The Church and the Jews in the XIIIth Century*, pp. 85–143. Translation of the most important bulls of Innocent III on the Jews.

Laffan, R. G. D., *Select Documents of European History*, I, pp. 100–101, "A Constitution of Innocent III on the Jews, 1199."

28.

The Jewess Who Became a Catholic
about 1220

ONE of the most popular collections of religious tales of the Middle Ages is *The Dialogue on Miracles*. In the thirteenth century it was probably the most widely read book of its type in Central Europe. The stories are in the form of a dialogue between a monk and a novice whom he is instructing. These "miracles" are valuable because they give us insight into the mind of the average medieval man and thus reflect his attitude to the Jew.

The selection below deals with the conversion of a Jewess and the subsequent attempts made by her father to secure her return. The author was Caesarius [d. about 1240], Prior at Heisterbach Abbey, near Bonn. He wrote his book in Latin about 1222.

ALSO OF A BAPTIZED JEWISH MAIDEN AT LOUVAIN

⟪MONK: A little while ago, the daughter of a Jew at Louvain was converted to the faith in the following manner. A cleric named Rener, chaplain to the Duke of Louvain, was in the habit of going to the house of this Jew to argue with him about the Christian faith. His daughter [Rachel], then a little girl, would often listen very eagerly to the discussion, and would weigh, as well as her intelligence allowed, both the arguments of the Jew, her father, and those of his clerical opponent; and so, little by little, she became, by the providence of God, imbued with the Christian faith. Being taught secretly also by the cleric, she became so far contrite as to say that she wished to be baptized. A woman was brought to her, who withdrew her secretly from her father's house; the cleric baptized and placed her in a convent of the Cistercian Order, called Park [near Louvain].

When her conversion became known, the infidel father was much grieved, and offered the Duke a great sum of money to restore to him his daughter, who, he complained, had been taken by stealth from his house. Now the Duke was quite willing to restore the girl, though a Christian, to her father, though a Jew; but the cleric Rener resisted him saying: "Sir, if you commit this crime against God and His church, never can your soul be saved." Dom Walter, the Abbot of Villers [south of Louvain], also opposed him.

The Jew, seeing that he was disappointed of the hope he had cherished from the Duke, is said to have bribed Hugo [de Pierrepont, d. 1229], the Bishop of Liège, who took the part of the Jew to such an extent, that he sent letters to the convent of nuns at Park, ordering them to restore his daughter to him. But when the Jew, accompanied by his friends and relations reached the convent, the maiden, who was established there, though she knew nothing of his coming, began to perceive a very evil odor, so that she said openly: "I do not know whence it comes, but an odor as of Jews is troubling me." [This is the *Foetor Judaicus*, the "Jewish stench," which Jews were said to possess.] Meanwhile the Jews were knocking at the window; and the abbess, as I believe, said to the girl: "Daughter Catherine," for so she had been named at her baptism, "your parents wish to see you." She replied, "That explains the odor I perceived; I will not see them"; and she refused to leave the house.

At the end of the year the Bishop of Liège was accused of this action of his before Dom Engilbert, Archbishop of Cologne [d. 1225], in the synod held by him, and he was ordered never again to trouble the aforesaid convent with regard to this girl who had been baptized. [A special council was held in Cologne about 1220 to try Hugo.] He was silenced for a time, but not really obedient; for not long afterwards he sent a letter summoning the young woman, under pain of excommunication, to come to Liège to answer the objections raised by her father. She came but under good protection. It was alleged, on the part of the Jew, that she was carried away and baptized by force when under age; and it was said to the girl: "Catherine, we have been told that you would gladly go back to your father, if you were allowed." She replied: "Who told you this?" and they answered: "Your father himself." Then in a clear voice she uttered these words: "My father truly has lied in his beard."

Now when the Jew's advocate [a Christian lawyer] continued to urge her, Dom Walter, the Abbot of Villers was much moved and said to him: "Sir, you are speaking against God and against your own honor. Be sure of this, that if you say one single word more against the girl, I will do all I can with the lord Pope, that you may never be allowed to speak in any cause again." [The lawyer is threatened with disbarment if he tries to win the father's case.] Then being frightened by this he said privately to the Abbot: "My lord Abbot, what harm does it do to you if I can manage to get money out of this Jew? I will say nothing that can possibly hurt the girl." But presently when he received his fees from the Jew, he said to him: "I do not dare to say another word in this case."

At the end of the year, when Dom Wido, Abbot of Clairvaux, was making his visitation in the diocese of Liège, he met the Bishop, warned him, and begged him to have respect for God and his own honor, and to cease from harassing a maiden already dedicated to Christ. To whom the Bishop replied: "My good lord Abbot, what has this case to do with you?" The Abbot answered: "It has a great deal to do with me, and for two reasons; first because I am a Christian, and next, because that convent in which she is living is of the lineage of Clairvaux." [This convent was a daughter institution of the Abbey of Clairvaux.] And he added, "I shall place this girl and her case under the protection of the lord Pope, and shall ground my appeal upon the letters written by you against her." At the time of the General Chapter [meeting], he sent to the Prior of Park, through our [Heisterbach] abbot, letters which he had obtained from the lord Pope against the Bishop [of Liège], so that, if by any chance the Bishop should attempt to harass the convent further on this girl's account, he might defend himself by these letters.

NOVICE: Just as, a little while ago, I was edified by the pity of the English bishop, so am I now scandalized by the avarice of him of Liège.

MONK: His defenders say that his persistence in this affair was due, not to love of money, but to zeal for justice. But it is difficult to believe this, because if he had been actuated by the motive of justice, he would certainly not have tried to force a baptized girl, a virgin consecrated to Christ and a nun in a Christian convent, to return to Jewish infidelity.

NOVICE: Yes, I fully agree with that.

BIBLIOGRAPHY

READINGS FOR ADVANCED STUDENTS

Parkes, J., *The Conflict of the Church and the Synagogue*. See Index under "Conversion to Christianity"; "Converts to Christianity."

JE, "Apostasy and Apostates from Judaism"; "Pierleoni."

ADDITIONAL SOURCE MATERIALS IN ENGLISH

Grayzel, S., *The Church and the Jews in the XIIIth Century*, pp. 287–291, documents dealing with the support of Jewish converts to Christianity.

Bland, C. C. S., *Miracles of the Virgin: Johannes Herolt Called Discipulus (1435–1440)*. Miracles XVIII–XIX and LXVI describe the conversion of Jews through the miraculous intervention of the Glorious Virgin Mary.

29.

The Burning of the Talmud
Paris, 1239–1248

A JEWISH convert to Christianity, Nicholas Donin, had denounced the "blasphemies" of the Talmud to Pope Gregory IX (1227–1241) who had thereupon (1239) ordered the prelates and rulers of France, England, and the Spanish and Portuguese lands to seize all Jewish books and to examine them. Louis IX, the pious young king of France (1226–1270) was the only one to pay heed to the papal mandate: the books in his land were seized on March 3, 1240.

In June of the same year four prominent French rabbis, led by Jehiel of Paris, were compelled to meet with Donin in a public disputation. The arguments of the Jews, however, were of no avail; the Talmud was condemned and was eventually burnt, probably both in 1242 and 1244.

The case was later reopened as is evidenced in the first selection quoted below: a Latin letter from the French papal legate, Odo of Chateauroux (d. 1273), to Pope Innocent IV (1243–1254). Odo had been asked by the Pope (1247) to investigate again the alleged anti-Christian character of the Talmudic writings. In his answer to Pope Innocent, Odo reluctantly agrees to do so and at the same time reviews the whole case since its beginnings in 1239. He also incorporates in this review a series of letters, one from Pope Gregory IX, dated June 9, 1239, ordering the archbishops of France to seize all Jewish works and another from Gregory to the Churchmen of Paris, dated June 20, 1239, ordering them to burn the confiscated works if they are found to contain any objectionable statements.

The second selection, from the year 1248, is a translation of Odo's final condemnation of the Talmud.

The third selection, unlike the formal Latin letters of Odo is a tale by the priestly chronicler, Thomas of Cantimpré. In his Latin treatise on virtues and vices, *Bonum universale de apibus* (about 1263), this zealous Dominican tells us in truly naive medieval fashion what befell the Archbishop Gautier who in 1240 tried to help the Jews save their books.

The ultimate result of the prohibition from studying the Talmud

145

was the cessation of rabbinic studies in northern France which had been famous for its Talmudic academies since the days of Rashi of Troyes.

1. *Odo to Innocent IV, 1247*

❡To the most holy father and lord, Innocent, high priest by the grace of God, from Odo, by divine goodness Bishop of Tusculum, legate of the apostolic throne. . . . :

Recently [1247] it pleased your Holiness to order me to have the Talmud and other books of the Jews displayed before me, to inspect them, and, after having inspected them, to show tolerance to the Jews with regard to those books which may seem worthy of tolerance because they are not injurious to the Christian faith, and to return these to the Jewish teachers.

In order that the proceedings which at one time took place about the said books may not be hidden from your Holiness, and lest it happen that anyone be fooled in this affair by the shrewdness and falsehoods of the Jews, let your Holiness know that at the time of the holy Pope Gregory [IX] of happy memory, a certain convert, by the name of Nicholas [Donin, about 1239], related to the said Pope that the Jews, not satisfied with the ancient Law which God had transmitted in writing through Moses, and even completely ignoring it, assert that a different Law, which is called "Talmud," that is "Teaching," had been given by God; and, they say, that it was handed down to Moses verbally and was implanted in their minds. [Donin, apparently, had Karaitic leanings.]

It was thus preserved unwritten until certain men came whom they call "sages" and "scribes," who, lest this [Talmudic] law disappear from the minds of men through forgetfulness, reduced it to writing the size of which by far exceeds the text of the Bible. In this are contained so many unspeakable insults that it arouses shame in those who read it, and horror in those who hear it. This too is the chief factor that holds the Jews obstinate in their perfidy. [The Talmud prevents Jews from becoming Christians.]

When he heard of these things, the Pope saw fit to write [June 9, 1239] to all archbishops of the kingdom of France, as follows: . . .

"Wherefore, since this [Talmud] is said to be the chief cause that holds the Jews obstinate in their perfidy, we thought that your Fraternity should be warned and urged, and we herewith order you by apostolic letters, that on the first Saturday of the Lent to come [March 3, 1240], in the morning, while the Jews are gathered in the synagogues, you shall, by our order, seize all the books of the Jews who live in your districts, and have these books carefully guarded in the possession of the Dominican and Franciscan friars. For this purpose you may invoke, if need be, the help of the secular arm; and you may also promulgate the sentence of excommunication against all those subject to your jurisdiction, whether clergy or laity, who refuse to give up Hebrew books which they have in their possession despite your warning given generally in the churches, or individually. . . ."

In the same manner he [Pope Gregory IX] wrote to all the archbishops of the kingdoms of England, Castile, and Leon. He also sent his letter to the King of Portugal. . . . Likewise [June 20, 1239] he sent orders to the Bishop and the Prior of the Dominicans and to the Minister of the Franciscan friars of Paris, as follows: . . .

"Wherefore, since this [Talmud] is said to be the most important reason why the Jews remain obstinate in their perfidy, we, through apostolic letters, order your Discretion to have the Jews who live in the kingdoms of France, England, Aragon, Navarre, Castile, Leon, and Portugal, forced by the secular arm to give up their books. Those books, in which you will find errors of this sort, you shall cause to be burned at the stake. By apostolic power, and through use of ecclesiastical censure, you will silence all opponents. You will also report to us faithfully what you have done in the matter. But, should all of you be unable to be present at the fulfillment of these instructions, someone of you, none the less, shall carry out its execution. . . ."

All books that had been intercepted were put under stamp and seal, and much more was found in the said books in the presence of Gautier, Archbishop of Sens of happy memory [d. 1241] and of the venerable fathers of Paris, of the Bishop of Senlis [Adam of Chambly, d. 1258] and of the Friar Geoffroy of Blèves [d. 1250], your chaplain, then regent of Paris, and of other teachers of theology, and even of Jewish teachers who, in the presence of these men, confessed that the above-named things were contained in their books. [On the contrary, Jehiel of Paris in 1240 denied that the statements referred to Christians.]

A careful examination having afterwards been made, it was discovered that the said books were full of errors, and that the veil covers the heart of these people to such a degree, that these books turn the Jews away not only from an understanding of the spirit, but even of the letter, and incline them to fables and lies. From this it is clear that the Jewish teachers of the kingdom of France uttered a falsehood to your Holiness and to the sacred fathers, the lords cardinals, when they said that without these books, which in Hebrew are called "Talmud," they cannot understand the Bible and the other precepts of their laws, in accordance with their faith. After the said examination had been made, and the advice of all the teachers of theology and canon law, and of many others, had been taken, all the said books which could then be gotten hold of, were consigned to the flames [probably in 1242] in accordance with the apostolic degree [of 1239].

It would therefore be most disgraceful, and a cause of shame for the apostolic throne, if books that had been so solemnly and so justly burned in the presence of all the scholars, and of the clergy, and of the populace of Paris, were to be given back to the masters of the Jews at the order of the pope—for such tolerance would seem to mean approval. . . .

All this have I recounted to your Holiness in these presents in order that the whole truth about the said books may be revealed to your Holiness. I have moreover asked the Jewish masters to show me the Talmud and all their other books; and they have exhibited to me five most vile volumes which I shall have carefully examined in accordance with your command.

11. *Condemnation of the Talmud by Odo, May 15, 1248*

℧Odo, by the Grace of God, Bishop of Tusculum, Legate of the Apostolic Throne, to All Whom these Presents May Reach, Greetings in the Lord:

Know ye all, that in Paris, on the Ides of May [the 15th], in the year of our Lord 1248, we inspected certain Jewish books called Talmud, and, in the presence of the Jewish masters and of those called for this purpose, we pronounced definite judgment as follows:

"In the name of Father, Son, and Holy Ghost, amen!

"Certain books by the name of Talmud having been presented by the Jewish masters to us armed with apostolic authority, we have examined these books and caused them to be carefully examined by men of discretion, expert in these matters, God-fearing, and zealous for the Christian faith.

"Whereas we found that these books were full of innumerable errors, abuses, blasphemies, and wickedness such as arouse shame in those who speak of them and horrify the hearer, to such an extent that these books cannot be tolerated in the name of God without injury to the Christian faith, therefore, with the advice of those pious men whom we caused to be gathered especially for that purpose,

"We pronounce that the said books are unworthy of tolerance, and that they are not to be restored to the Jewish masters, and we decisively condemn them.

"We are also possessed of full knowledge as to the place and time of other books not shown to us by the Jewish masters nor by us examined, although we have often made demands for them; and we shall do what there is to be done with regard to them. . . ."

III. *A Defender of the Talmud Dies, 1241*—CONCERNING THE SUDDEN DEATH OF AN ARCHBISHOP WHO HINDERED THE BURNING OF TALMUDIC BOOKS DECREED UNDER PENALTY OF DEATH BY SAINT LOUIS, THE KING OF FRANCE

❡I myself saw another archbishop in France [probably Gautier of Cornut, Archbishop of Sens], a man of letters and well-known, upon whom such a punishment fell by divine command:

The most pious of princes, King Louis of France, at the instigation of that very excellent preacher, Brother Henry of Cologne of the order of Friars Preachers, ordered about 1239, under penalty of death, that that most blasphemous book of the Jews, which is called the Talmud, be brought to Paris. In it, in many places, were written unheard of heresies and blasphemies against Christ and his mother. Accordingly, various copies of this book were brought to Paris to be burned [1240]. Thereupon the Jews went weeping to the archbishop, who was the supreme councillor of the king, and offered him money without limit for the preservation of the books. Corrupted by this, he went to the king, and soon turned the youthful mind to his own wish. Therefore, the books having been returned, the Jews set aside a solemn day to be observed every year, but in vain; for the spirit of God ordained otherwise, for a year later, on the same day and in the same place where the accursed books had been returned to the Jews—that is, in Vincennes near Paris—this archbishop, coming to the king's council, was seized with dreadful internal pain, and the same day with mighty groans passed away [1241]. Thereupon the king, with his whole train, fled from that spot, in terrible fear that he might be divinely smitten together with the archbishop. Not long afterwards, at the instigation of Brother Henry, whom we have mentioned, the books of the Jews were gathered, as before, under penalty of death, and burned in very great numbers. Note now, reader, that all the Eastern [Karaite] Jews consider as heretics and excommunicate those Jews who, against the law of Moses and the prophets, obtain and copy this book, which is called the Talmud. And nevertheless, a Christian archbishop defended such a book!

BIBLIOGRAPHY

REFERENCES TO TEXTBOOKS

Roth, pp. 197ff.; Sachar, pp. 195–197.

READINGS FOR ADVANCED STUDENTS

Graetz, III, pp. 563–580; Graetz-Rhine, III, pp. 341–347.
Popper, W., *The Censorship of Hebrew Books*, pp. 6–17.
JE, "Guillaume of Auvergne."

ADDITIONAL SOURCE MATERIALS IN ENGLISH

Grayzel, S., *The Church and the Jews in the XIIIth Century*, pp. 239–243, 251–253, 275–281, give the material dealing with the Church proscription of the Talmud.

30.

A Bull of Pope Gregory X
October 7, 1272

IN the last decade of the sixth century Pope Gregory I (590–604) laid down the principle that, though Christianity was to protect itself against the "evil" influence of the Jewish religion, it nevertheless had the obligation to preserve Jewry from the attacks and encroachments of Christians. This sentiment of the Church was prompted both by humaneness and by the desire to preserve Jewry as a proof of the truth of Christianity: the Hebrew Bible of the Jews "foretold" the coming of Jesus; the sufferings of the Jews were reputedly their punishment for the rejection of Jesus.

This principle of tolerance, which Gregory I had taken over from the later Roman Empire, became basic in the relations between Catholicism and Judaism. The Church, which had set itself up as the highest authority in the Christian world, frequently issued decrees in defense of Jewry. Beginning with Pope Calixtus II (1119–1124), if not before, and going down into the fifteenth century, a whole series of bulls appeared, threatening Christians with excommunication and other penalties if they converted Jews by force, exercised violence illegally against them, robbed them of their possessions, attacked them at their devotions, desecrated their cemeteries, or dug up and carried off their dead. The list of these offenses is important because it is typical of the annoyances to which the medieval Jew was exposed.

If the Jews were confronted by an unusual peril, the pope would repeat the usual stereotyped phrases of protest taken from the original bull of Calixtus II (about 1120) and would then insert a special paragraph to cover the specific problem of that day. Thus in 1247 and 1253 Innocent IV strongly discredited the ritual murder accusation: that Jews killed Christian children and partook of their blood on the Passover holiday. The need for papal bulls of defense was most urgent, for all through the thirteenth century there was virtually an epidemic of ritual murder accusations as a result of which dozens of Jewish men and women were put to death.

In 1272 Pope Gregory X (1271–1276) issued a typical, stereotyped bull into which he incorporated two significant statements: the first declared that the testimony of a Christian against a Jew had no validity unless it was confirmed by a Jew; the second was a most vigorous denunciation of the ritual murder charge. This refutation of the blood accusation, begun by Innocent IV in 1247, was repeated by various popes as late as Clement XIII in 1763. The different bulls in defense of Jewry were issued at the solicitation of the different Jewish communities in Europe and usually entailed a large expense. The continuous stream of papal decrees from about 1120 to 1763, however, would lead one to believe that they were of little lasting avail in coping with prejudice.

⟨Gregory, bishop, servant of the servants of God, extends greetings and the apostolic benediction to the beloved sons in Christ, the faithful Christians, to those here now and to those in the future. Even as it is not allowed to the Jews in their assemblies presumptuously to undertake for themselves more than that which is permitted them by law, even so they ought not to suffer any disadvantage in those [privileges] which have been granted them. [This sentence, first written by Gregory I in 598, embodies the attitude of the Church to the Jew.] Although they prefer to persist in their stubbornness rather than to recognize the words of their prophets and the mysteries of the Scriptures [which, according to the Church, foretold the coming of Jesus], and thus to arrive at a knowledge of Christian faith and salvation; nevertheless, inasmuch as they have made an appeal for our protection and help, we therefore admit their petition and offer them the shield of our protection through the clemency of Christian piety. In so doing we follow in the footsteps of our predecessors of blessed memory, the popes of Rome— Calixtus, Eugene, Alexander, Clement, Celestine, Innocent, and Honorius.

We decree moreover that no Christian shall compel them or any one of their group to come to baptism unwillingly. But if any one of them shall take refuge of his own accord with Christians, because of conviction, then, after his intention will have been manifest, he shall be made a Christian without any intrigue. For, indeed, that person who is known to have come to Christian baptism not freely, but unwillingly, is not believed to possess the Christian faith. [The Church, in principle, never approved of compulsory baptism of Jews.]

Moreover no Christian shall presume to seize, imprison, wound, torture, mutilate, kill, or inflict violence on them; furthermore no one shall presume, except by judicial action of the authorities of the country, to change the good customs in the land where they live for the purpose of taking their money or goods from them or from others.

In addition, no one shall disturb them in any way during the celebration of their festivals, whether by day or by night, with clubs or stones or anything else. Also no one shall exact any compulsory service of them unless it be that which they have been accustomed to render in previous times. [Up to this point Gregory X has merely repeated the bulls of his predecessors.]

Inasmuch as the Jews are not able to bear witness against the Christians, we decree furthermore that the testimony of Christians against Jews shall not be valid unless there is among these Christians some Jew who is there for the purpose of offering testimony.

[The church council at Carthage, as early as 419, had forbidden Jews to bear witness against Christians; Justinian's law of 531 repeats this prohibition. Gregory X here—in accordance with the medieval legal principle that every man has the right to be judged by his peers—insists that Jews can only be condemned if there are Jewish as well as Christian witnesses against them. A similar law to protect Jews was issued before 825 by Louis the Pious (814–840) of the Frankish Empire.]

Since it happens occasionally that some Christians lose their Christian children, the Jews are accused by their enemies of secretly carrying off and killing these same Christian children and of making sacrifices of the heart and blood of these very children. It happens, too, that the parents of these children or some other Christian enemies of these Jews, secretly hide these very children in order that they may be able to injure these Jews, and in order that they may be able to extort from them a certain amount of money by redeeming them from their straits. [Following the lead of Innocent IV, 1247, Gregory attacks the ritual murder charge at length.]

And most falsely do these Christians claim that the Jews have secretly and furtively carried away these children and killed them, and that the Jews offer sacrifice from the heart and the blood of these children, since their law in this matter precisely and expressly forbids Jews to sacrifice, eat, or drink the blood, or to eat the flesh of animals having claws. This has been demonstrated many times at our court by Jews converted to the Christian faith: nevertheless very many Jews are often seized and detained unjustly because of this.

We decree, therefore, that Christians need not be obeyed against Jews in a case or situation of this type, and we order that Jews seized under such a silly pretext be freed from imprisonment, and that they shall not be arrested henceforth on such a miserable pretext, unless—which we do not believe—they be caught in the commission of the crime. We decree that no Christian shall stir up anything new against them, but that they should be maintained in that status and position in which they were in the time of our predecessors, from antiquity till now.

We decree, in order to stop the wickedness and avarice of bad men, that no one shall dare to devastate or to destroy a cemetery of the Jews or to dig up human bodies for the sake of getting money. [The Jews had to pay a ransom before the bodies of their dead were restored to them.] Moreover, if any one, after having known the content of this decree, should—which we hope will not happen— attempt audaciously to act contrary to it, then let him suffer punishment in his rank and position, or let him be punished by the penalty of excommunication, unless he makes amends for his boldness by proper recompense. Moreover, we wish that only those Jews who have not attempted to contrive anything toward the destruction of the Christian faith be fortified by the support of such protection. . . .

Given at Orvieto by the hand of the Magister John Lectator, vice-chancellor of the Holy Roman Church, on the 7th of October, in the first indiction [cycle of fifteen years], in the year 1272 of the divine incarnation, in the first year of the pontificate of our master, the Pope Gregory X.

BIBLIOGRAPHY

REFERENCES TO TEXTBOOKS

Elbogen, pp. 102ff.; Roth, pp. 183ff.

31.

The Passau Host Desecration
1478

ONE of the basic rites of the Catholic Church is the Holy Communion. In this ceremony the Eucharist, consisting of the wine and the "Host" (a piece of consecrated bread), undergo a miraculous change. The Fourth Latern Council (1215) tells us that Jesus' "body and blood are verily contained in the sacrament of the altar under the species of bread and wine, the bread being transubstantiated into the body and the wine into the blood, by Divine Power."

Since according to Catholic doctrine the consecrated wafer becomes the "real" body of Jesus it was natural that these Hosts should become the subject of miracles.

In the thirteenth century when the doctrine of transubstantiation found general acceptance the belief began to grow that the Jews were desecrating the host: because of their hatred of Jesus, they desired to recrucify him; this they did, so it was said, by sticking needles and knives into the wafers which then began to bleed. The curious Jews, it would seem, wanted also to test the truth of Christianity, but the miracles that ensued from this act of defilement proclaimed to the astonished Jews the soundness of Catholic doctrine. Such was the general belief in the later Middle Ages.

One of the most notorious of such charges of host desecration occurred in Passau, Bavaria, in 1478. Christoff Eisengreisshamer, a Christian thief who specialized in robbing churches, confessed under torture that he had stolen some consecrated wafers on behalf of the Jews of Passau. Arrested, the Jews under torture confirmed the confession. They admitted, too, that they had sent some of the stolen sacramental wafers to Prague, Salzburg, and [Wiener-] Neustadt. They confessed that when they had stabbed the hosts, blood flowed from them; that the form of a child arose; and that when they tried to burn the wafers in an oven two angels and two doves appeared.

Ten of the arrested Jews were executed: four who converted to Christianity were treated mildly—merely beheaded. Four were burnt alive; two others, Pfeyl and Vettel, who were said to have stabbed and burnt the miraculous hosts, were first torn by glowing

155

pincers and then burnt. Christoff, the thief, after being plucked by
hot pincers, was also cremated alive. The majority of the Passau
Jews, about forty, then found it advisable to accept Christianity.

With the introduction of Protestantism and its rejection of transubstantiation, the accusation of host desecration disappeared from
Protestant lands; it still continued, however, in Catholic states.

No evidence that would stand in a court of law today has ever
been adduced to prove the truth of a charge of this nature.

The Passau synagogue was razed and in its place a church was
erected (1479–1484) to commemorate the miracle of the wafers and
to shelter the relics of the incident. One of the hosts that miraculously
escaped the stabbing and the fire was exhibited for years to crowds
of pilgrims who thronged to the new shrine. The knife that did the
stabbing was preserved and set in a beautiful monstrance and is still
being shown today. About 1480 an enterprising artist made some
rude woodcuts picturing this famous case, and, adding a German
text, he sold them to the crowds at the church in much the same
way that guidebooks and copies of the testimony of celebrated trials
are sold today to the curious and the morbid. The following account
is a translation of the early modern German text of this woodcut.

A HORRIBLE THING WHICH WAS DONE AT PASSAU BY THE JEWS, AS
    FOLLOWS:

ℂFourteen hundred and seventy-seven years after Christ's birth: at
that time the Right Reverend Prince and Lord, Lord Ulrich of
Passau, born von Nussdorf [d. 1480] was reigning.

It happened that a wanton and desperate fellow, usually known
as Christoff Eysengreisshamer, unmindful of his soul's salvation and
lusting for temporal goods, made an agreement, Judas-like, with
the Jews after inquiring whether if he brought them the Sacred
Host, the body of our Lord Jesus Christ, they would buy it.

The Jews—those enemies and blasphemers of the crucified true,
living God and of Mary his mother—lived at this time here in
Passau on the Ilz [River] behind St. Georgenberg. They had often
employed him and made use of him to go on errands and had dispatched him near and far. The Jews, these avaricious dogs, answered
[Christoff], out of the great hatred which they had to the Lord
Jesus our Savior, that he should go ahead and bring the Host and
they would pay him for it.

After the deal had been made, the seller and callous sinner, in
his wickedness, laid a snare for the Holy Sacrament. In the already
mentioned 'seventy-seventh year on the Friday before St. Michael's

day [September 26, 1477], he broke open the receptacle in which
the Host is reserved in St. Mary's church in Freyung-in-the-Abbey
[near Passau] and stole eight pieces of the Holy Sacrament, seized
hold of them with his sinful hands, and wrapped them in a kerchief.
He carried them on his person from that Friday till Sunday morning [September 28, 1477] and then in his faithlessness turned them
over to the Jews to whom he sold them for a *Rheinisch Gulden* [one
Gulden = 240 *Pfennige*], each Host thus amounting to thirty
Pfennig. This was an insult to the holy Christian Church [reminding
one that Judas sold Jesus for thirty pieces of silver].

The Jews—blasphemers of God—kept the Hosts and skeptically
brought them to their synagogue, seized hold of the body of Christ
with their sinful hands in order to crucify him with savage eagerness
and thus test the Christian faith. [If blood flowed from the wafer,
then it was the *real* body of Christ.] A Jew took a sharp knife, and
when he had stabbed the Host on the altar in the synagogue, blood
flowed out of it, and the face of a child appeared. The Jews, very
much frightened, took counsel and sent two sacraments to Prague,
two to [Wiener-] Neustadt, and two to Salzburg. And when they
threw [the remaining] two wafers into a glowing baker's oven they
saw two angels and two doves fly out of it.

Later the evil-doer [Christoff] was seized in the year 'seventy-
seven, before Lent [more correctly, 1478, before February 4], while
breaking into a church at Germannsberg. He was then led prisoner
to the episcopal palace at Passau, where he voluntarily confessed this
great crime, and told even more about the Jews. Thereupon the
above-mentioned devout Right Reverend Bishop of Passau, Ulrich,
who, as a Christian prince, was quite properly very much grieved by
this crime, decided to exact adequate punishment. He commanded
the noble and gracious knight, Lord Sebastian von der Alben—at
that time his Grace's marshal—to seize all the Jews of Passau and
to question them about the truth. [There were ten men seized.]
They all with one accord confessed, and showed the knife, the stone
[altar], the place, and the oven where they had committed and
perpetrated such a deed with the Holy Sacrament.

Four of them converted to the Christian faith and were brought
to justice on Tuesday after Judica in Lent of the 'seventy-seventh
year [more correctly, 1478, March 10]. The new Christians [the
four converts] were executed by the sword; the Jews, by fire; and
two of them were torn with pincers [and then burnt alive]. A few
weeks after the others, the seller [Christoff] was executed, as the
law demands, with glowing pincers—all of which he bore with

great patience, remorse, and devoutness, and also confessed publicly
all that he had done.

May God have pity on his soul and the souls of all the faithful.
Amen.

BIBLIOGRAPHY

REFERENCES TO TEXTBOOKS

Elbogen, pp. 106ff.

READINGS FOR ADVANCED STUDENTS

Lowenthal, M., *The Jews of Germany*, see Index, "Desecration of the Host,
Charges of."

JE, "Host, Desecration of."

ADDITIONAL SOURCE MATERIALS IN ENGLISH

Coulton, G. G., *A Medieval Garner*, pp. 716–719, "Shylock in Provence." A
sixteenth century account of a Jew who was flayed alive for having
"uttered several injurious words against the honor of the glorious Virgin
Mary."

Grayzel, S., *The Church and the Jews in the XIIIth Century*, pp. 137–139,
tells the story of Jews converted to Christianity through a miracle-work-
ing Host.

32.

Reuchlin's Appeal to Bonetto de Lattes
October–November, 1513

IN 1507 Johann Pfefferkorn, a fanatical and malignant converted Jew of dubious reputation, set out to destroy all Hebrew books except the Bible. He succeeded in 1509 in securing authority from the vacillating German emperor, Maximilian I (d. 1519), to confiscate them. However, in June, 1510, in order to help an influential courtier under financial obligation to the Jews, the German Emperor, himself, ordered the confiscated books to be returned.

In July, 1510, Johannes Reuchlin (1455–1522) of Pforzheim, a distinguished scholar and a student of Hebrew, was commissioned to make a study of the rabbinic writings in order to determine whether or not it was to the advantage of Christianity to destroy them. Reuchlin decided in favor of the Jewish works; in doing so he aroused the ire of the Dominican friars at Cologne, who had aligned themselves with Pfefferkorn. The Dominicans, who were preeminent in combatting heresy, looked askance at the study of Latin, Greek, and Hebrew by the humanists. They feared that the new learning would lead men away from the orthodoxy and from the authority of the Church.

In the first stage of the conflict (1510) the Jews of Germany were triumphant in that they saved their Talmudic writings. In fact, Pope Leo X (1513–1521) even permitted a Christian, Daniel Bomberg, to print the first edition of the Talmud at Venice (1520).

The second stage of the conflict affected the Jews only indirectly. The Dominicans, who may have treasured hopes of increasing their inquisitorial functions, attacked Reuchlin for his defense of Jewish writings; and in the ensuing conflict Germany was divided into two camps, Reuchlinists and anti-Reuchlinists. This struggle did a great deal to bring the Catholic Church into ill repute and thus helped to pave the way for the Protestant Reformation. The resultant breakdown of Church power ultimately brought toleration and emancipation to the Jew.

The following selection is a translation of a Hebrew letter which Reuchlin sent to Bonetto de Lattes (whose Hebrew name was Jacob ben Immanuel Provinciale), the Jewish physician-in-ordinary to Pope Leo X. Reuchlin had succeeded in October, 1513 in saving his book *Augenspiegel* from proscription by the Cologne Dominicans; but, fearing that these heresy hunters would summon him to trial again, he appealed for help in this letter written to de Lattes in late October or early November, 1513. He wanted the Jew to induce the Pope to keep the case out of the hands of the Cologne friars. However, he was willing, if necessary, to appear for trial in his own diocese or in a papal court of appeal. The appeal to de Lattes may have availed, for Reuchlin was tried in his own diocese and the arbiter, the Bishop of Speyer, acquitted him (1514).

Reuchlin was interested not in Jews but in Jewish literature. He did not like Jews.

❴To my master who sits in the seat of the wise; to the great luminary, the pillar of the Jewish exile; to him who shines in the skies, the skilled physician, my master and teacher *Mazzal Tob* (Bonetto in the Italian vernacular), of the province of Rome, the fit physician of the Pope. [*Mazzal Tob*, "Good luck," is a Hebrew pun on the Italian *Bonetto*.]

Among many who come to the gates of obeisance—entering in peace and going out in peace—I too am present; I, the insignificant one, who have signed at the bottom—than whom there is none lower, who prostrates himself to the ground.

Sir, after many greetings and by your leave, overcome by my inability to express myself properly and by my lack of understanding, I wish to inform your Excellency how during the past two years our lord, the Emperor—may his Majesty be exalted—visited the city of Cologne, a place where there is a great Christian university and some notable theologians. [The Emperor Maximilian was in Cologne for the Imperial Diet, July–November, 1512.]

These theologians all came together, frightened and excited, groaning and weeping, and cried aloud: "Help, O King and Emperor. There is in thine empire a certain people scattered abroad and dispersed and their laws are diverse from those of every people, and this is because of the Talmudic works they possess. [The Dominicans condemn the Jews in the words of Haman, Esther 3.] For in those books there are written a great many reproaches and blasphemies and curses and prayers against our faith and the leaders of our religion: the pope, the bishops, the theologians, the priests, and monks. And they pray and curse etc., after this fashion daily, as we have just said, not only against these, but also against the Emperor and King and princes and governors and against every one of our nations and our peoples. All this is due to the Talmudic writings.

"In addition there is another great evil that we must bear in mind: if these books did not exist, there would be but one religion, and everyone would believe in Jesus, our Messiah. It is those books alone that push them off the right road. Therefore 'it profiteth not the King to suffer them' [Esther 3:8]; and bearing in mind the interests of our religion and our churches, we advise and warn, if it seem good to the Emperor, that an order be issued to seize and turn over all the books of the Jews to the treasuries of the Emperor and King, through an officer appointed for this purpose. All of them should then be burnt, except the Biblical books, because they are the basic works of our religion.

"All Talmudic works, however, should be burnt in a burning fire so that they may not have any ground to curse thee our King, O Emperor our lord, nor any of our compatriots, nor to reproach nor blaspheme our God and our churches. Furthermore, this should be done for another purpose, more important than the others, namely, in order that all Jews will be able to call on the One God after all these books have been burned, for they have served as a screen between them and our religion, with the result that the Jews cannot recognize our Creator." [The Dominicans believed that the Jews would become Christians if the rabbinic writings were destroyed.]

The one who has compassed and done all this is a certain one of your people [Pfefferkorn] who deserted your religion. As is said in the Bible [Nahum 1:11]: "Out of thee came he forth, that deviseth evil against the Lord, that counselleth wickedness," and as it is also said [Isaiah 49:17]: "Thy destroyers shall go forth from thee."

And this apostate, *Meshummad* as you say in your language, had a number of letters from princes and bishops and particularly from a certain nun, the sister of our lord, the Emperor—may his Majesty be exalted. [Kunigunde, Maximilian's sister, was in a convent in Munich, Bavaria.] She not only wrote a letter, but, going personally before the Emperor, her brother, she bowed down to the ground and wept before him, saying: "O my lord and brother, pillar of the world and ruler of the nations, you are responsible for all the sins and transgressions that have been committed through these books because, though you have the power to stop this, you do not.

"What better proof do you want than this man who was originally of their faith and knows all the Talmudic writings? Therefore, my lord, I beseech your Majesty, in order that if you do this your name may live among the nations and kings and emperors who preceded you. How otherwise will it be known that you are faithful and loyal to our faith unless you do this which is right in the eyes of God and man? Therefore, for the reasons I have given, issue an order that in every place where those Talmudic writings are found they are to be seized and burnt." [Two decrees of confiscation were issued: in August and in November, 1509.]

Now, sir, as a result of such admonitions, requests, and supplications, the Emperor commanded that those books be confiscated and brought to the storehouses of the king, and they were. After this the Emperor said that he wished to secure advice as to what to do with these works, and he did. After he had been advised he sent me an official letter and adjured me by the imperial and royal decree that I should examine, search, and investigate whether such things are found in these books or not. I familiarized myself with them according to the poverty of my intellect and the limits of my comprehension. [A decree of July 6, 1510 authorized Reuchlin also to examine the Hebrew books.]

In accordance with that understanding which the Holy One blessed be He has granted me and with a great deal of effort on my part, I studied and learned these books because of the desire and the love which I have always had for studying and reading Hebrew books. I examined them, and I wrote [October, 1510] and responded to the command of the King to the effect that I did not know nor had I heard of such things in the Talmudic writings. The Talmudic works are divided into laws, statutes, and legends, and whoever wishes to believe them may believe them. And if such things of which this *Meshummad* speaks should be found, that particular book or books should be burnt; but there are a great many cabalistic and other important writings whose destruction would be a great loss. [He believed the cabala contained Christian doctrines.] Everything that that *Meshummad* has said, he has said only in order to provoke and to cause trouble.

And after our lord, the Emperor, read my opinion and my idea on the subject he commanded that those books that had been seized should be returned to the hands of their owners. [Reuchlin errs. The books had already been returned.] And indeed, sir, when that *Meshummad* and the scholars of Cologne University saw that it was through my advice that their plan had come to naught, they complained bitterly, saying that I was a heretic—not believing in our religion and denying its very principles. And it was not enough that they made a public outcry, but that *Meshummad*, that common and complete ignoramus, wrote against me a book full of errors and lies, attacking my honor and faith. [In the *Handspiegel*, "Hand-mirror," 1511, Pfefferkorn insinuates the Jews bribed Reuchlin.] Now I, in turn, in order to defend my honor, came back with an-other book, written in German, and I divided my arguments into a number of parts and gave the reasons for my ideas, and they wanted to burn that book which I composed. [This *Augenspiegel*, "Eye-glasses," 1511, was Reuchlin's answer to the *Handspiegel*.] (Those scholars, too, of that university have also written a book against me [1512, the *Articuli* of Arnold von Tungern] and have sent it to many everywhere in order to broadcast the attack on my honor and my faith. They have also brought this matter to the attention of the Inquisitor [Jacob van Hoogstraten of Cologne] and have slandered me.)

But when they saw that they were not able to put me into bad odor with the inquisitors so as to have my book burnt; that they were not able to rouse the public against me, as I have already mentioned; that in this matter I would submit myself and my cause to the papal court; and that they were not able to do anything against me; then they wrote a big book attacking me and sent it broadcast in order to revile me in the eyes of God and man. [Prob-ably the *Articuli sive propositiones* of Arnold von Tungern of the University of Cologne, 1512, mentioned above.]

Therefore, sir, inasmuch as I fear that they will summon me to appear in court outside my own town and province, and this would entail a huge expense, I would entreat your gracious favor. I have heard that your Excellency is daily at the papal quarters and that the body of his Holiness is in your skilled care. Therefore I would beg of your Excellency that you influence his Holiness, our lord, the Pope, that they should have no power or permission to compel me to appear before any other judge except the judges of my prov-ince, as is provided for by our statutes and laws. And if after this they wish to appear before his Holiness, our lord, the Pope, I am ready for anything: to answer them and to straighten out the matter properly. But to come to Cologne to their court, or to a neighboring court—that does not seem right to me, and it is not legal usage that I should try my case outside my own territory first. [In Cologne the Dominicans controlled the ecclesiastical courts.]

In this matter I know that I have found favor in the eyes of your Excellency and that not in vain have I labored and striven therein, for it was due to me that all the Talmudic writings were not burnt in Germany. I am convinced and believe that whatever slander was spread about these books was spread in order to gain notoriety.

Therefore, I do request and beg of you, as I have already said, that you do not refuse my petition, for you possess the power to do this and even more. And insofar as I am able, here at home, to serve your Excellency, or others for your Excellency's sake, I will do so whole-heartedly and willingly and gladly. Your Excellency has only to command and I will fulfill.

The One God knows this. May He maintain your Excellency and those under your protection in good condition and in sound health in accordance with your own wishes and the wish of your friend, the undersigned.

The humblest Gentile, who continually seeks your friendship and is at the service of your Excellency,

JOHANNES REUCHLIN of Pforzheim, Doctor.

BIBLIOGRAPHY

REFERENCES TO TEXTBOOKS

Roth, pp. 242–245; Sachar, pp. 227–228.

READINGS FOR ADVANCED STUDENTS

Graetz, IV, pp. 422–468; Graetz-Rhine, IV, pp. 277–316; Margolis and Marx, pp. 483–485.

Freimann, A., and F. Kracauer, *Frankfort* (Jewish Community Series), Chap. iv, "Pfefferkorn and the Dispute concerning Jewish Books (1509–1511)."

Hirsch, S. A., *A Book of Essays*, contains detailed essays on Reuchlin and Pfefferkorn.

Lowenthal, M., *The Jews of Germany*, Chap. x, "Reuchlin and Some Obscure Men."

JE, "Bonet de Lates"; "Hoogstraten, Jacob van"; "Pfefferkorn, Johann"; "Reuchlin, Johann von."

ADDITIONAL SOURCE MATERIALS IN ENGLISH

Epistolae obscurorum virorum; the Latin Text with an English Rendering, Notes, and an Historical Introduction by Francis Griffin Stokes. Here we have a complete translation of the famous letters poking fun at Pfefferkorn and his Dominican friends. Many of these letters throw light on the Reuchlin-Pfefferkorn controversy.

33.

Martin Luther and the Jews
1523–1543

THE struggle in Germany between Johannes Reuchlin and the Dominicans on the question of the preservation of some rabbinic writings led in part to the formation of a large body of public opinion that was decidedly anti-Catholic. It was this anti-Catholic group which Martin Luther (1483–1546), a monk, rallied about himself when he initiated the Protestant Revolution in 1517.

In a work written as early as 1523, *That Jesus Christ Was a Born Jew*, Luther was very sympathetic to the Jews because he hoped that he might induce them to become Protestants and thus prove to the world the superiority of Protestantism over Catholicism. This book appears to have been widely read, for there were in the first year of publication nine German prints in addition to a Latin edition.

Late in life Luther turned bitter against the Jews. The causes were many: the Jews did not flock to his new Christianity; on the contrary, they even presumed, occasionally, to convert Christians and dared to argue even with him on matters theological. Also, he was a sick man. His growing bitterness and sense of disillusionment finally vented itself in 1543 in a series of German anti-Jewish writings of which *Concerning the Jews and Their Lies* is a notorious example. There are no more bitterly anti-Jewish statements in all Christian literature than those which may be found in these writings of the disappointed rebel. His attacks were not original: they are drawn from older medieval writings some of which come from the pens of apostate Jews.

Josel of Rosheim, the Jewish advocate, protested vigorously against this bitter attack of Luther which, it seems, confirmed the exclusion of the Jews from Electoral Saxony and brought about a deterioration of their position in Hesse. Though unsuccessful in these two lands Josel did receive (1546) a charter from the Emperor Charles V which confirmed the rights and privileges of Jews throughout the German Empire.

Luther's anti-Jewish essays are still a frequently quoted source for modern anti-Semites.

I. THAT JESUS CHRIST WAS BORN A JEW—*1523*

❡I will therefore show by means of the Bible the causes which induce me to believe that Christ was a Jew born of a virgin. Perhaps I will attract some of the Jews to the Christian faith. For our fools— the popes, bishops, sophists, and monks—the coarse blockheads! have until this time so treated the Jews that to be a good Christian one would have to become a Jew. And if I had been a Jew and had seen such idiots and blockheads ruling and teaching the Christian religion, I would rather have been a sow than a Christian.

For they have dealt with the Jews as if they were dogs and not human beings. They have done nothing for them but curse them and seize their wealth. Whenever they converted them, they did not teach them either Christian law or life but only subjected them to papistry and monkery. When these Jews saw that Judaism had such strong scriptural basis and that Christianity [Catholicism] was pure nonsense without Biblical support, how could they quiet their hearts and become real, good Christians? I have myself heard from pious converted Jews that if they had not heard the gospel in our time [from us Lutherans] they would always have remained Jews at heart in spite of their conversion. For they admit that they have never heard anything about Christ from the rulers who have converted them.

I hope that, if the Jews are treated friendly and are instructed kindly through the Bible, many of them will become real Christians and come back to the ancestral faith of the prophets and patriarchs. . . . [Luther considered the heroes of the Old Testament good Christians.]

I would advise and beg everybody to deal kindly with the Jews and to instruct them in the Scriptures; in such a case we could expect them to come over to us. If, however, we use brute force and slander them, saying that they need the blood of Christians to get rid of their stench and I know not what other nonsense of that kind, and treat them like dogs, what good can we expect of them? [Mediaeval Christians believed in a *Foetor Judaicus*, a "Jewish stench."] Finally, how can we expect them to improve if we forbid them to work among us and to have social intercourse with us, and so force them into usury?

If we wish to make them better, we must deal with them not according to the law of the pope, but according to the law of Christian charity. We must receive them kindly and allow them to compete with us in earning a livelihood, so that they may have a good reason to be with us and among us and an opportunity to witness Christian life and doctrine; and if some remain obstinate, what of it? Not every one of us is a good Christian.

I shall stop here now until I see what the results will be. May God be gracious to us all. Amen.

II. CONCERNING THE JEWS AND THEIR LIES—*1543*

⟨What then shall we Christians do with this damned, rejected race of Jews? [The Jews were rejected by God since they refused to accept Jesus as the Messiah.] Since they live among us and we know about their lying and blasphemy and cursing, we can not tolerate them if we do not wish to share in their lies, curses, and blasphemy. In this way we cannot quench the inextinguishable fire of divine rage (as the prophets say) nor convert the Jews. We must prayerfully and reverentially practice a merciful severity. Perhaps we may save a few from the fire and the flames [of hell]. We must not seek vengeance. They are surely being punished a thousand times more than we might wish them. Let me give you my honest advice.

First, their synagogues or churches should be set on fire, and whatever does not burn up should be covered or spread over with dirt so that no one may ever be able to see a cinder or stone of it. And this ought to be done for the honor of God and of Christianity in order that God may see that we are Christians, and that we have not wittingly tolerated or approved of such public lying, cursing, and blaspheming of His Son and His Christians. . . . [Luther and others believed that the Jews cursed the Christians in their daily prayers.]

Secondly, their homes should likewise be broken down and destroyed. For they perpetrate the same things there that they do in their synagogues. For this reason they ought to be put under one roof or in a stable, like gypsies, in order that they may realize that they are not masters in our land, as they boast, but miserable captives, as they complain of us incessantly before God with bitter wailing.

Thirdly, they should be deprived of their prayer-books and Talmuds in which such idolatry, lies, cursing, and blasphemy are taught.

Fourthly, their rabbis must be forbidden under threat of death to teach any more. . . .

Fifthly, passport and traveling privileges should be absolutely forbidden to the Jews. For they have no business in the rural districts since they are not nobles, nor officials, nor merchants, nor the like.

Let them stay at home. I have heard that there is a rich Jew riding around the country with a team of twelve horses—he wants to be a Messiah—and he is exploiting princes, nobles, land, and people to such an extent that important people look askance at this. [This was "the wealthy Michael," court-Jew of Joachim II of Brandenburg, a famous commercial magnate of the time.] If you princes and nobles do not close the road legally to such exploiters, then some troop ought to ride against them, for they will learn from this pamphlet what the Jews are and how to handle them and that they ought not to be protected. You ought not, you cannot protect them, unless in the eyes of God you want to share all their abomination. . . . [Luther seems to be inciting the robber barons to attack the Jews on the roads. Michael, the wealthy Jew, was actually seized in 1549 by highwaymen acting as agents for some of the most prominent citizens of Magdeburg.]

Sixthly, they ought to be stopped from usury. [Usury means any degree of interest, not only an exorbitant rate.] All their cash and valuables of silver and gold ought to be taken from them and put aside for safe keeping. For this reason, as said before, everything that they possess they stole and robbed from us through their usury, for they have no other means of support. This money should be used in the case (and in no other) where a Jew has honestly become a Christian, so that he may get for the time being one or two or three hundred florins, as the person may require. This, in order that he may start a business to support his poor wife and children and the old and feeble. Such evilly acquired money is cursed, unless, with God's blessing, it is put to some good and necessary use. . . .

Seventhly, let the young and strong Jews and Jewesses be given the flail, the ax, the hoe, the spade, the distaff, and spindle, and let them earn their bread by the sweat of their noses as is enjoined upon Adam's children. For it is not proper that they should want us cursed *Goyyim* [Gentiles] to work in the sweat of our brow and that they, pious crew, idle away their days at the fireside in laziness, feasting, and display. And in addition to this, they boast impiously that they have become masters of the Christians at our expense. We ought to drive the rascally lazy bones out of our system.

If, however, we are afraid that they might harm us personally, or our wives, children, servants, cattle, etc. when they serve us or work for us—since it is surely to be presumed that such noble lords of the world and poisonous bitter worms are not accustomed to any work and would very unwillingly humble themselves to such a degree among the cursed *Goyyim*—then let us apply the same cleverness [expulsion] as the other nations, such as France, Spain, Bohemia, etc., and settle with them for that which they have extorted usuriously from us, and after having divided it up fairly let us drive them out of the country for all time. For, as has been said, God's rage is so great against them that they only become worse and worse through mild mercy, and not much better through severe mercy. Therefore away with them. . . .

To sum up, dear princes and nobles who have Jews in your domains, if this advice of mine does not suit you, then find a better one so that you and we may all be free of this insufferable devilish burden—the Jews.

BIBLIOGRAPHY

REFERENCES TO TEXTBOOKS

Elbogen, pp. 121–123; Roth, pp. 245–246; Sachar, pp. 227–229.

READINGS FOR ADVANCED STUDENTS

Graetz, IV, pp. 468–476, 540–552; Graetz-Rhine, IV, pp. 316–324, 375–388.
Abbott, G. F., *Israel in Europe*, Chap. xiv, "The Reformation and the Jews."
Box, G. H., "Hebrew Studies in the Reformation Period and after: Their Place and Influence," in E. R. Bevan and C. Singer, *The Legacy of Israel*, pp. 315ff.
Deutsch, G., *Jew and Gentile*, Chap. iii, "The Protestant Reformation and Judaism."
Lowenthal, M., *The Jews of Germany*, Chap. xi, "The Reformation."
Newman, L. I., *Jewish Influence on Christian Reform Movements*, pp. 617ff.; "Martin Luther's Debt to Jews and Judaism."
JE, "Luther, Martin."

ADDITIONAL SOURCE MATERIALS IN ENGLISH

The Table Talk of Martin Luther (Bohn's library). There is sufficient material in Luther's table talk to throw light on his attitude toward the Jews. See Index under "Jews."

34.

The Burning of the Talmud in Italy
1553

THE success of the Protestant Revolution frightened the Catholic Church. It submitted itself to an inner reformation that expressed itself not only in a tightening of church discipline but also in an increased severity towards Jews as non-Catholics. The first palpable expression of this renewed antagonism to the Jew was the confiscation of Hebrew books in Italy in 1553. Two rival Christian book-publishers who printed Hebrew books slandered each other at the papal court. For this purpose they employed apostate Jews who were supposed to be at home in Hebrew literature. Before this quarrel had run its course the Inquisition at Rome was led to investigate and to condemn the Talmud as an anti-Christian work. Thousands of copies of this and other rabbinic books were burnt throughout the country, and in the course of the next generation the Church gradually instituted a rigid censorship of all Hebrew books, old and new. In order, therefore, to protect themselves from the accusations of apostates, the Jews of Italy, in 1554, decided for the future to examine and censor their own books before printing them. The intolerance of the Inquisition in Italy and the rise of rival presses in other lands gradually minimized the influence of Italy as the center of Jewish printing.

The following account of the burning of the Talmud in Italy in 1553 is taken from *Emek Ha-Baka* ("The vale of tears"), a Hebrew martyrology, completed in 1575 by the Italian Jewish physician, Joseph Ha-Kohen (1496–d. about 1578). This interesting historian, Spanish by descent, papal-French by birth, Italian by adoption, is also known for his translation into Hebrew in 1557 of a Spanish work dealing with the Spanish possessions in America, the conquest of Mexico, and the history of Peru.

¶In those days certain scoundrels [apostates] went forth from our midst and did impute things that were not true against the Torah of the Lord our God and stiffened their neck and went astray from the Lord. They rejected the covenant which God had made with our fathers and followed after the Gentiles, concerning whom the Lord had commanded that they should not do like them. They provoked Him very much with their vanities and sinned heavily.

They brought up an evil report against the Talmud to the Pope Julius III [1550–1555], saying: "There is a certain Talmud widely spread among the Jews and its laws are diverse from those of all peoples. It calumniates your Messiah and it ill befits the Pope to suffer it." The impetuous Julius became very angry and his fury raged within him and he said: "Get hold of it and let it be burnt." No sooner had the command left his lips than the officers went forth, rushing out in haste, and entered the houses of the Jews and brought the books found there into the city-square and burnt them on the Sabbath day, on the festival of New Year in the year 5314, that is, 1553. And the children of Israel bewailed the burning which the enemies of God had kindled. [In Rome the books were burnt on Saturday, September 9, 1553.]

These are the names of those informers who were our troublers: Hananel da Foligno, Joseph Moro, Solomon Romano. O, Lord, do not blot out their sin. Deal with them in the time of thine anger.

Fleet messengers went forth to the tall and "tonsured" people [the clergy] throughout the Romagna so that in Bologna and Ravenna innumerable books were burnt on the Sabbath, and the children of Israel sighed and cried aloud but had no power to help themselves. In Ferrara and Mantua, too, the books were burnt by order of the Pope who commanded that they were to be destroyed. There was no one to save them in the day of the Lord's wrath. [A decree of September 12, 1553 ordered all Talmuds to be burnt.]

In Venice, too, the Pope reached out and did not withdraw his hand from destroying. A certain adversary and enemy there, who had also deserted the divine Torah, Eleazar ben Raphael, the physician, gnashed at them with his teeth. There, too, innumerable books were burnt in the month of Bul, that is, the eighth month [October or November, 1553]. They sought to lay their hands even on the Holy Scriptures in the ark, but the congregational heads stood in the breach and saved them from their hands.

And in all the rest of the places to which the command of the Pope came there was great mourning among the Jews and fasting and weeping and wailing. The house of Israel humbled themselves and cried out to God saying: "The Lord, He is righteous," and when they humbled themselves the fierce wrath of God turned from them and He would not destroy them altogether. In the Duchies of Milan and Montferrat they did not even make a search, for the command of the Pope was odious to Don Ferrante [Gonzaga, d.

1557], the Viceroy. The Lord made the chiefs of the community to be pitied in his eyes and no one listened to the voice of the Pope. (The corrector [who added notes to *The Vale of Tears*] says: The merit of the Talmudical academy which was in that cream of cities, Cremona, stood them in good stead. For verily the Lord raised up for them a redeemer, the great scholar, the honored Rabbi Joseph Ottolengo, who spread Torah in Israel. On them the wrath of the Lord did not fall, for their delight was in the law of the Lord; day and night they did not cease its study, and God saved them. It was not until the year 5319 [1559, when the Inquisition seized and burnt about 11,000 Hebrew volumes in Cremona] that the evil reached them, for then the academies came to an end and over them, too, passed the poisonous cup of reeling of the princes, and there was no longer peace for those who fight the battle of the Torah.) The Cardinal of Mantua [Ercole Gonzaga, d. 1563], the brother of Don Ferrante, also spoke to the Jews several times before he did anything at all in order that they might know what to do. Remember them, my God, for good.

The community leaders went to the Pope and he received them graciously in that he allowed them to keep the works of the later [Jewish] lawmakers, so as to leave them a remnant in the land, but he would not listen to them with respect to the books of the Talmud. And now, O Lord, consider and see for there is no might in us to stand before those who rise against us, neither know we what to do, but our eyes are upon you. [A bull of May 29, 1554 allowed Jews to keep all books except those containing supposedly anti-Christian statements. In 1564 even the censored Talmud was allowed.]

BIBLIOGRAPHY

READINGS FOR ADVANCED STUDENTS

Graetz, IV, pp. 561ff.; Graetz-Rhine, IV, pp. 394–400.

Amram, D. W., *The Makers of Hebrew Books in Italy*, Chap. xi, "The Quarrel of Giustiniani and Bragadini and the Condemnation of the Talmud."

Popper, W., *The Censorship of Hebrew Books*, Chap. v, "End of the 'Golden Era'—Destruction of the Talmud in Italy."

ADDITIONAL SOURCE MATERIALS IN ENGLISH

Finkelstein, L., *Jewish Self-Government in the Middle Ages*. The ordinances of Ferrara (1554) governing the printing of new Hebrew books may be found on page 304. They are also found in I. Abrahams, *Jewish Life in the Middle Ages*, 1932, pp. 85ff.

35.

The Spanish Inquisition at Work
1568

THE Spanish Holy Office, or Inquisition, was an ecclesiastical court that inquired into heresy and watched over the morals of Catholics. It had no authority over Jews unless they were already converts to Christianity or engaged in heretical activities. This court, which was under state control, was established in Castile in 1480, primarily in order to watch over these converts or Marranos, many of whom pretended to be Christians, but secretly practiced Jewish customs. The Inquisition authorities, fearing the influence of the unconverted Jews upon the Marranos, were instrumental in securing the expulsion of the Jews from Spain in 1492. Thousands of these Jews, however, became Marranos at this time, and thus also came under the jurisdiction of the Holy Office which watched and punished them.

The following account translated from the Spanish deals with Elvira del Campo, who in 1567 was caught practicing Jewish rites. She was tried in Toledo for not eating pork and for putting on clean linen on Saturdays. She admitted so doing, but although she was of Jewish origin she denied any intention of committing heresy. Character witnesses, including clergymen, testified that she was a good Christian. She probably was. Her Jewishness consisted simply of not eating pork and of observing some of the Sabbath customs because when eleven years of age her mother had so enjoined her.

Her father and husband, evidently both of Christian origin, knew nothing of all this. The witnesses who testified against her, servants and neighbors, said she went to mass and confession, was kind and charitable but would not eat pork. The chief witnesses were two of her husband's employees who lived in the house and had spied about the kitchen and in the cupboards. She was arrested early in July, 1567. She was at that time pregnant; her baby was born the end of August in prison and the case was not taken up again till the winter. We do not know what happened to the infant. On April 6, 1568 she underwent her first torture, a moderate one. Below is the official report of this torture as made by the secretary of the Inquisition.

This selection has been chosen, not merely because it gives an authenticated picture of the Inquisition at work, but because it demonstrates also how it was possible for the authorities to get innocent people to "confess" to the most horrible of non-existent crimes, such as the poisoning of wells and the murder of children for religious purposes.

⟨She was carried to the torture-chamber and told to tell the truth, when she said that she had nothing to say. She was ordered to be stripped [so as to allow free play for the torturing ropes] and again admonished, but was silent. When stripped, she said: "Señores, I have done all that is said of me and I bear false-witness against myself, for I do not want to see myself in such trouble; please God, I have done nothing." She was told not to bring false testimony against herself but to tell the truth. The tying of the arms was commenced; she said: "I have told the truth; what have I to tell?" She was told to tell the truth and replied: "I have told the truth and have nothing to tell." One cord was applied to the arms and twisted and she was admonished to tell the truth but said she had nothing to tell. Then she screamed and said: "I have done all they say."

Told to tell in detail what she had done she replied: "I have already told the truth." Then she screamed and said: "Tell me what you want for I don't know what to say." She was told to tell what she had done, for she was tortured because she had not done so, and another turn of the cord was ordered. She cried: "Loosen me, Señores, and tell me what I have to say: I do not know what I have done. O Lord have mercy on me, a sinner!" Another turn was given and she said: "Loosen me a little that I may remember what I have to tell; I don't know what I have done; I did not eat pork for it made me sick; I have done everything; loosen me and I will tell the truth." Another turn of the cord was ordered, when she said: "Loosen me and I will tell the truth; I don't know what I have to tell—loosen me for the sake of God—tell me what I have to say—I did it, I did it—they hurt me Señor—loosen me, loosen me, and I will tell it."

She was told to tell it and said: "I don't know what I have to tell —Señor I did it—I have nothing to tell—Oh my arms! release me and I will tell it." She was asked to tell what she did and said: "I don't know, I did not eat because I did not wish to." She was asked why she did not wish to and replied: "Ay! loosen me, loosen me—take me from here and I will tell it when I am taken away—I say that I did not eat it." She was told to speak and said: "I did not eat it, I don't know why." Another turn was ordered and she said: "Señor I did not eat it because I did not wish to—release me and I will tell it." She was told to tell what she had done contrary to our holy Catholic faith. She said: "Take me from here and tell me what I have to say—they hurt me—Oh my arms, my arms!" which she repeated many times, and went on: "I don't remember—tell me what I have to say—O wretched me!—I will tell all that is wanted, Señores—they are breaking my arms—loosen me a little—I did everything that is said of me."

She was told to tell in detail truly what she did. She said: "What am I wanted to tell? I did everything—loosen me for I don't remember what I have to tell—don't you see what a weak woman I am?—Oh! Oh! my arms are breaking." More turns were ordered and as they were given she cried: "Oh! Oh! loosen me for I don't know what I have to say—Oh my arms!—I don't know what I have to say—if I did.I would tell it." The cords were ordered to be tightened, when she said: "Señores have you no pity on a sinful woman?" She was told, yes, if she would tell the truth. She said: "Señor, tell me, tell me it." The cords were tightened again, and she said: "I have already said that I did it." She was ordered to tell it in detail, to which she said: "I don't know how to tell it, Señor, I don't know." Then the cords were separated and counted, and there were sixteen turns, and in giving the last turn the cord broke.

She was then ordered to be placed on the *potro* [a sort of ladder with sharp-edged rungs]. She said: "Señores, why will you not tell me what I have to say? Señor, put me on the ground—have I not said that I did it all?" She was told to tell it. She said: "I don't remember—take me away—I did what the witnesses say." She was told to tell in detail what the witnesses said. She said: "Señor, as I have told you, I do not know for certain. I have said that I did all that the witnesses say. Señores, release me, for I do not remember it." She was told to tell it. She said: "I do not know it. Oh! Oh! they are tearing me to pieces—I have said that I did it—let me go." She was told to tell it. She said: "Señores, it does not help me to say that I did it and I have admitted that what I have done has brought me to this suffering—Señor, you know the truth—Señores, for God's sake have mercy on me. Oh, Señor, take these things from my arms—Señor, release me, they are killing me."

She was tied on the *potro* with the cords, she was admonished to tell the truth, and the *garrotes* were ordered to be tightened. [Ropes, tightened by twisting-sticks, *garrotes*, cut deep into the flesh.] She said: "Señor, do you not see how these people are killing me?

Señor, I did it—for God's sake let me go." She was told to tell it.
She said: "Señor, remind me of what I did not know—Señores, have
mercy on me—let me go for God's sake—they have no pity on me—
I did it—take me from here and I will remember what I cannot
here." She was told to tell the truth, or the cords would be tightened.
She said: "Remind me of what I have to say for I don't know it—
I said that I did not want to eat it—I know only that I did not want
to eat it," and this she repeated many times. She was told to tell
why she did not want to eat it. She said: "For the reason that the
witnesses say—I don't know how to tell it—miserable that I am
that I don't know how to tell it—I say I did it and—my God!—how
can I tell it?" Then she said that, as she did not do it, how could she
tell it—"They will not listen to me—these people want to kill me
—release me and I will tell the truth."

She was again admonished to tell the truth. [The court wanted her
to confess she consciously practiced Judaism.] She said: "I did it, I
don't know how I did it—I did it for what the witnesses say—let
me go—I have lost my senses and I don't know how to tell it—loosen
me and I will tell the truth." Then she said: "Señor, I did it, I don't
know how I have to tell it, but I tell it as the witnesses say—I wish
to tell it—take me from here—Señor, as the witnesses say, so I say
and confess it." She was told to declare it. She said: "I don't know
how to say it—I have no memory—Lord, you are witness that if I
knew how to say anything else I would say it. I know nothing more
to say than that I did it and God knows it." She said many times:
"Señores, Señores, nothing helps me. You, Lord, hear that I tell the
truth and can say no more—they are tearing out my soul—order
them to loosen me." Then she said: "I do not say that I did it—I
said no more."

Then she said: "Señor, I did it to observe that Law." She was
asked what Law. [This is the Mosaic law.] She said: "The Law that
the witnesses say—I declare it all Señor, and don't remember what
Law it was—O, wretched was the mother that bore me." She was
asked what was the Law she meant and what was the Law that she
said the witnesses say. This was asked repeatedly, but she was silent
and at last said that she did not know. She was told to tell the truth
or the *garrotes* would be tightened, but she did not answer. Another
turn was ordered on the *garrotes* and she was admonished to say
what Law it was. She said: "If I knew what to say I would say it.
Oh Señor, I don't know what I have to say—Oh! Oh! they are killing me—if they would tell me what—Oh, Señores! Oh, my heart!"
Then she asked why they wished her to tell what she could not tell

and cried repeatedly: "O, miserable me!" Then she said: "Lord bear witness that they are killing me without my being able to confess." She was told that if she wished to tell the truth before the water was poured she should do so and discharge her conscience. [The mouth was distended by an iron prong, the nostrils were plugged, the *toca*, a linen funnel, was thrust down the mouth to conduct water trickling slowly from a jar. The victim strangled, gasped, and suffocated.]

She said that she could not speak and that she was a sinner. Then the linen *toca* was placed [in her throat] and she said: "Take it away, I am strangling and am sick in the stomach." A jar of water was then poured down, after which she was told to tell the truth. [If the torture lasted long enough the court nearly always got the confession it expected.] She clamored for confession, saying she was dying. She was told that the torture would be continued till she told the truth and was admonished to tell it, but though she was questioned repeatedly she remained silent. Then the inquisitor, seeing her exhausted by the torture, ordered it to be suspended.

Note

"Four days were allowed to lapse," says Lea, "for experience showed that an interval, by stiffening the limbs, rendered repetition more painful. She was again brought to the torture-chamber but she broke down when stripped and piteously begged to have her nakedness covered. The interrogatory went on, when her replies under torture were more rambling and incoherent than before, but her limit of endurance was reached and the inquisitors finally had the satisfaction of eliciting a confession of Judaism and a prayer for mercy and penance."

One of the judges who considered the case voted that she be sentenced to death but the majority decided on a lesser punishment. She was sentenced June 13, 1568 after having already been jailed for almost a year. She was to abjure her heresy publicly, wearing a penitential garment of yellow on which were two crosses, one on the breast, the other on the back. She was also sentenced to prison for three years, during which time she was to wear this penitential garment if she should ever happen to appear in public. After her sentence was served, this garment, the *sanbenito*, would be hung in the church together with her name to publish her disgrace. Her property was confiscated, and had she been a man she would not have been permitted to hold office or practice any of the better known trades or professions. Nor was she permitted ever to wear ornaments of gold and silver, or silken garments; or to carry arms or to ride on a horse. Frequently these disabilities were extended to include children and grandchildren.

After six months she was freed from prison, but "was beggared and ruined for life, and an ineffaceable stain was cast upon her kindred and descendants."

BIBLIOGRAPHY

REFERENCES TO TEXTBOOKS

Elbogen, pp. 84ff.; Roth, pp. 224ff.; Sachar, pp. 208ff.

READINGS FOR ADVANCED STUDENTS

Graetz, IV, pp. 308ff.; Graetz-Rhine, IV, pp. 189ff.; Margolis and Marx, pp. 460ff.

Adler, E. N., *Auto de fé and Jew*. A series of historical studies dealing primarily with the Inquisition and the Sephardic Jews.

Herculano, A., *History of the Origin and Establishment of the Inquisition in Portugal*. Tr. by J. C. Branner. A standard work.

Kohut, G. A., "Jewish Martyrs of the Inquisition in South America." *Publications of the American Jewish Historical Society*, IV (1894).

Lea, H. C., *A History of the Inquisition of Spain*, 4 vols. This standard work throws a great deal of light on the relation of the Inquisition in Spain to the Jews. Material dealing with the Jews in the New World may be found in Lea's *The Inquisition in the Spanish Dependencies*.

Roth, C., *A History of the Marranos*. The best work for a study of the Jewish relations to the Inquisition.

Catholic Encyclopedia, "Inquisition." A Catholic interpretation of this tribunal.

JE, "Auto da fé"; "Inquisition."

ADDITIONAL SOURCE MATERIALS IN ENGLISH

Adler, C., "Trial of Jorge de Almeida by the Inquisition in Mexico." *Publications of the American Jewish Historical Society*, IV (1894).

Fergusson, D., "Trial of Gabriel de Granada by the Inquisition in Mexico, 1642–1645." Edited with notes by C. Adler. *Publications of the American Jewish Historical Society*, VII (1899). Practically a complete record of the entire trial.

Lindo, E. H., *The History of the Jews of Spain and Portugal*, Chap. xxii. This chapter contains a list of indications whereby a secret Jew may be detected.

Wolf, L., *Jews in the Canary Islands. Being a Calendar of Jewish Cases Extracted from the Records of the Canariote Inquisition, etc.* A work as valuable as it is interesting.

36.

The Martyrdom of the Reizes Brothers
Lemberg, Poland, May 13, 1728

IT was discovered, probably early in 1728, that Jan Filipowicz, a Jewish convert to Christianity, had reverted to Judaism. The authorities ordered an investigation made. A number of prominent rabbis and laymen, hearing of their impending arrest, fled the city and country; others, however, were arrested, among them the two brothers, Hayyim and Joshua Reizes of Lemberg. They were accused of "tampering" with the faith of a Christian convert, of taking a cross from him and trampling it under foot, and of attempting to wipe away the chrism, the holy oil with which he had once been anointed. All these charges were capital offenses and the Reizes brothers (together with two others who succeeded in escaping) were found guilty. Filipowicz's confession was obtained after he had twice been put to the torture. Legend reports that in spite of severe torture, the Jews made no confession.

The sentence imposed on the Reizes brothers reads that "their tongues are to be torn out of their throats, and while still living they are to be quartered and then burnt." To escape this sentence Joshua committed suicide in prison by cutting his throat and it was only the corpse that was dragged through the streets and then cremated. For three days the Jesuit father Zóltowski tried to induce Hayyim to convert to Christianity, promising him escape from punishment. Hayyim persisted in his faith and the above sentence was carried out in every detail on May 13, 1728, on the eve of the feast of *Shabuot*. Filipowicz, the convert, had already been executed before this for his lapse.

The following account, describing the arrest and fate of these martyrs, is taken from the Hebrew minute-books of the burial society of Lemberg.

❡It happened like this: the rabbi, the great scholar and martyr, our master and teacher, Rabbi Hayyim Reizes—of blessed memory— was the president of the rabbinical academy of the twin communities here in Lemberg. Learning and prominence were both united in him for he was rich in worldly goods and was a great philanthropist, giving of his money generously to the poor and poverty-stricken. He was forty-one years old. His younger brother was a great student of Jewish lore and greatly renowned for his piety. He would afflict himself for years by [frequent] fasting. He was thirty-one years of age. (He was the father of the great scholar, the head of the academy in Lemberg, Mordecai Reizes.)

It happened that a certain Jew, who was not of our city and whose birthplace was not in our country—for he came from afar—had changed his religion, come here, repented of his sin, and had returned to his faith. This man, however, was arrested after this, for the matter had become known to the archbishop and the priests. When they asked him who it was that had enticed him to return to Judaism he answered that he was not acquainted with any one in our community. If, however, they would line up the men of the place he would walk in front of them and pick out the one who had misled him.

The archbishop therefore commanded that all the men of our community, including the scholarly rabbi, the president of the academy, and his brother, be lined up in the Jewish quarter. So the Catholic leader and the priests came and the apostate passed by [the Reizes brothers]. The priests and their chief had been told that the rabbi and his brother had enticed the apostate, and, inasmuch as he passed before Rabbi Hayyim Reizes, the president of the academy, and his brother Rabbi Joshua, and had said nothing, Rabbi Hayyim called out in Latin to the leader of the priests: "See, my lord, I am indeed innocent of this sin, and I have been suspected without cause." No sooner had the apostate heard this than he returned to his vomit and said: "Thou art the man, and your brother, too!"

They were immediately seized and sentenced to death and burning. The sentence against Rabbi Joshua—of blessed memory—was that he should be tied to the tail of a horse and dragged through the streets and highways. . . . They were in prison forty-one days and upon the eve of *Shabuot*, the day of sacrifice [May 13, 1728], these scholars, martyrs, and pious men were killed, being brutally stabbed to death and burnt.

May God avenge their blood and may their memory mount on high, so that their merits and righteousness may plead for us. Amen.

37.

The Punishment for Sacrilege
Nancy, France, June 17, 1761

JACOB ALEXANDRE was a feeble-minded Jewish beggar and good-for-nothing who flirted with the idea of converting himself and was even given instruction in Christianity by a priest of Longeville. On Monday, the 8th of June, 1761, he went into the church of St. Peter at Nancy and ate the holy wafer, or Host, administered during Communion. He probably did not realize that the eating of the Host by a Jew was a sacrilege punishable by death in Catholic states. This twenty-two year old moron was at once arrested and on the 17th of June sentenced by Stanislaus the Beneficent (1677–1766), Duke of Lorraine and Bar, to be hanged.

This severe sentence was not directed against him because he was a Jew; Christians also who ran athwart of the Church law were frequently executed. It is an interesting coincidence that during this very year Jean Calas, a Protestant merchant, was arrested on the false charge of murdering his own son to prevent him from becoming a Catholic. Calas was ultimately tortured, broken alive on the wheel, and then burnt to ashes. Voltaire interested himself in the Calas family and secured a revision of the case which proved the innocence of the unfortunate victim.

The findings of the court in the Alexandre case are reproduced below, from the French, as a typical illustration of the enforcement of canon law by the state and of the characteristic medieval severity imposed for infractions of Church law. That cases such as these were not infrequent is evidenced by the story of the martyrdom of the Reizes brothers described in the preceding chapter.

It was Alexandre's good fortune that he appealed his case to a higher court in Lorraine, for by a decision of July 2nd he was merely condemned to make public penance and to be sent to the galleys for life. He was accordingly taken to the church of St. Peter where he asked pardon, then he was taken to the place of execution where he was branded on the right shoulder by the hangman, and then he was dispatched to the galleys. This was twenty-eight years before the French Revolution after which, in all probability, a man could not even be arrested for the crime described below.

《I maintain, in the name of the King, that the said Jacob Alexandre, of the Jewish nation, has been adequately charged and convicted of having gone on the eighth day of the present month into the parochial church of St. Peter, in the suburbs of Nancy, that he presented himself at the altar, and that he received the Holy Communion at the hands of the curate. This constitutes a profanation so much the more punishable inasmuch as the aforesaid Jacob Alexandre had himself instructed in the holy mysteries of our religion. He knew that, being a Jew, he was committing an abominable crime by the profanation which he was perpetrating in receiving Our Lord before being baptized and by receiving all the sacraments necessary to approach the altar and to receive the Holy Communion.

I find the aforesaid Jacob Alexandre adequately charged and convicted of having asked for charity in our city—and moreover, in the guise of a converted Jew—and in that way to have won the sympathy of charitable people. This is a theft from the needy poor as well as an abuse of our religion.

As satisfaction for this, I demand that the aforesaid Jacob Alexandre be delivered into the hands of the executioner in order that, bareheaded, with a rope around his neck, his body covered with a white linen shirt, and holding in his hand a wax candle weighing two pounds, he may be conducted by the executioner before the cathedral church which is primatical in this city. [Through this garb and ceremonial he evidenced his penitence.]

There he shall make public penance, ask pardon of God, of his king, and of justice for the abominable crime he has committed. Then, in due order, he is to be conducted to the place of execution of this city in order to be hanged and strangled, on a gallows which will be erected there for that purpose, until death sets in. His corpse is then to be thrown into the fire to be burnt, and his ashes are to be scattered to the winds.

I sentence the aforesaid Jacob Alexandre to a fine of one hundred livres towards the domain of the King in the event that the confiscation of his property, out of which the expenses of the case have first been deducted, shall not have resulted in profit to the King. [His property is to be confiscated and if it is insufficient he is to be fined in addition.]

Jewry and the Individual Jew

A. JEWISH SELF-GOVERNMENT

38.

Jewish Autonomy in Babylon
about 1168

THE Jewish settlement in the valley of the Tigris-Euphrates dates back at least as far as the Babylonian Exile (586 B.C.E.). Probably at a very early period the exiles were given considerable self-rule. In later centuries the political leader, reputedly a descendant of the House of David, was called the Head of the Exile, or Exilarch. The spiritual and religious guides, the chiefs of the academies, were called *Geonim*, "Excellencies," an abbreviated title for "Head of the Academy which is the Excellency of Jacob." The political leaders, the exilarchs, were given considerable authority to rule, tax, and to judge the Jews wherever the power of the reigning Gentile dynasty extended, and in the days of the califs of Bagdad, during the Middle Ages, the Jews affected to believe that Mohammed, the prophet of Islam, had granted their leaders many privileges. Though the exilarch was nominally the political leader of the Jews, he was often in conflict with a *Gaon* who sought power for himself. Despite the oppressive exactions of some individual exilarchs the Jews were very proud of their Davidic rulers who represented them as a people at the court of the calif.

The following account from the Hebrew itinerary of the Jewish traveler, Benjamin of Tudela in Navarre, describes the exilarchate in the twelfth century under the Abbaside califs. Benjamin was in Bagdad about the year 1168.

℘ In Bagdad there are about forty thousand Jews, and they dwell in security, prosperity, and honor under the great Calif [al-Mustandjid, 1160–1170], and amongst them are great sages, the Heads of the Academies engaged in the study of the Law. . . . At the head of the great academy is the chief rabbi, Rabbi Samuel the son of Ali. He is the "Head of the Academy which is the Excellency of Jacob." He is a Levite, and traces his pedigree back to Moses our teacher. [The *Gaon* Samuel ben Ali held office from about 1164 to 1193. After the death of the exilarch he became the real ruler of the Jews in the Near East. Nine other scholars who devoted their time to teaching and communal administration are next listed.] . . .

These are the ten scholars, and they do not engage in any other work than communal administration; and all the days of the week they judge the Jews their countrymen, except on Monday, when they all appear before the chief rabbi Samuel, the Head of the Academy Excellency of Jacob, who in conjunction with the other scholars judges all those that appear before him.

And at the head of them all is Daniel the son of Hisdai, who is styled "Our Lord, the Head of the Exile of all Israel." [Daniel, the Exilarch, was in office from about 1160 to about 1174.] He possesses a book of pedigrees going back as far as David, King of Israel. The Jews call him "Our Lord, Head of the Exile," and the Mohammedans call him *Saidna ben Daoud* ["noble descendant of David"], and he has been invested with authority over all the congregations of Israel at the hands of the Emir al Muminin, the Lord of Islam [the calif at Bagdad]. For thus Mohammed commanded concerning him and his descendants; and he granted him a seal of office over all the congregations that dwell under his rule, and ordered that every one, whether Mohammedan or Jew or belonging to any other nation in his dominion, should rise up before the exilarch and salute him, and that any one who should refuse to rise up should receive one hundred stripes.

And every Thursday when he goes to pay a visit to the great Calif, horsemen—non-Jews as well as Jews—escort him, and heralds proclaim in advance: "Make way before our Lord, the son of David, as is due unto him," the Arabic words being *Amilu tarik la Saidna ben Daoud*. He is mounted on a horse, and is attired in robes of silk and embroidery with a large turban on his head, and from the turban is suspended a long white cloth adorned with a chain upon which the seal of Mohammed is engraved.

Then he appears before the Calif and kisses his hand, and the Calif rises and places him on a throne which Mohammed had ordered to be made in honor of him, and all the Mohammedan princes who attend the court of the Calif rise up before him. And the exilarch is seated on his throne opposite to the Calif, in compliance with the command of Mohammed to give effect to what is written in the Law: "The sceptre shall not depart from Judah, nor the ruler's staff from between his feet, as long as men come to Shiloh; and unto him shall the obedience of the peoples be." [Genesis 49:10. Many Jews interpreted this verse to mean that there will always be a Jewish ruler somewhere till the Messiah comes.]

The authority of the exilarch extends over all the communities of Babylon, Persia, Khorasan and Sheba which is El-Yemen, and Diyar

Kalach [Bekr] and all the land of Mesopotamia, and over the dwellers in the mountains of Ararat and the land of the Alans [in the Caucasus], which is a land surrounded by mountains and has no outlet except by the iron gates which Alexander made, but which were afterwards broken. Here are the people called Alani.

His authority extends also over the land of the Sawir, and the land of the Turks, unto the mountains of Asveh and the land of Gurgan [near the Caspian Sea], the inhabitants of which are called Gurganim who dwell by the river Gihon, and these are the Girgashites who follow the Christian religion. Further it extends to the gates of Samarkand, the land of Thibet, and the land of India.

In respect of all these countries the exilarch gives the communities power to appoint rabbis and overseers who come unto him to be consecrated and to receive his authority. [The *Hazzan*, or overseer, was then an important official of the synagogue.] They bring him offerings and gifts from the ends of the earth. He owns hospices, gardens, and plantations in Babylon, and much land inherited from his fathers, and no one can take his possessions from him by force. He has a fixed weekly revenue arising from the hospices of the Jews, the markets and the merchants, apart from that which is brought to him from far-off lands. The man is very rich, and wise in the Scriptures as well as in the Talmud, and many Israelites dine at his table every day. [Daniel the Exilarch, in a letter dated 1161, complains of his poverty, but that was seven years before Benjamin came to Bagdad.]

At his installation, the exilarch gives much money to the Calif, to the Princes and the officials. On the day that the Calif performs the ceremony of investing him with authority, the exilarch rides in the second of the royal equipages, and is escorted from the palace of the Calif to his own house with timbrels and fifes. The exilarch appoints the Head of the Academy [by placing his hand upon his head, thus installing him in his office]. The Jews of the city are learned men and very rich.

In Bagdad there are twenty-eight Jewish synagogues, situated either in the city itself or in Al-Karkh [the business section of greater Bagdad] on the other side of the Tigris; for the river divides the metropolis into two parts. The great synagogue of the exilarch has columns of marble of various colors overlaid with silver and gold, and on these columns are sentences of the Psalms in golden letters. And in front of the ark are about ten steps of marble; on the topmost step are the seats of the exilarch and of the princes of the House of David. The city of Bagdad is twenty miles in circumference, situated in a land of palms, gardens, and plantations, the like of which is not to be found in the whole land of Babylon. People come thither with merchandise from all lands. Wise men live there, philosophers who know all manner of wisdom, and magicians expert in all manner of witchcraft.

BIBLIOGRAPHY

REFERENCES TO TEXTBOOKS

Elbogen, pp. 20ff., 49ff.; Roth, pp. 120ff.
Golub, J. S., *Medieval Jewish History*, Sec. II; Sec. IV, "Jewish Self-Government," etc.

READINGS FOR ADVANCED STUDENTS

Graetz, III. See Index under "Exilarch," and "Exilarchate"; Margolis and Marx, pp. 235–236.
Abrahams, I., *Jewish Life in the Middle Ages*, 1932, Chap. iii, "Communal Organization."
JE, "Academies in Babylonia"; "Babylonia"; "Bagdad"; "Community, Organization of"; "Exilarch."

ADDITIONAL SOURCE MATERIALS IN ENGLISH

Adler, M. N., *The Itinerary of Benjamin of Tudela*. The complete translation of the itinerary of this famous Jewish traveller. Information on life and government in Babylon may also be found in the itinerary of Rabbi Petachia of Ratisbon (1170–1187), translated in E. N. Adler, *Jewish Travellers*.
Finkelstein, L., *Jewish Self-Government in the Middle Ages*. Part II, texts and translations, is very helpful for a study of the self-government of the medieval Jew in Europe.
Halper, B., *Post-Biblical Hebrew Literature*, "The Installation of an Exilarch," II, pp. 64–68.
Millgram, A. E., *An Anthology of Mediaeval Hebrew Literature*, Chap. vi, "How the Mediaeval Jews Governed Themselves (Legal Literature)." This section contains material concerning Jewish self-government.

39.

The Ban of Solomon Ben Adret
1305

THE study of the philosophy and the natural sciences of the Greeks and the Arabs led many Jews in southern France and in Spain to examine critically the most sacred beliefs of Judaism. Some even denied the divine authority of the Bible. Philosophical and religious radicalism threatened the very foundations of the orthodoxy so zealously guarded by the rabbinic leaders.

As a result of this situation conflict arose between the liberals and the orthodox. For a time the battle centered around Maimonides' philosophical writings which many orthodox declared heretical. Bans and counter-bans were hurled. The orthodox were so convinced of the heretical nature of Maimonides' *Guide for the Perplexed* and his *Book of Knowledge* that in 1233–1234 they induced the Dominican monks to burn them.

This struggle between the forces of science and the forces of tradition, a struggle that had already begun with the first contacts of Jewish and Islamic culture, reached an acute stage in the late thirteenth and the early fourteenth centuries. The battle line extended from Spain to Palestine. Rabbi Solomon ibn Adret (1235–1310), the rabbi of Barcelona and a scholar of international repute, was finally led to issue a vigorous ban against those who studied religious philosophy and certain of the natural sciences before they were twenty-five years old, and against their teachers. It was felt that if a man "filled his belly" with Jewish lore till twenty-five he could safely study anything else after that.

Ibn Adret, who was by nature a traditionalist, believed that scientific and philosophic studies, unless carefully controlled, undermined religious beliefs. He realized, too, that pious, naive Christians resented Jewish skepticism. The ban he issued in 1305, although authoritative only for his community Barcelona, gradually found acceptance in other cities and lands. It was, however, the growing Christian intolerance, more than anything else, that led Jews to neglect all but rabbinic studies.

The introduction to this Hebrew ban of Ibn Adret is a composite of flowery Biblical phrases used metaphorically. It is not an unusual style for this type of pronouncement.

Woe to mankind because of the insult to the Torah!
For they have strayed far from it.
Its diadem have they taken away;
Its crown have they removed.

[It is an insult to the Torah to prefer the sciences to
Jewish religious teachings.]

Every man with his censer in his hand offers incense
Before the Greeks and the Arabs.

[Many students are worshipping at the shrine of Greek
and Arabic science and philosophy.]

Like Zimri they publicly consort with the Midianitess
And revel in their own filth!

[Even as Zimri of old consorted with the seductive Midianitess, Numbers 25, Jews now flirt with heresy.]

They do not prefer the older Jewish teachings
But surrender to the newer Greek learning the prerogatives due
    their Jewish birthright.
They turn not back,
But act like strangers [to their own teachings],
And like satyrs, at the head of all the streets
They dance to these [foreign ideas],
And even teach them to their children.
Therefore, when we saw the fowler's snare even in the remote parts
    of the earth,
And the dove [the Torah] compelled to make her nest in the sides
    of the pit's mouth,
We trembled and said:
"The disease [heresy] is spreading!"
So now we have risen and made a covenant with the Lord and the
    Torah of our God,
Which we and our fathers have accepted on Sinai,
Not to let anything strange come among us,
Nor let the nettle and the thistle [that is, heretical ideas] spring up
    in our palaces.
Servants are we, servants of the Lord!
The Lord, He has made us.
His are we.

Therefore have we decreed and accepted for ourselves and our
children, and for all those joining us, that for the next fifty years,
under threat of the ban, no man in our community, unless he be

twenty-five years old, shall study, either in the original language or in translation, the books which the Greeks have written on religious philosophy and the natural sciences. [However, original Jewish works on philosophy and science, even those of Maimonides, may be read at any age. Mathematical works from the Greek were also probably permitted.]

It is also forbidden for any member of our community to teach any Jew under twenty-five years of age any of these sciences lest they drag him away from the law of Israel which is superior to all these teachings. How can a human being not be afraid to judge between the wisdom of man, who builds only on analogy, argument, and guess, and between the wisdom of the Superior Being, between whom and us there is hardly any comparison? Can a human being, who inhabits but a perishable body, think of sitting in judgment on God, who created him, by saying—God forbid—"This He can do, and this He cannot do"? This, certainly, would lead one to complete heresy and from this, indeed, may every student of the Torah be delivered!

We have, however, excluded from this our general prohibition the science of medicine, even though it is one of the natural sciences, because the Torah permits the physician to heal. [Medicine was then a common profession among Jews.]

Over the scroll of the Law and in the presence of the whole community, we have agreed, on the Sabbath of the portion, "These are the words," in the year 5065, to ban these things. [This portion, Deuteronomy 1, was read on Saturday, July 31, 1305.]

Solomon ben Abraham, of blessed memory, the son of Adret.
Etc.,
Etc.

BIBLIOGRAPHY

REFERENCES TO TEXTBOOKS

Elbogen, pp. 114ff.; Sachar, pp. 178–183.

READINGS FOR ADVANCED STUDENTS

Graetz, III, pp. 522ff., 618–634; IV, pp. 1–51; Graetz-Rhine, III, pp. 370ff.; Margolis and Marx, pp. 392ff.

Epstein, I., The "Responsa" of Rabbi Solomon ben Adreth of Barcelona (1235–1310) as a Source of the History of Spain. Chap. vii: "Excommunications."

Sarachek, J., *Faith and Reason: The Conflict over the Rationalism of Maimonides.* A detailed study of the anti-Maimunist agitation.

JE, "Adret, Solomon ben Abraham"; "Excommunication"; "France" (pp. 460–461).

ADDITIONAL SOURCE MATERIALS IN ENGLISH

Halper, B., *Post-Biblical Hebrew Literature,* "Epistle Prohibiting Anyone under Twenty-Five Years of Age To Study Philosophy," II, pp. 176–182. This letter is the second of a series of three statements, including the notorious ban, which Solomon ben Abraham Adret issued on the subject of the study of the. sciences.

The ban against Spinoza may be found on pp. 17–18 of F. Pollock, *Spinoza: His Life and Philosophy,* 2nd edition, and on pp. 141–142 of L. Browne, *Blesséd Spinoza.*

40.

Sumptuary and Other Police Laws
1416–1740

THE Jewish community exercised its power by enacting various police laws which controlled such matters as moral conduct, the prices of goods, and particularly private expenditures for clothes and jewels. Sumptuary laws, those directed primarily against extravagance in personal attire, were motivated largely by fear of Gentile envy, but also by the desire to keep poor Jews from living beyond their means. Dressing like one's Gentile neighbor was frowned upon also, for it was felt that an assimilation in dress was the first step toward an assimilation in ideas. In addition, since Talmudic times national calamities in Jewry were the signal for more sobriety in living, and it goes without saying that the strong ethical and ascetic spirit of the medieval Jewish leaders was opposed to any ostentation.

The following series of sumptuary and police laws are taken from a number of countries to show how common this type of legislation was. The examples given below are varied for the sake of diversity, for, as a matter of fact, the regulations in force in most Jewish communities were very much alike. And not only the Jews, but the Christians, too, were concerned with the problem of luxury and petty vices: the medieval Christian legislation of the Church, state, and town abounds in enactments of this nature.

The first group of laws, originally in Hebrew, is taken from the decisions of a group of Italian Jews who met at Forli on Wednesday, May 18, 1418. These men, representing the chief communities of central and northern Italy, had first met in Bologna in 1416, and had there been empowered, as a national Jewish commission, to guide the destinies of Italian Jewry for the next ten years.

The second selection, originally in Castilian, is an abstract from the legislation which was enacted May 2, 1432 at Valladolid by a national Jewish Castilian assembly.

The third group of laws, originally in Yiddish, is taken from the 1595 community constitution of the Jews of Cracow; the fourth selection, originally in Hebrew, is a decision of the national Jewish Council of Lithuania for the year 1637.

The fifth, originally in Yiddish, includes several laws from the legislation of the French Jewish community of Metz from 1690 to 1697. During this seven year period, five separate ordinances were issued by its Jewish leaders; thus we see that these laws were made only to be broken! The sixth decree, originally in Hebrew, is taken from the 1740 "ornament and garment" ordinance of the town of Carpentras in papal-France.

1. Forli, Italy, May 18, 1418

❲In order also to humble our hearts, and to walk modestly before our God, and not to show off in the presence of the Gentiles, we have agreed that from today, until the termination of the time already mentioned [1426], no Jew or Jewess of the above recorded Jewish communities, towns, or villages shall be so arrogant as to wear a fur-lined jacket, unless, of course it is black. Also the sleeves must not be open, nor be lined with silk, for that would be arrogant. These fur-lined jackets, however, other than black, may still be worn, provided that the sleeves and the garments themselves are closed at the sides and at the back. [Thus the expensive lining will not be seen and not excite envy.] . . .

Likewise no woman shall openly wear any girdle or belt if its silver weighs more than ten ounces.

II. Valladolid, Spain, May 2, 1432

❲No son of Israel of the age of fifteen or more shall wear any cloak of gold-thread, olive-colored material or silk, or any cloak trimmed with gold or olive-colored material or silk, nor a cloak with rich trimmings nor with trimmings of olive-colored or gold cloth.

This prohibition does not include the clothes worn at a time of festivity or at the reception of a lord or a lady, nor at balls or similar social occasions.

Because of the diversity of custom among the communities in regard to the wearing apparel, we find it impracticable to make a general ordinance which shall provide for all the details that ought to be included, and we therefore ordain that each community shall make such ordinances on the subject so long as this Ordinance endures, as will keep before their minds that we are in Dispersion because of our sins, and if they desire to establish more rigorous rules than this they have the power to do so. [The motivation for simplicity in dress here is religious sobriety, not fear of envy.]

III. *Cracow, Poland, 1595*

⟪It is forbidden to go through the streets at night playing on musical instruments, nor shall any one, whether householders, young men, or boys, shout or yell in the streets.

If a person does such things, or if a fight breaks out at night, or if someone attacks a citizen or injures his home, the night-watch are required to awaken one or two of the officials who are expected to get up immediately and to admonish the people to go home. If, however, they have been very violent, the officials have the authority to put them under arrest till the morning, when the chief officials of the community—may their Rock and Redeemer guard them— will settle their case.

1615–1616

One is permitted to wear only two rings on weekdays, four on the Sabbath, and six on the holidays. Both men and women are absolutely forbidden to wear precious stones. An exception is made in the case of a pregnant woman who is permitted to wear a ring with a diamond because of its curative powers. Otherwise no exception will be made, under penalty of three ducats. [Some precious stones were reputed to possess magical healing qualities. Baba Batra 16b.]

IV. *Lithuania, September 4, 1637*

⟪With respect to banquets: Inasmuch as people are spending too much money unnecessarily on festive meals [at marriages, circumcisions, etc.], every Jewish community and settlement which has a rabbi is expected to assemble its officers and rabbi and to consider the number of guests which it is suitable for every individual, in view of his wealth and the occasion, to invite to a festive meal. No one is permitted to come to a banquet unless he has been invited by the beadle. In a settlement where there is no rabbi the nearest Jewish court will enact such an ordinance for them.

V. *Metz, France, 1690*

⟪Shoes or other footgear in red or blue leather, or in any other color except black and white, are forbidden to every one. The same rule applies to footgear of velvet or any other stuff, fringed or stitched, which is likewise forbidden.

1692

It has been learned that many women are having veils embroidered in the city by non-Jews. This circumstance may give rise to a great deal of jealousy and animosity—for, till now, the non-Jews might have supposed that the gold worn by Jewesses on their garments and clothes was imitation, while now they are positive that it is genuine. For this reason announcement is made and notice is given that beginning today, no person—man, woman, or girl—is permitted to have any veils, hats, borders of cloaks, or any other object of dress made or embroidered by non-Jews, whether directly or through an intermediary. Those who have given some to be done outside by non-Jews must immediately recover these objects under penalty of a fine of twenty *Reichsthaler* for the benefit of the poor, and the administration itself will have them taken back from the non-Jews.

1694

It has also been decided that all women ought to wear a cloak and veil when going to the synagogue. Women who are not yet fifteen years old may go to the synagogue without cloak or veil, but as soon as they reach the age of fifteen they are subject to the rule. . . .

It is necessary to add that all fashionable styles of arranging the hair or those recently devised are also forbidden.

1697

Young men and women, and particularly servants of both sexes, are not allowed to go to a dance at night without having been invited, under penalty of a fine of one *Reichsthaler*. [Laws against servants served to preserve class distinctions.]

VI. *Carpentras, Papal-France, March 22, 1740*

⟮It was also agreed that grown-ups and young men are not permitted to wear a wig with curls. [Wigs without ringlets, however, are allowed.] Those, however, who return from a journey are allowed to go through the ghetto wearing the wig with curls which they used on their trip. When they come home, however, they must change it; if they have no other in the house they are given three days to get another. [On trips Jews often dressed like Gentiles to avoid being annoyed.]

BIBLIOGRAPHY

READINGS FOR ADVANCED STUDENTS

Abrahams, I., *Jewish Life in the Middle Ages*, 1932, Chap. xv, "Costume in Law and Fashion"; Chap. xvi, "The Jewish Badge."

Roth, C., "Sumptuary Laws of the Community of Carpentras," *JQR*, N. S., XVIII (1927–1928). An instructive study.

JE, "Costume"; "Sumptuary Laws."

ADDITIONAL SOURCE MATERIALS IN ENGLISH

Finkelstein, L., *Jewish Self-Government in the Middle Ages*. See Index under "Clothes," "Clothing," "Dress."

41.

Josel of Rosheim
Germany, 1537–1547

AN important personage in medieval Jewry was the *shetadlan* (advocate). It was the duty of the *shetadlan* to intercede with the authorities to remove disabling laws or to avert impending ills. Josel of Rosheim in Alsace (d. 1554) was the most famous *shetadlan* of his age. By means of the pen, the spoken word, and a winning personality he worked for the Jews throughout the Germanic lands, using his influence with the Emperors Maximilian I (1493–1519) and Charles V (1519–1556) to protect Jewry at a time when both Protestantism and Catholicism were opposing it.

The following account tells of his attempts to persuade the rulers of Saxony and Brandenburg not to drive the Jews out of their territories. It is part of the Hebrew memoirs in which Josel has described his efforts on behalf of his fellow-Jews.

ℂIn the year 297 (1536–1537) the Elector John Frederick of Saxony was about to outlaw us and not allow the Jewish people even to set foot in his country. This was due to that priest whose name was Martin Luther—may his body and soul be bound up in hell!—who wrote and issued many heretical books in which he said that whoever would help the Jews was doomed to perdition. [The Hebrew for Luther is a pun and may be read, the "impure one." Josel in politics was pro-Catholic and looked upon Luther as a heretic.] Through his many tales Luther stirred up so much trouble between the rulers and their peoples that the Jews could hardly maintain themselves. [Luther, angry that the Jews refused to become Protestants, had by now turned against them.]

With the approval of our rabbis I was given some letters of high recommendation from certain Christian scholars, even from Strasbourg, and I set out to find the Elector in Meissen or Thuringia. [Among other letters Josel had one to Luther from Capito, the Strasbourg Protestant, but Luther refused to meet Josel or intercede for the Jews.] But I did not succeed in presenting the letters until the Elector came to Frankfort where he met with other rulers, particularly the Margrave [Joachim II] of Brandenburg who also intended to expel all his Jews. [German princes met in Frankfort in 1539 to discuss a possible peace between the Catholics and Protestants.] However, through the course of events and because of disputations which I had in the presence of Christian scholars, I succeeded in convincing the rulers, by means of our holy Torah, not to follow the views of Luther, Butzer, and his gang, with the result that the rulers even confirmed our old privileges. [Butzer, a Protestant preacher, at first a friend of the Jews, turned against them bitterly in 1538.]

In addition a miraculous piece of good luck now happened to us for it was discovered and made known to many, and particularly to the Margrave Joachim II, that all those martyred Jews who had been burnt at the stake during his father's time, in 270 (1510)—thirty-eight souls—had been burnt alive because of a lying, evil, false accusation! [In the days of Joachim I, 1499–1535, a thief falsely implicated the Brandenburg Jews in a church theft, host desecration, and a ritual murder. Thirty-eight Jews were then burnt alive in Berlin.] For the thief [Paul Fromm] had already confessed his lie, but an evil, cruel enemy, the bishop, had ordered the priest not to tell the Margrave of the thief's confession. [Bishop Jerome, said nothing to Joachim I, because Jerome and others wanted the Jews expelled.]

As a result of hearing all these things the princes changed their minds and allowed the Jews to stay in their lands. Up till now [about 1547] Joachim II has kept his word, but Saxony has gone back on its promise and has done much harm by outlawing us [1536 and 1543]. Because of this God has rewarded him amply by bringing him low. [The Elector John Frederick of Saxony was imprisoned in 1547 after his defeat by the Emperor Charles V.]

Blessed be the Lord who avenges His people.

BIBLIOGRAPHY

REFERENCES TO TEXTBOOKS

Elbogen, pp. 132ff.; Roth, pp. 235ff.

READINGS FOR ADVANCED STUDENTS

Margolis and Marx, pp. 547–548.
Lowenthal, M., *The Jews of Germany*, pp. 161–173.
JE, "Josel of Rosheim."

42.

The Shulhan Aruk
1564–1565

JEWS, throughout the Middle Ages and up to modern times, were organized along communal lines as a corporate body. Each Jewry was a separate and distinct group wherever it was found, and was recognized as such by law. The state determined its relation to Jewry as a body through a constitution which it gave the Jews; the Jews, however, in their inner life, governed themselves in accordance with Talmudic-rabbinic law. This rabbinic law, which was universally accepted by the Jews, was codified several times before it reached its most definitive and popular form in the *Shulhan Aruk*, the "Set Table" of Joseph Caro (1488–1575). This is an abbreviated form of his larger work, *Bet Yosef*, the "House of Joseph," a critical legal commentary. The *Shulhan Aruk* was first published in Venice, 1564–1565.

Caro, a Sephardic scholar who lived in the Ottoman Empire after the expulsion from Spain and died in the mystic community of Safed in Palestine, was one of the greatest rabbinic authorities of his generation. During his day Jewish religious unity was threatened by the welter of conflicting opinions in matters of observance, and it is not improbable that he hoped through his two chief legal works to bring about a unity in world Jewish practice that would hasten the advent of the Messiah. The *Shulhan Aruk* did not at once find the universal acceptance which Caro had hoped for; it met with resistance in eastern Europe and was adopted only after a struggle and after it had been modified by Moses Isserles (about 1530–1572), the famous rabbi of Cracow who added notes incorporating the religious customs of German and East European Jewry.

The *Shulhan Aruk* contains four sections. *Orah Hayyim*, the "Way of Life," deals with the religious worship of the Jew at home and in the synagogue. *Yoreh Deah*, the "Teacher of Knowledge," treats of ritual slaughter, dietary laws, forbidden practices, burial and mourning customs, and the like. *Eben Ha-Ezer*, the "Stone of Help," gives the marriage and divorce laws, and *Hoshen Ha-Mishpat*, the "Breastplate of Judgment," codifies the civil law and the court

200

procedure. Illustrations are given below from the four sections of this code which is still authoritative in the life of the Orthodox Jew.

ORAH HAYYIM: LAWS OF THE PURIM SCROLL

694. The law of Purim funds designated for the poor. Herein are four paragraphs.

    1. Every man is duty bound to give at least two gifts, to two poor people. . . .

    2. One may not divert Purim funds to any other charity, but the poor man may do whatever he wants with the money he receives.

    3. We need not investigate in giving any Purim money, but may bestow it upon any one who reaches out his hands to receive it. In places where it is the custom to give Purim money to non-Jews also, it is all right to follow the custom.

    4. Where there are no poor, one is permitted to retain one's Purim funds and then give them away wherever one wishes.

695. The laws of the Purim banquet. Herein are four paragraphs.

    2. On Purim a person should drink until he doesn't know the difference between, "Cursed be Haman," and "Blessed be Mordecai."

NOTE [by Isserles]: Some authorities say that it is not necessary to get as drunk as all that, but merely to drink more than one's normal allowance, so that he may fall asleep, and because he is asleep not know the difference between "Cursed be Haman" and "Blessed be Mordecai." It is immaterial whether one drinks a whole lot or a little, as long as his thoughts are directed to God. No one should fast on Purim except to prevent a bad dream from coming true. There are some people who are accustomed to wear their Sabbath and holiday clothes on Purim and that is a good custom. . . . Some authorities say that if a man injures his neighbor as a result of too much Purim "joy" he is free from paying damages.

2. Every man should seek to marry a worthy woman. Herein are eleven paragraphs.

    1. No man should marry a woman in whom there is any blemish.

NOTE: Any one who marries a tainted woman for the sake of money will have children who will not turn out well. But if a woman is not disqualified for a man, and if he wishes to marry her for her money, he is permitted to. . . . If a person had been promised a large sum of money at his engagement and has not received it, he must not desert his bride because of it. Nor shall one quarrel too much about his wife's property, for he who does so will not prosper, nor will his marriage be successful, for the money that a man gets with his wife does not really belong to him after all. Any man who marries for this reason is called a "fortune-hunter." However, one may accept what his father- or mother-in-law is generous enough to give him without any fear that the marriage will not prosper.

EBEN HA-EZER: LAWS OF PROPAGATION

1. The laws about propagation, and that one should not be without a wife. Herein are fourteen paragraphs.

 3. Every Jew is commanded to get married at eighteen, and he who gets married earlier is observing the commandment in the very best way. But no one ought to get married before thirteen, for this would be lust. Under no circumstances should one pass his twentieth birthday without getting married, and if a person passes his twentieth birthday and doesn't care to get married, the court shall compel him to marry in order that he may fulfill the command of propagation. However, if he is busied with the Torah and concerned about it, and is afraid to get married lest he be troubled too much about making a living, and therefore have to neglect his study of the Torah, he is permitted to delay.

NOTE: But nowadays it is not the practice to compel a man to get married.

YOREH DEAH: LAWS CONCERNING IDOLATRY

157. What are the sins which a man must not commit even if his life is at stake. Herein are three paragraphs.

 2. A Jew is forbidden to say that he is a Gentile in order to avoid being killed. But he is allowed to put on different clothes during a period of persecution in order that

they should not recognize that he is a Jew, inasmuch
as he does not say that he is a Gentile.

NOTE: . . . . To dress like a Gentile in order that one may not
be recognized as a Jew, and thus get out of paying tolls and the
like, is forbidden.

LAWS ABOUT CONVERTS

268. How to make converts, men or women, and the laws about
      the marriage of a convert. Herein are twelve paragraphs.

    2. If a man wants to become a Jew they say to him: "What
    has prompted you to come to convert yourself? Don't
    you know that Jews are now oppressed, prostrate, mis-
    treated, undergoing suffering?" If he answer: "I know,
    and I am not worthy to join you," then they accept him
    without further delay and inform him of the principles
    of Judaism, namely, the unity of God, and the prohibi-
    tion of idolatry. This they discuss with him at length.
    [Yebamot 47a. Practically all the laws of the *Shulhan
    Aruk* are of Talmudic origin.]

HOSHEN HA-MISHPAT: LAWS OF FRAUDULENT REPRESENTATION AND MISTAKES IN PURCHASES

231. One must not deceive in measure or weight. How to make
      measures and weights. How to weigh. The obligation to ap-
      point officers in charge of measures and markets. Herein are
      twenty-eight paragraphs.

    2. The courts are required to appoint officers who shall
    regularly visit the shops, and whomever they shall find
    using a deficient measure or weight or inaccurate scale
    they shall be permitted to flog and to fine, as it shall
    appear proper to the court.

LAWS OF THEFT

356. It is forbidden to buy anything from a thief. The law regard-
      ing one who buys from a known thief, or a thief who is not
      known as such. Herein are ten paragraphs.

    1. It is forbidden to buy any stolen goods from a thief,
    for such a purchase would be a great sin, inasmuch as

the purchaser thus encourages wrongdoers and incites them to further thefts, for if there were no purchaser there would be no thief.

NOTE: One is forbidden to assist a thief in any possible way.

BIBLIOGRAPHY

REFERENCES TO TEXTBOOKS

Elbogen, pp. 151ff.; Roth, pp. 261ff.; Sachar, pp. 236ff.

READINGS FOR ADVANCED STUDENTS

Graetz, IV. See Index under "Karo, Joseph"; Graetz-Rhine, IV, pp. 437ff.; Margolis and Marx, pp. 519-522, 536-537.

Waxman, M., *A History of Jewish Literature*, II, pp. 144ff.: "The *Shulhan Aruk* of Joseph Karo."

JE, "Caro, Joseph b. Ephraim"; "Isserles, Moses ben Israel"; "Law, Codification of."

ADDITIONAL SOURCE MATERIALS IN ENGLISH

There is no complete English translation of the *Shulhan Aruk*, but there is available now a very satisfactory translation of the Talmud, the basic work, of which the *Shulhan Aruk* is to a large extent an epitome. This is the Soncino Press (London) edition of *The Babylonian Talmud*.

43.

The Council of Four Lands and the Lithuanian Council
about 1582–1764

THE Jews of Poland, as a separate ethnic and religious minority, had enjoyed a large measure of self-rule since the second half of the thirteenth century. However, after the middle of the sixteenth century, the Polish kings encouraged the organization of their Jews into groups even more compact, primarily because it became easier for the rulers to collect the taxes due from their Jewish subjects. Polish Jewry was from that time on ruled by a group of laymen and rabbis who were called the *Waad arba arazot*, the "Council of Four Lands." The four lands were Great Poland, Little Poland, Red Russia (East Galicia and Podolia), and Volhynia. Lithuania, originally a part of the Council, had its own central organization beginning with 1623.

The Council of Four Lands had a great deal of influence: it governed the economic life of the Jews, protected Polish Jewry at the court of the king and in the Polish parliament, collected the taxes due the state, regulated religious observances, organized courts, and itself sat as a court of last appeal. In short, it controlled practically every phase of the fiscal, economic, administrative, religious, cultural, social, and spiritual life of the greatest Jewish community in the world. It was practically a Jewish state in Poland.

In the eighteenth century as Poland declined, the Council declined with it and fell heavily into debt. It was abolished in 1764 both in Poland and in Lithuania by the Polish parliament which then hoped by direct taxation to increase its income from its Jewish citizens.

The first account following is taken from *Yewen mezulah* ("The miry depth"), a contemporary Hebrew account of Polish Jewish life and suffering in the first half of the seventeenth century. The author is Nathan Hannover, a Polish rabbi who was killed in 1683. His glowing account of Jewish communal life in Poland is not without a touch of exaggeration.

The second selection deals with the bankruptcy laws of the Council of Four Lands; the third includes a series of laws of the independent Lithuanian Council. All these laws were originally promulgated in Hebrew.

1. Philanthropy and Justice among Polish Jews, about 1648

❡And now I shall begin to describe the organization of Polish Jewish life which was entirely of a righteous, upright, proper, and enduring character.

It is said in the treatise on the *Fathers* [the Mishnaic ethical tractate Abot 1:2, 18]: Simon the Just was one of the last survivors of the Great Synagogue. He used to say: "Upon three things the world is based; upon the Torah, upon the religious service, and upon the practice of charity." Rabban Simon ben Gamliel used to say: "By three things is the world preserved; by justice, by truth, and by peace." All these six pillars upon which the world stands were found in the land of Poland. . . .

THE PILLAR OF CHARITY

There was no limit to the practice of charity in the land of Poland. First, as to the sheltering of strangers. If a scholar or a preacher, a guest, should happen to come even to a community where they issue meal and lodging tickets for strangers, he would not have to degrade himself by accepting a ticket but could go to some officer of the community and stay wherever he liked. [The system of ticket-relief did away with the humiliation of begging. But a scholar was spared even the need for tickets.] Then the beadle of the community would come and get his credentials and show them to the treasurer or to the executive officer in charge that month. They then would give him a gift—whatever they thought proper—and would respectfully send it to him through the beadle, and he would then lodge with some citizen as long as he wished.

With other wayfarers who received tickets it was thus: they would be given a note and could lodge with a householder—whose turn it now was—as many days as they wished. At the very least, every order was good for three days. They would give them eat and drink, evening, morning, and afternoon, and when they were about to continue on their way they would provide them with food for the journey and send them on from town to town by horse and wagon.

If young students or lads or householders or girls came from other towns or distant lands, they would at once clothe them. He who wanted to learn a trade would be turned over to a master-workman and he who wanted to do domestic service would be given housework to do. [A large proportion of the Polish craftsmen were Jews.] If a person wanted to study, they would hire a teacher to instruct him, and afterwards, when he had become a worthwhile student, some rich man would take him into his home, give him his daughter to wife along with many thousands of gold pieces as a dowry, and would dress him royally. And who, if not the rabbinical students, are to be regarded as royalty? Then, even after the marriage, he would be sent away from home to study in the great academies. After two or three years, when he returned to his home, his father-in-law would maintain a school for him in his own house and would spend money lavishly that distinguished scholars might come there for years until he also was appointed president of an academy in some community.

And even if the young man was not at first a good student but had an apt mind for learning so that there was a prospect of his developing as a scholar if he studied, some rich man with a young daughter would occasionally turn up and give him food and drink and clothes and all that he needed, as he would for his own son, and hire a teacher for him until he had become a worthwhile student. Then he would give him his daughter to wife as I have described above. There is no finer practice of charity than this.

There were, likewise, some very fine laws providing for the poor girls in every province, and no girl, no matter how needy she was, ever reached her eighteenth year without being married off. Many pious women busied themselves with this good work. May God give them their reward and have mercy on the remnant of Israel!

THE PILLAR OF JUSTICE

Justice obtained in Poland just as in Jerusalem before the destruction of the Temple. There were courts in every town, and if people did not care to try their case before the court of their own town they could go to a nearby court. And if they did not care to try their case before a nearby court, they could go to a superior court, for in every province there was a higher court, as for example, the highest court for the Ukraine and Volhynia was in the metropolis, Ostrog, just as the capital city, Lemberg, was the seat of the chief court for the province of Red Russia. And so there were many other large communities and each one of them served as the seat of the chief court for its district.

If, however, different communities, through their leaders, would start litigation among themselves, in order to try their case they would have to appear before the leaders of the Four Lands—may their Rock and Redeemer guard them—who met twice a year. This was an assembly which included one official picked from among the leaders of every town. They, in turn, were joined by six outstanding rabbinical scholars of Poland, and all these together were known as the Council of Four Lands. They used to hold sessions annually at the Lublin fair between Purim and Passover, and at the Yaroslav fair in the month of Ab or Ellul. [Thus they met in the early spring and in the late summer at the fairs where thousands of Jews gathered.]

The leaders of the Four Lands were just like the Sanhedrin [of old which met in the Temple] in the Hewn Chamber for they had the power to judge every Jew in the kingdom of Poland: to issue prohibitions, to enact ordinances, and to punish people as they saw fit. Every difficult case was brought to them and they decided it. In order to lighten their task, the leaders of the Four Lands would choose judges from the various provinces and these men were called Provincial Judges. All civil cases would come before these Provincial Judges, but cases that involved fines, the priority of possession, and other difficult matters were tried by the leaders of the Four Lands themselves—may their Rock and Redeemer guard them. The law suit of a Jew would never come before Gentile judges, nor before the court of any magnate, nor before the king himself—may his glory be exalted. [The Jews, like the nobles and the burghers, insisted on the right to their own courts.] If, however, a Jew should attempt to try his case before the judges of the Gentile courts, he would be severely reproached for he made it appear that [Deuteronomy 32:31] "our enemies are our judges."

ii. *Bankruptcy Laws of the Council of Four Lands, Lublin, February —March 1624*

⟨The following are the ordinances of the leaders of the Four Lands —may their Rock and Redeemer guard them—with reference to bankrupts. [Bankruptcies were frequent: the Gentile merchant guilds made it difficult for Jews to make a living.]

1. If a bankrupt debtor should offer to make a settlement for his debts with his creditors, then the ban is to be published against him and for a whole year he is to be considered under the ban and unfit to offer testimony and to take an oath. [This severe law purposed to make bankrupts disgorge hidden resources.] He is to be imprisoned for a whole year and shall not be appointed to any office for any religious work. If he already has an office he is to be removed from it, and he shall not be called up to the Torah

for a whole year [or] until he repay all his notes to his creditors.

2.   No man is allowed to do any business with such bankrupts, and if he violates this injunction he will injure only himself, for he will himself lose the right of legal action against the bankrupt with whom he is involved.

3.   The creditors may take away all the clothes which the bankrupt has made for his wife within the year that he became a bankrupt. The bankrupt shall also lose the rights of citizenship in the Jewish community. [This would probably limit his right to remain in the city and do business there.]

4.   Even if some creditor should make a concession to a bankrupt, and even if he had shaken hands on it, the creditor is always able later to sue him and, through the courts, get back the money conceded. The handshake shall always be regarded as having been void from the very start, on the ground that the court has the right to declare void any such concession.

5.   When the ban is pronounced in the synagogue against bankrupts, the man's wife and children must be present in the synagogue at the moment when the ban is pronounced. [The fear of such an ordeal would tend to lessen bankruptcies.]

6.   Wherever the leaders of any community will not carry out these above mentioned ordinances with reference to bankrupts, they shall be condemned to pay a fine of two hundred ducats which will not be remitted and will be used for the ransom of captives. They will also be compelled to pay that debt [of the bankrupt].

III. *Laws of the Lithuanian Council Governing Tax Collections and Recourse to Courts, September 4, 1623*

⊄The chiefs, the leaders of every community, shall appoint two men in their towns who shall busy themselves with the collection of the "poll" tax [a sum paid by the Jewish people as a whole to the state], the taxes for the support of the corporate Jewish organization, and the *powrotne* [another state] tax, in order that everything being prepared and ready on time, no injury—God forbid —should accrue to the Jewish government. These men shall have the power and authority in matters of taxation to punish, and to confiscate, attach, and seize goods as pledge without the least interference on the part of any communal chief or leader. But if these two men should be lax in the collections they will be held responsible for all injuries that may happen to the Jewish government.

A Jew who entertains the thought of summoning a Gentile before the King's Court, or before the High Criminal Court, or before the local courts, or before the district courts, shall do nothing until he first presents his problems to the leaders of his city. And similarly when Gentiles summon him before the King's Court or before the High Criminal Court, he must first come to the officers of his community and pay attention to all that they will command him. [This action was motivated by the desire of the Jewish authorities to maintain peaceful relations with the Gentiles.]

Laws Dealing with Sabbath Buying and Jewish Farmers, August 22, 1628

In all places where there is market day on the Sabbath the nearest Jewish court shall take care to warn Jews and to keep them from violating the prohibition to buy on the Sabbath. It shall teach them that which is allowed and that which is forbidden, so that they shall not profane the Sabbath, and it shall punish publicly those who thereby desecrate and violate the Sabbath.

Those who control estates: villages or hamlets, shall appear before the rabbinical authority of the nearest Jewish court to get instruction as to what work is forbidden on the Sabbath in order not to sin. [The law refers to Jews who owned or leased farms or estates.] They shall also get instruction in the matter of castration of their cattle and fowls, the raising of hogs, the distilling of brandy on the Sabbath, and in similar matters and laws. They must secure a rule of guidance from a rabbinic authority as to how they shall conduct themselves, under penalty of one hundred ducats to be given to charity, to say nothing of additional punishments and prosecution.

A Law Governing the Work of Gentile Farm Hands on the Jewish Sabbath, August 29, 1632

If a man holds an estate and requires ploughing, sowing, harvesting, and other types of labor several days a week from the Gentiles who live in his villages and hamlets, he must be very careful to substitute some other day of the week for the Sabbath so that these Gentiles will not work on the Jewish rest day. If, however, he has Gentile laborers from his villages and towns who are employed permanently, by the week, without any interruption, then he must go to the nearest Jewish judge to get instruction as to how he shall proceed and what he shall do, and shall receive a rule of guidance from him.

BIBLIOGRAPHY

REFERENCES TO TEXTBOOKS

Elbogen, pp. 136–139; Roth, pp. 264–272, 305–307; Sachar, pp. 223–225, 240–241.

READINGS FOR ADVANCED STUDENTS

Graetz, IV, pp. 631–649, V, pp. 1–17; Graetz-Rhine, V, pp. 1–37, 82–96; Margolis and Marx, pp. 532–546, 551–557.

Dubnow, S. M., *History of the Jews in Russia and Poland*, I, Chap. iv, "The Inner Life of Polish Jewry at Its Zenith"; Chap. v, "The Autonomous Center in Poland during Its Decline (1648–1772)"; Chap. vi, "The Inner Life of Polish Jewry during the Period of Decline."

Karpeles, G., *Jewish Literature and Other Essays*, pp. 272–292, "A Jewish King in Poland." A legend that throws light on Polish governmental anarchy in the sixteenth century.

JE, "Council of Four Lands"; "Lithuania"; "Russia."

ADDITIONAL SOURCE MATERIALS IN ENGLISH

Finkelstein, L., *Jewish Self-Government in the Middle Ages*. Contains national communal statutes. See pp. 257–264, 348–375, etc.

44.

The Constitution of the
Jewish Community of Sugenheim Town
Franconia, 1756

IN 1756, Frederick the Great promulgated his famous *Reglement* or constitution for Prussian Jewry. That same year, two imperial barons in an obscure village in Franconia signed a constitution for the Jews of their *Judengasse*. The Frederician document concerns itself with a Jewry numbering thousands of souls; the Sugenheim document concerns itself with a tiny community of twelve householders, all told.

The Sugenheim constitution was granted by the local barons who wanted to regulate the life of the Jewish subjects, keep them from quarreling with one another, and help them conduct themselves decorously in their new synagogue which had just been built (1755).

Here we have the simplest type of communal organization: an executive committee of three has almost complete authority. There were two communal heads (*parnasim*) and a treasurer (*hekdesh gabbai*). The two *parnasim* represented the two groups of Jews of the two jointly ruling barons. Each baron had six Jewish families. The only paid synagogal or communal official was the cantor who was spiritual leader, teacher, ritual meat slaughterer, *Schulklopfer*, *hôtelier*, and cantor. The group was too small to support a rabbi. The Jews were not rich, but made a comfortable living trading with the neighboring farmers and gentry.

This charter, originally in German, gives us an authentic, unvarnished picture of a typical south German Jewish community in pre-emancipation days. We learn not only of their quarrels and factions, but also of their simple living, their fine philanthropy, and their sturdy religiosity.

⟪Inasmuch as the Jews here in our town of Sugenheim are not yet provided with a fixed code of laws—as a result of which much quarreling and confusion have developed among them and both of the local lords have been annoyed several times—therefore both of the jointly ruling lords (namely, the Right Honorable Imperial-Immediate Baron, Sir Christoph Friedrich, Baron of Seckendorff,

Lord of Sugenheim Town. . . . and also the Right Honorable Imperial-Immediate Baron, Sir Christoph Wolfgang Philipp, Baron of Seckendorff, Lord of Sugenheim Town) have deigned to confer the present communal constitution on the local Jewish community. They are to be guided by it in their conduct of their synagogal and other Jewish ceremonies in their newly-built communal synagogue, and in the punishment, according to circumstances, of the malicious and the stubborn. As follows:

I. SYNAGOGUE WILL BE HELD ON MONDAYS AND THURSDAYS

Inasmuch as one must go to the synagogue on Mondays and Thursdays, every one who remains at home on such days and does not go to the synagogue must pay a fine of one *Kreuzer* to the Jewish treasury. [On Monday and Thursday the Torah is also read.]

II. THE PUNISHMENT IF ONE DOES NOT COME TO THE SYNAGOGUE ON THE MINOR DAY OF ATONEMENT

If a member of the community does not come to the synagogue on the Minor Day of Atonement [the day before New Moon], and cannot prove either that he was dispatched somewhere by our gracious master, or that he had some other business duties outside of town which could not be postponed, then he shall either be fined a quarter of a pound of wax for the benefit of the communal treasury, or he shall not be called up [to the Torah reading] for a month. [The wax was used for synagogue candles.]

III. THE CANTOR SHALL CALL [PEOPLE] TO THE SYNAGOGUE REGULARLY

Whenever there is to be a religious service the cantor shall call people to the synagogue regularly so that no one may excuse himself because of ignorance. If, however, the cantor forgets this and does not call people on the appointed days, he is to be fined ten *Kreuzer* the first time, and if he blunders frequently he is to be fined fifteen to twenty *Kreuzer*, or mayhap even dismissed.

IV. THE PUNISHMENT FOR ONE WHO INDULGES IN IDLE TALK IN THE SYNAGOGUE

No householder shall gossip in the synagogue. From [the prayer at the beginning of the morning service] "Blessed be He who hath said" to the "Eighteen Benedictions" [toward the end], he shall not speak a word with anyone but shall recite his prayers in reverence. After the "Eighteen Benedictions" one may speak when absolutely necessary, but idle talk is forbidden under threat of a fine of a quarter of a pound of wax for the Jewish treasury.

V. NO HOUSEHOLDER IS TO LEAD IN PRAYER ON THE HIGH HOLIDAYS

No householder is to lead in prayer on the High Holidays [New Year's Day and the Day of Atonement]. A cantor is to conduct the services unless the entire community is content to use a lay leader.

VI. PENALTY FOR WRANGLING IN THE SYNAGOGUE

He who wrangles with another in the synagogue and acts abusefully and shamefully must pay a fine of twenty *Kreuzer,* half of which goes to the civil authorities and the other half to the Jewish communal treasury.

VII. PENALTY FOR QUARRELING, FIGHTING, AND STRIKING ONE ANOTHER IN THE SYNAGOGUE

If, however, anyone should quarrel with, fight, or strike someone in the synagogue, he is without fail to be fined a florin, half of which is to go to the civil authorities, and half to the Jewish treasury. If the two communal leaders and the treasurer should ignore the matter, for reasons of personal friendship, then each one of them is to be fined a pound of wax should the other householders report their partiality.

VIII. CALLING PEOPLE TO THE TORAH IN THE SYNAGOGUE

On Mondays and Thursdays, two Levites and one Israelite; on Saturday, however, three Levites and three Israelites are to be called to the Torah, according to rank, one after another. [Jews were called to the reading of the Torah in the following order on the basis of descent: Cohen ("priest"), Levite, and other Israelites.] But on *Rosh Hashanah, Yom-Kippur,* and on the first and last days of *Sukkot, Pesah,* and *Shabuot,* every one is called to the Torah: a Levite is called up each time together with an Israelite. The normal order in summoning people to the Torah is disregarded.

IX. CONCERNING THE CALLING OF NEW RESIDENTS TO THE TORAH

When a new resident comes to our town, he is called up last after the other householders, since he is the most recent arrival.

If a man should treat another shamefully while calling him to the Torah, or in connection with his being called to the Torah, he is to be fined a quarter of a pound of wax which is to go to the Jewish treasury. If, however, there should be any act of violence, then the punishment is to be meted out as prescribed in Article VII. [The fines meted out were a not inconsiderable source of income to both the Jewish and general community.]

X. CONCERNING THE CALLING OF GUESTS TO THE TORAH

If a wayfarer or guest happens to be in the synagogue and, as a courtesy, is called to the Torah with the result that a householder is left out, then that householder has the right to be called up at the next week-day or Sabbath service. [Jews were jealous of the privilege of reading the weekly Pentateuchal portion.]

XI. CALLING ONE TO THE TORAH BECAUSE OF MARRIAGE, SPECIAL RELIGIOUS SERVICES, ETC.

If a person becomes *bar mizwah* [at thirteen one becomes a full Jew, a "man of duty"] or becomes engaged, or is given a party on a Sabbath by his fiancée, or becomes a godfather, or has a circumcision feast, or if his wife rises from childbed, then he has the right on that Sabbath or holiday to be called to the Torah.

XII. WHAT ONE [CALLED TO THE TORAH] MUST CONTRIBUTE TO THE JEWISH TREASURY

Since no one is to have this honor for nothing, he is to have the officiant recite some blessings for which he is to pledge a gift for the upkeep of the synagogal buildings, namely, a quarter of a pound of wax which he is to pay immediately after the Sabbath. Similarly, the man who helps preside at the service is to be called to the Torah only on the weekday and on the Sabbath after he relinquishes office, under threat of the ban. [This ban amounted to exclusion from synagogal activities.] However, as long as he is a functionary in the service, he must not call himself to the Torah unless he has received permission from the entire community.

XIII. CONCERNING THE PURCHASE OF SYNAGOGAL HONORS

The first bid for a synagogal honor must be two *Pfennig* and then raised by the householders. He who offers most gets it, and whatever he offers for it must be paid, if the bid is made in the presence of the entire community. He, however, who does not pay can be banned by the two communal leaders and the communal treasurer. That communal honor which one buys on *Simhat Torah* for an entire year [such as supplying wine gratis for the service] must be paid for within six weeks under threat of the ban.

XIV. THE FINE FOR WRANGLING ABOUT BOOKSTANDS

If a couple of congregants quarrel over a bookstand or, even more, engage in fisticuffs, each one is to be fined a florin, half of which is to go to the civil authorities, and half to the Jews. The men who have quarreled are to move to the back of the synagogue, opposite one another, and there be kept for a year. [The bookstands in the synagogue were assigned according to rank. These individual, portable reading desks were a frequent cause of strife.]

XV. THE FINE FOR MOVING BOOKSTANDS

He who dares maliciously to move another's bookstand and to get in the way of a man who takes the [usual] three steps backward [at the finish of the "Eighteen Benedictions"] has to pay a fine of a quarter of a pound [of wax], to prevent disorder from occurring in the synagogue, but on the contrary everything should move along quietly and decorously. If, however, the fine does not serve as a warning to a turbulent congregant who continues in his malice in spite of it, then he is to be banned.

XVI. CONCERNING THE FEES FOR BECOMING A MEMBER OF THE JEWISH COMMUNITY

Every newcomer who moves in after the building of the local synagogue or will in the future receive the protection [of the civil authorities] must give eighteen Rhenish florins as "entry money," laying it down in cash. A local Jewish young man [who seeks communal rights] must pay four florins; a local Jewish young woman, eight florins. Money so procured will be used for the benefit of the community.

XVII. CONCERNING THE COMMUNAL TREASURER

A different person is to serve as communal treasurer every year and is to take his turn in accordance with his rank. He is also to be free from rendering a formal account of what he receives and what he disburses, inasmuch as one householder has confidence in the other that in this matter every one will act in accordance with his Jewish conscience and will not defraud the treasury.

THE AUTHORITY OF THE COMMUNAL CHIEFS AND THE COMMUNAL TREASURER

This communal treasurer shall have the power, together with the two communal chiefs, jointly to impose the ban as well as the fines contained in this communal constitution. They may also be assured of the aid of the civil authorities against the unruly.

XVIII.

In turn the [two] communal leaders must help the treasurer, as far as possible, in the collection of the moneys, and not allow the arrears to pile up. Indeed, the refractory are to be banned to compel them, in this or some other permissible fashion, to pay the treasury.

XIX. THE HIRING OF A CANTOR

The majority of the votes of the Jewish residents of the town and of those who have children to teach shall decide in the hiring of the cantor. However, they must select an able person, one who can serve well as the schoolmaster and understands ritual slaughtering thoroughly. He must also be able to account for his origin and for his conduct in the past by means of the proper documents. [Communities frequently had sad experiences with scamps.]

XX. THE WAGES OF A CANTOR AND THE TEACHING OF THE CHILDREN

The cantor's wages are to be made up of three parts, namely, one-third [to be paid] by the pupils, one-third by taxation [of wealth], and one-third [a fixed sum for all] by the family heads. He is required to teach a lad till he is thirteen, a girl till she is eleven. One studying the Five Books of Moses is to be taught one hour a day; a child studying the prayer book, one half-hour daily; and one learning the alphabet, a quarter of an hour daily.

XXI. PAYING THE CANTOR

Every householder living here, if he has a child, is expected to contribute as much to the cantor as he would if he sent a child to
school to begin its studies. This applies even to those who have
children too young to begin their studies.

XXII. DISCHARGING A CANTOR

A cantor is not to be discharged immediately at the request of a few
householders who dislike him. Inasmuch as the cantor is selected
by the majority vote of the Jews who live in the place and of those
who send their children to school, he is, therefore, to be discharged
only by these groups.

XXIII.

The local Jewry has come to an understanding, the fifth of September of this year, with respect to the taxation that:

Eyssig agrees to pay the taxes on........	2600 florins,
Jacob Callmann, on.....................	3000
Meyer Jacob, on.......................	1800
Gump, on	900
Löw, on	1400
Lässar, on	600
Beerlein Callmann, on.................	900
Simon Göz, on	200
Nathan Lazarus, on	400
Nathan Salomon, on	100
Joseph, on	150
Hirsch, on	350

This arrangement is to last for a three year period. However, if
a legacy should fall to one or the other in the intervening period he
is to be assessed again. On the other hand what one gains through
trade in such a three-year period is not to be included in the funds
to be taxed. The civil authorities have acquiesced in this agreement.

XXIV. MAZZAH FLOUR

Inasmuch as the expenses, which rise from the milling of the *mazzah*
flour and the cleansing of the mill, have up till now not been met
[by the levy] on the amount milled, for one has been expected to
pay only as much as his neighbor [no matter how much flour was

milled]: therefore this unjust procedure has been changed so that in the future the expenses are to be met in accordance with the amount of work done.

XXV. CONTRIBUTIONS TO THE SYNAGOGUE

The amount necessary to support the synagogue in the future will be met, half by taxation of wealth and half by [equal payments by individual] families.

XXVI. MEAL TICKETS FOR WAYFARERS

Inasmuch as wayfarers are not allowed to travel on the festivals and holidays they are to be given additional meal tickets on these days. If any of the wayfarers are ill and cannot be sent on, they are to be lodged with the cantor. The food, however, is to be supplied every day by a different householder who may then credit himself with a meal ticket. [Each resident was expected to supply a number of meals to wayfarers.]

BURIAL OF WAYFARERS

If such a wayfarer should die and have no means to provide for his burial, the expense is to be borne by the communal treasury.

XXVII. REPARTITION OF THE MEAL TICKETS

The meal tickets are to be levied [as follows]: eight for every family head and two for every hundred florins capital. Since [in levying meal tickets] only half a man's wealth is assessed, the communal chiefs and the treasurer are responsible that the proper number of tickets is assigned. However, the cantor is to apportion them properly and impartially so that the poorer [citizens of the town] do not have too heavy a burden and the richer do not have too few [meals to supply]. Whenever it shall be proved that the cantor has done wrong [in favoring the rich against the poor in assigning meal orders] he shall be fined a pound of wax for the communal treasury. [The town's twelve Jewish families were to give 220 free meals a year. The burden of this philanthropy would, of course, fall on the richer Jews of the community. A similar statute of the community of County Wied-Runkel warned the Jewish authorities against exploiting the poorer citizens in apportioning meal orders.]

XXVIII. PURIM

No one shall dare mask himself or run around in clown's garb or with candles and torches on Purim under penalty of a florin to be paid the civil authorities. [Such hilarity often ended in a row.]

SIMHAT TORAH

And on *Simhat Torah* the Jews and Jewesses shall stop their sport of throwing [fruits and candies to the parading children] under pain of penalty of a quarter pound of wax to the Jewish treasury and a half a florin to the civil authorities.

XXIX. BUSINESS ON SUNDAY AND HOLIDAYS

Under threat of a fine of a florin to the civil authorities no Jew shall presume, on the Christian Sunday, festivals, or holidays (either before or after divine services), to run into the house of a Christian or to watch for him on the street and to induce him to do business under the pretext that he will make a good profit. On the contrary, just as the Jews rest on their Sabbath even so shall they allow the Christians to observe their Sunday and holidays quietly.

XXX. PRAYER IN THE SYNAGOGUE FOR THE CIVIL AUTHORITIES

Inasmuch as it is the duty and obligation of every subject to pray for the civil authorities, therefore the local Jewry, as a whole, shall offer prayers in their synagogue for both of the honorable lords [of Sugenheim] and, to be sure, according to the religious formula approved by the gracious rulers.

XXXI. THE PENALTY FOR THE UNRULY

If any individual shall venture to oppose these regulations he shall be specially cautioned and warned against punishment by the communal chiefs and the treasurer. If he nevertheless does not obey he is at once to be placed under the ban.

XXXII. THE PUBLICATION OF THIS COMMUNAL CONSTITUTION

In order that no householder may be able to excuse himself through ignorance, the communal chiefs shall have the cantor read this communal constitution to all the householders, publicly, word for word, in the synagogue, right now and then every year at Pentecost and relate its entire contents exactly and without deviation.

In witness whereof and for further authentication, the honorable, gracious, baronial rulers have graciously deigned to confirm this communal constitution with their esteemed signature in their own hand and with the impression of their hereditary baronial seal.

Sugenheim Town, the 30th of December, in the year 1756.

Signed: CHRISTOPH FRIEDRICH
Baron of Seckendorff
[SEAL]

Signed: CHRISTOPH WOLFFGANG PHILIPP
Baron of Seckendorff
[SEAL]

BIBLIOGRAPHY

READINGS FOR ADVANCED STUDENTS

Abrahams, I., *Jewish Life in the Middle Ages*, 1932, Chap. i, "The Centre of Social Life"; Chap. ii, "Life in the Synagogue"; Chap. iii, "Communal Organization."

ADDITIONAL SOURCE MATERIALS IN ENGLISH

El libro de los acuerdos. Being the Records and Accompts of the Spanish and Portuguese Synagogue of London from 1663 to 1681. Translated. . . . by L. D. Barnet. This work includes the seventeenth century constitution of the Sephardic Jewish community of London.

Margoliouth, M., *The History of the Jews in Great Britain*, III, pp. 234ff.: "Translation of the Enactments of the Sacred Congregation of the Great Synagogue of London." This is a detailed congregational constitution of English Ashkenazic Jews of the pre-emancipation period.

Jewry and the Individual Jew

B. JEWISH SECTS, MYSTICS, AND MESSIAHS

45.

The Messiah in Crete
about 431

FROM pre-Christian days and even down to the present the Jewish people have looked forward to the coming of a Messiah of the house of David—a Messiah who would redeem the Jews from their suffering and lead them in glory back to a new Palestine. Almost every century has brought forward would-be saviors, some undoubtedly sincere, who, tragically enough, brought only disappointment and disillusionment to expectant masses.

The false Messiah described below is one of the first known in the Diaspora. He appeared in the island of Crete about 431 and found acceptance, possibly under the influence of a Talmudic computation (Sanhedrin 97b) that the Son of David would come about the year 440. His career is described in the Greek *Ecclesiastical History* of Socrates Scholasticus, whose book covers church and general history from 305 C.E. to 439 C.E. Socrates, a native of Constantinople, and a contemporary of the events which he describes, died about 440.

⟨About this period a great number of Jews who dwelt in Crete were converted to Christianity through the following disastrous circumstance. A certain Jewish impostor pretended that he was Moses, and had been sent from heaven to lead out the Jews inhabiting that island, and conduct them through the sea: for he said that he was the same person who formerly preserved the Israelites by leading them through the Red Sea. During a whole year therefore he perambulated the several cities of the island and persuaded the Jews to believe such assurances. He moreover bid them renounce their money and other property, pledging himself to guide them through a dry sea into the land of promise. Deluded by such expectations, they neglected business of every kind, despising what they possessed, and permitting any one who chose to take it. [In the Messianic era everything would be plentiful; money would not be needed.]

When the day appointed by this deceiver for their departure had arrived, he himself took the lead, and all followed with their wives

225

and children. He led them therefore until they reached a promontory that overhung the sea, from which he ordered them to fling themselves headlong into it. Those who came first to the precipice did so, and were immediately destroyed, some of them being dashed in pieces against the rocks, and some drowned in the waters. And more would have perished, had not the providence of God led some fishermen and merchants who were Christians to be present. These persons drew out and saved some that were almost drowned, who then in their perilous situation became sensible of the madness of their conduct. The rest they hindered from casting themselves down by telling them of the destruction of those who had taken the first leap.

When at length the Jews perceived how fearfully they had been duped, they blamed first of all their own indiscreet credulity, and then sought to lay hold of the pseudo-Moses in order to put him to death. But they were unable to seize him, for he suddenly disappeared: which induced a general belief that it was some malignant fiend, who had assumed a human form for the destruction of their nation in that place. In consequence of this experience many of the Jews in Crete at that time, abandoning Judaism, attached themselves to the Christian faith.

BIBLIOGRAPHY

READINGS FOR ADVANCED STUDENTS

Greenstone, J. H., *The Messiah Idea in Jewish History*, Chap. iii, "The Talmudic Period."
Silver, A. H., *A History of Messianic Speculation in Israel*, Chap. i, "The Talmudic Period."
Encyclopaedia of Religion and Ethics, "Messiahs (Pseudo-)."
JE, "Pseudo-Messiahs."

46.

The Medieval Jewish Kingdom of the Chazars
740-1259

ABOUT the year 740, many of the Chazars, a powerful Turkish tribe occupying the steppes of southern Russia, became converts to Judaism. More than two centuries later, the report of the existence of this Jewish kingdom aroused the curiosity of Hasdai ibn Shaprut (about 915-970). Ibn Shaprut was not only the personal physician of the Spanish Califs Abd-al-Rahman III (912-961) and his son Hakam II (961-976) but was also inspector-general of customs and an adviser in foreign affairs. To satisfy his curiosity he wrote to the ruler of the Chazars about 960 and some time later received an answer from Joseph, the reigning king. The letters of Hasdai and Joseph, both originally written in Hebrew, are given below in extract.

Fragments of the Chazar kingdom persisted into the thirteenth century.

I. THE LETTER OF RABBI HASDAI, SON OF ISAAC IBN SHAPRUT, TO THE KING OF THE CHAZARS, *about 960*

⟪I, Hasdai, son of Isaac, son of Ezra, belonging to the exiled Jews of Jerusalem in Spain, a servant of my lord the King, bow to the earth before him and prostrate myself towards the abode of your Majesty from a distant land. I rejoice in your tranquility and magnificence and stretch forth my hands to God in heaven that He may prolong your reign in Israel. . . .

Praise be to the beneficent God for His mercy towards me! Kings of the earth, to whom his [Abd-al-Rahman's] magnificence and power are known, bring gifts to him, conciliating his favor by costly presents, such as the King of the Franks, the King of the Gebalim, who are Germans, the King of Constantinople, and others. All their gifts pass through my hands, and I am charged with making gifts in return. [Ibn Shaprut, who knew several languages, received these embassies.] Let my lips express praise to the God of heaven, who so far extends His lovingkindness towards me, without any merit of my own, but in the fullness of His mercies!

I always ask the ambassadors of these monarchs who bring gifts, about our brethren the Israelites, the remnant of the captivity, whether they have heard anything concerning the deliverance of those who have languished in bondage and have found no rest. [He was anxious to know if the "lost ten tribes" existed as an independent Jewish state anywhere.]

At length mercantile emissaries of Khorasan [a land southeast of the Caspian Sea] told me that there is a kingdom of Jews which is called Al-Chazar. But I did not believe these words for I thought that they told me such things to procure my goodwill and favor. I was therefore wondering, till the ambassadors of Constantinople came [between 944 and 949] with presents and a letter from their king to our king, and I interrogated them concerning this matter.

They answered me: "It is quite true, and the name of that kingdom is Al-Chazar. It is a fifteen days' journey by sea from Constantinople, but by land many nations intervene between us; the name of the king now reigning is Joseph; ships sometimes come from their country to ours bringing fish, skins, and wares of every kind. [The Chazars, great traders, got their wares from the Russians to the north.] The men are our confederates and are honored by us; there is communication between us by embassies and mutual gifts; they are very powerful; they maintain numerous armies with which they occasionally engage in expeditions." When I heard this report I was encouraged, my hands were strengthened, and my hope was confirmed. Thereupon I bowed down and adored the God of heaven. [Hasdai was happy: Christians could no longer say the Jews were without a country as a punishment for their rejection of Jesus.]. . . .

I pray for the health of my lord the King, of his family, and of his house, and that his throne may be established for ever. Let his days and his sons' days be prolonged in the midst of Israel!

II. THE LETTER OF JOSEPH THE KING, SON OF AARON THE KING, THE TURK
—MAY HIS CREATOR PRESERVE HIM—TO THE HEAD OF THE AS-
SEMBLY, HASDAI, THE SON OF ISAAC, SON OF EZRA—*about 960*

℃. . . .I wish to inform you that your beautifully phrased letter was given us by Isaac, son of Eliezer, a Jew of the land of Germany. [Isaac carried it through Germany, Hungary, and Russia to Chazaria.] You made us happy and we are delighted with your understanding and wisdom. . . . Let us, therefore, renew the diplomatic relations that once obtained between our fathers, and let us transmit this heritage to our children. [Joseph believed the Chazars had once had diplomatic relations with the Spanish Arabs.]

You ask us also in your epistle: "Of what people, of what family, and of what tribe are you?" Know that we are descended from Japhet, through his son Togarmah. [In Jewish literature Togarmah is the father of all the Turks.] I have found in the genealogical books of my ancestors that Togarmah had ten sons. These are their names: the eldest was Ujur, the second Tauris, the third Avar, the fourth Uguz, the fifth Bizal, the sixth Tarna, the seventh Chazar, the eighth Janur, the ninth Bulgar, the tenth Sawir. [These are the mythical founders of tribes that once lived in the neighborhood of the Black and Caspian Seas.] I am a descendant of Chazar, the seventh son.

I have a record that although our fathers were few in number, the Holy One blessed be He, gave them strength, power, and might so that they were able to carry on war after war with many nations who were more powerful and numerous than they. By the help of God they drove them out and took possession of their country. Upon some of them they have imposed forced labor even to this very day. The land [along the Volga] in which I now live was formerly occupied by the Bulgarians. Our ancestors, the Chazars, came and fought with them, and, although these Bulgarians were as numerous as the sand on the shores of the sea, they could not withstand the Chazars. So they left their country and fled while the Chazars pursued them as far as the Danube River. Up to this very day the Bulgars camp along the Danube and are close to Constantinople. The Chazars have occupied their land up till now. [The Chazars, known since the second century, dominated southern Russia during the early Middle Ages.]

After this, several generations passed until a certain King arose whose name was Bulan. He was a wise and God-fearing man, trusting in his Creator with all his heart. He expelled the wizards and idolators from the land and took refuge in the shadow of His wings. . . . After this his fame was spread broadcast. [Bulan probably ruled about 740. He was the first Jewish Chazar ruler.] The kings of the Byzantines and the Arabs who had heard of him sent their envoys and ambassadors with great riches and many great presents to the King as well as some of their wise men with the object of converting him to their own religion. [The Byzantines and Arabs hoped to stop the raids of the Chazars by converting them.]

But the King—may his soul be bound up in the bundle of life with the Lord his God—being wise, sent for a learned Israelite. The King searched, inquired, and investigated carefully and brought the sages together that they might argue about their respective religions. Each of them refuted, however, the arguments of his opponent so that they could not agree. When the King saw this he said to them: "Go home, but return to me on the third day. . . ."

On the third day he called all the sages together and said to them: "Speak and argue with one another and make clear to me which is the best religion." They began to dispute with one another without arriving at any results until the King said to the Christian priest: "What do you think? Of the religion of the Jews and the Moslems which is to be preferred?" The priest answered: "The religion of the Israelites is better than that of the Moslems."

The King then asked the kadi [a Moslem judge and scholar]: "What do you say? Is the religion of the Israelites, or that of the Christians preferable?" The kadi answered: "The religion of the Israelites is preferable."

Upon this the King said: "If this is so, you both have admitted with your own mouths that the religion of the Israelites is better. Wherefore, trusting in the mercies of God and the power of the Almighty, I choose the religion of Israel, that is, the religion of Abraham. If that God in whom I trust, and in the shadow of whose wings I find refuge, will aid me, He can give me without labor the money, the gold, and the silver which you have promised me. As for you all, go now in peace to your land." [This account of Bulan's conversion is apparently legendary. Another Hebrew source tells us that Judaism was adopted by the Chazars when a Jewish general was made king. Jewish fugitives from Constantinople also made many converts in Chazaria.]

From that time on the Almighty helped Bulan, fortified him, and strengthened him. He circumcised himself, his servants, attendants, and all his people. [Arabic sources say the royal family and nobility became Jews, but only a part of the people.] Then Bulan sent for and brought from all places wise men of Israel who interpreted the Torah for him and arranged the precepts in order, and up to this very day we have been subject to this religion. May God's name be blessed and may His remembrance be exalted for ever!

Since that day [about 740] when my fathers entered into this religion, the God of Israel has humbled all of their enemies, subjecting every folk and tongue round about them, whether Christian, Moslem, or pagan. No one has been able to stand before them to this day [about 960]. All of them are tributary. [But only about ten years later Joseph was defeated by the Russians, 969.]

After the days of Bulan there arose one of his descendants, a king,

Obadiah by name, who reorganized the kingdom and established the Jewish religion properly and correctly. He built synagogues and schools, brought in Jewish scholars, and rewarded them with gold and silver. [The Jewish scholars could have come from Bagdad and Constantinople.] They explained to him the Bible, Mishnah, Talmud, and the order of divine services. The King was a man who revered and loved the Torah. He was one of the true servants of God. May the Divine Spirit give him rest!

He was succeeded by Hezekiah, his son; next to him was Manasseh, his son; next to him was Hanukkah, the brother of Obadiah; next Isaac, his son; afterwards, his son Zebulun; then his son Moses; then his son Nissi; then his son Aaron; then his son Menahem; then his son Benjamin; then his son Aaron II; and I, Joseph, the son of Aaron the King, am King, the son of a King, and the descendant of kings. [These kings probably had Turkish names besides their Hebrew ones.] No stranger can occupy the throne of my ancestors: the son succeeds the father. This has been our custom and the custom of our forefathers since they have come into existence. May it be the gracious will of Him who appoints all kings that the throne of my kingdom shall endure to all eternity.

You have also asked me about the affairs of my country and the extent of my empire. I wish to inform you that I dwell by the banks of the river known as the Itil [Volga]. At the mouth of the river lies the Caspian Sea. The headwaters of the river turn eastward, a journey of four months distance.

Alongside the river dwell many tribes in cities and towns, in open as well as fortified places. . . . Bear in mind that I dwell at the delta of the Itil and, by God's help, I guard the mouth of the river and do not permit the Russians who come in ships to enter into the Caspian so as to get at the Moslems. Nor do I allow any of their [the Moslems'] enemies who come by land to penetrate as far as Derbend. [Derbend, an Arab city, was the gate through which the nomads in Russia hoped to rush through and raid the rich towns of Asia Minor.] I have to wage war with them, for if I would give them any chance at all they would lay waste the whole land of the Moslems as far as Bagdad. . . .

You have also asked me about the place where I live. I wish to inform you that, by the grace of God, I dwell alongside this river on which there are situated three capital cities. The queen dwells in one of them; it is my birthplace. It is quite large, built round like a circle, the diameter of which is fifty parasangs. [The King lived on an island in the Volga; there were also towns on both banks.]

Jews, Christians, and Moslems live in the second city. Besides these there are many slaves of all nations in it. It is of medium size, eight square parasangs in length and breadth.

In the third I reside with my princes, officers, servants, cupbearers, and those who are close to me. It is round in shape and its diameter is three parasangs. The river flows within its walls. This is my residence during the winter. From the month of Nisan [March-April] on we leave the city and each one goes forth to his vineyards, fields, and to his work. . . .

You mention in your letter that you yearn to see my face. I also would very much like to see your pleasant countenance and the rare beauty of your wisdom and greatness. Would that it were according to your word. If it were granted me to be associated with you and to behold your honored, charming, and pleasant countenance, then you would be my father and I your son. According to your command would all my people be ruled, and according to your word and discreet counsel would I conduct all my affairs. Farewell.

BIBLIOGRAPHY

REFERENCES TO TEXTBOOKS

Roth, pp. 158–159, 264–265.

READINGS FOR ADVANCED STUDENTS

Graetz, III, pp. 138–141, 214–230; Graetz-Rhine, III, pp. 99–130; Margolis and Marx, pp. 308–312, 525–526.

Dubnow, S. M., *History of the Jews in Russia and Poland*, I, "The Kingdom of the Khazars," pp. 19–29.

Frazer, J. G., *Garnered Sheaves*, Part I, Chap. x, "The Killing of the Khazar Kings."

Mann, J., *Texts and Studies in Jewish History and Literature*, I, pp. 3ff.: "Hisdai ibn Shaprut and His Diplomatic Intervention on Behalf of the Jews in Christian Europe."

JE, "Chazars"; "Hasdai abn Yusuf ibn Shaprut."

ADDITIONAL SOURCE MATERIALS IN ENGLISH

Halper, B., *Post-Biblical Hebrew Literature*, "The Four Captives," II, pp. 123–126. A legendary description of the arrival of Rabbi Moses b. Enoch, one of the first Jewish scholars to come to Arabic Spain. He was a contemporary of Hasdai ibn Shaprut.

Miscellany of Hebrew Literature, I, pp. 92ff.: "The Epistle of R. Chisdai, Son of Isaac (of Blessed Memory), to the King of the Cusars," and "The Answer of Joseph, King of the Togarmi, etc." Another translation of the king's answer has been made by H. Hirschfeld, *Judah Hallevi's Kitab al Khazari*, 1931, pp. 272–279.

47.

Anan and the Rise of Karaism
Babylon, about 760

THE appearance in the seventh century of Islam, a world religion, stimulated Jews and Christians to examine their own beliefs more carefully. Moreover, the later development of philosophic thought in the Arab world made men more critical of established religions. In the Jewish world such criticism of Judaism expressed itself in the formation of a number of petty heretical sects, some of which had their roots in the heterodox thought of the preceding seven or eight centuries and now again became active. Practically all of them, whether old or new, had this in common: they were opposed to Talmudism, to the system of law and ritual as developed by the rabbis on the basis of the Bible.

The opposition on the part of some of these anti-nomistic sectaries to the superstitions, to the crude concepts of the deity, to the naive mysticism and demonology of an appreciable number of rabbinic Jews brought a certain amount of freedom of thought and a healthy provocative criticism into Jewish thinking in the Middle Ages.

Anan ben David, a notable Babylonian Jew, rallied many of the dissatisfied elements in Jewry around him about 760, and created a new sect called the Ananites. He attempted to throw overboard rabbinic tradition, law, and ritual, and he called for a return to the Bible, which every individual was to interpret according to his own intellectual powers. Though Anan instituted some changes in calendation, marriage, dietary legislation, liturgy, and the like, he did not reject the basic religious principles of Judaism.

By the ninth century these sectaries, who had by now made inroads into the Rabbanites and had produced some eminent scholars, were called *Karaim*, Karaites, "followers of the Bible," and it is by this name that the last remnants of this group, about twelve thousand, are known today.

It is now almost impossible to determine, with any degree of accuracy, what actually happened in the eighth century when Anan seceded from rabbinical Judaism. The Karaites and their rabbinical opponents, the Rabbanites—like the later Protestants and Catholics

—disliked each other so cordially that it was difficult for either side to write dispassionately.

The first selection below, translated from the Hebrew, is a Rabbanite account of the rise of Anan. Its facts, in general, are accurate. It is thought to be the work of the great Saadia, and may be an extract of his Arabic *Refutation of Anan* written in Egypt in 905 when he was but twenty-three years of age.

The second account, also Rabbanite, comes from the pen of the Spanish Jewish historian, Abraham ibn Daud, who in 1161 finished his Hebrew *Line of Tradition*. It is not improbable that his history was written to show the authenticity of rabbinic tradition, and thus to confute the Karaites who had been making proselytes in Spain.

The third account comes from *Orah Zaddikim* ("The path of the righteous"), a bibliographical work written in Hebrew by Simhah Isaac Luzki, a Karaite scholar. Though this book was written as late as 1757—just about a thousand years after the rise of Anan—nevertheless it follows older Karaitic historical traditions. According to this tradition, which is at least as early as the tenth century, the Karaites are the original Jews, and the Rabbanites or Pharisees are but one of a group of heretics who have been perverting the original Jewish religion since the days of Jeroboam I, about 933 B.C.E.! Anan is thus not the founder of a heresy, but the last great Jewish reformer. This entire concept of Jewish history is, of course, false.

The fourth selection is taken from the Hebrew missionary and propagandistic pamphlet, *Tokahat Megullah* ("An open rebuke"), written 960–1000 by the Jerusalem Karaite, Sahl ben Mazliah. The extract given here is an attack on rabbinic tradition and an appeal to the individual to turn directly to the Bible, and, on the basis of his own reasoning, determine the laws which he must observe.

1. *A Rabbanite Account of the Origin of Karaism, 905 (?)*

⟪Anan had a younger brother whose name was Hananiah. Now Anan was greater than his brother in knowledge of the Torah and older in years, but the scholars of that generation were not willing to set him up as exilarch [ruler of the Babylonian Jews] because of the unmitigated unruliness and irreverence which characterized him. The sages, therefore, turned to Hananiah his brother because of his great modesty, shyness, and fear of God, and made him exilarch. Then Anan became incensed, he and every scoundrel that was left of the Sadducean and Boethusian breed [sectaries of the latter days of the Second Temple], and he secretly determined to make a

schism [in Judaism] because he feared the government of that day.
These heretics appointed Anan as their exilarch. [Schismatics who
created new religions were tolerated; heretics were not.]

This matter was made known to the authorities on a Sunday and
it was ordered that he be put into jail until Friday, when he was to
be hanged, for he had rebelled against the government [in not accepting Hananiah, the calif's appointee]. There, in the prison, he met
a certain Moslem scholar [probably Abu Hanifa, d. 767, a famous
divine], who was also imprisoned, and was to be hanged also on that
very Friday, for he had rebelled against the religion of Mohammed.
The Moslem gave him a piece of advice, and this is what he said
to him: "Are there not in the Torah commands which may permit
of two interpretations?" Anan answered: "There certainly are."
Then he said to him: "Take some point and interpret it differently
from those who follow your brother Hananiah; only be sure your
partisans agree to it, and don't fail also to give a bribe to the vizier.
Perhaps he'll give you permission to speak. Then prostrate yourself
and say: 'My lord King, have you appointed my brother over one
religion or two?' And when he will answer you: 'Over one religion,'
then say to him: 'But I and my brother rule over two different religions!' Then you'll surely be saved, if you'll only make clear to
him the religious differences between your faith and the faith of
your brother, and if your followers agree with you. Talk like this
and when the King [al-Mansur, 754–775] hears these things, he'll
keep quiet."

Anan thereupon set out to deceive his own group and said to
them: "Last night Elijah appeared to me in a dream and said to me:
'You deserve to die because you have transgressed against that which
is written in the Torah.' " [Elijah, says Anan, told him to go back to
the laws of the Torah, the Bible.]

Through his sharp sophistry he taught them these things, and in
order to save himself from violent death and to win a victory he
spent a lot of money bribing his way until the King gave him permission to speak. Then he began saying: "The religion of my
brother is dependent, in making the calendar, on astronomical calculation of the months and year, but my religion is dependent on
the actual observation of the new moon and the signs of the ripening
grain." Now since that king made his calculation, too, through actual
observation of the new moon and the signs of the ripening grain,
he was pacified and reconciled to Anan. [In making the calendar the
Rabbanites employed mathematics; the Karaites, observation of
natural phenomena.]

II. *Abraham ibn Daud's Account of Anan, about 1161*

⟨Anan and Saul his son—may the name of the wicked rot—lived in the days of Yehudai Gaon [of Sura, 760–764]. This Anan was a descendant of the house of David and a scholar originally, but people discovered something wrong in him, and for this reason he was not appointed *gaon* [head of a Jewish academy], and the fates decreed that he should not become exilarch either.

Because of the envy and chagrin in his heart he prepared the way for a great deal of trouble later by misleading and enticing the Jews away from the traditions of the sages which had been handed down by the prophets through reliable witnesses, as we have been showing in this book. Thus he became a "scholar who rebelled against the decisions of the highest authorities" in that he refused to hearken to the judges. [This was a capital crime. Sanhedrin 11:1.] He composed books and raised disciples, and of his own accord devised statutes that are no good, laws by which man cannot live.

III. *A Karaitic Account of Anan, 1757*

⟨Now this is what happened in the days of Anan the Prince, peace be unto him, a saintly and pious man. He was the greatest and most prominent scholar of all the Jewish sages and a very distinguished student of the written law [Bible] and the oral law—the Mishnah and Talmud—and of the sciences and astronomy, too, and withal a very pious and humble man, perfect and upright, fearing God and turning aside from evil. He was an aristocratic prince, notable in family and position, of the seed of David the king, peace be unto him, a chief and a great man in Israel, acceptable to the majority of his brethren, seeking the welfare of the people of God and speaking peace to all the children of Israel. [This description of Anan's scholarship and virtues is probably exaggerated.]

Anan, of blessed memory, lived in Bagdad and belonged to the party of the *Zaddikim*. [The *Zaddikim* are the "Righteous," but the Rabbanites called them *Zedukim*, Sadducees, "heretics."] Because of his great wisdom and his unusual saintliness and modesty the whole house of Israel, the two groups, the "Righteous" and the Pharisees chose him and appointed him to be prince of God in their midst, president of the court, and exilarch. It was the custom in those days that under the authority of the Arab sovereign then ruling in Bagdad that the Jewish prince, as presiding judge and exilarch, took the place of a king over all the Jewish exiles.

When, with the consent of both the Arab king and the Jewish people, Anan the Prince had been appointed presiding judge and exilarch of all the Jews in the Arab dominions, he clothed himself with a cloak of zeal and was very jealous for the Lord of Hosts, the God of Israel, and for His perfect and true Torah which had been in the possession of the Pharisees for so many generations and years. [The Rabbanites, however, say Anan was never appointed exilarch by them.] He desired to restore the crown of the Law to its pristine glory and began to preach in public and to argue against the oral law, the Mishnah, to deny it and to repudiate it completely. Now when the whole assembly of the Pharisees saw all this and heard this, these accursed scoundrels gathered themselves together and rose up against him and conspired to murder him. But since they feared the King too much to murder Anan, they went and defamed and slandered him to the monarch, saying that he had rebelled against the law of the land and deserved death. But God, blessed be He, finding Anan's heart perfect before Him, gave him favor and love in the eyes of the King, who had compassion on him and saved him from their hands so that he was left alive.

When Anan the Prince saw that the Pharisees would not hearken to his advice and would not accept his legislation, and were not willing to go back to the truth, he scorned the position of exilarch, loathed the leadership, and besought the King to give him permission to go to the Holy City—may it be rebuilt and reestablished speedily in our days—where he might settle and build a synagogue. God, blessed be He, gave him favor in the eyes of the king, who granted all he asked.

Then Anan the Prince rose up, left his home, forsook his inheritance and all the wealth which he had acquired in Babylon, and took with him his sons, disciples, associates, and all his friends and acquaintances, and they all went to Jerusalem, the Holy City, and settled there. [The Rabbanites have no record that Anan settled in Jerusalem.] There he built a synagogue, a temple of God, a temple in miniature—which is still standing there today in the possession of our brethren the Karaites (may their Rock and their Redeemer guard them)—where they might weep and pray in the evening, morning, and afternoon, and in the three nightly watches, and make confession of our sins and iniquities and the iniquities of our fathers. [These were Karaitic "mourners for Zion."] Thus they fulfill that which is written in the Bible [Isaiah 62:6–7]: "I have set watchmen upon thy walls, O Jerusalem. They shall never hold their peace day nor night: 'Ye that are the Lord's remembrancers, take ye no rest and give Him no rest, till He establish and till He make Jerusalem a praise in the earth.' "

Now when Anan, the saintly Prince, saw that the Pharasaic group was growing and increasing and that the sect of the "Righteous" was continually diminishing and losing ground, he feared lest in the future the true Torah be forgotten completely, and lest in the course of time the assembly of the "Righteous" go over to the Pharisees—God forbid. Therefore he decreed that his disciples and all his friends and acquaintances, the assembly of the "Righteous," should separate, divide, and cut themselves off from the Pharasaic group completely, by a most complete division and separation and an absolute secession. He forbade us to eat their food because they do not guard themselves against the many kinds of ritual uncleanliness, and because they eat carcasses and animal fats that are forbidden in the Torah. Similarly he forbade us to marry with them because they have broken down the barriers against incest which are forbidden us under penalty of divine punishment—[Hosea 5:7] "They have dealt treacherously against the Lord, for they have begotten strange children"—and because they have other errors and crazy ideas. [He considered as incestuous marriages between relatives of the husband and relatives of the wife.]

iv. *A Karaitic Attack on Rabbinical Tradition, 960–1000*

⟨Know, my Jewish brethren, that every one is responsible for himself, and God will not hearken to the words of him who tries to justify himself, saying: "Well, my teachers taught me to do this," any more than he listened to the excuse of Adam who said [Genesis 3:12–13]: "The woman whom Thou gavest to be with me, she gave me of the tree, and I did eat." Nor will God accept the excuse of the man who says: "The sages fooled me," any more than he tolerated the excuse of Eve when she said: "The serpent beguiled me, and I did eat."

And just as He gave to each his due, and exercised His judgment on each one of them, so will He do to any one who argues in that manner, as it is written [Zechariah 10:3]: "Mine anger is kindled against the shepherds, and I will punish the he-goats." The "shepherds" are the leaders, and the "he-goats" are those who are led. Realize, therefore, that he who attempts to justify himself, saying: "I walked in the ways of my fathers," will find that this excuse will not help him at all. Did not our God, blessed be He, answer [Zechariah 1:4]: "Be ye not as your fathers"? And did He not further say [Psalm 78:8]: "They shall not be as their fathers, a stubborn and rebellious generation."

This is to tell us that we are not bound to follow in the ways of our fathers in every respect, but we must reflect on their ways and compare their actions and their laws to the words of the Torah. If we see that the teachings of our fathers are exactly like the words of the Bible, then we must accept them and pay attention to them. We must follow them and dare not change them. But if the teachings of our fathers are different from the Bible, we must cast them out, and must ourselves seek and investigate and think about the commands of the Torah. [This is the basic principle of Karaism.] That which is written in the Torah of Moses—peace be unto him—about the commandments and other things does not require any sign or witness to show us whether or not it is true; but that which our fathers have told us requires proof and a responsible witness so that one may determine if it is true or not, and only that law which is proved to us will we perform, for thus it is written [Hosea 10:12]: "Sow to yourselves according to righteousness, reap according to mercy." [Biblical law is to be followed literally; the validity of rabbinic law requires constant substantiation. Yet the Karaites, too, soon found it impossible to follow the Bible literally.]

And you, O House of Israel, have mercy on yourselves, and have compassion on your children. Behold the sun [of Karaism] is rising and the light is shining! Choose the good way in which is found the living waters and walk therein. Do not walk in a dry and weary land [of rabbinic law] where there is no water!

Do not say, how shall we do this? How can we follow the commandments if the Karaites themselves disagree? Which one of them shall we follow [in the interpretation of the law]? [The answer is that] the Karaites do not say that they are leaders. They have made no arbitrary innovations to lead the people as they might like, but they investigate and examine the Torah of Moses and the books of the prophets—of blessed memory—and even look into the works of the sages of old.

Therefore they [the Karaites] merely say to their Jewish brothers: "Learn, investigate, search, and inquire and do that which has been demonstrated to you through valid proof and which agrees with your reason." Do not say: "How is this possible?"; for this is what our Rock desires and wishes of us, and it is incumbent upon us to perform that commandment which becomes valid only through our understanding by proof and testimony, and not by arbitrary will. [It is one's duty to think for himself.]

BIBLIOGRAPHY

REFERENCES TO TEXTBOOKS

Elbogen, pp. 50ff.; Roth, pp. 151ff.; Sachar, pp. 161ff.
Golub, J. S., *Medieval Jewish History*, Sect. iv, "New Sect Challenges Oral Law," etc.

READINGS FOR ADVANCED STUDENTS

Graetz, III, pp. 127–159; see "Karaism" and "Karaites" in Index;
 Graetz-Rhine, III, pp. 33–70; Margolis and Marx, pp. 258–263; see "Karaites" in Index.
Mann, J., "New Studies in Karaism," *Yearbook: Central Conference of American Rabbis*, XLIV (1934), pp. 220–241.
Waxman, M., *A History of Jewish Literature*, I, Chap. xiii, "Karaite Literature"; II, Chap. viii, "Karaite Literature."
Encyclopaedia of Religion and Ethics, "Karaites."
JE, "Karaites."

48.

Aaron the Mystic, of Bagdad
about 870

ACCORDING to old Jewish traditions Aaron ben Samuel Ha-Nasi of Bagdad was a noted scholar, mystic, and wonder-worker who left his native Babylon, about the middle of the ninth century, and wandered westward to Palestine and finally to southern Italy. There he not only spread Talmudic learning but also imparted his secret lore to a few trusted friends, and thus became the "father of mysteries" for European Jewry.

The following obviously mythical account of one of his adventures in Benevento is found in the Hebrew rimed prose chronicle of Ahimaaz. This family history, called *A Book of Genealogies*, was written in 1054.

⊄There came from Bagdad [the center of world Jewish culture in the early Middle Ages], from our beloved ones, [Aaron] an esteemed man of distinguished family, an illustrious scholar, warding off wrath from the descendants of those that sleep in Hebron [the patriarchs, the ancestors of the Hebrews]. . . . He made use of his wonder-working wisdom to do very difficult and astonishing things. When he reached Benevento the entire community came out as one man to welcome him.

On the Sabbath, an esteemed young man arose to read the prayers before Him that dwelleth on high. He chanted with pleasing voice. When he reached the words "Praise ye the Lord who is to be praised," his voice lingered on the sound, but he did not pronounce God's name. The master at once realized that the reader was actually a dead man, and it is known [Psalm 115:17] that the dead do not praise God. "Stop!" he at once commanded in a loud voice. "Do not give praise, for thou art not permitted to recite prayer before God."

Then he began to question the youth, to plead with him in the name of his Maker, saying: "Tell me and do not fear, do not conceal from me what thou hast done, confess the truth before the Creator of the Spirit, glorify the God of glory, give thanks to Him in the midst of the congregation, and so acquire a portion in the world to come, and in this world be without sin. Thou wilt then be free from transgression, winning for thyself blessings, the well ordered world to come, and the good appointed for the righteous among His people, for those that fear God and honor His name."

Immediately he answered: "I have indeed sinned, and trespassed against God; I have rebelled and transgressed and done wrong. If you are willing to bear the burden of the sin which your servant has committed [I will confess]." And all of them were willing to bear all that he imposed upon them. Thereupon he confessed, giving thanks to God; and thus told what he had done and what had happened to him.

He said: "Hear me, O people of God, my teachers and masters, leaders and elders, sages and scholars, princes and nobles, old and young, I will tell you plainly all that happened.

"In my time there was a Jew named Rabbi Ahimaaz who went to Jerusalem, the glorious city, three times, to fulfill his vow. [Ahimaaz, a south Italian scholar, lived about 868. Pious Jews in those days wished to pilgrimage to Palestine at least three times during their lifetime.] On each pilgrimage he took 100 pieces of gold with him [probably a donation from Italian Jews], as he had vowed to the Rock of his salvation, to give aid to those who were engaged in the study of His law, and to those who mourned the ruined house of His glory. [There was a group of ascetics in Jerusalem that mourned the loss of the Temple and prayed for its restoration. They were supported by charity.]

"As he set out on his third pilgrimage, he asked my mother for me, saying: 'Let him go with me, to keep me company and help me on the way. I will bring him back to thee; at my hands thou mayest require him; if I do not bring him back to thee, I shall have sinned before God, I and my children.' Then we set out on our journey rejoicing, without a thought of sadness.

"As we were sitting at the table of the scholars in study with the head of the academy, the teachers of the Law exclaimed: 'Let us give praise, in pleasant and fervent song, with love and devotion to Him that is adored by myriads.' They looked at their disciples seated before them; the head of their school turned to them and said: 'Let the young man in our midst, who has come with our colleague Rabbi Ahimaaz, cheer us and delight our heart with the flow of his knowledge and the utterance of his thoughts.' Then I began reverently to give praise in psalm and song to Him that putteth on light as a garment.

"There sat one of the elders in meditation, intently listening to my chanting. He began to weep bitterly. Rabbi Ahimaaz, looking at him, noticed his actions, and arising from the company went over to him and begged him to tell why he wept. The elder simply told him that God had decreed that, in a little while, the young man would surely die. When the good man heard this his eyes filled with tears, he rent his clothes and tore out his hair, and exclaimed before them all: 'I have no place among the living; I have sworn to his mother that I would bring him back to her, without mishap or harm; how can I return to my house, if the lad is not with me? The oath which I have taken will be the means of blighting my hope and my ardent expectation.'

"Seeing his affliction and his bitter weeping, they wrote the Holy Name that was written in the Sanctuary; they made an incision in the flesh of my right arm, and inserted the Name where the flesh had been cut. [Through the proper use of the four-lettered Name of God: YHWH, it was said that one could perform miracles.] So I came away in peace and returned home to my mother. While Rabbi Ahimaaz was alive I wandered from land to land. [This reminds one of "the wandering Jew."] Living since that time, I can live forever if I so desire, for no man can know the place of the Name unless I reveal it. But I will show it to you; I am in your hands; deal with me as seems right in your eyes."

So they brought the grave clothes; he approached and put them on; he showed them where the master had made the incision, and took the Name out of it. His body became lifeless; the corpse crumbled in decay as from the dissolution of many years, the flesh returned to the dust.

BIBLIOGRAPHY

READINGS FOR ADVANCED STUDENTS

Waxman, M., *A History of Jewish Literature*, I, Chap. xii, "Mysticism."

ADDITIONAL SOURCE MATERIALS IN ENGLISH

Coulton, G. G., *A Medieval Garner*, pp. 280ff., "The Wandering Jew." This is Matthew of Paris' account of Cartaphilus, the wandering Jew.

Salzman, M., *The Chronicle of Ahimaaz*, from which the above selection is taken, contains other materials throwing light on mystical practices in Jewish life of the time.

The Zohar, 5 vols., Soncino Press, London, is a very satisfactory translation of this basic medieval cabalistic work.

49.

Practical Cabala
about 900–1400

THROUGHOUT the entire history of Judaism, magic, incantations, and conjurations have played a great part in the life of the masses. In contradistinction to metaphysical, reflective cabala, this dabbling in magic was called practical cabala. The rabbis frowned on this type of folk-religion, but it flourished in spite of them. These magical formulae are not necessarily Jewish in origin; they are common to all peoples and religions and are as old as the hills.

The first four selections below are from a mixed Hebrew and Aramaic handbook of magic called *The Sword of Moses*. This work was well known in Asia and Africa in the tenth century and is probably much older. The fifth selection comes from *The Wisdom of the Chaldeans*, a Hebrew astrological text which is no later than the fourteenth century and is probably much older.

The Sword of Moses, tenth century

I.   To conjure a spirit write on a laurel-leaf: "I conjure thee, Prince whose name is Abraksas, in the name of SLGYY HWH YH GUTYUS HWH AFRNUHH HWH ASGNUHH HWH BTNUSYY HWH that thou comest to me and revealest to me all that I ask of thee, and thou shalt not tarry." And the one conjured by thee will come down and reveal himself to thee.

II.   If you wish to kill a man, take mud from the two sides of the river and form it into the shape of a figure, and write upon it the name of the person, and take seven branches from seven strong palm-trees and make a bow from reed with the string of horse-sinew, and place the image in a hollow, and stretch the bow and shoot with it, and at each shot say ATTRS B' SHLUMYM MYBGSS B' SHUTTYAYA may "X" be destroyed. [For "X" insert the name of your enemy.]. . . .

III.   To walk upon the water without wetting the feet, take a leaden plate and write upon it HBKSHFHYAL YHWHH ASRGHYAL YHWHH HZASNHYAL YHWHH MUDDGHYAL YHWHH and place it in thy girdle, and then you can walk. [Jewish folk tradition says Jesus was able to walk on water through the power of magic.]

244

IV.   Against any enemy. Write upon a new-laid egg, on a Naza-
rene cemetery: "I conjure you, luminaries of heaven and earth, as
the heavens are separated from the earth, so separate and divide 'X'
from his wife 'X,' and separate them from one another, as life is
separated from death, and sea from dry land, and water from fire,
and mountain from vale, and night from day, and light from darkness, and the sun from the moon; thus separate 'X' from 'X' his
wife, and separate them from one another in the name of the twelve
hours of the day and the three watches of the night, and the seven
days of the week, and the thirty days of the month, and the seven
years of *Shemittah*, and the fifty years of Jubilee, on every day.
[Every seventh year is a *Shemittah* year. After seven *Shemittahs*
comes the Jubilee, the fiftieth year.] In the name of the evil angel
Tmsmael, and in the name of the angel Iabiel, and in the name of the
angel Drsmiel, and in the name of the angel Zahbuk, and in the
name of the angel Ataf, and in the name of the angel Zhsmael, and
in the name of the angel Zsniel, who preside over pains, sharp pains,
inflammation, and dropsy, and separate 'X' from his wife 'X,' make
them depart from one another, and that they should not comfort
one another, swiftly and quickly."

v. *The Wisdom of the Chaldeans, fourteenth century*—HOW TO
MAKE SOMEONE FALL IN LOVE WITH YOU

⟪On the sixth day Anael functions. He is the ruler appointed on
all manner of love. This ruler is in the likeness of a woman. She
has in one hand a mirror in which she beholds herself, and in the
other a comb with which she is combing her head. She, like unto
other angels, has serving angels; she also holds her hands outstretched.
At her right arm serves an angel whose name is Arbiel, on the left
one called Niniel, over her head one whose name is Lahabiel, and
at her feet one called Ahabiel.

   If thou wishest to employ him [Anael], make a tablet of fine
silver, draw upon it the likeness of a woman in accordance with
the woman thou likest; then write on her shoulder her name and
the name of her mother, and the name of the one who loves her,
and that of his mother, and draw her hands outstretched. Draw
then under her right arm the figure of a nice young man, and write
on his shoulder Arbiel; under her left arm draw the image of
another young man and write on his forehead Niniel; behind her
draw the image of a man with red ink and write on his shoulder
Lahabiel.

The use of this picture of the woman on the tablet is that it gains for thee the love of that man or woman whom thou desirest with a strong and unbreakable love. Thou hast only to touch this tablet and they will run after thee and fulfill thy desire, especially that woman whose name thou hast written on the tablet.

And thou must utter the following conjuration: "I conjure thee, Anael (thou and thy servants who are called by thy name, and whose name is included in theirs, viz.: Arbiel, Niniel, Ahabiel and Lahabiel), in the name of Uriel, with the countenance flaming all round, inflame so-and-so with my love and with my strong affection, and may her destiny be united with mine in the same manner as Adam was united to Eve. May she not have any chance to eat or to drink, or to sleep, or to stand, or to sit, before she is in love with me. . . . and until she comes to me and fulfills all my wishes and desires." Then warm the tablet on the fire and thou wilt see marvellous things.

If the person in question is a man, then say: "That he may fulfill my wish," viz., this or that thing. On the back of the tablet write *Sit*, for this is his [Anael's] Seal, and write it in the hour of Venus.

BIBLIOGRAPHY

READINGS FOR ADVANCED STUDENTS

Encyclopaedia of Religion and Ethics, "Magic (Jewish)."
JE, "Amulet"; "Magic."

ADDITIONAL SOURCE MATERIALS IN ENGLISH

Gaster, M., *Studies and Texts in Folklore, Magic, Medieval Romance, Hebrew Apocrypha and Samaritan Archaeology*, 3 vols. The collected writings of the greatest authority on medieval Jewish magic. *The Sword of Moses* and *The Wisdom of the Chaldeans*, from which the selections above have been extracted, are also reprinted in this collection.

50.

David Alroy, False Messiah
about 1146–1147

THE crusades, which began in the eleventh century, stimulated Messianic movements all over the world. Both in Christian and Moslem lands the Jews looked forward to the coming of the Messiah and the return to the Holy Land. Persecutions at the hands of Christian crusaders and Moslem fanatics, the Christian conquest of Palestine, the political changes in the map of Asia Minor, the oppressive taxation—all these things induced in the Jews of almost every land the hope that the day of their redemption had also come. Self-proclaimed Messiahs arose to lead the expectant masses back to Jerusalem.

Among these false Messiahs was David Alroy, who lived in Persia, probably during the Second Crusade, 1146–1147. Through skilful propaganda he appealed to the warlike Jewish mountaineers of northern Persia to support him in revolt. But a violent death brought an end to him and to his far-reaching plans.

There are two important accounts of the career of David Alroy; the one by Benjamin of Tudela, the twelfth century Spanish traveller; the other by Samuel ibn Abbas, a contemporary Moslem writer. Ibn Abbas, a very learned physician and mathematician who had become a Moslem, was originally a Jew. Full of zeal for Islam, he wrote an attack on Judaism in 1169 under the title, *The Silencing of the Jews and the Christians through Rational Arguments*. In this Arabic work Ibn Abbas describes the Messianic agitation for no other purpose than to poke fun at the credulous Jews. Nevertheless we have preferred his account, biased though it is, to that of Benjamin of Tudela because it is simpler and probably more accurate.

⟨We are going to tell a story of the haste with which the Jews accepted the false and the fictitious, which shows how little discernment they have. The following incident happened in our time among the finest, cleverest, and shrewdest among them, namely, the Jews of Bagdad. A swindler, a young Jew, a man of fine features, whose name was Menahem ben Solomon but who was known by the name of Ibn al-Ruhi, grew up in the neighborhood of Mosul. [As a Mes-

sianic pretender he took the name of David. Al-Ruhi or Alroy may
mean "the inspired one." Even Menahem ben Solomon may be a
Messianic name and not a real one.]

In comparison with the mass of Jews who lived in that section
of the territory of Mosul called Amadia, he passed for a scholar in
Jewish law. The commandant of the citadel there was very fond
of this rogue and liked him because he held a good opinion of him,
and because he considered him as well-versed in religious matters as
Alroy wished to appear. The commandant himself enjoyed his
visits. This gave the rogue the desire to secure the position of this
officer, whom he considered such an imbecile that he imagined he
could attack the citadel, take it, and make a fortress out of it.
[Alroy, a cultured man, was more probably a patriot than a rogue.]

He therefore wrote to the Jews who live in the territory of Azer-
baijan and its borders since he knew that the Jews of Persia were
more ignorant than all others. He mentioned in his letters that he
had arisen in order to free the Jews from the power of the Moslems.
[Alroy was really leading a rebellion of the desperate Persian Jews
against their Moslem overlords. Jerusalem was his goal.]

In his approach he made use of all sorts of cunning and deceit.
Among the things which he devised I have seen that which has in
substance the following meaning: "Perhaps you will say: Why is
our help called for? Is it for battle or for war? No, we do not want
you for battle or for war. You merely have to appear before this
commander in order that the envoys of the princes who have come to
this court may see you." At the end of the letters there was written:
"It is proper that every one of you have a sword or some other
weapon on his person concealed under his clothes." [Through his
skilled secretary he appealed to all the Jews of the Near East to rally
about him.]

The Jews of Persia and the inhabitants of the area of Amadia and
the territory of Mosul consented, and they came to him with their
sharpened weapons so that he had a large force present. The commandant held such a good opinion of him that he thought all these
people had come merely for the purpose of visiting this scholar
whose fame, he fancied, had reached them. He finally discovered
their intentions, but since he did not care to spill blood, he killed
only the swindler who had incited the revolt. The others wandered
about aimlessly after having suffered misfortune, calamities, and
poverty. [The account by Benjamin of Tudela, however, implies
that Alroy was successful against the Persians until his own father-
in-law assassinated him for the sake of a huge reward.]

As obvious as these facts are to every intelligent person, they are nevertheless not yet clear to the Jews, and the Jews of Amadia hold Alroy even today in higher esteem than many of their prophets. Many consider him to be the expected Messiah himself, and I have seen many Persian Jews in Khoi, Selmas, Tibriz, and Maragha who invoke his name in the most holy of oaths. [It was in Maragha that Ibn Abbas had the vision which influenced him to become a Moslem.] The Jews of Amadia are in all things more vigorous opponents and enemies of the other Jews than the Christians. In that section there is even a sect which derives its origin from the above-mentioned impostor, Menahem.

About the time that the people in Bagdad heard of Menahem, two crafty deceivers among the Jewish scholars of the city forged letters in his name in which they announced to the Jews of Bagdad the redemption which they had been awaiting of old and designated a night in which they would all fly to Jerusalem together. The Bagdad Jews, in spite of their supposed intelligence and their boasted critical spirit, listened to this and allowed themselves to be misled into accepting it as the truth. Their wives brought their possessions and jewelry to both men, in order that these might distribute them in their name to those who in their judgment were worthy of them. In this manner the Jews spent the largest portion of their fortune. [The Jews intended that their wealth be distributed for charity in order to merit the coming of the Messiah.]

They procured green garments for themselves, and they came together that night on the roofs, waiting for the moment, when, as they hoped, they would fly from there to Jerusalem on angels' wings. [Green is the symbol of resurrection and of God's mercy.] The women began to scream because of their suckling infants, for fear that they would fly away before their children, or their children before them, and thus the little ones, because of delay in getting suck, might suffer hunger. The Moslems there were amazed at this, wondering what could have happened to the Jews, and did not oppose them until they discovered to what unbelievable assurances the Jews had surrendered themselves. [Later on the Moslems and Christians laughed at the Jews for trying to fly without wings.]

The Jews continued to move to and fro in preparation for their flight until they were disillusioned by the break of dawn and by the departure of the deceivers who had already left with their riches. Now the deception was clear to them, and they realized how far these men had carried their villainy. This year was called the "Year of Flying Away," and both old and young date from it.

[This anecdote of the credulous Bagdad Jews seems mythical inasmuch as a similar story was told of the Jews and of Moslem heretics in preceding centuries.]

This occurrence is sufficient to cover them with lasting disgrace and eternal shame. That which I have just narrated is complete enough and will suffice to silence them and to shut their mouths because of that which is to be condemned in them.

BIBLIOGRAPHY

REFERENCES TO TEXTBOOKS

Golub, J. S., *Medieval Jewish History*, Sec. IV, "Messianic Pretenders—Abu Isa," etc.

READINGS FOR ADVANCED STUDENTS

Graetz, III, pp. 428–435.
Greenstone, J. H., *The Messiah Idea in Jewish History*, Chap. iv, "The Rise of Rationalism."
Silver, A. H., *A History of Messianic Speculation in Israel*, Chap. iii, "The Period of the Crusades (11–12c.)."
Encyclopaedia of Religion and Ethics, "Messiahs (Pseudo-)."
JE, "Alroy, David"; "Pseudo-Messiahs."

ADDITIONAL SOURCE MATERIALS IN ENGLISH

Adler, M. N., *The Itinerary of Benjamin of Tudela*, pp. 54–56, contains an account of David Alroy as seen through the eyes of a Jew who visited the haunts of Alroy a few years after his death.

51.

David Reubeni and Solomon Molko
1524–1532

IN 1524 there appeared in Rome one David Reubeni, who professed to be the ambassador of a brother, Joseph, the king of a group of Jewish tribes in a distant land. Reubeni declared that his mission was to secure aid—and particularly cannon-founders and gunsmiths—from the Christians of Europe, and to enlist the Christians in an alliance against the common enemy, the Turks. Through this cooperation with the Christians, Reubeni believed, the Jews could hope to regain Jerusalem for themselves; so he appealed to the Pope, to Portugal, the great colonial power of the day, and to Charles V of the Holy Roman Empire and Spain. It was a bold and daring venture conceived in the spirit of the Renaissance.

Some scholars maintain that this Jewish ambassador was an impudent impostor. They point out that his Hebrew diary abounds in Germanisms, precluding the possibility of his coming from the Orient. There is no doubt that Reubeni did not represent a Jewish state, although it is not at all impossible that he was an emissary of some Jews of the Arabian Peninsula who looked to Christendom for help against the advancing Turks.

While in Portugal Reubeni met Diogo Pires (about 1500–1532), a youthful New Christian who was an official in the court of appeals. Pires, or Solomon Molko as he later called himself, was so moved by the appearance of the Jewish ambassador that he returned to the faith of his fathers and fled from Portugal. In Italy these two worthies joined in a common appeal to Charles V. Their enterprise failed.

Reubeni wrote a rather detailed diary which is still extant, but a more succinct account of these two men is to be found in the writings of the Jewish historian, Joseph Ha-Kohen (1496–1578). In 1553 Joseph had finished a large history called *A History of the Kings of France and the Ottoman Rulers*. Far more important for the story of the Jews is his Hebrew martyrology, *Emek Ha-Baka* ("Vale of tears"), which Joseph completed in its final form in 1575. It is from this book that the following account of Reubeni and Molko has been taken.

℀In those days [1525] there appeared at the court of the King of Portugal a Jew, David by name, from a distant land, India [Arabia]. And David said to him: "I am a Hebrew and I fear the Lord God of the heavens. My brother, the king of the Jews, has sent me here to you, my lord King, for help. And now help us that we may go to fight Sulaiman the Turk, so that we may take the Holy Land out of his power." [Reubeni wanted Palestine for the Jews.]

The King answered him: "Let thy coming be in peace. Now go and I will send you to the archbishop and I will do whatever he says." So David left him and spent a short time in Lisbon. The Marranos believed his words, saying: "He is our redeemer, for the Lord has sent him," and many gathered about him and they honored him exceedingly. [The oppressed Marranos, thinking he had come to deliver them from their oppressors, kissed his hands and showered attentions on him.]

Then that man journeyed from that place and passed through Spain, and wherever he passed many of the Marranos, who were scattered there, flocked to him, and this ultimately became a stumbling block to them. [The Marranos who flocked to him were no doubt later turned over to the Inquisition.] Then he passed on to France and went to Avignon, and from that place he journeyed and came to Italy. He made embroidered banners on which he wrote the Holy Names, and at that time many believed in him.

David came also to Bologna, Ferrara, and Mantua and declared that with the consent of the Christian kings he was going to take all the Jews in those cities with him back to his homeland. He also spoke to the Pope about this matter and the Jews became very frightened. They would ask him: "What shall we do with our wives now if we go to war? How about our children whom they have borne?" He would answer: "There are many such in our land. Do not be afraid for there is no restraint to the Lord to save." He also made up a letter and said: "My brother, the king, sent it to me and it is written and sealed with the signet of the king." [His brother Joseph, he said, was king of the Jewish tribes of Gad, Reuben, and Manasseh.] But there came a day when his secret was discovered and people no longer believed in him, for he decreed decrees of naught. [The people lost faith in him.]

A shoot came forth from Portugal—Solomon Molko was his name—of the stock of the Jews who had been scattered there since the days of the forced conversions. [Most Portuguese Jews had been forced to become Christians in 1497.] He was at that time a very young man, one of the secretaries of the king. When Solomon saw this man David, God touched his heart; he returned unto the Lord, the God of our fathers, and he circumcised himself.

In those days Solomon knew nothing of the Torah of God or the Holy Writings; but after he was circumcised, God gave wisdom to him, and to the amazement of many people almost immediately he became wiser than all other men. [There was then no Inquisition in Portugal to prevent the secret-Jews from studying Hebrew.] He then crossed over to Italy and dared to speak of the Torah of our God in the presence of kings and he did not hide his face from them. He went to Turkey [where he studied Cabala]. Then he returned to Rome [1530] where he spoke with Clement, the Pope [1523–1534], who showed him favor in spite of the wishes of the theologians of the Church. The Pope gave him a permit, written and sealed in his name, allowing him to settle wherever he wanted and to declare himself a Jew.

Solomon became very learned in cabalistic lore, and he would utter beautiful and charming words, for the spirit of God spoke in him and His word was on his tongue continually. He would constantly draw beautiful thoughts from the depths of the cabalistic well and would write them down on tablets and send them to his friends in Salonica where they would print them. [His *Sermons*, on cabalistic themes, were published there in 1529.] He preached in public in Bologna and other places, and many flocked to him to listen to his wisdom and to try him with questions. Solomon, however, answered all their questions; nothing was hidden from him which he could not tell them. They saw the wisdom of Solomon and they said: "The report which we heard about you is true. In fact your wisdom greatly exceeds the report which we have heard about you."

Many were envious of him but they were not able to cause him any injury in Italy, for he was beloved in the sight of the princes. He joined himself to David and they were united at that time. [Both were in Venice, 1530, seeking help for the Jewish people. Solomon also wanted to publish some books.]

Now in addition Solomon wrote for the wise the visions he had seen, as I have already described in my book, *A History of the Kings of France and the Ottoman Rulers*. There you may see of his troubles, his experiences, and how he wrote concerning David as follows: "I have heard people say that Prince David has come to Italy and him, too, have some of the wicked of our Jews slandered. I thought that when I would see him he would teach me understanding; but just the very opposite happened, for he asked me questions. Still I don't rely on that for I know he is a great sage. As for that which he was accustomed to say, that he knew no lore or Torah—well, that was in order to fool the people, and also to find out how I would act toward him. Since this was his intention I always acted toward him as a servant toward his master." Thus far the words of Solomon in his letter as I have written in my history book.

And it came to pass after this that Solomon undertook to speak in detail to the Emperor [Charles V, 1519–1556] on religious matters. And while the Emperor was in Regensburg he took the trip and spoke with him there. [The chief problem of the Imperial Parliament at Regensburg in 1532 was the war against the Turks. Reubeni and Molko probably suggested that the Jews and Marranos arm themselves and help fight the Moslems.] The Emperor remained firm and would not listen to him, being impatient, and even issued an order to put him and his friend Prince David and his men into prison. [Josel of Rosheim, the German Jewish leader, had warned Molko to avoid the Catholic Emperor.] They remained there for a few days until the Emperor returned to Italy. Then he brought them back, shackled on wagons, to Mantua where they were put into jail. The Emperor then spoke with his advisers, and when they found Solomon guilty and deserving death, the Emperor commanded: "Take him out and let him be burnt." [Solomon was to be burnt as a renegade Christian.]

And so one day they put a gag into Solomon's mouth and took him outside. The whole city was in an uproar because of him, and the fire was burning. One of the officers of the Emperor then spoke: "Remove the gag from his mouth for I have a message to him from the King"; and they did so. Then he said to him: "The Emperor has sent me to you, Sir Solomon, to say: 'If you turn back from this, your way, you will be forgiven, and he will spare your life and you shall live before him. But if not, this evil decree will be executed against you.'"

But Solomon did not stir or move before him, but answered like a saint, like an angel of God: "My heart is bitter and vexed for the days that I spent in the Christian religion. Do now what is pleasing in your eyes, but let my soul return to the house of its Father as it was in my childhood, for then I was better off than now." This roused their fury against him and they cast him upon the faggots that were on the fire, sacrificing him to God like a burnt offering that is completely consumed. [He was burnt at the stake late in 1532.] And God smelled the sweet savor and gathered his pure soul to His Garden of Eden, and he was with Him as a nursling, playing before Him at all times. His servants, however, they took out of jail and let them go free. The only one left in the toils was his friend the Prince, David Reubeni, whom they still kept under guard. When the Emperor returned to Spain he took David with him and put him into prison, where he died. After this they burnt many of the Marranos in Spain because of this David Reubeni and his dreams.

Many people in Italy at that time believed that Rabbi Solomon Molko had been saved through his wisdom from the hands of those who sought to destroy his life, and that the fire had no power over his body. [Molko had once before escaped the fires of the Inquisition. Some thought he escaped this time also.] There was even one person who affirmed under oath in the presence of the congregation that for eight days after the burning Solomon stayed in his home and thence went his way without ever being seen again. But the Lord God knows! Would that I could truthfully and honestly write here in this book whether his words were true or not.

BIBLIOGRAPHY

REFERENCES TO TEXTBOOKS

Roth, pp. 241–242; Sachar, pp. 238–240.

READINGS FOR ADVANCED STUDENTS

Graetz, IV, pp. 491–512; Graetz-Rhine, IV, pp. 338–354; Margolis and Marx, pp. 504–507.

Adler, E. N., *Auto de fé and Jew*, Chap. v, "Embassy from Jews in India," Chap. vi, "David Reubeni in Portugal."

Brod, M., *Reubeni, Prince of the Jews*. This is a good historical novel. Part one is entirely fictional as far as Reubeni is concerned, but is useful for a picture of life in a medieval German Jewish community. Part two attempts to assimilate the known data about Reubeni and Molko.

Greenstone, J. H., *The Messiah Idea in Jewish History*, Chap. v, "The Development in the Kabbalah."

Roth, C., *Venice* (Jewish Communities Series), pp. 72–79.

Encyclopaedia of Religion and Ethics, "Messiahs (Pseudo-)."

JE, "Molko, Solomon"; "Pseudo-Messiahs"; "Reubeni, David."

ADDITIONAL SOURCE MATERIALS IN ENGLISH

Adler, E. N., *Jewish Travellers*, pp. 251–328, has a translation of the diary of David Reubeni.

Halper, B., *Post-Biblical Hebrew Literature*, "A Jew Who Claims To Belong to the Ten Tribes Visits Italy," II, pp. 230–234. This is a contemporary account of Reubeni by Abraham Farissol.

52.

Isaac Luria, the Cabalist
1534–1572

SPAIN was the chief center in the Middle Ages for the study
of the *Zohar* and other cabalistic works, but after the expulsion in
1492 new centers for mystical studies arose. Most famous among
them was the town of Safed in the hills of Galilee. The greatest
of the cabalists here was Isaac Luria [1534–1572], a native Palestinian
of Italian-German origin. His followers, who looked upon him as
almost superhuman, called him the *Ari*, the "Lion." The initials ARI
stand for *Ashkenazi Rabbi Isaac*, the "German Rabbi Isaac."

Luria, in his system of cabala, laid emphasis upon transmigration
of souls, repentance, asceticism, the power of prayer, Messianism,
intense religious concentration, and sincere, high-minded living.
He himself wrote very little, but his oral teachings, his personality,
his religious practice, and the legends that have clustered about him
have all influenced Jewry to this day. His chief disciple, Hayyim
Vital Calabrese (1543–1620), a Palestinian of Italian origin, is most
responsible for the spread of the Lurianic cabala.

The first selection following, a short biography of Luria, is taken
from the Hebrew letters which Shlimel ben Hayyim Meinsterl
Dresdnitz began to send from Safed in 1606. Shlimel was a devout
follower of Luria and gleaned his information from the disciples of
the "Lion" himself. Despite their legendary cast—strongly reminiscent of the New Testament gospels—these letters contain some
authentic data of the life of this important historic figure.

The second selection, which so clearly portrays the social conscience of Luria, is taken from an ethical and liturgical work, *Hemdat
Yamim* ("Desire of days"), first published in 1731–1732. Though
this book is usually ascribed to the notorious mystic Nathan Benjamin Ghazzati (1644–1680), it is probably the work of the seventeenth century Italian Jewish cabalist, Israel Solomon Longhi.

1. *A Short Biography of the "Lion," 1607*

⟨First, I would like to say something about the loftiness of the
"Lion," Rabbi Isaac—of blessed memory—although what I say

256

amounts to only a drop in the bucket. During his youth he lived in Egypt although he was born in Jerusalem. At his birth Elijah, of blessed memory, appeared to his father—for he was very pious, as was his mother too—and said to him: "Take heed, now, on the day of the circumcision, not to circumcise this child until you see me standing beside you in the synagogue."

Now when the eighth day came and they took the child to the synagogue for the circumcision the father looked around on all sides for Elijah but did not see him there. By some sort of a pretext, the father delayed for about a half an hour or more and kept the congregation standing. They wondered why he held off so long and finally they all rebuked him. He, however, paid no attention to their complaint but waited till finally Elijah did come. He said to the father: "Sit down on the chair," and the father sat down with the infant in his arms. [Elijah was the patron saint at circumcisions and sat on a special "Elijah chair."] Then Elijah came, sat down on the father's lap, took the child from the parent, put him on his own lap and held him with his own two arms. The man who performed the circumcision went ahead with his work and saw nothing, of course, but the father. After the child had been circumcised Elijah returned him to the father, saying: "Here is your child. Take good care of him for a great light shall shine forth from him upon all the world."

Later when he was still a lad his father died. Because of poverty he went down to Egypt to the home of his uncle who was a very rich man. [His uncle Mordecai Francis was a wealthy tax-collector.] Luria developed into a brilliant student noted for his keenness, powers of argumentation, and sound reasoning, so that by the time he was fifteen years of age he was superior to all the sages of Egypt in his understanding of and his ability to debate in Talmudic law. His uncle then gave him his daughter to wife. After the marriage he studied alone with our honored teacher, Rabbi Bezalel Ashkenazi [d. about 1591], for seven years, and after this he studied by himself for six years. In addition to this, for two years in succession, he kept himself in seclusion in a certain house built along the Nile river and sanctified himself by an unusual piety. He was altogether alone and spoke with no one. On the eve of the Sabbath, just before it grew dark, he would return to his home, but even here, too, he would talk to no one, not even his wife, except when it was absolutely necessary, and then only in Hebrew and very briefly.

It was there on the banks of the Nile that he merited for himself the descent of the Holy Spirit. At times Elijah the prophet revealed himself to him and taught him the [cabalistic] secrets of the Torah, and he was found so worthy that throughout the night his soul would mount on high, and troops of ministering angels would come to guard him on the way till they had led him into the heavenly assembly, and there they would ask of him in which college he wished to study. . . . [There were schools in heaven, also.]

After these two years of extreme asceticism in Egypt, Elijah appeared to him. Luria was at that time only thirty-six years of age; and he was thirty-eight years old when, from here in Safed—may it be rebuilt and reestablished speedily in our days—he was summoned to the Academy on High, because of our many sins. Elijah had said to him: "The time of your death is approaching. And now go up to Safed. There you will find a certain scholar whose name is Rabbi Hayyim Calabrese—may God guard and deliver him. Anoint him in your stead. Lay your hands upon him and teach him all your lore for he will take your place. The sole purpose of your coming into the world has been to "improve" the soul of Rabbi Hayyim, for it is a precious one. [Blemished souls can be "improved" through good deeds and the help of the saints.] Through you he will merit wisdom, and a great light shall shine forth from him upon all Israel. I assure you that I will reveal myself to you whenever you need me; I will lay bare before you the secrets of the upper and the nether worlds, and God, too, will pour out upon you his Holy Spirit a thousand times more than you are able to acquire here in Egypt."

All these things did our Master Luria—of blessed memory— reveal to our teacher Rabbi Hayyim Calabrese, and he in turn revealed them intimately to a chosen few of his associates in Palestine. But our teacher Hayyim, however, wrote in the book which he composed that it appeared to him that Luria was the Messiah ben Joseph but the Master would not admit it to him because of his exceeding humility. However his disciples could surmise it from what Luria had told them. . . . [Messiah ben Joseph is the forerunner of the Davidic Messiah.]

Luria knew all the deeds of men and even their thoughts. He could read faces, look into the souls of men, and recognize souls that migrated from body to body. He could tell you about the souls of the wicked which had entered into trees and stones or animals and birds; he could tell you what commandments a man had fulfilled and what sins he had committed since youth; he knew wherein a sinful man had been punished by God and would prescribe "improvements" to remove a moral blemish, and knew just when such a moral defect had been corrected. He understood the chirping of birds, and through their flight he divined strange things, as is referred to in the verse [Ecclesiastes 10:20]: "For a bird of the air shall carry the voice, and that which hath wings shall tell the matter." All of this he acquired because of the piety, asceticism, purity, and holiness that he had exercised since his youth.

11. *Abraham Galante's Theft, Safed, 1569–1572*

❡He who fears the word of the Lord will take care to see that his business is carried on honestly in order that he shall not sin through false representation or through theft. He should at all times renounce his own in favor of his neighbor and in this way he can be sure that that which belongs to his neighbor will not come into his possession. It is impossible to do business so as to be exactly correct and to stick to the middle of the road and not to take something from your neighbor or he from you. Therefore, he who fears the word of God and who dreads divine punishment for theft will renounce a little of what he really has coming to him, for if he does not it is inevitable that he will take something, if only a trifle, of what he comes across.

In the days of Luria—of blessed memory—the late Rabbi Abraham Galante had asked the Master to give an "improvement" to his soul. [Galante, who died at Safed in 1588, was a wealthy Italian cabalist.] The Master was very timid about doing so because of Galante's outstanding position, until finally the latter said to him: "If you do not declare unto me everything that you see on my forehead then I will adjure you by God to inform me!" Luria then turned to look at his forehead and said: "There is a possibility, my lord and teacher, that you are guilty of theft." [The mystics believed that sin leaves its mark on the forehead.]

Galante was immediately terribly frightened and cried out: "Whither shall I carry my shame since I am guilty of the crime of theft," and went home out of sorts and displeased and put on sackcloth and ashes. He then sent and summoned all the garment workers in his employ [he was a manufacturing weaver], and when they came to him they found their employer clad in sackcloth sitting on the earth, and they were very much distressed.

"Can you not realize and understand that I am only a human being and have no desire to go to Gehenna because of you," he said to them. "Now if you will examine most carefully the accounts of your wages for the work you have done for me, I will appreciate it. If there is nothing due you, then leave me."

"What demands can we make of you for payment?" they responded. "Ever since we have been in your employ we have lacked nothing and do not expect to lack anything. God's blessing has rested upon us; we have had more than enough to eat, and there is no one of us who keeps accounts."

"Nevertheless," he then replied, "it is obvious that I am guilty of the crime of theft since you refuse to make your just demands for moneys due from me. Now I am therefore going to put some money before you and I want every one of you to take whatever you want and to forgive me for all that I have taken that belongs to you, and I, in turn, will forgive you."

He put the money before them, but they were not willing to stretch out their hands to take even a single penny. One woman, however, did put out her hand and take two pennies, and then altogether they called out and said: "We completely forgive you, down to the last penny, etc."

Galante then arose and went to the synagogue of the Master— may his memory endure in the world to come—who hurried out to meet him and said to him: "Why, my lord, were you so exceedingly fearful?" To which Galante answered: "Is it a small matter to feel that I may possibly be guilty of theft? Now if I have found favor in your sight take a look at my forehead and see whether it carries the sign of anything."

"There is no sign of sin," responded the Master and then revealed to Galante the mystery of how it came about that there was a suspicion of theft, by informing him that it was because of that woman who stretched out her hand and took the two pennies. The error arose out of the fact that that woman did the finest work and was superior to the other weavers and should have received more, but was only paid the same wages as the other craftsmen. "But in the heavens above," said Luria, "where they are very particular about such things, they held it against you and stamped the account in writing on your forehead!"

BIBLIOGRAPHY

REFERENCES TO TEXTBOOKS

Elbogen, pp. 148–149; Roth, pp. 260–261; Sachar, pp. 232–236.

READINGS FOR ADVANCED STUDENTS

Graetz, IV, pp. 617–630; Graetz-Rhine, IV, pp. 442–453; Margolis and Marx, pp. 518–524.

Schechter, S., *Studies in Judaism*, Second Series, "Saints and Saintliness," pp. 148ff.; "Safed in the Sixteenth Century, etc.," pp. 202ff.

JE, "Cabala"; "Luria, Isaac ben Solomon Ashkenazi"; "Vital, Hayyim."

53.

Shabbethai Zebi, False Messiah
1666

O F all the pseudo-Messiahs who appeared in Jewish life, Shabbethai Zebi was the most notorious and was the most widely acclaimed. Hundreds of thousands of Jews, both the cultured and the mob, accepted him as the long awaited savior and redeemer of Israel. The times were ripe for him: central Europe and its Jewry with it had been devastated by the Thirty Years' War; East European Jewry had been literally decimated by a series of massacres beginning in 1648. In such periods of suffering the Jewish people always looked forward to a return to a Palestine where a free Jewish state would be established that would serve as a refuge for the myriads of unassorted and panic-stricken Jews.

Cabalists reckoned 1648 as the Messianic year; Christian mystics thought it would be 1666. Thus when Shabbethai Zebi was proclaimed Messiah by frenzied followers and astute propagandists, he found a ready, wildly enthusiastic reception. His charming personality, his fine appearance, his pleasant singing voice, and his cabalistic learning all made him the idol and the hope of a crushed and yearning people.

Shabbethai Zebi probably had no original mystical philosophy of his own; he was a follower of the Lurianic school of mystical thought. His immediate followers who, after his death, created a secret Moslem-Jewish sect (the *Dönmeh*) and who conceived of him as God incarnate, crossed beyond the periphery of Judaism. The Frankists, another Shabbethaian group, also left the faith ultimately, although unwillingly. However, there remained within the fold of Judaism even up to the nineteenth century some outstanding individuals in Central Europe who were not unsympathetic to Shabbethaian Messianism.

The following account of the life and work of Shabbethai Zebi is from the pen of Sir Paul Rycaut (1628–1700), an English diplomat who saw many years of service in the Ottoman Empire and wrote in his *History of the Turkish Empire* of events at first hand. Rycaut, who tries to be fair, thought Zebi was an impostor; however, it is questionable that the false Messiah was a conscious charlatan.

ANNO 1666

❡We shall begin this year with the strange rumor and disturbance of the Jews, concerning Shabbethai Zebi, their pretended Messiah which, for being most principally acted in Turkey, may properly belong to the history of this time and place. . . .

According to the predictions of several Christian writers, especially of such who comment upon the *Apocalypse* or *Revelations* [13:18], this year of 1666 was to prove a year of wonders, of strange revolutions in the world, and particularly, of blessing to the Jews. . . .

Strange reports flew from place to place of the march of multitudes of people from unknown parts into the remote deserts of Arabia, supposed to be the ten tribes and a half, lost for so many ages. That a ship was arrived in the northern parts of Scotland, with her sails and cordage of silk, navigated by mariners who spoke nothing but Hebrew, and with this motto on their sails, "The Twelve Tribes of Israel." . . .

In this manner millions of people were possessed when Shabbethai Zebi first appeared at Smyrna, and published himself to the Jews for their Messiah, relating the greatness of their approaching kingdom, the strong hand whereby God was about to deliver them from bondage, and gather them from all parts of the world. It was strange to see how this fancy took and how fast the report of Shabbethai and his doctrine flew through all parts where Jews inhabited, and so deeply possessed them with a belief of their new kingdom and riches, and many of them with promotion to offices of government, renown, and greatness; that in all places from Constantinople to Buda (which it was my fortune that year to travel) I perceived a strange transport in the Jews, none of them attending to any business, unless to wind up former negotiations, and to prepare themselves and families for a journey to Jerusalem. All their discourses, their dreams, and disposal of their affairs tended to no other design but a reestablishment in the Land of Promise, to greatness and glory, wisdom and doctrine of the Messiah [Shabbethai], whose origin(al), birth, and education is first to be recounted.

Shabbethai Zebi was son of Mordecai Zebi, an inhabitant and natural of Smyrna who gained his livelihood by being broker to an English merchant in that place; a person who before his death was very decrepit in his body, and full of the gout and other infirmities. But his son Shabbethai Zebi, addicting himself to study and learning, became a notable proficient in the Hebrew and Arabic languages. And especially in divinity and metaphysics he was so cunning a sophister that he vented [expressed] a new doctrine in their Law, and drew to the profession of it so many disciples as raised one day a tumult in the synagogue; for which afterwards he was, by censure of the Hakams (who are the expounders of the Law), banished out of the city. [The Smyrna rabbis expelled this Messianic pretender between 1651–1654.]

During the time of his exile he traveled to Thessalonica, now called Salonica. . . . And being now free from the encumbrances of a family, his wandering head moved him to travel through the Morea [southern Greece], thence to Tripoli in Syria, Gaza, and Jerusalem. . . . and meeting there with a certain Jew called Nathan, a proper instrument to promote his design, he communicated to him his condition, his course of life, and intentions to declare himself the Messiah of the world, so long expected and desired by the Jews. [Beginning in 1665, Nathan Benjamin of Gaza brilliantly propagandized the gospel of Shabbethai.]

This design took wonderfully with Nathan; and because it was thought necessary, according to Scripture and ancient prophecies, that Elijah was to precede the Messiah, as St. John Baptist was the forerunner of Christ, Nathan thought no man so proper to act the part of the prophet as himself. And so no sooner had Shabbathai declared himself the Messiah, but Nathan discovers himself to be his prophet, forbidding all the fasts of the Jews in Jerusalem, and declaring that the Bridegroom [the Messiah] being come, nothing but joy and triumph ought to dwell in their habitations; writing to all the assemblies of the Jews to persuade them to the same belief. And now the schism being begun, and many Jews really believing what they so much desired, Nathan took the courage and boldness to prophesy that [in 1666] one year from the 27th of Kislew. . . . the Messiah was to appear before the Grand Signior [the Sultan of Turkey], and to take from him his crown, and lead him in chains like a captive. . . .

And now all the cities of Turkey, where the Jews inhabited, were full of the expectation of the Messiah; no trade or course of gain was followed. Every one imagined that daily provisions, riches, honors, and government were to descend upon him by some unknown and miraculous manner. An example of which is most observable in the Jews at Thessalonica, who now full of assurance that the restoration of their kingdom and the accomplishment of the times for the coming of the Messiah was at hand. . . . applied themselves immediately to fastings; and some in that manner beyond the abilities of nature, that having for the space of seven days taken no sustenance, were famished. [The Jews did penance to speed the coming of the Messiah.]

Others buried themselves in their gardens, covering their naked bodies with earth, their heads only excepted, remained in those beds of dirt, until their bodies were stiffened with the cold and moisture. Others would endure to have melted wax dropt upon their shoulders; others to roll themselves in snow and throw their bodies in the coldest season of the winter into the sea, or frozen waters. But the most common manner of mortification was first to prick their backs and sides with thorns and then to give themselves thirty-nine lashes. All business was laid aside; none worked or opened shop, unless to clear his warehouse of merchandise at any price. Who[ever] had superfluity in household stuff sold it for what he could. . . .

In the heat of all this talk and rumor came Shabbethai Zebi [in 1665] to Smyrna, the city of his nativity, infinitely desired there by the common Jews; but by the Hakams or Doctors of their Law, who gave little or no credence to what he pretended, [he] was ill received, not knowing what mischief or ruin this doctrine and prophecy of a new kingdom might produce. . . . Shabbethai gained ground daily; and the Grand Hakam [Aaron Lapapa] with his party, losing both the affection and obedience of his people, was displaced from his office, and another [Hayyim Benveniste] constituted. [Benveniste was] more affectionate and agreeable to the new prophet, whose power daily increased by those confident reports of his enemies being struck with frenzy and madness, until [the enemies,] being restored to their former temper and wits by him, became his friends, admirers, and disciples. . . .

Shabbethai Zebi, having thus fully fixed himself in Smyrna and filled other places with the rumors of him, declared that he was called by God to visit Constantinople, where the greatest part of his work was to be accomplished. [Shabbethai was expected to overthrow the Sultan and to take Palestine.] In order whereunto he privately shipped himself with some few attendants on a Turkish *saik* [a two-masted sailing vessel] in the month of January, 1666, lest the crowd of his disciples and such who would press to follow him should endanger him in the eyes of the Turks, who already began to be scandalized at the reports and prophecies regarding his person. . . .

The great vizier [Ahmed Köprülü] then also at Constantinople (being not yet departed on his expedition for Candia [Crete]), having heard some rumors of this man and the disorder and madness he had raised amongst the Jews, sent two boats (whilst the *saik* was detained by contrary winds) with commands to bring him up prisoner to the Port; where accordingly Shabbethai, being come, was committed to the most loathsome and darkest dungeon in the town, there to remain in farther expectation of the vizier's sentence. The Jews were not at all discouraged at this illtreatment of their prophet, but rather confirmed in their belief of him, as being an accomplishment of the prophecy of those things which ought to precede his glory and dominion. [According to tradition the Messiah was to suffer before being acclaimed.] . . .

In this manner Shabbethai Zebi remained a prisoner at Constantinople for the space of two months; at the end of which the vizier having designed his expedition for Candia, and, considering the rumor and disturbance the presence of Shabbathai had made already at Constantinople, thought it not secure to suffer him to remain in the imperial city, whilst both the Grand Signior and himself were absent. And [he] therefore changed his prison to the Dardanelli, otherwise called the castle of Abydos. . . . opposite to Sestos, places famous in Greek poetry. This removal of Shabbethai from a worse prison to one of a better air confirmed the Jews with greater confidence of his being the Messiah, supposing that had it been in the power of the vizier or other officers of the Turks to have destroyed his person, they would never have permitted him to live unto that time. . . .

With this consideration and others preceding, the Jews flocked in great numbers to the castle where he was imprisoned, not only from the neighboring parts, but also from Poland, Germany, Leghorn, Venice, Amsterdam, and other places where the Jews reside; on all whom, as a reward of the expense and labors of their pilgrimage, Shabbathai bestowed plenty of his benedictions, promising increase of their store and enlargement of possessions in the Holy Land.

So great was the confluence of the Jews to this place that the Turks thought it requisite to make their advantage thereof, and so not only raised the price of their provisions, lodgings, and other necessaries, but also denied to admit any to the presence of Shabbethai unless for money, setting the price sometimes at five, sometimes at ten dollars, or more or less, according as they guessed at the abilities and zeal of the person. By which gain and advantage to the Turks, no complaints or advices were carried to Adrianople either of the concourse or arguments amongst the Jews in that place, but rather all civilities and liberties indulged unto them, which served as a farther argument to ensnare this poor people in the belief of their Messiah. . . . [The Turkish tolerance of Zebi made people think he was the Messiah.]

But to return again to Shabbethai Zebi himself, we find him still remaining a prisoner in the castle of Abydos upon the Hellespont, admired and adored by his brethren with more honor than before, and visited by pilgrims from all parts where the fame of the coming of the Messiah had arrived. Amongst which one from Poland named Nehemiah Cohen was of special note and renown, learned in the Hebrew, Syriac, and Chaldee, and versed in the doctrine and cabala of the Rabbins as well as Shabbethai himself: one (of whom it was said), had not this Zebi anticipated the design, esteemed himself as able a fellow for to act a Messiah as the other.

Howsoever, it being now too late to publish any such pretense, Shabbethai having already prepossessed the office and with that the hearts and belief of the Jews, Nehemiah was contented with some small appendage or relation to a Messiah, and therefore to lay his design the better, desired a private conference with Shabbethai. These two great Rabbins being together, a hot dispute arose between them. . . . And thereupon the dispute grew so hot, and the controversy so irreconcilable, as was taken notice of by the Jews, and controverted amongst them as every one fancied.

But Shabbethai being of greater authority, his sentence prevailed, and Nehemiah was rejected as schismatical and an enemy to the Messiah, which afterwards proved the ruin and downfall of this imposture. For Nehemiah, being thus baffled, and being a person of authority and a haughty spirit, meditated nothing but revenge; to execute which to the full, he took a journey to Adrianople, and there informed the chief ministers of state and officers of the court, who (by reason of the gain the Turks made of their prisoner at the castle on the Hellespont) heard nothing of all this concourse of people and prophecies of the revolt of the Jews from their obedience to the Grand Signior. . . .

A *chaouse* or messenger was immediately dispatched to bring up Shabbethai Zebi to Adrianople, The *chaouse* executed his commission after the Turkish fashion in haste, bringing Shabbethai in a few days to Adrianople, without farther excuse or ceremony, not affording him an hour's space to take a solemn farewell of his followers and adorers, who now were come to the vertical point of all their hopes and expectations.

The Grand Signior, having by this time received divers informations of the madness of the Jews and the pretenses of Shabbethai, grew big with desire and expectation to see him; so that he no sooner arrived at Adrianople, but the same hour he was brought before the Grand Signior. . . . The Grand Signior. . . . declared that, having given public scandal to the professors of the Mahometan religion and done dishonor to his sovereign authority by pretending to withdraw from him so considerable a portion as the land of Palestine, his treason and crime could not be expiated without becoming a Mahometan convert: which if he refused to do, the stake was ready at the gate of the seraglio to impale him.

Shabbethai, being now reduced to his last game and extremity (not being in the least doubtful what to do, for to die for what he was assured was false was against nature and the death of a mad man), replied with much cheerfulness that he was contented to turn Turk and that it was not of force, but of choice; having been a long time desirous of so glorious a profession, he esteemed himself much honored that he had an opportunity to own it first in the presence of the Grand Signior [September, 1666]. . . .

The news of Shabbethai turning Turk and of the Messiah to a Mahometan quickly filled all parts of Turkey. The Jews were strangely surprised at it, and ashamed of their easiness of belief, of the arguments with which they had persuaded others, and of the proselytes they had made in their own families. Abroad they became the common derision of the towns where they inhabited. The boys hooted after them, coining a new word at Smyrna (*poustai!*) which every one seeing a Jew, with a finger pointed out, would pronounce with scorn and contempt; so that this deceived people for a long time after remained with confusion, silence, and dejection of spirit.

And yet most of them affirm that Shabbethai is not turned Turk, but his shadow only remains on earth, and walks with a white head, and in the habit of a Mahometan; but that his body and soul are taken into heaven, there to reside until the time appointed for accomplishment of these wonders. And this opinion began so commonly to take place, as if this people resolved never to be undeceived, using the forms and rules for devotion prescribed them by their Mahometan Messiah. Insomuch that the Hakams of Constantinople, fearing the danger of this error might creep up and equal the former, condemned the belief of Shabbethai being Messiah as damnable, and enjoined them to return to the ancient method and service of God, upon pain of excommunication. . . .

And thus the . . . Jews [returned] again to their wits, following their trade and profession of brokage as formerly, with more quiet and advantage than the means of regaining their possessions in the Land of Promise. And thus ended this mad frenzy amongst the Jews, which might have cost them dear, had not Shabbethai renounced his Messiahship at the feet of Mahomet [IV. Sultan, 1648–1687].

These matters were transacted in the years 1665 and 1666, since which Shabbethai hath passed his time devoutly in the Ottoman court. . . . In this manner Shabbethai passed his days in the Turkish court, as some time Moses did in that of the Egyptians; and perhaps in imitation of him cast his eyes often on the afflictions of his brethren, of whom, during his life, he continued to profess himself a deliverer; but with that care and caution of giving scandal to the Turks, that he declared, unless their nation became like him, that is, renounce the shadows and imperfect elements of the Mosaical law, which will be completed by adherence to the Mahometan, and such other additions as his inspired wisdom should suggest, he should never be able to prevail with God for them or conduct them to the Holy Land of their forefathers.

Hereupon many Jews flocked in, some as far as from Babylon, Jerusalem, and other remote places, and casting their caps on the ground, in presence of the Grand Signior, voluntarily professed themselves Mahometans. Shabbethai himself, by these proselytes gaining ground in the esteem of the Turks, had privilege granted him to visit familiarly his brethren, which he employed in circumcising their children the eighth day, according to the precept of Moses, preaching his new doctrines, by which he hath confirmed many in their faith of his being the Messiah, and startled all with expectation of what these strange ways of enthusiasm may produce. But none durst publicly own him, lest they should displease the Turks and the Jews, and incur the danger of excommunication from one, and the gallows from the other. [Shabbathai's Jewish-Moslem followers still exist today as the Dönmeh, "apostates."]

BIBLIOGRAPHY

REFERENCES TO TEXTBOOKS

Elbogen, pp. 150ff.; Roth, pp. 309–313; Sachar, pp. 242–245.

READINGS FOR ADVANCED STUDENTS

Graetz, IV, pp. 118–167, 206–231; Graetz-Rhine, V, pp. 153–182, 218–235; Margolis and Marx, pp. 558–577.

Greenstone, J. H., The Messiah Idea in Jewish History, Chap. vi, "The Effects of Kabbalistic Speculation."

Kastein, J., The Messiah of Ismir, Sabbatai Zevi. A biography, of the modern dramatic type, which leans very heavily on the best sources. This work is by no means a definitive study.

Silver, A. H., A History of Messianic Speculation in Israel, Chap. vii, "The Seventeenth Century."

Encyclopaedia of Religion and Ethics, "Messiahs (Pseudo-)."

JE, "Dönmeh"; "Ghazzati, Nathan Benjamin ben Elisha ha-Levi"; "Pseudo-Messiahs"; "Shabbethai Zebi b. Mordecai."

ADDITIONAL SOURCE MATERIALS IN ENGLISH

Rycaut, P., *The History of the Turkish Empire, from the Year 1623, to the Year 1677*, London, 1687, pp. 174–184. This source, from which the above selection has been taken, is probably the most accurate contemporary account of Shabbethai Zebi.

[Evelyn, J.,] *The History of the Three Late Famous Impostors, viz. Padre Ottomano, Mahomed Bei, and Sebatai Sevi*, London, 1669. Evelyn probably plagiarized his material from reports which Rycaut had submitted prior to 1669.

54.

The Rise of the *Hasidim*
Eastern Europe, about 1735–1740

IN Poland in the eighteenth century, anarchy, the growth of religious hatred, and the difficulties in the economic life led to a deepening of the mystical spirit on the part of the Jewish masses who looked to God for help. There were quite a number of mystics, Messianic pretenders, and spiritual heroes who ministered to a desperate people and promised them relief. Israel ben Eliezer (about 1700–1760) was one of these spiritual heroes.

Sometime between 1735 and 1740 he set about to spread his teachings. He had been a synagogue watchman, a schoolteacher, a ritual slaughterer, and an innkeeper, and now he became a writer of amulets, an exorciser, an herb-doctor, a miracle worker, and above all a physician of the soul. He was called the BeSHT, the *Baal Shem Tob*, which may be translated, the "Good Master of the Name," the one who employs the Name of God for good purposes only. From the city of Miedzyboz in Podolia, where he spent the last years of his life, his teachings spread all over eastern Europe until his movement, Hasidism ("pietism"), became one of the most powerful and vigorous in all Jewry.

Hasidism was not a revolt against the Jewish religion but against its leaders and their interpretation of it. The Besht taught a new way to worship God. He taught the spiritually hungry masses an inner service of the heart through intense personal prayer to a God who is present in all things. He preached humility, and decried asceticism, although he had himself practiced asceticism in his earlier days. He appealed for joy and ecstasy in all religious service; he stressed a love of nature. He insisted that spiritual perfection comes not through learning but through personal devoutness, and thus the humblest ignoramus can come as close to God as the greatest rabbinic scholar. Through the example of his own tender and kind life, through his gentle satires and simple parables, he made Judaism meaningful for the masses at a time when its human qualities were being neglected by its rabbinic leaders.

Like Isaac Luria, an earlier mystic, he wrote no books.

The first two selections given below are taken from the Hebrew *Shibhe ha-Besht* ("Praises of the Besht"), the first biography of the founder of Hasidism, published in 1814, about fifty-four years after the death of its hero. Though the book abounds in legends and miracles it contains passages which portray the Besht as he really was. The first selection covers the period from his boyhood to the beginning of his public ministry, about 1735. The second reflects his attitude toward tainted money.

The third selection, a reminiscence of the great Hasidic leader by his own grandson Baruch of Miedzyboz (about 1750–1811), portrays clearly his disapproval of asceticism. It is found in Baruch's *Buzina de-Nehora* ("The lighted lamp"), a Hebrew collection of Baruch's comments and remarks.

1. *The Career of the Besht before He Began His Public Ministry, about 1700–1740*

⟪And it came to pass after the death of the Besht's father, that, as the lad grew up, the Jews of the community [of Okop, in Podolia, where he was born] were kind to him because his father had been very dear to them. They therefore turned him over to a teacher for instruction, and he made rapid progress in his studies. It was a habit of his, however, to study for several days and then to run away from school. Then they would have to search for him and would find him sitting alone in the forest. They ascribed this to the fact that he was an orphan, that he had no one to look after him, and that he had to shift for himself. They would therefore bring him back again to his teacher. And so it happened a number of times: he would run away to the woods in order to be alone there, until finally they lost interest and abandoned the plan of giving him to a teacher. And thus the lad grew up in an unusual manner.

He hired himself out to be a teacher's assistant, to take the children to school and back, and to lead them to the synagogue, and to recite with them in a pleasant voice: "Amen, may His great Name be blessed," the "Sanctification," and the "Amens." [He was now about twelve years of age.] This was his work—holy labor with children whose breath is without sin. And all the while the children strolled along he would sing with them in a sweet voice and with great pleasure and he was heard afar off. . . .

And then he became a watchman in the synagogue. This was his wont: as long as the people in the synagogue were awake he would sleep, and when those who had been awake slept, then he, who had been asleep, awoke and carried on his work—perfect work [probably cabalistic study]—until the time came when the people arose again. Then he would go back to sleep, and thus they thought that he had slept all through that night from beginning to end. . . .

[Israel now began to study cabala with a rabbi's son who had come to the village.]

When the people of the community saw that Israel was studying with the son of the rabbi, they said that surely the merit of Israel's father had brought it about that the rabbi's son should come to this town and befriend him. It seemed to them that Israel was following the right path, so they gave him a wife, but it was not very long before his wife passed away. . . .

After this he struck out on a new path for he went away from that place to a town near the holy community of Brody where he became a successful teacher. He found favor in the eyes of all, for he was a very distinguished scholar and such a great sage that all the affairs of the community were decided and determined by him. [This account of his scholarship is exaggerated.] If there happened to be a dispute between people and they came to him he would so settle their case that both the innocent and the guilty would be satisfied with him, for he appealed to them out of the fullness of his wisdom so that all were pleased. . . .

[The Good Master of the Name now came to Brody in Galicia to seek the bride to whom he had been secretly affianced by her late father. Her brother Gerson had objected to her marriage with this apparently untutored man.]

Then said Rabbi Gerson to his sister: "Truly, I am very much ashamed of your husband. If you care to divorce him I will be happy; but if not I will buy you a horse so that you may move on with him and dwell wherever you wish for I cannot stand the disgrace." To this she agreed, and they wandered about until finally he fixed on a place where she could dwell, but he himself wandered alone among the great hills, the [Carpathian] mountains.

This is how he made a living. Two or three times a week she used to come to him with the horse and wagon, then he would dig brick-clay which she would take to the city, and in this way she earned her living. The Good Master of the Name used to fast for long stretches and whenever he wished to eat he would dig a little hole in the ground, then put some flour and water in it, and it would become baked through the heat of the sun. This was all the food he ate after his fast. And he spent all his time in seclusion.

After seven years of living in seclusion among the mountains, had passed, and the time drew nigh for him to reveal himself, he journeyed with his wife to the holy community of Brody, to his brother-in-law, the rabbi, our master the teacher Rabbi Gerson. When they arrived the rabbi greeted his sister enquiring: "Where have you been?" She answered him, saying: "We wandered about from town to town and encountered a great deal of trouble." So he became very sorry for his sister and settled them near his house and employed the Good Master of the Name as his servant. . . .

Then said Rabbi Gerson: "I can't even get this sort of service out of him, for he is no good at any sort of work." After this, therefore, Rabbi Gerson leased for him a tavern in a village that he might be able to make a living there. There he attained a high degree of perfection for he built a solitary hut for himself in the woods and there he used to pray and to study both day and night throughout the week. Only on Sabbath days did he come home. At home he had white garments for the Sabbath, and also a bath house as well as a place to take a ritual bath. [His life now seems to be patterned consciously after that of Isaac Luria.] It was his wife who was busy making a living, and God dispensed blessing and prosperity on the works of her hands. They were most courteous in their treatment of wayfarers and in providing them with food and drink. Whenever guests would arrive she would send for her husband, and he would come and serve them. But no one really knew anything about him. . . .

After this he fixed his residence in the holy community of Tluste [Galicia, about 1735] and was also a teacher there. He could not get ten men together for a [regular religious] service in his home, but he invited a few to his house and prayed with them there. He used to wear a garment of the coarsest cloth and his toes used to stick out of the holes in his shoes, for he was very poor. Before he prayed he would take a ritual bath, even in the dead of winter, and while he prayed perspiration in beads as big as beans would drop from him [because he prayed so earnestly].

Sick people would frequently come to see him but he did not care to receive them until the following incident happened. Once they brought an insane man—or perhaps it was a woman—to him, but he would not see him. That night it was revealed to him that he had passed his thirty-sixth year, and in the morning he checked the figures and found out it was correct. So then he received that insane person and cured him. He gave up the profession of teaching and took my father-in-law, of blessed memory, as his secretary. [One of the compilers of this book was a son-in-law of the Besht's secretary, Alexander.]

From then on people began to journey to him from all places.

[The Besht now, about 1740, entered upon his public ministry and finally settled in Miedzyboz where he preached his gospel.]

II. *Tainted Money*

⦗I have heard from the rabbi [of Ilincy?] that in a certain scroll of the Law they were always finding mistakes. They corrected it constantly, but nevertheless they kept on finding errors in it. They showed this scroll of the Torah to the Good Master of the Name, and he said that it had been ordered and paid for with money that is called "rake-off" money. This means that each time people would play cards for money they would give a coin, as rent for the use of the rooms, to the master of the house. The master of the house saved this money and for it had that scroll of the Torah written. And [the Besht was right for] this is really what had happened. The Good Master of the Name said further that this scroll could not be made right, but would forever be unfit even if they would correct it ever so many times.

III. *Fasting and True Religion*

⦗Commenting on Psalm 107:18: "Their soul abhorred all manner of food," Baruch of Miedzyboz [a grandson of the Besht] said that they once asked the Good Master of the Name: "What is the essence of religious service? Do we not know and have not our fathers told us that in ancient days pious men used to fast from one Sabbath to another? But now you have stopped this sort of thing for you have said that every man who fasts will some day have to justify himself and that he will be considered a sinner inasmuch as he has plagued his soul. Now, therefore, tell us what is the essence of religious service."

Thereupon the Good Master of the Name answered them: "I have come to this world to point out another way whereby man may attract to himself these three things, namely, love of God, love of Israel, and love of Torah. And there is no need to practice asceticism!"

BIBLIOGRAPHY

REFERENCES TO TEXTBOOKS

Elbogen, pp. 156–157; Roth, pp. 313–315; Sachar, pp. 263–267.

READINGS FOR ADVANCED STUDENTS

Graetz, V, pp. 374–394; Graetz-Rhine, V, pp. 339–350; Margolis and Marx, pp. 581–588.

Buber, M., *Jewish Mysticism and the Legends of Baalshem.* "The Life of the Chassids," pp. 1–38. The balance of the book is devoted to Hasidic legends as reworked by Buber.

Dubnow, S. M., *History of the Jews in Russia and Poland,* I, pp. 220–241.

Ginzberg, L., *Students, Scholars and Saints,* Chap. vi, "The Gaon, Rabbi Elijah Wilna."

Minkin, J. S., *The Romance of Hassidism.* One of the best accounts in English.

Schechter, S., *Studies in Judaism,* First Series, 1896, Chap. i, "The Chassidim"; Chap. iii, "Rabbi Elijah Wilna, Gaon."

Waxman, M., *A History of Jewish Literature,* III, pp. 18ff.

JE, "Ba'al Shem-Tob, Israel b. Eliezer"; "Hasidim, Hasidism."

ADDITIONAL SOURCE MATERIALS IN ENGLISH

Levin, M., *The Golden Mountain: Marvellous Tales of Rabbi Israel Baal Shem and of His Great-Grandson, Rabbi Nachman, etc.* Through these stories one may derive some concept of the dream world of the *Hasidim.*

Solomon Maimon: an Autobiography, pp. 151–186. A critical account of Hasidism by a contemporary.

55.

An Attack on the *Hasidim*
Shklov, Russia, December 31, 1786

THE rapid growth of the Hasidic movement startled the rabbinic leaders and their followers. As *Mitnaggedim* ("opponents"), they objected to the separatistic tendencies of the *Hasidim*, and to their changes in dress, in the religious service, and in their method of slaughtering. The *Mitnaggedim* resented the revolt against the authority of the rabbis; they dreaded the neglect of scholarship, and they feared the enthusiasm of the ignorant masses for cabalistic and mystic teachings. The movement smacked too much of Shabbethaianism, Frankism, and even moral laxity.

Under the influence of the great rabbinic scholar, Elijah of Vilna (1720–1797), the Jews of both Vilna and Brody issued severe edicts against the *Hasidim* in 1772. These two manifestoes are the precursors of a whole series of similar pronouncements all through eastern Europe; and as these proved ineffective, more severe denunciations and bans tending to read the *Hasidim* out of Judaism were published.

The following circular is typical of the attacks which failed to stop the progress of the movement. It was issued in 1786 by the anti-Hasidic community of Shklov, in Moghilef, in White Russia. The leaders of this town were moved to action probably because of the successes of the Hasidic leader, Shneor Zalman (1748–1812), and because of the missionary activity of one Isaac Zaslaver who was associated with an unqualified ritual-meat slaughterer.

In 1804 the Russian government gave the new group legal status, and gradually the *Mitnaggedim* and *Hasidim* learned to tolerate each other. The *Hasidim* still exist to the number of hundreds of thousands and are a powerful influence in East European Jewish life.

ℭBecause of our many sins, worthless and wanton men who call themselves *Hasidim* have deserted the Jewish group and have set up a so-called place of worship for themselves. And thus, as every one knows, they worship in a most insane fashion following a different ritual which does not conform to the religion of our holy Torah, and they tread a path which our fathers have never trod. In addition to this the works of their teachers have, unfortunately,

276

recently been published [1780–1784], and it is obvious to us that all of their writings are opposed to our holy Torah and that they contain misleading interpretations. The exaggerations and stories of miracles that are described in their books are particularly evident and obvious lies, and far be it from us to place any trust in any such exaggerated statements. And behold, as a result of this great misfortune, a fire has been kindled, unfortunately, in the midst of Jewry, and there is a breaking away from the obligations imposed by the Torah. [Some *Hasidim* laughed at some of the Jewish laws.]

Therefore, we, the undersigned, are in agreement that every community is most urgently bound to adopt rigorous measures—carrying with them every possible penalty—in order to put into effect all the protective and defensive measures described below. And these details are to be officially recorded in the minute-books of every community and city that they may serve as a charge and as a memorial for future generations, so that our Jewish brethren may avoid the evil customs and laws of the *Hasidim.*

The following are the protective measures which were adopted at our session:

1. We order that a fast and public prayer be instituted on the 25th of the month of Tebet of the current year [January 15, 1787] in all communities. [The purpose of this prayer and public fast was to avert the evils of heresy.]. . . .

2. All possible measures are to be adopted to put an end to the prayer-meetings of the heretics in all communities, so that they will be deprived of the possibility of common assembly.

3. Careful watch is to be maintained that no one should study their literature, and search is to be made with this purpose in mind.

4. We fully confirm the validity of the ordinances which were issued in Brody and in Vilna [1781] and which deal with the prohibition of pilgrimages to the heads of the sect.

5. What their ritual slaughterers kill may not be eaten, the meat of such slaughtering is to be considered carrion, and the instruments used are to be considered polluted and forbidden. Meat brought into one city from another place is to be considered carrion unless it is accompanied by a certificate from a reliable person who is not a member of the Hasidic group. [This article would break off social relations with the *Hasidim.*]

6. Supervisors to see that all the above mentioned provisions are carried out should be appointed in every city.

7. No one is to shelter any member of this sect.

8. No member of the above mentioned sect may bring suit in a Jewish court. No community may permit any one of them to hold a position as cantor or rabbi, and it goes without saying that no one of them may teach our children.

9. It is to be announced in all communities that any one who knows anything, good or bad, about the *Hasidim* must bring his information to the court.

We, the undersigned, are unanimous with respect to all these measures.

Shklov, Sunday, the 10th of Tebet, 5547 [December 31, 1786].

MOSES, *son of Rabbi Yudel.*

Etc., etc., etc., etc.

BIBLIOGRAPHY

REFERENCES TO TEXTBOOKS

Elbogen, pp. 156–157; Roth, pp. 313–315; Sachar, pp. 263–267.

56.

The Frankists
1755-1817

THE conversion of Shabbethai Zebi to Islam did not put an end to his influence. Many of his half-Jewish, half-Moslem followers, known to the Turks as *Dönmeh* ("apostates"), exist to this day in the Balkans and in the Near East.

These Shabbethaians were particularly active in the eighteenth century in Poland as a result of the economic suffering and physical persecution which the Jews experienced there. Many Jews, because of their distress, persisted in looking forward to the speedy coming of a Messiah who would bring them redemption. These mystics were led by an adventurer, Jacob Frank (about 1726-1791), a Podolian Jew who joined the *Dönmeh* in Salonica and later returned to Poland in 1755 to organize these sectarians. These Frankists, the secret group which he dominated, believed in a peculiar mixture of Jewish, Moslem, and Christian dogmas. It was at the same time ascetic and libertinistic. It fought rabbinic leadership and law and substituted the cabalistic *Zohar* for the Talmud as its authoritative guide and mentor.

In the years 1759 and 1760 over seven hundred of the Frankists embraced Christianity. Though the group continued its propaganda for many years among the Jews of eastern and central Europe, it exerted no appreciable effect on Jewry as a whole. With the death of Jacob Frank's daughter, Eva, the "Holy Lady," in 1817, this Shabbethaian sect faded from the scene.

The first account given below is taken from the Hebrew work, *Dibre Binah* ("Words of Wisdom"), a polemical work against the Shabbethaians and the Frankists. It was written by Ber of Bolechow (1723-1805), a Galician Jew, who not only records the arguments which the Talmudic Jews had with these Contra-Talmudists or Zoharites but also describes the early life of Frank and some of the beliefs of his sect. Unlike most of his Jewish contemporaries, Ber tried to be fair in his judgment of the Frankists.

The second account is taken from the German memoirs of the famous mineralogist, Karl Cäsar von Leonhard, who in his youth had seen the notorious Jacob Frank in Offenbach and had heard a great deal about him.

1. *Frank and His Ideas, Poland, 1755–1759*

❡These two men [Mordecai Stryzow and Zeeb Bendits] had been sent on a mission to Salonica by their entire group—believers in Shabbethai Zebi—in order that they might see and greet their Messiah, Berechiah, who had succeeded Shabbethai Zebi and had permitted them to do the forbidden things mentioned above. [It was rumored that Berechiah had encouraged immorality.] But when they came to the city of Salonica and found Berechiah in bed, sick of the disease of which he ultimately died, these two messengers then remained there and were not sent back to Poland. They did, however, write a letter to the men of their [Shabbethaian] sect reporting that Berechiah had died and that his holy soul had departed while discussing the mysteries and secrets of the Torah. Through the laying on of hands he had ordained the rabbi and scholar, our master, Rabbi Jacob Frank, the son of Loeb, the bookbinder of the city of Korolówka.

Some people say that his father was a distiller of whiskey, and that he himself had been a teacher's assistant who had wandered about from town to town and from province to province studying until he arrived finally at the city of Salonica. There he studied the *Zohar* intensively under the men of the sect until he acquired a rich knowledge in the *Zohar* and became widely known as a scholar of cabalistic lore. It was for this reason that Berechiah ordained him and that he succeeded him as described above. About the year 5615 [1755]. . . . he rose up and came to Poland. . . . and visited all the cities wherever any members of that group were found. Many of them followed him until he had acquired a large flock. . . .

[Excommunicated in 1756 because of anti-rabbinism, the Frankists appealed to the Catholic Church for sympathy and pointed out through the following confession of faith how close they were to Christianity. It was on the ground of these theses that a disputation took place in Kamenetz-Podolsk on June 20–27, 1757 between the Jews and the Frankists.]

1. We believe everything that God has commanded in the ancient law of Moses and everything that he has taught us therein.

2. It is impossible to understand and to know the holy Torah thoroughly by mere human reason and without the "grace" of God. [This thesis points to Christian theological influence.]

3. The Talmud, which is full of unheard of slanders against God, must be abandoned and disregarded.

4. There is One God and He has created everything.

5. And this God is One, undivided in essence, although three in manifestation. [Such trinitarianism can be traced in some cabalistic writings.]

6. God is able to clothe himself in the body of man and thus be subjected to all vicissitudes except sin.

7. In accordance with the words of the prophets Jerusalem will never be rebuilt.

8. The Messiah, whose coming has been predicted by all the prophets, will never reappear.

9. God himself has borne the punishment for the sin of the first Adam and has thus removed the curse from the latter and all his descendants in the succeeding generations. God is the Messiah who has incarnated himself. [Christianity too believes that its Messiah atoned for the innate sin which mankind inherited through Adam.]

[In May, 1759, the Frankists, about to become Catholics, asked for the following concessions from the Church. The Church, however, refused to compromise; nevertheless, many of the Frankists accepted baptism, although unwillingly.]

And these are the terms which they sought in the petition which was written in the month of Iyyar 5519 [May 1759]:

1. That the conversion shall take place in Lemberg, close to the time of the contracts, that is, during the festival of Three Kings [January 6, 1760. Many Polish nobles came on this day to the Lemberg fair and made their contracts. The Frankists hoped the rich nobles would serve as godfathers and befriend them].

2. That they should not be compelled to shave their beards and earlocks.

3. That they should be permitted to wear the Jewish garb.

4. That they be allowed to use Jewish names together with their Christian names, as for instance, Andrew and Woelfila.

5. That they should not intermarry with the Gentiles but only among themselves. [The Frankists, it seems, did not really want to become Christians.]

6. That they should not have to eat swine's flesh.

7. That they should rest both on the Sabbath and on Sunday like the Christians.

8. That they should be allowed at all times to study the *Zohar* and the other cabalistic works.

9. On the basis of the Talmud they would like to prove seven theses, some of which confirm the Christian faith, and the seventh of which proves the evil of the Talmud which ought to be burnt.

[This disputation between the Jews and the Frankists took place in Lemberg, July 17—September 10, 1759.]

11. *The Latter Days of Frank, 1760–1791*

⟨At the time of which I speak, 1788, there appeared in the vicinity of Offenbach [near Frankfort on the Main] a most strange and mysterious figure. He became the object of curiosity, of astonishment and, in fact, there was something phenomenal about him. I might be accused, perhaps, of being incomplete if I should forget to describe this matter.

By permission of the Prince of Isenburg, a Baron Frank settled in the city. Some called him count, and some even wanted to make a prince out of the man. He moved into a princely mansion and lived in a brilliant, magnificent style. The furnishings of his house were the most costly and luxurious, the steps were covered with soft carpets: everything had a festive appearance. Frank maintained a guard of honor, and his retinue soon increased so that it amounted to a thousand persons: men, women, girls, and children. Here his adherents found a safe meeting place, a friendly reception, and abundant support. All of them lived quietly and peacefully at the expense of their chief who bore all their responsibilities. They formed a small world—fond of life, but not of work. Not a single one of these people followed any line of business. Shabbethaian Jews, bringing gifts, pilgrimaged in masses from eastern Europe to Offenbach. . . . Frank lived secluded together with his children, a daughter and two sons. . . .

In order to supplement this account I must relate what we have heard from time to time of the details of the earlier life of Frank. . . . Frank was arrested. . . . Because he was a Christian who was faithful to his Jewish adherents and made converts, he was taken to Czenstochowa on the Warthe. [He was imprisoned here as a Christian heretic, 1761–1773.] He remained there for several years under close arrest and received his freedom only when the Russians conquered this fortress.

Encouraged by the support that he had received before this and striving ever higher, our soldier of fortune traversed Poland, Bohemia, and Moravia, spreading his religious teachings everywhere. He extorted funds from his like-minded adherents and gradually acquired huge sums so that finally he traveled about with a numerous train like a prince. His followers, from private secretary to stable boy, were, without exception, converted Jews.

In Vienna. . . . he displayed a pomp and lived in a style far exceeding the fortune of a private citizen. No one knew the source of his financial affluence and for this reason the police thought it advisable to expel him, although they had no other cause for apprehension.

The chief of the "Non-Jews" now chose Brünn [Moravia, 1773] as his residence and the "brethren" provided for him so generously that often whole barrels full of money were brought to him. Here Frank would always say his prayers out in the open. He would ride out in a magnificent carriage, surrounded by his horsemen who were puffed up with the pride of wealth and who like Uhlans were dressed in green and red. On their long lance points they had military pennants with the emblem of the sun and moon, eagles and stags. A most peculiar ceremony took place after prayer: a trooper, who had followed the master's carriage and who was mounted on a stately steed that was decked with innumerable bells, would pour water out of a leather sack on to the spot where the prayers had been offered up.

Another attempt to establish himself in Vienna ended, like the first, in failure. Frank was not tolerated by the police although he resorted to a number of artifices; among others, pretending that a princess from the North was supporting him.

Four years after he had succeeded in settling in Offenbach death unexpectedly severed all relations. [He was in Offenbach from 1788–1791.] Frank died suddenly of an apoplectic stroke. This was the fatal turning point for the family's fortunes. The hopes of the children were not fulfilled; this affliction plunged them into anxiety and grief, and they became impoverished. Their financial income was exhausted, and they were compelled to go into debt.

Did all illusion vanish with the hero of the play, or had his successors not studied their rôles sufficiently well? The sect lost its hold in Germany.

BIBLIOGRAPHY

REFERENCES TO TEXTBOOKS

Roth, p. 313; Sachar, pp. 244–245.

READINGS FOR ADVANCED STUDENTS

Graetz, V, pp. 271–290; Margolis and Marx, pp. 583ff.
Dubnow, S. M., *History of the Jews in Russia and Poland*, I, pp. 211–220.
JE, "Frank, Jacob"; "Pseudo-Messiahs."

Jewry and the Individual Jew
C. JEWISH NOTABLES

57.

Saadia
882–942

Fʀᴏᴍ 300 to 1000 Babylonia was the center of Jewish life. There the Jews had a political head in the exilarch and great religious leaders in the *geonim*, who were the presidents of the Talmudic academies of Sura and Pumbedita. These schools influenced Jewish religious life all over the world during the days of the Abbaside caliphate, whose capital was at Bagdad (750–1258).

One of the most famous of these academy heads was Saadia ben Joseph (882–942), who was born in the district of Faiyum in Upper Egypt. He was one of the greatest intellects in Jewry, and the first outstanding scholar to fuse together the Arabic and the Hebraic cultures. This creative scholar is noted for his many writings which touch almost all subjects: rabbinic law, poetry, liturgy, grammar, mysticism, polemics, chronology, Bible, and philosophy. His best known books were a translation of the Bible into Arabic and a philosophic work called *Emunot we-Deot* ("Beliefs and Opinions"), both of which are still popular. Most of his works were written in Arabic. After wandering and teaching in Egypt, Palestine, and Syria, he came to Babylon (921), became *Gaon* of the academy at Sura (928), and soon was engaged in a bitter controversy with the exilarch who had appointed him.

The story of this struggle, which reflects the character of Saadia, is given below. This account, now extant only in Hebrew, was originally written in Arabic by Nathan the Babylonian about 960 and is part of a work of a rather popular nature dealing with the Jews of Bagdad.

⟨When the president of the academy at Sura died, the Exilarch [David ben Zakkai] was considering whom he would induct into the office and had decided on either our master Saadia of Faiyum or Zemah ben Shahin. The latter was a learned man of a distinguished family. The Exilarch had sent first to Nissi Naharwani to be the head of the academy but he answered: "It cannot be. The head of the academy is called the 'Light of the World' while I am blind."

"Well, then, what is your opinion in this matter?" the Exilarch said to him. "Do what you like," he answered him. The Exilarch then told him what he thought of doing, that his choice had fallen on either our master Saadia or on Zemah ben Shahin. Nissi told him to appoint Zemah ben Shahin and not Saadia, even though the latter was a great man and a distinguished scholar. "He fears no man, however," he said, "and kowtows to no one because of his great wisdom, his spirit, his eloquence, and his fear of sin." "Well," answered the Exilarch, "my decision is already made. I have decided on our master Saadia of Faiyum."

"Do what you like," answered Nissi. "The first one to listen to his words and study with him will be myself. And I shall be the first to accept him." So they inducted him into office at that time in the presence of Kohen Zedek and the scholars of the Pumbedita academy, and they appointed him chief of the college at Sura. [Kohen Zedek was the head of the rival academy of Pumbedita, then in Bagdad. He opposed Saadia, who was appointed to Sura, 928.]

But it was not long before a quarrel broke out [about 930] between the Exilarch and Saadia, and Bagdad was divided into two parties. All the wealthy of Bagdad, the scholars of the academies, and the prominent people of the city sided with Saadia, ready to help him by means of their money and their influence with the king, his princes, and advisers.

There was, however, a very influential man in Bagdad, Caleb [Chalaf] ibn Sargado by name, who was a supporter of the Exilarch. He gave 60,000 *zuz* of his fortune—for he was a rich man—to remove Saadia from office, but he did not succeed, for the sons of Netira and all the wealthy of Bagdad were with Saadia. [Sahl and Isaac Netira, influential bankers in Bagdad, were known for their generosity to the Jewish and Moslem poor. Saadia had taught Sahl.] The fact is that this Caleb was jealous of Saadia, for though Caleb was eloquent and very learned and knew an answer or two for every question, Saadia knew ten times more, and for this reason Caleb envied him. [Caleb wanted the Sura appointment. Later he became head of Pumbedita and thus achieved his ambition of presiding over one of the great Babylonian academies.]

The roots of the quarrel between Saadia and the Exilarch were some property that belonged to some men who were within the jurisdiction of the Exilarch, and a large sum of money which fell to them through inheritance and which they desired to divide. They quarreled about it until they voluntarily agreed to give to the Exilarch ten per cent of all that fell to them by inheritance, in order to remove all complaints against themselves and to settle the case.

This ten per cent which they gave to the Exilarch as his share amounted to seven hundred goldpieces, so he issued the documents for them, sealed them, and ordered them to go to the heads of the academies who would confirm them. [The legal papers of the Exilarchs had to be confirmed by the heads of the great academies of Sura and Pumbedita.]

When the documents reached Saadia he examined them and saw things in them that did not seem right to him. Nevertheless he spoke to the men courteously: "Go to Kohen Zedek, the head of the Pumbedita academy, and let him sign this document first; then I will do so." Now he only said this in order to cover up the unseemly thing which was obvious to him but which he did not wish to make public. They did as he commanded them and went to Kohen Zedek, the head of the Pumbedita academy, and he put his seal on them.

After Kohen Zedek had done this, they came back to Saadia to have him also sign and confirm them. "Why do you want my signature?" asked Saadia of them. "You already have the signatures of the Exilarch and of Kohen Zedek, the head of the Pumbedita academy. You don't need my signature." "Why don't you sign?" they countered. "I don't know," he answered, and refused to reveal the reason to them, until they adjured him many times to tell them what he found wrong in their documents. He could not violate his oath to hide anything from them; hence he told them what he found wrong in the papers and why they were invalid.

They then returned to the Exilarch and told him about it, so he sent Judah, his son, and said to him: "Go tell Saadia, in my name, that he should sign the documents." Judah, the son of the Exilarch, went and told Saadia, in the name of his father, to sign the papers. "Return and tell your father," Saadia answered, "that it is written in the Bible [Deuteronomy 1:17]: 'You must never show partiality in a case.'" So the son went back and his father said to him: "Tell Saadia to sign the papers and not to be a fool." The youth returned to Saadia and spoke to him respectfully. He did not repeat the words of his father but begged and entreated Saadia to seal the documents for fear lest a quarrel arise between Saadia and his father. But Saadia refused.

The Exilarch sent to him many times, but the son did not want to reveal to Saadia all that his father had really told him to say. He made every effort to persuade him to sign the documents so as to avoid a break between Saadia and his father on account of this. However, when his father tired him out with all this coming and going, he became angry and raised his hand against Saadia saying: "If you don't sign the papers, as my father wants you to, I'll hit you."

No sooner had the words left the mouth of the youth than the servants of Saadia dragged him outside the door and closed the gates in his face. With tears streaming down his cheeks he came back to his father who asked him what had happened. He told him the whole story. As soon as his father heard this he deposed Saadia and appointed Joseph, son of Jacob, to be head of the academy of Sura in his stead. But Saadia, too, when he heard of the action taken, in turn excommunicated the Exilarch and sent for Hasan, that is Josiah, the brother of David ben Zakkai, to be Exilarch in place of his brother.

This brother held the office for three years and died, but the quarrel between Saadia and the Exilarch, however, was dragged out for seven years, until a certain case turned up between two men who were wrangling at law. The one chose Saadia as judge, the other selected the Exilarch. The Exilarch sent for the man who had chosen Saadia to come before him and they beat him badly. [The Exilarch's ban against Saadia forbade anyone to employ him as a judge.]

With his clothes torn, the wounded man went about crying to the whole community telling them what had happened to him. They took the matter very much to heart, for it was established custom that academy heads had no power over any man who was under the authority of the Exilarch, nor did the Exilarchs have any control over any one who was under the authority of the academy heads. No one had the right to contest the legality of the action of the other in any matter that lay within the jurisdiction of the other. And if a man was a stranger in the country, hailing from a foreign land, and not coming under the jurisdiction of the one or the other, he had the right to turn to whichever one he wished.

Since this man who was cudgeled was not under the jurisdiction of the Exilarch, the community was incensed at what had happened to him. All of them went to Bishr ben Aaron—the father-in-law of Caleb ibn Sargado—who was a great man in Babylon and one of the important men of his city [probably a member of the "Bene Aaron," court-bankers], and they told him how far this quarrel had gone among the Jews and how serious were the things that had happened. "Do something. It all depends on you," they said to him. "We're with you. Perhaps we'll be able to stop this quarrel which is only being kept up by your son-in-law Caleb ibn Sargado." [Sargado had written a diatribe against Saadia in which he made

beaten up a club

nasty insinuations. Saadia called him *celeb*, dog, instead of Caleb or Chalaf. Street-brawls between the two factions were frequent. Saadia himself was assaulted.]

Bishr went to the most prominent Jews, gathered them together in his home, and in the presence of them all spoke to the Exilarch who was also there: "What is this that you are doing? How long will you persist in this dispute and not fear divine punishment? Fear your God and stay out of trouble, for you know how far a quarrel can go. Now consider how you can improve your relations with Saadia. Make your peace with him and don't cherish any grudge against him."

The Exilarch responded with a peaceful answer that he would do as advised. Then Bishr got up, went to the home of Saadia, brought him and his followers who accompanied him to his house, and repeated to him the very words he had spoken to the Exilarch, and he also responded favorably. The Exilarch with all his adherents and his men were in one house, and our master, Saadia, with his party and all his men were in another house opposite it, but both houses were in the courtyard of this Bishr who went from one to the other with words of peace.

Then men, the leaders of the community, got up and divided themselves off into two groups. The one group escorted the Exilarch, and the other, Saadia; and these two marched from their respective sides until they met. Then they kissed and embraced each other. All this happened during the Fast of Esther [the day before Purim, February 27, 937]. When this matter between the two was settled, Bishr, rejoicing that they had made peace through his mediation, begged them and those standing there with them to spend the night with him and read the scroll of Esther in his home. But neither the Exilarch nor Saadia was willing to do this. "Then let Saadia dine with me or let me dine with him," suggested the Exilarch. They cast lots between them and the lot fell to the Exilarch, that Saadia should go with him, and so he did. He went to his home, took Purim dinner with him, and spent two days in his company, and departed on the third day in joy and in good spirit.

After the reconciliation had taken place between them and the quarrel had ceased, Joseph son of Jacob, whom the Exilarch had kept as college head in place of Saadia all the years of the dispute, now remained at home. Nevertheless the salary that he used to get as college president was not withheld from him, but sent to his house. The Exilarch, David ben Zakkai, died [about 940] and they sought to appoint his son [Judah] in his place, but he only lived seven months after his father and also passed away. He [Judah] had a young son, about twelve years of age, and Saadia took him into his home and kept him in school until Saadia himself died. [Saadia died of melancholia, 942.]

BIBLIOGRAPHY

REFERENCES TO TEXTBOOKS

Elbogen, pp. 52ff.; Roth, pp. 154ff.; Sachar, pp. 164ff.

Golub, J. S., *Medieval Jewish History*, Sec. IV, "A Great *Gaon*—Saadiah," etc.

READINGS FOR ADVANCED STUDENTS

Graetz, III, pp. 187ff.; Graetz-Rhine, III, pp. 71–95; Margolis and Marx, pp. 264–272.

Malter, H., *Saadia Gaon: His Life and Works*. The standard work on Saadia.

Encyclopaedia of Religion and Ethics, "Se'adiah."

JE, "Saadia b. Joseph."

58.

Paltiel of Egypt
about 952–about 976

ONE of the most interesting sources for the study of medieval Jewish life is a family history written in rimed Hebrew prose and known as *A Book of Genealogies*. It was composed in 1054 by Ahimaaz, a native of southern Italy, who describes in it the history of his distinguished family during the preceding two centuries.

Probably the most significant figure among his ancestors was Paltiel, who died about 976. According to Ahimaaz, Paltiel ultimately became vizier under the Fatimite Califs Al Muizz (953–975) and Al Aziz (976–996), whose empire extended at times from Morocco to the borders of Mesopotamia.

Ahimaaz is not an accurate historian; much that he tells us is legend. Nevertheless, it seems hardly to be doubted that Paltiel played an important part at the court of Al Muizz, the conqueror of Egypt, as astrologer, financial agent, and personal adviser. A different medieval source ascribes his rise, in part, to his skill as a physician. The following account from the Ahimaaz chronicle describes the life of this notable Jew.

⟨In those days [952] the Arabians with their armies, with Al Muizz as their commander, overran Italy. [There is no other record that Al Muizz himself ever came to Italy.] They devastated the entire province of Calabria, and reached Oria, on the border of Apulia; they besieged it, defeated all its forces; so that the city was in dire distress; its defenders had no power to resist; it was taken by storm; the sword smote it to the very soul. They killed most of its inhabitants, and led the survivors into captivity. And the commander inquired about the family of Rabbi Shephatiah. [Shephatiah was an ancestor of Paltiel. Legend tells how he once saved the Jews of Oria from persecution at the hands of the Emperor Basil, 867–886.] He sent for them and had them appear before him. And God let them find grace in his eyes. He bestowed His kindness upon Paltiel, His servant, and let him have favor before him. And Al Muizz brought him to his tent, and kept him at his side, to retain him in his service. [Since our records show that Al Muizz did not really come to

Italy, Paltiel probably entered his service in some other manner.]

One night the commander and Paltiel went out to observe the stars. As they were gazing at them, they saw the commander's star consume three stars, not all at one time, but in succession. And Al Muizz said to him: "What meaning dost thou find in that?" Paltiel answered: "Give thy interpretation first." The commander replied: "The stars represent the three cities, Tarentum, Otranto, and Bari, that I am to conquer." Paltiel then said: "Not that, my Lord; I see something greater; the first star means that thou wilt rule over Sicily; the second, that thou wilt rule over Ifrikiya and the third, that thou wilt rule over Babylonia [Egypt]." Al Muizz at once embraced him and kissed him, took off his ring and gave it to him, and took an oath saying: "If thy words come true, thou shalt be master of my house and have authority over all my kingdom."

Before seven days had passed, a message was brought to Al Muizz. The princes of Sicily sent messengers to him saying: "Know that the Emir is dead. Come thou in haste and assume authority and dominion over us." He thereupon gathered his troops; with all the captains of his army he embarked on his ships and crossed over into their country, and became their ruler. [Sicily was finally conquered by the Moslems in 965, during the reign of Al Muizz.] Then he had faith in the words of Paltiel, and did not depart from his advice, either to the left or to the right; he appointed him master over his house and domain. He entered his service as his vizier.

Some time after, Al Muizz went to Ifrikiya, leaving his brother as ruler over Sicily; and Paltiel went with him. There he grew in eminence, and added to his fame; he was second in power to the Calif; his renown spread through all the cities. . . .

Upon the death of the ruler of Egypt [Kafur, d. 968], the elders of Egypt, through reliable couriers, wise and chosen messengers, sent a letter authorized by the princes and nobles and the people of the cities and villages to Al Muizz, Calif of the Arabians, in which they said: "We have heard of thy mighty deeds, the violence of thy wars, which thou hast waged in thy wisdom, of thy sagacity in which thou excellest the princes that formerly ruled over the kingdom of Egypt. Now, come to us, be king over us, with the consent of our princes and all the eminent men of our country; we will be thy subjects, thou shalt be our king." [Jacob ibn Killis, d. 990, a Jewish convert to Islam, later vizier of Egypt, was among those who advised the Calif in his conquest of Egypt.]

Al Muizz considered the proposal; Paltiel was summoned; and they took counsel together as to what they should do, for it was a long journey, through a barren and desolate land; all the way there was no water; no supplies of food; no tents or places of shelter. [They had to cross the Sahara and Libyan deserts.] Paltiel set out in advance and established the camps; he erected bazaars and places for lodging, appointed merchants for them, and supplied them with bread, water, fish, meat, garden produce, and everything necessary for soldiers coming from the distant cities. Then the Calif and princes and courtiers set out; they pitched the tents of their encampment three miles from Cairo. [Their camp became the city of Cairo. The original town was called Fustat.]

All the nobles of Egypt joyfully came forth to greet them, their chiefs and governors, their officials and princes and the masses of the people as well. They came up to him and prostrated themselves. He made them take an oath of allegiance, by their law, and accepted their hostages, princes of the people. Then Paltiel entered Egypt with a division of the forces, detailed them on the walls and towers, that they might guard the city, the palace and public buildings, and appointed sentinels to be on guard, day and night, on the outskirts and the borders. [The triumphal entry of the army of invasion was on July 7, 969.] And then the Calif with all his army marched in. The nobles and all the people gathered about him, and again swore allegiance to him. He walked into the court and took his seat in his palace, on the throne of his dominion and majesty. They put the sceptre into his hand, and the royal crown upon his head, and he reigned over the kingdom of the South [Egypt] after his heart's desire. [The Calif did not arrive in Cairo till June, 973. The actual conquest in 969 was made by his general Djawhar, whom some scholars identify with Paltiel.]

Once, on the Day of Atonement, when Paltiel was called to read from the Torah, the whole assemblage arose and remained standing in his presence, the sages, the scholars that were in the school, the young students and the elders, the lads and children; the entire community was standing. [In Bagdad the people rose when the Exilarch read the Torah. Paltiel probably had a similar position.] He called to them saying: "Let the old be seated and the young stand. If you refuse, I will sit down and refuse to read, for this does not seem right to me."

When he finished reading, he vowed to the God of his praise 5000 dinars of genuine and full value; 1000 for the head of the academy and the sages, 1000 for the mourners of the sanctuary, 1000 for the academy of *geonim* at Babylon, 1000 for the poor and needy of the various communities, and 1000 for the exaltation of the Torah, for the purchase of the necessary oil. [There is also a tradition that he built a synagogue on the site of the Temple at Jerusalem.]

In the morning he arose early and hurried, for he was always zealous in observing the law, that his evil inclination might not prevail over him to prevent his carrying out his good intention; he engaged men and horses and mules, and provided guards, and sent them forth with the caravans that travelled through the deserts. And they delivered the gold pieces, as Paltiel their master had ordered, and distributed them among the schools and synagogues, and the mourners of Zion and the poor of the communities of Israel. [The "mourners of Zion" were ascetics who prayed in Jerusalem for the restoration of the Temple and the coming of the Messiah.]

The growth of his authority which the king, through his bounty, had bestowed upon him over his royal domain, having appointed him ruler over the kingdom of Egypt and of Syria as far as Mesopotamia, and over all the land of Israel as far as Jerusalem, his eminence and power and wealth with which the king had honored and distinguished him, are recorded in the chronicles of the kingdom of Egypt. [Paltiel was not only vizier but in all probability also the political head of the Jews. He bore the title of *Nagid* or "Prince" of the Jews in the Fatimite Empire, which then extended from Sicily, over North Africa, to Syria.]

BIBLIOGRAPHY

READINGS FOR ADVANCED STUDENTS

Mann, J., *The Jews in Egypt and in Palestine under the Fatimid Caliphs*, I, pp. 13–19, 49, 64, 72.

Marx, A., "Studies in Gaonic History and Literature," *JQR*, N.S., I (1910–1911), pp. 78–85.

JE, "Paltiel."

ADDITIONAL SOURCE MATERIALS IN ENGLISH

Salzman, M., *The Chronicle of Ahimaaz*, from which the above selection is taken, contains additional materials on Paltiel and other members of this notable family.

59.

Samuel Ha-Nagid, Vizier of Granada
993– d. after 1056

ONE of the most famous of the Jewish notables of Moslem Spain was Samuel Ha-Levi, who is also known as Samuel Ha-Nagid. Beginning life as a shopkeeper, Samuel Ha-Levi ultimately became the chief minister at the court of Granada. By virtue of this office he became the political head of the Jews in Granada and probably thus received the title *Nagid* ("Prince"), his name becoming Samuel Ha-Nagid. He served his community as rabbi and did a great deal to further Jewish learning throughout the world.

Samuel was a fine linguist, a scholar, a diplomat, and a distinguished soldier. His reputation in the Middle Ages was based mainly on his excellent poetry, some of which was written even on the battle-field.

The following account of his life is taken from *Sefer Seder ha-Kabbalah* ("The Line of Tradition"), a Hebrew historical work written by Abraham ibn Daud of Toledo in 1161.

❡One of the great disciples of Rabbi Enoch [d. 1014] was Rabbi Samuel Ha-Levi, the Prince, the son of Joseph, who was known as Ibn Nagdela, of the community of Cordova. He was an unusually fine Talmudic scholar and was also well versed in Arabic literature and language. He was of the type that could occupy a high position in the royal palace.

Samuel was a merchant, supporting himself with great difficulty, until the devastating days in Spain which followed the fall of the Amirid kingdom when the Berbers secured the power. [The civil war, which began in Spain in 1009, reached its climax in 1012 in the sack of Cordova by the Berbers.]

It was then that the land of Cordova began to decline and its inhabitants fled. Some of them ran away to Saragossa, where their descendants are even now; some fled to Toledo and their descendants are known there even to this day.

This Rabbi Samuel Ha-Levi fled to Malaga. There he had a shop and was a petty merchant. His shop happened to be near the palace of Ibn al-Arif, the vizier of King Habbus [1019–1038], the son of

Maksan, the King of the Berbers, in Granada. At the request of a
maid servant of the vizier, Samuel used to write letters for her to her
master the vizier, Abu al-Kasim ibn al-Arif. This latter saw his
letters and was amazed at his wisdom.

Some time later this vizier, Ibn al-Arif, got permission of his king,
Habbus, to return to his home in Malaga. There he asked the people
of his house: "Who used to write those letters that came to me
from you?" "A certain Jew," they answered, "who comes from the
community of Cordova and lives near your palace—he used to write
them for us." Immediately the secretary issued a command and they
rushed Rabbi Samuel Ha-Levi to him. "It is unbecoming for you
to sit in a shop," he said to him. "Stay here with me." He did so and
became his secretary and adviser.

The vizier used to advise the King according to the advice given
by Rabbi Samuel Ha-Levi, of blessed memory. All his advice was
as though it came from God, and the King Habbus prospered
through it very much. After some time the vizier, Ibn al-Arif, became mortally ill, and King Habbus, who came to visit him, said to
him: "What shall I do? Who will advise me in the wars which encompass me?" "I have never advised you," he answered him, "out of
my own mind, but at the suggestion of this Jew, my secretary.
Take care of him, and he will be as a father and a minister to you.
Do whatever he advises you, and God will help you." So after the
death of the vizier, King Habbus took Rabbi Samuel Ha-Levi and
brought him to his palace and he became his vizier and councillor.

In the year 4780 [1020] he was in the palace of the King Habbus.
[Samuel was already an important official before 1020.] The King
had two sons: the name of the elder was Badis, and the younger,
Bulukkin. All the Berber princes favored Bulukkin, the younger
son, as the successor, but all the rest of the people favored Badis.
The Jews, too, and among them Rabbi Joseph ibn Migas, Rabbi
Isaac ben Leon, and Rabbi Nehemiah, who was called Escafa, three
Granada notables, favored Bulukkin, but Rabbi Samuel Ha-Levi
favored Badis.

On the day that King Habbus died, the Berber princes and their
distinguished men rose in the morning to crown his son Bulukkin.
Bulukkin, however, immediately went and kissed the hand of his
elder brother Badis. Thus Badis was crowned in the year 4787 [1027]
and the face of his enemies turned black like the bottom of a pot,
and against their will they had to crown Badis. [Badis was really
crowned in 1038 and died in 1073.]

After this Bulukkin regretted that he had made his brother king and kept on getting the upper hand over his brother Badis, with the result that King Badis was unable to do a thing, big or small, without his brother's interference. But after this his brother Bulukkin became sick, and the King gave orders to the physician not to cure him. The physician obeyed, and Bulukkin died. Thus was the kingdom established in the hands of Badis. These three distinguished Jews of the city, whom we have mentioned, fled to the land of Seville [then hostile to Granada].

Rabbi Samuel Ha-Levi was appointed Prince in the year 4787 [1027], and he conferred great benefits on Israel in Spain, in north-western and north-central Africa, in the land of Egypt, in Sicily, even as far as the Babylonian academy, and the Holy City, Jerusalem. All the students who lived in those lands benefited by his generosity, for he bought numerous copies of the Holy Scriptures, the Mishnah, and the Talmud—these, too, being holy writings. [Ibn Daud here refutes the Karaites who denied the authority of the Mishnah and the Talmud.]

To every one—in all the land of Spain and in all the lands that we have mentioned—who wanted to make the study of the Torah his profession, he would give of his money. He had scribes who used to copy Mishnahs and Talmuds, and he would give them as a gift to students, in the academies of Spain or in the lands we have mentioned, who were not able to buy them with their own means. [Printing was not yet invented. Manuscripts were very expensive.] Besides this, he furnished olive oil every year for the lamps of the synagogues in Jerusalem. He spread the knowledge of the Torah [Jewish learning] very widely and died an old man, at a ripe age, after having acquired the four crowns: the crown of the Torah, the crown of high station, the crown of Levitical descent, and what is more than all these, the crown of a good name merited by good deeds. He died in the year 4815 [1055] and his son, Rabbi Joseph Ha-Levi, the Prince, succeeded him. [It is more probable that Samuel died in 1056 or later when Joseph (b. 1035), succeeded him as vizier.]

Of all the good traits of his father, Joseph lacked but one. He was not humble like his father because he grew up in riches, and he never had to bear the yoke [of poverty and discipline] in his youth. He was proud to his own hurt, and the Berber princes were jealous of him, with the result that on the Sabbath, on the 9th of Tebet in the year 4827 [Saturday, December 30, 1066], he and the community of Granada were murdered. [About 1500 families were killed. This is the first known massacre of Jews in Spain by Moslems.]

All those who had come from distant lands to see his learning and his greatness mourned for him, and the lament for him spread to all lands and to all cities. Since the days of the ancient rabbis—of blessed memory—who wrote the *Scroll of Fasts* and decreed that the 9th of Tebet should be a fast, the reason for the decree was never known. But from this incident we know that they were directed by the Holy Spirit to fix this day. After his death his books and treasures were scattered and dispersed throughout the world. So also were the disciples whom he had raised up. After his death they became the rabbis of Spain and the leaders of the generation.

BIBLIOGRAPHY

REFERENCES TO TEXTBOOKS

Elbogen, pp. 56–57; Roth, pp. 160–161; Sachar, pp. 171–172.

READINGS FOR ADVANCED STUDENTS

Graetz, III, pp. 254–264, 273–280; Graetz-Rhine, III, pp. 131–139, 147ff.; Margolis and Marx, pp. 313–317, 321.

Dozy, R., *Spanish Islam*. See Index under "Samuel Ha-Levi" and "Joseph, son of Samuel Ha-Levi."

Sassoon, D. S., "Diwan of the Vizier Samuel Hannaghid," *The Jewish Chronicle*, (London), March 28, 1924, literary supplement no. 39.

JE, "Samuel ha-Nagid."

60.

Rashi
Northern France, about 1100

Rabbi SOLOMON BAR ISAAC (RaSHI) of Troyes (1040–
1105) is probably the best known medieval Jewish scholar. He
attained this popularity, which he still retains in Jewry, through
his Biblical and Talmudic commentaries which are noted for their
terseness, clarity, and erudition. Most of his life was spent in his
native town of Troyes, where he encouraged the Biblical and Talmudic studies which his descendants carried on and which made of
northern France one of the great centers of rabbinic scholarship
in the twelfth and thirteenth centuries.

He supported himself probably through the manufacture and
sale of wine and at the same time, no doubt, acted as rabbi in Troyes,
then one of the chief business towns of Europe. Some of his legal
decisions are interesting because they throw light on the times in
which he lived and in addition give us an insight into the character
of this notable scholar.

The first selection given below is a brief *teshubah* ("answer") to
the *sheelah* ("question") of a woman who wishes to know if she is
to be considered married according to the Jewish religion. She and
her husband, both Jews, had contracted a Jewish marriage with witnesses, at a time when both had been forced to embrace Christianity,
probably during the days of the First Crusade. It was during this
same period that Rashi lost many friends and relatives at the hands
of the fanatical crusaders.

The second selection is a decision of Rashi in the case of a
woman who has been driven from her home, unjustly, by an
unscrupulous husband. These *teshubot* or "answers" to legal and
ritual problems were written in Hebrew.

1. *Forced Converts to Christianity During the Days of the First Crusade, 1096–1105*

❦Herewith do I, the undersigned, answer him who has questioned
me concerning the marriage of a certain girl who was married at
a time when she and the groom, as well as the witnesses to the

ceremony, had already been forced by Gentiles to disavow the Jewish religion.

I am of the opinion that this woman requires a bill of divorcement before she can marry another man. The marriage of a Jew who has even voluntarily become an apostate and then marries is legal [according to Jewish law]. For it is said [Joshua 7:11]: "Israel has sinned," meaning [Sanhedrin 44a] that even though he has sinned he is still an Israelite. How much the more is this true in the case of all these forced converts who at heart are still loyal to God. Notice in this particular case how their final conduct reflects their original attitude, for as soon as they were able to find some form of escape they returned to Judaism. And even though the witnesses may have led a loose life while living among the non-Jews and may be suspected of the iniquities of the Gentiles, nevertheless their testimony to the marriage does not thereby become invalid. . . .

Peace! Solomon the son of Rabbi Isaac.

11. *Rashi Defends an Unfortunate Woman, before 1105*

⟨Two people came to argue their case before Rabbi Solomon. The wife complained that her husband had divorced her but had not treated her in accordance with Jewish custom. He answered: "I have divorced you in accordance with the law. You have no claim, not even to the amount stipulated in the marriage contract, for I was deceived when I married you. It is evident that you are afflicted with skin trouble, and the signs of this disease appear on you, on your nose; and your face in general is breaking out with boils. Before your marriage you yourself suffered from this disease which you got from your family, some of whom are also afflicted with this sickness, and when I married you I was unaware of your hidden defects."

"It's not so," she answered. "I was a hale and hearty woman when entering into marriage, and as for your saying that signs of a skin disease are visible on me, that is not so and never will be, for my whole body is in a healthy condition." There were, however, two warts that had appeared on her face due to the suffering and vexation which she had experienced after her husband had driven her from his house, but concerning this a number of members of the community, who had known the husband for many years and had heard nothing of this trouble, testified: "She was a healthy woman when she entered into marriage, and we have never noticed any signs of skin trouble."

The following decision was given by the rabbi in this dispute: First let me extend my greetings to those who have directed this question to me. Inasmuch as no physical defects were noticeable in this woman while she was in her father's house, and they have developed only since her marriage, in her husband's house, he has therefore no claim against her on the ground that she was physically unfit.

That man is conducting himself in a bad way and has shown that he is not acting like one of our father Abraham's children whose nature it is to be kind to his fellowman, and particularly so to his own flesh with whom he has entered the covenant of marriage. If that husband had set his mind on keeping his wife as much as he had set his mind on getting rid of her, her charm would have grown on him. Behold our rabbis have said [Sotah 47a]: "Every spot has a charm for those who live in it," even though it may be cursed with bad water and barren land. Similar is the charm exerted by a woman on her husband, and happy the man who has been fortunate enough to get such a wife and to acquire through her a share in life eternal. Even among those who deny God we find many who do not reject their wives and whose wives in turn act in like manner toward them, for they believe that the good they do serves as an expiatory sacrifice for the sins they have committed. But this fellow, though a member of the household of our Father in heaven, has acted cruelly toward the wife of his youth as God himself can testify.

According to the law of right it is incumbent upon him to treat her as custom prescribes for all Jewish women; and if he does not care to receive her back in kindness and in respect, then he must divorce her and pay her the entire amount stipulated in her marriage contract.

BIBLIOGRAPHY

REFERENCES TO TEXTBOOKS

Elbogen, pp. 112–114; Roth, pp. 174–175; Sachar, pp. 185–186.

READINGS FOR ADVANCED STUDENTS

Graetz, III, pp. 286–289, 308–310; Graetz-Rhine, III, pp. 159–165; Margolis and Marx, pp. 356–358.

Liber, M., *Rashi*. A brief rounded-out picture of the man and his writings.

Waxman, M., *A History of Jewish Literature*, I, pp. 192–195.

JE, "Rashi (Solomon bar Isaac)."

61.

Rashi's Grandson and the Crusaders
France, May 8, 1147

RABBI JACOB BEN MEIR (about 1100–1171), called Rabbenu Tam ("Our master, the perfect one"), was probably the outstanding Jewish scholar of France in his day. On his mother's side he was a grandson of the famous Rashi. He lived in the town of Rameru, near Troyes, in eastern France. He was by profession a money-lender; his leisure he devoted to his studies and to his communal activities. Because of his scholarship, his character, and his family prestige, his moral authority in Western and Central Europe was tremendous. Jacob lived through the terror of the Second Crusade (1146–1147) and, later, the burning of the Jews at Blois (1171).

The following account is taken from *A Book of Historical Records*, a Hebrew historical work by Ephraim ben Jacob (1132–about 1200), a German Jewish Talmudist and poet of note. It describes Jacob ben Meir's harrowing experiences during the trying days of the Second Crusade.

⟨On the second day of the Feast of Weeks [*Shabuot*, May 8, 1147] the French crusaders got together at Rameru, entered the house of our teacher Jacob (may he live long), took everything he had there, and even tore up the scroll of the Law in his presence. They got hold of him, led him out to the fields, condemned him because of his religion, and conspired against him to put him to death. Five times on the head they wounded him, and in doing so they said to him: "You are the greatest man in Israel; therefore we are taking vengeance on you because of him who was hanged [Jesus], and we are going to wound you just as you Jews inflicted five wounds on our God." [The five wounds are the stigmata of Jesus: four on the hands and feet, and one on the right side.]

His pure soul would have left him had it not been for the kindness of our Creator who had mercy on His Torah, and brought it about that a high official, who was to prove of help to Jacob, should be on the road that led through that field. Rabbi Jacob called to him and bribed him with a horse worth five gold pieces. The official then turned and appealed to the crusaders and cajoled them saying:

"Leave him to me today; I'll talk to him. Perhaps he'll be persuaded so that we can allure him to our faith. If he doesn't consent, rest assured that I'll turn him over to you tomorrow." They did so and the danger was averted. Because God had compassion on His people, He was merciful to him who taught them His holy Torah.

As far as the other communities of France are concerned, we have not heard that a single man was killed or forced into baptism. [Bernard of Clairvaux, the man behind the Second Crusade, opposed any violence toward the Jews.] However they did lose much of their wealth, for the King of France had issued an order that every one who volunteered to go on the crusade to Jerusalem would be forgiven the debts he owed the Jews. Now since most loans of the French Jews were given on trust, without surety, they lost their money. [The King, in line with the papal decree of Eugene III, 1146, probably remitted the interest alone, but the crusaders no doubt refused to pay the principal as well.]

BIBLIOGRAPHY

READINGS FOR ADVANCED STUDENTS

Graetz, III, pp. 375–381; Graetz-Rhine, III, pp. 224–229; Margolis and Marx, pp. 363–369.
JE, "Crusades, The"; "Jacob ben Meir Tam."

ADDITIONAL SOURCE MATERIALS IN ENGLISH

Robinson, J. H., *Readings in European History*, I, pp. 337–340 cites the privileges granted to crusaders by Pope Eugene III in 1146, and Innocent III in 1215.

62.

Maimonides
1135–1204

RABBI MOSES BEN MAIMON (RaMBaM) was the most eminent Jewish philosopher of the Middle Ages. His most famous books are: an Arabic commentary to the Mishnah; a Hebrew law code, the *Mishneh Torah* ("Repetition of the Law"); and the Arabic philosophical work, *The Guide for the Perplexed*. Maimonides, who was born in Cordova in 1135, was compelled when still a lad to flee from Spain because of the persecutions of the fanatical Almohades. After a series of misfortunes and wanderings in northern Africa and Palestine he finally settled in Egypt, in Fustat-Cairo, in 1165, where he became a court physician.

The extracts from his letters that follow give a clear picture of the man and his activity. The first letter below is an answer to Joseph ibn Djabir of Bagdad who had written to Maimonides for enlightenment on certain questions. Ibn Djabir, who knew only Arabic, could not consult Rambam's Hebrew code, the *Mishneh Torah*. The second letter is in answer to Samuel ibn Tibbon of southern France, who was translating the *Guide for the Perplexed* into Hebrew and wished to come to Egypt to visit the famous philosopher. Both of these letters were originally written in Arabic.

1. *Maimonides' Letter to Ibn Djabir, about 1191*

❡"I have set the Lord always before me."

We have received the letter of the honored and esteemed elder, the disciple Joseph ben Abul-Kheir (may his soul find rest in paradise) who is known as Ibn Djabir. He mentions in it that he is an ignoramus in Jewish things. However, it is clear to us from his letter that he is making a strong effort to study Jewish lore and that he is busying himself considerably with our Arabic commentary to the Mishnah, although he does not understand the code that we have written, that is to say, the *Mishneh Torah*, because it is in Hebrew. He also mentions that he has heard of certain scholars— may God protect them—who are there in Bagdad and who have attacked us in those things which he mentions and he wishes to answer them. [The *gaon* of Bagdad, Samuel ben Ali, attacked the views of Maimonides on resurrection.] Ibn Djabir also entreats us to write to him in order to help him in his studies and this we now do.

First let me tell you—may God maintain your worth and add to your success—that you are not an ignoramus but our disciple and friend, and so is every one who strives to cleave to the study of the Torah even though he understands but one verse or one law. It makes no difference whether one understands it through the Hebrew or Arabic or Aramaic: the thing is to understand the subject matter in whatever language it be, and this is even more true of commentaries and codes. The important fact is that you should busy yourself learning. Of any man who neglects his study or has never learnt anything it is said [Numbers 15:31]: "He has despised the word of God." Likewise any one, even though he be a great scholar, who is too lazy to increase his learning, fails to fulfill the positive commandment to study the Torah. This is as important as all other commandments put together.

In general I would like to tell you that you ought not underestimate yourself nor despair of attaining perfection. There were great scholars who began to study when they were already advanced in years and became what they were. [Tradition says Akiba, died about 132 C.E., was forty years old when he began to study.]

You ought to learn this section of the book in the original Hebrew in which we have composed it, for it is not hard to understand and very easy to learn. And after you have trained yourself in one part you will understand the entire work. [Ibn Djabir is advised to learn Hebrew from the *Mishneh Torah* and to use this code to solve his difficulties.] Under no circumstance do I desire to translate it into Arabic, for then all of its charm would be lost.

As a matter of fact I now wish to translate my [Arabic] commentary to the Mishnah and the *Book of Precepts* into the Holy Tongue. Surely then I will not translate this code into Arabic. Don't even ask it of me. [Maimonides wanted to preserve Hebrew as the Jewish national tongue.] At all events you are my brother. May God aid you and favor you with true perfection and treasure up for you the happiness of this world and the next. . . .

Moses, the son of Maimon of blessed memory.

II. *Maimonides' Letter to Samuel ibn Tibbon, 1199*

⟨Only the Blessed Creator of the World knows how I have been able to write this letter to you! I have had to run away from my fellow-men, isolating myself in some hidden nook. At times I have even had to lean for support against the wall, at other times I have had to write lying down on account of my excessive weakness, for my bodily vigor is sapped. I am pretty well advanced in years. [He was now 64 years old.]

But with respect to your wish to come here to me, I cannot but say how greatly your visit would delight me, for I truly long to commune with you, and would anticipate our meeting with even greater joy than you, although I am worried about your taking such a dangerous sea trip. [Storms and pirates were the dangers.]

Yet I must advise you not to expose yourself [to the perils of the voyage], for beyond seeing me, and my doing all I could to honor you, you would not derive any advantage from your visit. Do not expect to be able to confer with me on any scientific subject for even one hour, either by day or by night, for the following is my daily occupation:

I dwell in Fustat, and the Sultan resides at Cairo [originally a suburb of the older Fustat]; these two places are two Sabbath days' journeys distant from each other. [A Sabbath day's journey is two thousand paces.] My duties to the ruler [the regent al-Afdal, son of Saladin] are very heavy. I am obliged to visit him every day, early in the morning; and when he or any of his children, or any of the inmates of his harem, is indisposed, I dare not quit Cairo, but must stay during the greater part of the day in the palace.

It also frequently happens that one or two of the royal officers fall sick, and I must attend to their healing the entire day. Hence, as a rule, I repair to Cairo very early in the day, and even if nothing unusual happens, I do not return to Fustat until the afternoon. Under no circumstances do I return earlier. Then I am almost dying with hunger. I find the antechambers filled with people, both Jews and Gentiles, important and unimportant people, theologians and bailiffs, friends and foes—a mixed multitude, who await the time of my return.

I dismount from my animal, wash my hands, go forth to my patients, and beg and entreat them to bear with me while I partake of some slight refreshment, the only meal I take in the twenty-four hours. Then I go forth to attend my patients, write prescriptions and directions for their several ailments. Patients go in and out until nightfall, and sometimes even, I solemnly assure you, until two hours in the night [eight o'clock] or even later. I converse with, and prescribe for them while lying down on my back from sheer fatigue; and when night falls, I am so exhausted, I can scarcely speak.

In consequence of this, no Israelite can speak with me or have any private interview with me, except on the Sabbath. On that day, the whole congregation, or at least, the majority of the members, come to me after the morning service, when I instruct them as to their proceedings during the whole week; we study together a little until noon, when they depart. Some of them return, and read with me after the afternoon service until evening prayers. In this manner I spend that day. I have here related to you only a part of what you would see, if by God's aid you were to visit me.

Now, when you have completed for our brethren the translation you have commenced—and now that you have begun this good work you ought to finish it—I beg that you will come joyfully to visit me, but not with the hope of deriving any advantage from your visit as regards your studies; for my time is very limited. . . .

May your happiness, my dear son and pupil, increase and grow great, and may salvation be granted to our afflicted people. Written by Moses, the son of Maimon, the Sephardi [Spaniard] of blessed memory, on the 8th of Tishri, 1511 according to the Seleucide era [September 30, 1199]. Peace!

BIBLIOGRAPHY

REFERENCES TO TEXTBOOKS

Elbogen, pp. 58–60; Roth, pp. 175–177; Sachar, pp. 178–183.

READINGS FOR ADVANCED STUDENTS

Graetz, III, pp. 446–493; Graetz-Rhine, III, pp. 260–292; Margolis and Marx, pp. 337–345.

Friedenwald, H., "Moses Maimonides the Physician," *Bulletin of the Institute of the History of Medicine*, III (1935) no. 7, July.

Husik, I., *A History of Mediaeval Jewish Philosophy*, Chap. xiii, "Moses Maimonides." A good study of Maimonides, the philosopher.

Waxman, M., *A History of Jewish Literature*, I. See Index under "Maimonides."

Yellin, D., and I. Abrahams, *Maimonides*. A brief but adequate picture of the most notable medieval Jew.

Zeitlin, S., *Maimonides*. One of the best of the recent works on this great philosopher and codifier.

Encyclopaedia of Religion and Ethics, "Maimonides."

JE, "Ibn Tibbon: Samuel ben Judah ibn Tibbon"; "Moses ben Maimon."

ADDITIONAL SOURCE MATERIALS IN ENGLISH

Adler, H., "Translation of an Epistle Addressed by R. Moses Maimonides to R. Samuel ibn Tibbon," *Miscellany of Hebrew Literature*, I, pp.

219ff. This is a more complete translation of Maimonides' letter to Samuel ibn Tibbon which has been quoted above in abstract.

Book of Mishnah Torah . . . by . . . Moses son of Maimon. Tr. by Rabbi Simon Glazer. This is a translation of the first of the fourteen books of Maimonides' law code.

Gorfinkle, J. I., *The Eight Chapters of Maimonides on Ethics.* This work is an attempt by Maimonides to reconcile Aristotelian and rabbinic ethics.

Maimonides, Moses, *The Guide for the Perplexed,* tr. by M. Friedländer. This *Guide* is Maimonides' outstanding philosophical work.

63.

Ethical Wills
Twelfth and Fourteenth Centuries

MANY Jews were in the habit of writing wills, in Hebrew, in which they imparted instruction of an ethical and religious nature to their children and to their descendants. Such ethical testaments were not uncommon among Moslems and Christians at this time.

Many of these Jewish ethical wills, such as *A Father's Admonition*, which follows, are valuable for the insight they give us into the cultural and social life of the individual Jew of some particular land at some specific period. Others, such as the *Testament of Eleazar of Mayence*, are valuable in that they reflect the moral and ethical views of a pious Jew.

The *Admonition* of Judah ibn Tibbon (1120–about 1190) is thus particularly important because it throws light on the intellectual interests of a cultured Spanish Jew. Judah ibn Tibbon was born in Granada; he migrated to Lunel, in enlightened southern France, probably because of the religious bigotry of the fanatical Moslem Almohades. He was the "father of translators" from Arabic into Hebrew. His son, Samuel ibn Tibbon (about 1150–about 1230), for whom this lofty though rather querulous *Admonition* was written, succeeded in becoming an even greater translator than his father. Samuel's most valuable piece of work is the translation from Arabic into Hebrew of Maimonides' *Guide for the Perplexed*.

The *Testament of Eleazar of Mayence*, parts of which follow as the second selection, is the work of the simple and frank German Jew, Eleazar ben Samuel Ha-Levi of Mayence, who died in his native city on the first day of the Jewish New Year of 1357.

I. A FATHER'S ADMONITION—*The Ethical Will of Judah ibn Tibbon, France, about 1160–1180*

℘My son, list to my precepts, neglect none of my injunctions. Set my admonition before thine eyes; thus shalt thou prosper and prolong thy days in pleasantness! . . . .

Thou knowest, my son, how I swaddled thee and brought thee up, how I led thee in the paths of wisdom and virtue. I fed and

311

clothed thee; I spent myself in educating and protecting thee. I sacrificed my sleep to make thee wise beyond thy fellows and to raise thee to the highest degree of science and morals. These twelve years I have denied myself the usual pleasures and relaxations of men for thy sake, and I still toil for thine inheritance. [After the death of his wife the father devoted his time to Samuel, his son.]

I have honored thee by providing an extensive library for thy use, and have thus relieved thee of the necessity to borrow books. Most students must bustle about to seek books, often without finding them. But thou, thanks be to God, lendest and borrowest not. Of many books, indeed, thou ownest two or three copies. I have besides made for thee books on all sciences, hoping that thy hand might find them all as a nest. [The father probably compiled reference books for the use of the son.]

Seeing that thy Creator had graced thee with a wise and understanding heart, I journeyed to the ends of the earth and fetched for thee a teacher in secular sciences. I minded neither the expense nor the danger of the ways. Untold evil might have befallen me and thee on those travels, had not the Lord been with us!

But thou, my son! didst deceive my hopes. Thou didst not choose to employ thine abilities, hiding thyself from all thy books, not caring to know them or even their titles. Hadst thou seen thine own books in the hand of others, thou wouldst not have recognized them; hadst thou needed one of them, thou wouldst not have known whether it was with thee or not, without asking me; thou didst not even consult the catalogue of thy library. . . .

Therefore, my son! Stay not thy hand when I have left thee, but devote thyself to the study of the Torah and to the science of medicine. But chiefly occupy thyself with the Torah, for thou hast a wise and understanding heart, and all that is needful on thy part is ambition and application. I know that thou wilt repent of the past, as many have repented before thee of their youthful indolence. . . .

Let thy countenance shine upon the sons of men; tend their sick, and may thine advice cure them. Though thou takest fees from the rich, heal the poor gratuitously; the Lord will requite thee. Thereby shalt thou find favor and good understanding in the sight of God and man. Thus wilt thou win the respect of high and low among Jews and non-Jews, and thy good name will go forth far and wide. Thou wilt rejoice thy friends and make thy foes envious. For remember what is written in the *Choice of Pearls* [53:617, of Ibn Gabirol]: "How shall one take vengeance on an enemy? By increasing one's own good qualities." . . . .

My son! Examine regularly, once a week, thy drugs and medicinal herbs, and do not employ an ingredient whose properties are unknown to thee. I have often impressed this on thee in vain. . . .

My son! I command thee to honor thy wife to thine utmost capacity. She is intelligent and modest, a daughter of a distinguished and educated family. She is a good housewife and mother, and no spendthrift. Her tastes are simple, whether in food or dress. Remember her assiduous tendance of thee in thine illness, though she had been brought up in elegance and luxury. Remember how she afterwards reared thy son without man or woman to help her. Were she a hired nurse, she would have earned thy esteem and forbearance; how much the more, since she is the wife of thy bosom, the daughter of the great, art thou bound to treat her with consideration and respect. To act otherwise is the way of the contemptible. The Arab philosopher [probably Al-Ghazali, 1058–1112] says of women: "None but the honorable honoreth them, none but the despicable despises them.". . . .

If thou wouldst acquire my love, honor her with all thy might; do not exercise too severe an authority over her; our Sages [Gittin 6b] have expressly warned men against this. If thou givest orders or reprovest, let thy words be gentle. Enough is it if thy displeasure is visible in thy look; let it not be vented in actual rage. Let thy expenditure be well ordered. It is remarked in the *Choice of Pearls* [1:3]: "Expenditure properly managed makes half an income." And there is an olden proverb: "Go to bed without supper and rise without debt." Defile not the honor of thy countenance by borrowing; may the Creator save thee from that habit! . . . .

Examine thy Hebrew books at every New Moon, the Arabic volumes once in two months, and the bound codices once every quarter. [Arabic and Latin were the languages of science in Spain, the Provence, and southern Italy.] Arrange thy library in fair order, so as to avoid wearying thyself in searching for the book thou needest. Always know the case and the chest where the book should be. A good plan would be to set in each compartment a written list of the books therein contained. If, then, thou art looking for a book, thou canst see from the list the exact shelf it occupies without disarranging all the books in the search for one. Examine the loose leaves in the volumes and bundles, and preserve them. These fragments contain very important matters which I collected and copied out. Do not destroy any writing or letter of all that I have left. And cast thine eye frequently over the catalogue so as to remember what books are in thy library.

Never intermit thy regular readings with thy teacher; study in the college of thy master on certain evenings before sitting down to read with the young. Whatever thou hast learned from me or from thy teachers, impart it again regularly to worthy pupils, so that thou mayest retain it, for by teaching it to others thou wilt know it by heart, and their questions will compel thee to precision, and remove any doubts from thine own mind.

Never refuse to lend books to anyone who has not the means to purchase books for himself, but only act thus to those who can be trusted to return the volumes. [Before the invention of printing each book was written by hand and was therefore expensive.] Thou knowest what our sages said in the Talmud, on the text: "Wealth and riches are in his house; and his merit endureth for ever." [Ketubot 50a applies this verse, Psalm 112:3, to one who lends his copies of the Bible.] But, [Proverbs 3:27] "Withhold not good from him to whom it is due," [you owe it to your books to protect them] and take particular care of thy books. Cover the bookcases with rugs of fine quality, and preserve them from damp and mice, and from all manner of injury, for thy books are thy good treasure. If thou lendest a volume, make a memorandum before it leaves thy house, and when it is returned, draw thy pen over the entry. Every Passover and Tabernacles [that is, every six months] call in all books out on loan. . . .

I enjoin on thee, my son, to read this, my testament, once daily, at morn or at eve. Apply thy heart to the fulfilment of its behests, and to the performance of all therein written. Then wilt thou make thy ways prosperous, then shalt thou have good success.

II. TESTAMENT OF ELEAZAR OF MAYENCE, *Germany, about 1357*

❦These are the things which my sons and daughters shall do at my request. They shall go to the house of prayer morning and evening, and shall pay special regard to the *tefillah* [the "Eighteen Benedictions"] and the *shema* [Deuteronomy 6:4]. So soon as the service is over, they shall occupy themselves a little with the Torah [the Pentateuch], the Psalms, or with works of charity. Their business must be conducted honestly, in their dealings both with Jew and Gentile. They must be gentle in their manners and prompt to accede to every honorable request. They must not talk more than is necessary; by this will they be saved from slander, falsehood, and frivolity. They shall give an exact tithe of all their possessions; they shall never turn away a poor man empty-handed, but must give him what they can, be it much or little. If he beg a lodging over night, and they know him not, let them provide him with the where-withal to pay an innkeeper. Thus shall they satisfy the needs of the poor in every possible way. . . .

If they can by any means contrive it, my sons and daughters should live in communities, and not isolated from other Jews, so that their sons and daughters may learn the ways of Judaism. Even if com-pelled to solicit from others the money to pay a teacher, they must not let the young of both sexes go without instruction in the Torah. Marry your children, O my sons and daughters, as soon as their age is ripe, to members of respectable families. [Boys of thirteen and girls of twelve were considered ready for marriage.] Let no child of mine hunt after money by making a low match for that object; but if the family is undistinguished only on the mother's side, it does not matter, for all Israel counts descent from the father's side. . . .

I earnestly beg my children to be tolerant and humble to all, as I was throughout my life. Should cause for dissension present itself, be slow to accept the quarrel; seek peace and pursue it with all the vigor at your command. Even if you suffer loss thereby, forbear and forgive, for God has many ways of feeding and sustaining His creatures. To the slanderer do not retaliate with counter-attack; and though it be proper to rebut false accusations, yet is it most desir-able to set an example of reticence. You yourselves must avoid ut-tering any slander, for so will you win affection. In trade be true, never grasping at what belongs to another. For by avoiding these wrongs—scandal, falsehood, money-grubbing—men will surely find tranquillity and affection. And against all evils, silence is the best safeguard. . . .

Be very particular to keep your houses clean and tidy. [These ideas are interesting coming from a man who lived through the Black Death of 1349.] I was always scrupulous on this point, for every injurious condition and sickness and poverty are to be found in foul dwellings. Be careful over the benedictions; accept no divine gift without paying back the Giver's part; and His part is man's grateful acknowledgment. [Pay God for His blessings by blessing Him.]. . . .

On holidays and festivals and Sabbaths seek to make happy the poor, the unfortunate, widows and orphans, who should always be guests at your tables; their joyous entertainment is a religious duty. Let me repeat my warning against gossip and scandal. And as ye speak no scandal, so listen to none; for if there were no receivers there would be no bearers of slanderous tales; therefore the reception and credit of slander is as serious an offense as the originating of it. The less you say, the less cause you give for animosity, while [Proverbs 10:19] "in the multitude of words there wanteth not transgression.". . . .

I beg of you, my sons and daughters, my wife, and all the congregation, that no funeral oration be spoken in my honor. Do not carry my body on a bier, but in a coach. Wash me clean, comb my hair, trim my nails, as I was wont to do in my lifetime, so that I may go clean to my eternal rest, as I went clean to synagogue every Sabbath-day. If the ordinary officials dislike the duty, let adequate payment be made to some poor man who shall render this service carefully and not perfunctorily. [The dead were washed by the *Hebra Kaddisha*, "Holy Brotherhood".]

At a distance of thirty cubits from the grave, they shall set my coffin on the ground, and drag me to the grave by a rope attached to the coffin. [This is a symbolic punishment to atone for sins committed during lifetime, and, probably, to anticipate the punishments of Hell, *hibbut ha-keber*.] Every four cubits they shall stand and wait awhile, doing this in all seven times, so that I may find atonement for my sins. Put me in the ground at the right hand of my father, and if the space be a little narrow, I am sure that he loves me well enough to make room for me by his side. If this be altogether impossible, put me on his left, or near my grandmother, Yuta. Should this also be impractical, let me be buried by the side of my daughter.

BIBLIOGRAPHY

READINGS FOR ADVANCED STUDENTS

Lazarus, M., *The Ethics of Judaism*, 2 vols. This study limits itself primarily to Biblical and Talmudic sources.

Schechter, S., *Studies in Judaism*, Third Series, pp. 1-24, "Jewish Saints in Mediaeval Germany."

Waxman, M., *A History of Jewish Literature*, II, pp. 271-300.

JE, "Ethics."

ADDITIONAL SOURCE MATERIALS IN ENGLISH

Abrahams, I., *Hebrew Ethical Wills*, 2 vols. A fine collection of medieval Jewish ethical wills.

Millgram, A. E., *An Anthology of Mediaeval Hebrew Literature*, Chap. iv, "What the Mediaeval Jews Considered the Highest Good (Ethical Literature)."

64.

The Oath of Amatus
1559

AMONG the many eminent Jewish physicians of the Middle Ages, Amatus Lusitanus occupies a high place. He was born in Portugal in 1511, a crypto-Jew, and pursued his medical studies at the Spanish University of Salamanca. It was very probably fear of the impending Portuguese Inquisition that induced him to migrate first to Antwerp in Belgium (about 1533), and then to Italy where he was compelled to wander from town to town. His renown as a physician and scientist brought him the patronage of the family of Pope Julius III and of the Pope himself, but he found it advisable, finally, to leave for Salonica, a Moslem city, where he openly proclaimed his adherence to the Jewish faith.

Amatus was distinguished in the fields of anatomy, surgery, and internal medicine and also did excellent work in the related fields of pharmacology and botany. He lectured on medicine at the school in Ferrara for several years and enjoyed at the same time an extensive and lucrative practice. While still in his twenties he was a widely sought-after physician in Antwerp, and tells us that after curing the Portuguese Consul of tertian fever he was given a fee of three hundred gold ducats, a huge sum. One of his prescriptions contained thirty-three ingredients: that he obtained cures after such heroic treatment is indeed a tribute to his own skill if not to the toughness of some of his patients.

In his Latin *Centuries* which ran to seven volumes, each dealing with one hundred medical cases, he discusses the history and the treatment of each individual case. At the end of the *Sixth Century* he gives his physicians oath. It speaks for itself.

⟨I swear by the Eternal God and by His ten most holy commandments, which were given on Mount Sinai through Moses as lawgiver after the people had been freed from their bondage in Egypt, that I have never, at any time, done anything in these my treatments save what inviolate faith handed down to posterity; that I have never feigned anything, added anything or changed anything for the sake of gain: that I have always striven after this one thing, namely, that

317

benefit might spread forth to mankind; that I have praised no one, and censured no one merely to indulge in private passions, unless zeal for truth demanded this. If I lie, may I incur the eternal wrath of God and his angel Raphael [the angel of healing], and may nothing in the medical art succeed for me according to my desires.

Concerning the remuneration, furthermore, which is commonly given to physicians, I have not been anxious for this, but I have treated many, not only zealously, but even without pay: and have unselfishly and unswervingly refused several rewards offered by many people; and have rather sought that the sick might, by my care and diligence, recover their lost health than that I might become richer by their liberality. All men have been considered equal by me of whatever religion they were, whether Hebrews, Christians, or the followers of the Moslem faith. [The Church law that Jews must not treat Christian patients was not always observed.]

As concerns loftiness of station, that has never been a matter of concern to me, and I have accorded the same care to the poor as to those born in exalted rank. I have never brought about sickness; in diagnosis I have always said what I thought to be true. I have unduly favored no venders of drugs, except perhaps those whom I knew to surpass the others by reason of their skill in their art or because of their natural qualities of mind. In prescribing drugs I have exercised moderation in proportion as the powers of the sick man allowed. I have revealed to no one a secret entrusted to me; I have given no one a fatal draught. No woman has ever brought about an abortion by my aid; nothing base has been committed by me in any house where I was practicing; in short, nothing has been done by me which might be considered unbecoming an excellent and famous physician.

I have always held up to myself Hippocrates and Galen, the [ancient Greek] fathers of the medical art, as examples worthy of being followed by me, and the records of many other excellent men in the medical art have not been scorned by me. In my method of studying I have been so eager that no task, however difficult, could lead me away from the reading of good authors, neither the loss of private fortune, nor frequent journeys, nor yet exile, which, as befits a philosopher, I have thus far borne with calm and invincible courage. [Amatus, seeking freedom, fled from Portugal to Belgium, to Italy, and then to Turkey.] And the many students which I have thus far had I have always considered my sons, and have taught them very frankly, and have urged them to strive to conduct themselves like good men.

I have published my books on medical matters with no desire for profit, but I have had regard for this one thing, namely, that I might, in some measure, provide for the health of mankind. Whether I have succeeded in this, I leave to the judgment of others. At all events, I have held this always before me, and have given it chief place in my prayers.

Given at Thessalonica, in the year of the world 5319 [1559].

BIBLIOGRAPHY

READINGS FOR ADVANCED STUDENTS

Friedenwald, A., "Jewish Physicians and the Contributions of the Jews to the Science of Medicine," *Publications of the Gratz College,* I (1897), pp. 107ff.

Friedenwald, H., "Ethics of the Practice of Medicine from the Jewish Point of View," *Johns Hopkins Hospital Bulletin,* XXVIII (1917), No. 318.

—— "Montalto. A Jewish Physician at the Court of Marie de Medicis and Louis XIII," *Bulletin of the Institute of the History of Medicine,* III (1935), No. 2, February.

JE, "Juan Rodrigo de Castel-Branco"; "Medicine."

ADDITIONAL SOURCE MATERIALS IN ENGLISH

Grayzel, S., *The Church and the Jews in the XIIIth Century,* contains a letter, p. 347, regarding a Jewish oculist called to attend a member of the French royal family.

Nohl, J., *The Black Death,* pp. 203–204, contains a complaint of the Jewish community at Prague, 1714, that the Christian physicians of the Prague University will not attend them in their ghetto, and the denial of the medical faculty.

65.

Joseph Nasi Rebuilds Tiberias
1564

JOSEPH NASI was a Marrano banker who had by gradual stages moved from his native Portugal to Turkey where he openly professed his Judaism. He was a distinguished financier and an intimate friend of the crown prince, later Sultan Selim II (1566–1574) of the Ottoman Empire, who made him Duke of Naxos.

Joseph, through his influence with Prince Selim, secured the grant of the village of Tiberias in Palestine. It may be that he had some hopes of creating a Jewish city-state in this Palestinian town which he attempted to people with Jewish refugees, particularly Italians, fleeing from Christian persecution. The modernism of Nasi is shown by his intention to make these colonists self-supporting through the production of silk and by the manufacture of fine woolens in which he hoped to compete with the Venetian manufacturers. For reasons unknown this colonization never succeeded; Joseph, a skilful politician, had many irons in the fire.

The story of this attempt to establish a self-supporting Jewish colony on the shores of the Lake of Galilee is told by Joseph Ha-Kohen (1496–1578) in his well known Hebrew chronicle of Jewish history, *The Vale of Tears*.

⟨Don Joseph Nasi came to Ferrara with those who had escaped from the iron furnace, Portugal. He lived there for a short time and then went on to Turkey, where he found favor in the eyes of Sultan Sulaiman, who loved him very much. [From Portugal he had gone to Antwerp and then on to Venice, to Ferrara, and finally to Turkey, which he reached about 1553.] The Sultan gave him the ruins of Tiberias and seven of the villages about it [1563], appointing him prince and chief over them at that time. Don Joseph sent Rabbi Joseph ben Ardut, his agent, there to rebuild the walls of the city.

Ardut went and found favor also in the eyes of the Prince [Selim], who gave him a daily allowance of sixty aspers. The Sultan sent eight of his own household with him, together with an order, written and sealed with the royal signet, recommending him to the Pashas of Damascus and Safed, as follows: "Do everything that this man requires of you." Hence an order was issued by authority of the Sultan, as follows: "All builders and laborers in those villages must report for the rebuilding of Tiberias. He who does not appear will be punished."

There was plenty of building stone there, for Tiberias had been a very great city before it was destroyed. Indeed in the days of Rabbi Ammi and Rabbi Assi [about 300 C.E., at which time Tiberias was the cultural center of Palestine] there had been thirteen synagogues in it. The inhabitants of those seven villages were commanded to prepare mortar in generous quantities to carry on the work. There was also plenty of sand there, for the Sea of Galilee is nearby.

But the Arabs were envious of them, and a certain old noble arose and cried out to the inhabitants of that region: "Don't allow them to rebuild this city, for there will be trouble later. I have indeed found written in a very old book that when the city, whose name is Tiberias, is rebuilt, our religion will be destroyed, and we shall be the sufferers." They heeded him and refused to go on with the building of the walls, with the result that the work on the walls of Tiberias ceased.

Joseph ben Ardut, being very grieved, went to the Pasha of Damascus and complained before him: "I regret, my lord, but the inhabitants of the villages absolutely refuse to obey the command of the Sultan." Terrified, the Pasha hastened to send men there who seized two of the leaders and executed them in order that those left might see and be afraid, and not act rebelliously any more.

Again they started to dig in order to rebuild the walls of the city, and they found a large stone and under it a ladder descending into the ground. There they found a large church [probably a crusaders' church] full of marble statues and altars after the fashion of the Christian churches. The four slaves of Don Joseph whom the prince had given of those taken captive in the wars with Djelabi smashed it to pieces and filled the place with dirt. [These slaves are probably part of the thousands taken by the Sultan in 1535 from his deposed finance-officer Iskanderdjelabi and his father-in-law. Among the slaves seized was Muhammed Sokolli, later vizier and enemy of Nasi.] At that time were also found three bells which the Christians had hidden in the days of Guy, the last Christian king who ruled in that country when the enemy went up against them. They made cannons of them. [Tiberias, in possession of the crusaders, had been besieged by Saladin; Guy, 1186–1187, the last king of Jerusalem, was defeated nearby.]

The circumference of the city of Tiberias, which they rebuilt, was fifteen hundred cubits, and the work was finished in the month of Kislew, in the year 5325 [November-December 1564]. And Don Joseph rejoiced very much and gave thanks to God.

At his command they planted very many mulberry trees there to feed silk worms. He also ordered wool to be brought from Spain to manufacture garments just like the clothes they made in Venice, for the man Don Joseph was very great, and his fame spread throughout the land.

BIBLIOGRAPHY

REFERENCES TO TEXTBOOKS

Roth, pp. 253–258; Sachar, pp. 221–223.

READINGS FOR ADVANCED STUDENTS

Graetz, IV, pp. 593–629; Graetz-Rhine, IV, pp. 403–453; Margolis and Marx, pp. 486–487, 503, 512–518.

Kaufmann, D., "Don Joseph Nassi, Founder of Colonies in the Holy Land, and the Community of Cori in the Campagna," JQR, O.S., II (1890), pp. 291 ff.

Lewisohn, L., The Last Days of Shylock. A sound historical novel touching on the attempt of Joseph Nasi to rebuild Tiberias.

Roth, C., Venice (Jewish Communities Series), pp. 82–93.

JE, "Nasi, Joseph, Duke of Naxos"; "Turkey."

66.

Mordecai Meisel, Financier and Philanthropist
Prague, Bohemia
1528–1601

Mordecai Meisel (1528–1601), who was born and died in Prague, was one of the outstanding Jewish financiers and philanthropists of his day. His wealth was enormous, and for generations "I'd like to be as rich as Meisel" was a line in a folk-song sung in the ghettos of Europe. He made his fortune in articles of luxury, merchandise, real estate, but, primarily, through large loans to the Austrian state, then engaged in a series of wars with the Ottoman Empire. His career, in some respects, is paralleled later on by that of the first two generations of the Rothschilds.

He was one of the first of the great court-Jews and used his influence with the Hapsburg rulers to protect the Jews of Prague.

The first selection below is taken from *Zemah Dawid* ("Sprout of David"), a history of the Jews and Gentiles to the year 1592, written in Hebrew by the Prague Jewish historian, David Gans (1541–1613). It is a description of Mordecai Meisel, now in his sixty-fifth year. This description is valuable in that it gives us a picture of the qualities which the Jews of Central Europe in the sixteenth century admired in their leaders, and thus in turn gives us an insight into the ideals of the Jewish masses themselves.

The second selection, translated from the German, is taken from the Fugger news-letters, a motley collection of current events, assembled by the great sixteenth century banking and industry firm of the Fuggers, or by other agencies. This particular piece of news describes the confiscation of the wealth of Mordecai Meisel a few days after his death. Only three years before his death Meisel had received a written guarantee from the Emperor that his property would pass on to his heirs without any interference by the state. This is an adequate commentary on the times.

1. *Meisel the Philanthropist, 1592*

¶Mordecai Meisel is one of the walls and pillars of the synagogue, a prince of givers, a father to the poor, who seeks the welfare of his people and is beloved by the mass of his brothers. He has been a leader among the merchants. The greatness of his deeds deserves to be recorded; therefore I have thought it fit, in closing this book, to record some of his acts in order that they may be remembered in every city, generation, and family, so that his memory may not fade from our children because of all the fine charitable things that he did for us here in this holy community of Prague.

Out of his own means he built the High Synagogue, a temple in miniature, as it were, for honor and glory. He also donated many Torah scrolls, together with their finely wrought gold and silver ornaments: some to our community, some to Poland, and some to Jerusalem, the holy city. He also built the public bath-house, and the pool, too, that serves for the ritual bath, as well as a hospice for the needy and afflicted poor. He also laid stone pavements for all the streets of the Jewish quarter, all of this with his own money and at his own expense.

In addition to all these things he was also generous enough to build the great synagogue, majestic in its splendor, which has not its equal for beauty in the entire Jewish diaspora. It rests on twenty pillars, all of them of hewn stone, and now, just at the time that this, my book, is being finished, the work on it is also being completed. Those in charge of the building, led by the skilled, intelligent, and honored Joseph Wahl and Hirz Zoref [Juda Goldschmied de Herz, d. 1625], have figured out that he expended more than ten thousand thalers in its erection. [The Meisel Synagogue was dedicated *Simhat Torah*, 1592.]

Now all these things that have been mentioned have been for the good of the public; his private benefactions are too numerous to mention; no book is big enough to contain all the deeds of charity he daily performs. He has been accustomed to encourage the study of the Torah and its students through liberal aid and support, for he honors the scholars with gifts and fine presents. Does he not give food to the hungry, and choice meats, flour, fats, and other things necessary for the poor when the holidays come around? He is like a protecting wall to the sickly poor, for he lends his money to the penniless of our city, and thus enables them to make a living. During the past Hanukkah he lent them eight hundred thalers at one stroke. He has clothed the naked many a time: the majority of the poor of our city, all in one shade, too. Every year he has picked two poor girls by lot and married them off [by giving them dowries. He had no children of his own.]

I want to mention one more public benefaction and with this finish my statement. During the past two years, this prince, the honored Mordecai Meisel, has expended—during the course of these two years—the generous sum of more than twenty thousand thalers for the building of the above mentioned synagogue, for aid and loans which were sent to the poor of Posen, for loans to the poor of our city and for dowries for the daughters of our people. [After the Posen fire of 1590, Meisel lent the Jews there 10,000 gulden.]

Let it not enter the mind of anyone who is not here with us, that these words of mine are to some extent exaggerated in order to swell his praise, after the fashion of [I Samuel 18:7]: "Saul hath slain his thousands, and David his ten thousands." On the contrary, we have been sparing, as far as it was possible, in our recital of his virtues and his good deeds. Indeed the sage has already said: "Things that are well known require no proof." For hundreds and thousands of our people know that of all the things that I have mentioned there is not a single one that has not happened, for all of them are correct, and there is not among them even a hair's breadth of fault or lie. You, intelligent reader, investigate the past. Was there ever found a man like him, such a princely and liberal giver? Will not his righteousness exist forever?

In connection with all his good deeds we ought to mention his two wives. The first, who has long since died, Dame Eva, of blessed memory, was an intelligent God-fearing woman. She left behind her a good name because of her many virtues, humility, and wisdom. She was charitable and liberal with her money. His second wife, Dame Frumet—long may she live—is also a fine person, the crown of her husband. She is a God-fearing woman, one worthy of praise. Her hand is always open to satisfy the hungry. Her husband can always rely on her to strengthen, support, encourage, and lead him in all good endeavor. [Frumet Lekarz, the second wife, died in 1625.] May God requite them according to their work, and may their merit intercede for them and for us throughout all time. Amen.

II. *The Confiscation of Mordecai Meisel's Wealth, Prague, March, 1601*

⟪From Prague, the 5th Day of April, 1601.

A short time ago there died here the Jew Meisel. [He died during the night between the 13th and 14th of March.] Notwithstanding that he had left his imperial Majesty ten thousand florins, and much cash also to the hospital for poor Christians and Jews, his imperial Majesty on the following Saturday, viz., the Sabbath of the Jews, ordered Herr von Sternberg, at that time President of the Bohemian Chamber, to enter the Jew's house forcibly and to seize everything there was. The widow of Meisel handed this over willingly, for she had already set aside and hidden the best part of the treasure. That which was taken away came to forty-five thousand florins in cash, besides all manner of other things, such as silver plate, promissory notes, jewels, clothes, and all kinds of coins.

After this, however, the President, against whom the Jewess and the sons of the two brothers of Meisel had raised a strong protest to the privy councillors, was not satisfied with all this money and booty, and no doubt at the command of his Majesty, once more broke into the house at night. [These two nephews, both named Samuel, were to have been the heirs.] The son of one of the brothers was taken prisoner, secretly led away, and tortured in such guise that he confessed to the executioners, as a result of which the following substance was handed to the Bohemian Chamber:

```
80,000 ordinary single ducats of 2 florins apiece make ........160,000 florins
 5,000 pure golden Portugalese of 20 florins apiece make ......100,000 florins
15,000 pure golden [English] Rosenobles of 4 florins 5 kreuzer
       apiece ................................................. 61,250 florins
30,000 [Salzburg] turnip ducats of 2 florins apiece make ...... 60,000 florins
10,000 Styrian ducats of 2 florins apiece make ................ 20,000 florins
60,000 silver thalers of 70 kreuzer apiece make ............... 70,000 florins
Together with the above-mentioned ..........................    45,000 florins
Make altogether ........................................516,250 florins
```

[This was an enormous sum for those days.]

BIBLIOGRAPHY

READINGS FOR ADVANCED STUDENTS

Margolis and Marx, pp. 547–548.

Elwenspoek, C., *Jew Süss Oppenheimer. The Great Financier, Gallant, and Adventurer of the 18th Century*. A rather lurid picture of the well known court Jew, Joseph Süss Oppenheimer, who lived in the eighteenth century. Lion Feuchtwanger's novel, *Power*, dealing with Oppenheimer, is well worth reading.

Philipson, D., *Old European Jewries*, Chap. v, "The Judenstadt of Prague."

Sombart, W., *The Jews and Modern Capitalism*. An interesting study of the contributions of Jews to modern capitalism. Sombart's theory that Jews are largely responsible for the rise of capitalism has been severely criticized.

JE, "Court Jews"; "Meisel: Mordecai Marcus Meisel"; "Oppenheimer, Joseph Süss."

67.

An Accident and Its Consequences
Poland, about 1600

THE Tatar inroads into southern Poland in the sixteenth and seventeenth centuries compelled the Poles to arm themselves in defense. Jews, like their fellow-citizens, learned to handle "big guns" and "little guns," blunderbusses and pistols, and, of course, accidents happened. The following selection discusses such an accident and its consequences. It is in the form of a legal "question" and "answer" and is found in the Hebrew *responsa* or "answers" of Maharam Lublin (d. 1616).

Maharam is an abbreviated form of the name and title, "Our master, Rabbi Meir." This Polish worthy, who held important positions in Cracow, Lemberg, and Lublin, was one of the outstanding rabbinical minds in an age that produced many eminent Talmudists. He is notable, however, not merely for his tremendous learning, but also for his brilliant analytic method, for his independent, critical thinking, and for his succinctness and clarity of expression. His reputation extended all through Europe, for his opinions were sought all the way from Italy to Turkey.

In his private life Maharam was a wealthy business man. In his personal relations he was proud and even arrogant; in his decisions he was frequently lenient, as the following selection clearly indicates.

QUESTION

⟪This deals with a man of low spirit, a man of pains and sickness, mentally distraught because of an unfortunate incident which, as it were, God caused to happen to him in line with the old proverb: "From the wicked cometh forth wickedness." [I Samuel 24:13. The implication here is that he was stricken with disease because of his bad character.]

This happened during the time when, because of the Tatars, there were disturbances in Volhynia such as are customary in the cities situated in that district. At this time by command of the general and the officers every man there was expected to be ready with his weapon in his hand to engage in battle and to fight the Tatars.

It happened then on a certain day that the man in question was trying out his gun, as musketeers usually do. He was shooting with his weapon, which in German is called *Büchse* [gun], through a window in his house at a target that was fixed on the wall in his yard. But just then a man coming from the street into that yard and wishing to enter that house ran into the area just described and was unfortunately killed, without having been seen and certainly without having been aimed at. For the man who did the shooting had never seen the unfortunate fellow, as was later made clear by evidence offered in court on his behalf by people of his city. It was further testified that the Gentile who was the officer of the Jewish musketeer and his superior—for he was in charge of ten men—had stationed himself outside to warn off any one who might wish to enter the yard. Indeed he had done so in this case, too, for he had shouted at that man and had warned him not to enter there, as was made clear in court.

Now this musketeer has come to me, weeping and crying in the bitterness of his soul, and has willingly offered to take upon himself any penance for the calamity which, unfortunately, happened through him. [He wished to do penance by going into exile, although innocent.] Now I saw that he was a sick man, for he had just recovered from a skin disease—may you never get it—and that he was weak of foot, and that he did not have the strength to wander from town to town as would be required of a real penitent. In addition to this he is burdened with sons and daughters who are dependent on him for their support, and he lives among Gentiles in a village. [There were no other Jews to look after his children.] Therefore I have set my mind to enquire and to search about and to find some support among the teachings of our rabbis, of blessed memory, as to how to lighten his exile.

ANSWER

. . . Now, aside from any other reason or argument, the subject of our discussion is very much like a case of an unavoidable accident, for the person in question had relied on the guard who was stationed outside, even though he was a Gentile, to warn everyone who might enter, as indeed he did. But that unfortunate victim, however, disobeyed at the cost of his life, as was testified.

Now considering these circumstances, and in view of his [the musketeer's] poor physical condition, I have seen fit to lighten his exile to the degree that he should wander about in the towns which are in his immediate neighborhood, as is indicated in the sheet of penance which I have written for him. In addition, on every Monday and Thursday [when there are special synagogue services], he must go, from the village where he lives, to the next largest Jewish community to recite the confessions of sin and to be whipped, all this as indicated in the next paragraph.

Namely, first he is to go to the holy community of Ostrog and to lie down at the threshold of the synagogue as every one goes out, and then he is to be whipped and to make confession for his sins. [In the Middle Ages both Jews and Gentiles employed these means of penance.] Afterwards he is to go to the holy community of Vinnitsa, after that to Zaslavl, then to Ostropol, then to Sinyava, and finally to the holy community of Konstantinov, and shall also do that which is prescribed above. [These towns are in southwestern Russia, in the Ukraine.]

On every Monday and Thursday thereafter he must come on foot from the village in which he is living to the synagogue of the holy community of Konstantinov and sit behind the door. Then he is to be whipped and is to make confession and to fast every day [till evening] until a half year is passed, and he must frequently fast for three days and three nights straight.

But when I saw that this was more than his strength could bear, for he was a sick man, I again lightened his penance to the effect that he should fast only three days in every seven, but that he should not eat meat or drink strong drink the entire week, except on the Sabbaths and holydays, nor sleep on mattresses and pillows on week days. Also he was not to put on a clean garment, nor to take a bath, nor to cleanse his hair but once every month; nor was he to go to any feast or trim his hair. Now whatever I have lightened is because he is a man of pains and sickness and cannot walk from town to town and because he also has sons and daughters dependent on him for their support.

These are the words of the busily-engaged MEIR.

68.

The Memoirs of Glückel of Hameln
1646–1719

GLÜCKEL of Hameln (1646–1724) is one of the most interesting characters in German Jewish history. Despite the fact that she was a business woman of enterprise and real ability, she found time to rear and to marry off twelve of her thirteen children, allying them with the most notable Jewish families of Europe.

During the years 1691–1719 Glückel, who had removed from Hameln to Hamburg, wrote her memoirs in Judaeo-German. This work of hers is a most unusual one, for autobiography is rare in Jewish literature in this age, and as a medium of self-expression by a woman of this period it is altogether unique.

For an insight into the social, economic, and cultural life of the Jews of Central Europe in the period 1650–1725 these memoirs are almost invaluable. They give us an intimate picture of the family life of the average well-to-do Jew, his relation to the state, his business problems, his religious background, and his spiritual life.

The first selection given below illustrates one of the dangers incident to pawnbroking; the second recounts the story of a Wandsbeck Jew who became a thief, yet had the courage to die on the gallows rather than save his life by conversion to Christianity.

1. *The Dangers of Pawnbroking, about 1645*

⟨Now my father—the memory of the righteous is a blessing—had been married, as has already been mentioned, to a woman named Reize before he married my mother. She is said to have been a good person and a prominent woman, and to have kept a big house. Eventually she died, but left my father no children. She had an only daughter before this so that my father got a stepdaughter with his first wife. This girl did not have her equal in beauty and in good deeds; she knew French fluently, a fact which once stood my father in good stead. [The study of French by Jewish children was not uncommon in Germany in this age of Louis XIV.]

My sainted father once held a pledge from a notable on which he had lent 500 Reichsthalers. It happened after a time that the

330

notable returned with two other prominent men and wanted to redeem his pledge. My father, who had no suspicions, went upstairs and got it. His stepdaughter was at the clavicymbalum [a precursor of the piano], playing in order that the notables might not find the wait too tedious. The notables stood beside her and said to one another: "When the Jew comes down with our pledge we'll take it without paying for it and escape." This they said in French, not thinking that the girl would understand.

In the meantime, as my father came down with the pledge, the girl began to sing [in Hebrew] in a loud voice: "As you value your life, no pledge! Today he is here and tomorrow he runs away." Unfortunately in her haste she couldn't get anything else out. Thereupon my father said to the notable: "Sir, where is the money?" To which the notable answered: "Give me the pledge." To which my father responded: "I won't give the pledge until I get the money." Then the notable said to the others: "Comrades, we have been betrayed. The slut must know French." And uttering threats they ran out of the house.

The next day the notable came alone and paid my father the principal and the interest on the pledge and said: "You have benefited much and you have invested your money well in that you had your daughter taught French." And with this he went his way.

My sainted father kept this stepdaughter with him and treated her as if she were his own child. He married her off, making a good match for her: he got the son of Calman Aurich for her. Unfortunately she died while giving birth to her first child. [The Calmans of Aurich were wealthy court-Jews. A son of a Calman of Aurich became Baron de Picquigny and Vicomte de Amiens in 1774.]

A few days later [after she was buried] some one robbed her, taking her shroud. After she had appeared in a dream and had revealed what had happened to her, they went to the grave and found out that that is what had occurred. The women hurried and sewed her another shroud, and as they were sitting, sewing, the maid came into the room and cried out: "For God's sake, hurry up with your sewing! Can't you see the corpse sitting with you?" But the women saw nothing. When they had finished they gave the corpse its shroud and it never returned but remained at peace.

11. *The Thief Who Died a Martyr, about 1670*

❡Now my daughter Hannah (may her days be long!) grew up and became quite a clever child. Perhaps I'll tell about her later.

At that time an East Indiaman with many uncut diamonds fell into the hands of the King of Denmark and lay at Glückstadt. Since every sailor on it had diamonds, the Jews went to Glückstadt and did business and made good profits.

There were two Jews there who knew that a citizen in Norway had a large batch of these diamonds. They took evil counsel together, regrettably, and formed a partnership to get the diamonds out of that house where they were kept. It seems to me that the owner was a baker who had gotten them very cheaply.

So these two—this bad lot—came to Norway. At once they made a careful search for the man who had the diamonds and managed to get into his home. Gradually they became so friendly with this burgher that they found out where he kept his treasures, got the best of him, and took everything away from him. The man had sheltered them in his home.

The next morning they left the house and rented a skiff and thought they had made a good job of it all. But the Almighty did not want this to succeed. When the burgher arose the next morning and asked about his two guests, the servant told him that they had left the house quite early. The burgher was rather disturbed for whoever has such a treasure is always worried. Therefore he went to the chest where he kept his treasures but found nothing. He immediately took it for granted that his two guests had done this to him. He ran straight for the sea and asked some boatmen if they had not seen two Jews pulling out. "Yes," said one of them to him, "Such-and-such a boatman took them away about an hour ago." He hired a boat immediately, put in four oarsmen, and started after them. It was not very long before they sighted the boat with the thieves, but when the thieves saw that they were being followed they threw the whole treasure into the sea.

In short, the burgher overhauled them and they had to go back with him although they argued a great deal with him, saying: "Consider what you're about. We are honest folk. It will not be discovered that we have any of the stuff. You are doing us an injustice. We'll hold you responsible for this." They had thrown the stuff into the water in order the better to deny the charges, but it is written in our Ten Commandments: "Thou shalt not steal!" Therefore, God, blessed be He, did not help them and they were again brought back to the place from which they had fled. They denied everything the while they were being stripped naked and everything was being carefully searched. But all this did not help them.

They were put to such severe torture that finally they had to confess that they had done it, and that when they had seen that they were being pursued, they had thrown the diamonds into the sea, thinking that when they would be searched and nothing found on them, they would be able, by their denial, to get away with it. But, as has been said, God did not want this to happen and both were condemned to the gallows.

The one thief immediately accepted the Christian faith [and saved his life]. The other had been a pious man all his life and also had a pious father and mother. He came from Wandsbeck [on the outskirts of Hamburg]. He did not want to change his religion and chose to sacrifice his life. I knew him and his parents well, and all his life he had behaved himself as a pious, honest man. He must have been led astray by the other fellow, who was never any good, and so it was inevitable, unfortunately, that he should come to a bad end. Surely his soul is in Paradise for he must have actually attained future life through his conduct in his last hour.

Out of respect for his family I don't want to give his name, but the whole story is well known in Hamburg. The Holy One, blessed be He, will surely have accepted his martyrdom favorably, for he surrendered his life for God. He could have escaped just as easily as his companion but he fulfilled the commandment [Deuteronomy 6:5]: "Thou shalt love the Lord thy God with all thy soul [even though you die a martyr to prove your love of God]." Hence his death must have been an expiation of all of his sins. Therefore every one should learn from this example and not allow the evil inclination to seduce him with filthy lucre.

BIBLIOGRAPHY

READINGS FOR ADVANCED STUDENTS

Lowenthal, M., *The Jews of Germany*, Chap. xii, "Grand Dukes in Jewry."
Schechter, S., *Studies in Judaism*, Second Series, 1908. "The Memoirs of a Jewess of the Seventeenth Century," pp. 126–147.

ADDITIONAL SOURCE MATERIALS IN ENGLISH

Lowenthal, M., *The Memoirs of Glückel of Hameln*. Probably the best source available for the economic and social life of the Jew in Central Europe in the seventeenth and eighteenth centuries.

69.

Baruch Spinoza, Philosopher
1632–1677

$\mathbb{B}$ARUCH SPINOZA was born in Amsterdam of a family of Portuguese Jewish-Christians who had returned to Judaism. His philosophic and religious radicalism brought down upon him at an early age the wrath of the Sephardic Jewish community. He was finally excommunicated when he was but twenty-four years old. The Jewish leaders in Amsterdam—some of them men of a broad general culture—took this decisive step not only because of religious conservatism, and not only because of their love for the faith for which their very brothers and sisters had suffered martyrdom, but also because they feared that the resentment by the orthodox Dutch Christians of Spinoza's heresies might imperil the civil and economic status of all Dutch Jews.

Spinoza's great works are his *Theologico-Political Tractate*, published anonymously in 1670, and his *Ethics*, published after his death. In the *Theologico-Political Tractate* he pleaded for freedom of thought; in the *Ethics* he developed the pantheism which is so pronounced a characteristic of his philosophy. Toward Judaism he was most bitter and censorious.

The following biographical sketch of Spinoza is translated from the Dutch biography of Colerus (Johann Köhler), a Lutheran preacher at the Hague, a younger contemporary of the philosopher. His sketch of Spinoza (1705) is not the oldest, nor is it authentic in every aspect, but it is one of the most interesting and detailed, and remarkably fair for an orthodox Christian from whose viewpoint Spinoza was an enemy of religion.

A SHORT, BUT TRUE BIOGRAPHY OF BENEDICTUS DE SPINOZA. COMPOSED OF AUTHENTIC RECORDS AND THE ORAL TESTIMONY OF PERSONS STILL LIVING BY JOHANNES COLERUS, GERMAN PREACHER OF THE LUTHERAN COMMUNITY AT THE HAGUE

SPINOZA'S DESCENT AND FAMILY

❰This world famed philosopher Baruch de Spinoza was born at Amsterdam the 24th of November, in the year 1632. . . . Called

Baruch by his Jewish parents, he changed his name himself, when he forsook Judaism, and called himself Benedictus de Spinoza in his writings and letters. What is commonly said, that he was poor and of a very mean extraction, is not true. His father, a Portuguese Jew, was in very good circumstances, and a merchant at Amsterdam, where he lived upon the Burgwal, in a good house near the Old Portuguese Synagogue. Besides, his civil and handsome behaviour, his relations, who lived at ease, and what was left to him by his father and mother, prove that his extraction, as well as his education, was above that of the common people. Samuel Carceres, a Portuguese Jew, married the youngest of his two sisters. The name of the eldest was Rebeckah, and that of the youngest Miriam [d. 1651]. . . .

SPINOZA'S FIRST STUDIES

Spinoza showed from his childhood, and in his younger years, that nature had not been unkind to him. His quick fancy and his ready and penetrating wit were easily perceived. Because he had a great mind to learn the Latin tongue, they gave him at first a German student as a master. But afterwards in order to perfect himself in that language, he made use of the infamous Francis Van den Ende [hanged in Paris as a rebel, 1674], who taught it then in Amsterdam, and practis'd physick at the same time: That man taught with good success and a great reputation; so that the richest merchants of that city intrusted him with the instruction of their children, before they had found out that he taught his scholars something else besides Latin. For it was discovered at last, that he sowed the first seeds of atheism in the minds of those young boys. This is a matter of fact, which I cou'd prove, if there was any necessity for it, by the testimony of several honest gentlemen, who are still living, and some of whom have been elders of the Lutheran Church at Amsterdam. Those good men bless every day the memory of their parents, who took care in due time to remove them from the school of so pernicious and so impious a master. . . .

HE APPLIES HIMSELF TO THE STUDY OF THEOLOGY, AND THEN TO PHILOSOPHY

Spinoza, having learn'd the Latin tongue well, applied himself to the study of theology for some years. In the mean time his wit and judgment encreased every day: So that finding himself more disposed to enquire into natural causes, he gave over theology, and

betook himself altogether to the study of philosophy. He did for a
long time deliberate about the choice he shou'd make of a master,
whose writing might serve him as a guide in his design. At last, having
light upon the works of Descartes [rationalist philosopher, d. 1650],
he read them greedily; and afterwards he often declared that he had
all his knowledge of natural philosophy [science] from him. He
was charmed with that maxim of Descartes, which says that nothing
ought to be admitted as true, but what has been proved by good and
solid reasons. From whence he drew this consequence that the
ridiculous doctrine and principles of the Rabbins cou'd not help him
in his studies, because they are only built upon the authority of the
Rabbins themselves, and because what they teach does not proceed
from God, as they pretend without any ground for it, and without
the least appearance of reason. [Spinoza turned against rabbinic
Judaism.]

From that time he began to be very much reserved amongst the
Jewish teachers, whom he shunned as much as he cou'd. He was
seldom seen in their synagogues, which exasperated them against
him to the highest degree; for they did not doubt but that he wou'd
soon leave them, and make himself a Christian. Yet, to speak the
truth, he never embraced Christianity, nor received the holy baptism.
And tho he had frequent conversations with some learn'd Men-
nonites [a pacifistic Protestant sect], as well as with the most eminent
divines of other Christian sects, yet he never declared for, nor profest
himself to be a member of any of them.

Monsieur Bayle says in the biography of Spinoza [in *The Historical
and Critical Dictionary*], translated by F. van Halma, pp. 6–8, that
the Jews offered him a pension a little while before his desertion, to
engage him to remain amongst 'em, and to appear now and then in
their synagogues. This Spinoza himself affirmed several times to the
Sieur Van der Spyck, his landlord, and to some other persons; adding
that the pension, which the Rabbins design'd to give him, amounted
to 1000 florins. But he protested at the same time, that if they had
offered him ten times as much, he wou'd not have accepted of it,
nor frequented their assemblies out of such a motive; because he was
not a hypocrite, and minded nothing but truth.

Monsieur Bayle tells us that he happen'd one day to be assaulted
by a Jew, as he was coming out of the playhouse, who wounded him
in the face with a knife, and that Spinoza suspected that the Jew
design'd to kill him, tho his wound was not dangerous. But Spinoza's
landlord and his wife, who are still living, give me quite another
account of it. They had it from Spinoza himself, who did often tell

them, that one evening as he was coming out of the Old Portuguese Synagogue, he saw a man by him with a dagger in his hand; whereupon standing upon his guard, and going backwards, he avoided the blow, which reached no farther than his cloaths. He kept still the coat that was run thro' with the dagger, as a memorial of that event. This occurrence induced him to take up his residence outside of Amsterdam where he could quietly continue his studies in the natural sciences. [Some scholars question the authenticity of this attack.]

HE WAS EXCOMMUNICATED BY THE JEWS

He had no sooner left the communion of the Jews, but they prosecuted him juridically according to their ecclesiastical laws, and excommunicated him [July 27, 1656]. He himself did very often own that he was excommunicated by them, and declared, that from that time he broke all friendship and correspondence with them. Monsieur Bayle and Dr. Musaeus [professor of theology at Jena] report this also. Some Jews of Amsterdam, who knew Spinoza very well, have also confirmed to me the truth of that fact, adding, that the sentence of excommunication was publickly pronounced by the old man *Hakam Aboab*, a Rabbin of great reputation amongst 'em. [Isaac Aboab was also *hakam*, or rabbi, in Brazil, 1642.] I have desired in vain the sons of that old Rabbin to communicate that sentence to me; they answered me, that they could not find it amongst the papers of their father, but I cou'd easily perceive that they had no mind to impart it to me. . . .

SPINOZA LEARNS A TRADE OR A MECHANICAL ART. . . .

Spinoza . . . learned a mechanical art before he embraced a quiet and retir'd life, as he was resolv'd to do. He learned therefore to make glasses for telescopes, and for some other uses, and succeeded so well therein, that people came to him from all parts to buy them; and if necessary he could have made his living therefrom. A considerable number of those glasses, which he had polished, were found in his cabinet after his death, and sold pretty dear, as it appears by the register of the auctioneer who was present at the sale of his goods.

After he had perfected himself in that art, he apply'd himself to drawing, which he learn'd of himself, and he cou'd draw a head very well with ink, or with a coal. I have in my hands a whole book of such draughts, amongst which there are some heads of several considerable persons, who were known to him, or who had occasion to visit him. Among those draughts I find in the 4th sheet a fisherman having only his shirt on, with a net on his right shoulder, whose attitude is very much like that of Massanello, the infamous head of the rebels of Naples, as it appears in the history pictures. [Tommaso Aniello, Neapolitan liberator, was assassinated in 1647.] Which gives me occasion to add, that Mr. Van der Spyck, at whose house Spinoza lodged when he died, has assured me, that the draught of that fisherman did perfectly resemble Spinoza, and that he had certainly drawn himself. I do not for certain reasons wish to mention the considerable persons, whose heads are likewise to be found in this book, amongst his other draughts.

Thus he was able to maintain himself with the work of his hands, and to mind his study, as he design'd to do. So that having no occasion to stay longer in Amsterdam, he left it, and took lodgings in the house of one of his acquaintance, who lived upon the road from Amsterdam to Auwerkerke. He spent his time there in studying, and working his glasses. When they were polished, his friends took care to send for them, to sell 'em, and to remit his money to him.

HE WENT TO LIVE AT RYNSBURG, AFTERWARDS AT VOORBURG, AND AT LAST AT THE HAGUE

In the year 1664 [better 1660–1661] Spinoza left that place, and retired to Rynsburg near Leyden, where he spent all the winter, and then he went to Voorburg [April 1663], a league from the Hague, as he himself says, in his 30th [17th] letter written to Peter Balling. He lived there, as I am informed, three or four years; during which time, he got a great many friends at the Hague, who were all distinguisht by their quality, or by civil and military employments. They were often in his company, and took a great delight in hearing him discourse.

It was at their request that he settl'd himself at the Hague at last [1670], where he boarded at first upon the Veerkaay, at a widow's whose name was Van Velen [de Werve], in the same house where I lodge at present. The room wherein I study, at the further end of the house backward, up two pair of stairs, is the same where he lay, and where he did work and study. He wou'd very often have his food brought into that room, where he kept sometimes two or three days, without seeing any body. But being sensible that he spent a little too much for his boarding, he took a room upon the Pavilioengracht, behind my house, at Mr. Henry Van der Spyck's, whom I have often mention'd, where he took care to furnish himself with food and drink, and where he lived a very retired life, according to his fancy.

HE WAS VERY SOBER, AND VERY FRUGAL, IN FOOD AND DRINK

It is scarce credible how sober and frugal he was all the time. Not that he was reduced to so great a poverty, as not to be able to spend more, if he had been willing; he had friends enough, who offered him their purses, and all manner of assistance. But he was naturally very sober, and could be satisfied with little; and he did not care that people shou'd think that he had lived, even but once, at the expence of other men. What I say about his sobriety and good husbandry may be prov'd by several small reckonings, which have been found amongst his papers after his death. It appears by them, that he lived a whole day upon a milk-soop done with butter, which amounted to three stivers, and upon a pot of beer of three half stivers. Another day he eat nothing but gruel done with raisins and butter, and that dish cost him four stivers eight pennies. [Being tubercular he no doubt lived on a diet.] There are but two half pints of wine at most for one month to be found amongst those reckonings, and tho he was often invited to eat with his friends, he chose rather to live upon what he had at home, tho it were never so little, than to sit down at a good table at the expence of another man.

Thus he spent the remaining part of his life in the house of his last landlord, which was somewhat above five years and a half. He was very careful to cast up his accounts every quarter; which he did, that he might spend neither more nor less than what he could spend every year. And he would say sometimes to the people of the house, that he was like the serpent, who forms a circle with his tail in his mouth [thus making both ends meet]; to denote that he had nothing left at the years end. He added, that he design'd to lay up no more money than what would be necessary for him to have a decent burying; and that his heirs would inherit nothing from him; they did not deserve it.

HIS PERSON, AND HIS WAY OF DRESSING HIMSELF

As for his person, his size, there are still many people at the Hague, who saw and knew him particularly. He was of middle size, he had good features in his face, the skin somewhat black, black curl'd hair, long eye-brows, and of the same colour, so that one might easily know by his looks that he was descended from Portuguese Jews.

He was plain and simple in his cloaths and paid little attention how he was dressed. One of the most eminent councellors of state went to see him, and found him in a shabby morning-gown, whereupon the councellor blam'd him for it, and offer'd him another. Spinoza answer'd him, that a man was never the better for having a finer gown. To which he added: "It is unreasonable to wrap up things of little or no value in a precious cover."

In his way of living, and in his social relations he was quiet and retiring. He knew admirably well how to be master of his passions; he was never seen very melancholy, nor very merry. He had the command of his anger, and if at any time he was uneasy in his mind, it did not appear outwardly; or if he happen'd to express his grief by some gestures, or by some words, he never fail'd to retire immediately, for fear of doing an unbecoming thing. He was besides, very courteous and obliging in his daily relations; he would very often discourse with his landlady, especially when she lay in [with child], and with the people of the house, when they happen'd to be sick or afflicted; he never fail'd then to comfort 'em, and exhort them to bear with patience those evils which God assigned to them as a lot.

He put the children in mind of going often to church, and taught them to be obedient and dutiful to their parents. When the people of the house came from church, he wou'd often ask them what they had learn'd, and what they cou'd remember of the sermon. He had a great esteem for Dr. Cordes, my predecessor; who was a learned and good natured man, and of an exemplary life, which gave occasion to Spinoza to praise him very often. Nay, he went sometimes to hear him preach, and he esteem'd particularly his learned way of explaining the Scripture, and the solid applications he made of it. He advised at the same time his landlord and the people of the house not to miss any sermon of so excellent a preacher.

It happen'd one day, that his landlady ask'd him whether he believed she cou'd be saved in the religion she profest; he answered: "Your religion is a good one; you need not look for another, nor doubt that you may be saved in it, provided, whilst you apply your self to piety, you live at the same time a peaceable and quiet life."

When he staid at home, he was troublesome to nobody; he spent the greatest part of his time quietly in his own chamber. When he happen'd to be tired by having applyed himself too much to his philosophical meditations, he went downstairs to refresh himself, and discoursed with the people of the house about any thing that might afford matter for an ordinary conversation, and even about trifles. He also took pleasure in smoaking a pipe of tobacco; or, when he had a mind to divert himself somewhat longer, he look'd for some spiders, and made 'em fight together, or he threw some flies into the cobweb, and was so well pleased with that battel, that he wou'd sometimes break into laughter. He observed also, with a microscope, the smallest insects and flies, from whence he drew such consequences as seem'd to him to agree best with his discoveries. [That Spinoza fed flies to spiders as a form of diversion seems hardly justifiable. More probably he was engaged in experimentation.]

He was no lover of money, as I have said, and he was very well contented to live from hand to mouth. Simon de Vries of Amsterdam, who expresses a great love for him, in the 26th [8th] letter, and calls him his "most upright friend," *amicum integerrimum*, presented him one day, with a summ of two thousand florins, to enable him to live a more easie life; but Spinoza, in the presence of his landlord, desired to be excused from accepting that money, under pretence that he wanted nothing, and that if he received so much money, it wou'd infallibly divert him from his studies and occupations.

The same Simon de Vries being like to die [1667], and having no wife nor children, design'd to make him his general heir; but Spinoza wou'd never consent to it, and told him that he shou'd not think to leave his estate to any body but to his brother, who lived at Schiedam, seeing he was his nearest relation, and natural heir.

This was executed, as he proposed it; but it was upon condition that the brother and heir of Simon de Vries shou'd pay to Spinoza a sufficient annuity for his maintenance; and that clause was likewise faithfully executed. But that which is particular is that an annuity of 500 florins was offered to Spinoza by virtue of that clause, which he would not accept, because he found it too considerable, so that he reduc'd it to 300 florins. That annuity was regularly paid him during his life; and the same de Vries of Schiedam took care after his death to pay to Mr. Van der Spyck what Spinoza owed him, as it appears by the letter of John Rieuwertz, printer at Amsterdam, who was employed in that affair. It is dated the 6th of March, 1678, and directed to Van der Spyck himself. [Spinoza was thus not altogether dependent on his lens-grinding for his livelihood.]

When Spinoza's father had died [1654] and the estate was to be divided, his sister(s) [and his nephew] sought to exclude him and not to permit him his share. But he compelled them by law. However, when it came to the actual division, he allowed them to keep everything and took nothing for his use save a good bed upon which to lie and a curtain for it.

BIBLIOGRAPHY

REFERENCES TO TEXTBOOKS

Sachar, pp. 245–248.

READINGS FOR ADVANCED STUDENTS

Graetz, V, pp. 86–109, 166–167; Graetz-Rhine, V, pp. 136–148, 181–182; Margolis and Marx, pp. 495–500.

Abbott, G. F., *Israel in Europe*, Chap. xvi, "In Holland."

Browne, L., *Blesséd Spinoza*. This popular biography is useful for the Jewish background of the young Spinoza.

Milman, H. H., *The History of the Jews*, II, pp. 448–455.

Pollock, F., *Spinoza: His Life and Philosophy*, 2nd ed., 1912. A standard work.

Waxman, M., "Baruch Spinoza's Relation to Jewish Philosophical Thought and to Judaism," *JQR*, N.S., XIX (1928–1929), pp. 411–430.

JE, "Amsterdam"; "Spinoza, Baruch."

ADDITIONAL SOURCE MATERIALS IN ENGLISH

Colerus, J., *The Life of Benedict de Spinosa*, London, 1706. This English translation—made from a French translation—is reprinted in Pollock's *Spinoza*, pp. 387ff.

70.

Solomon Maimon in Poland
1760–1765

SOLOMON MAIMON (about 1754–1800) is an intriguing
figure of the eighteenth century. He was a Jewish scholar, a brilliant
philosopher, and a—ne'er-do-well. Solomon ben Joshua was his
original name, but, it seems, out of admiration for his ideal, the great
Maimonides, he called himself Solomon Maimon. During the last
years of his life his *Autobiography*, in German, was published, and
here he describes, among many other things, his early experiences
in his native Poland. His book is, therefore, a valuable, intimate
picture, by a trained observer, of the sad state of the inner life of the
Polish Jew just before the partition of the Polish Republic.

Three selections have been chosen from his work: a description
of a Polish Jewish school as he knew it; the comico-tragic story of
his marriage as a child; and several anecdotes of a famous Polish
magnate and his relations to "his" Jews.

1. *A Polish Jewish School of the Middle Eighteenth Century*

⟪My brother Joseph and I were sent to Mirz to school. My brother,
who was about twelve years old, was put to board with a schoolmaster of some repute at that time, by name Jossel. This man was
the terror of all young people, "the scourge of God"; he treated
those in his charge with unheard of cruelty, flogged them till the
blood came, even for the slightest offense, and not infrequently tore
off their ears, or beat their eyes out. [Though corporal punishment
was the rule, such brutality was uncommon.] When the parents of
these unfortunates came to him, and took him to task, he struck
them with stones or whatever else came to hand, and drove them
with his stick out of the house back to their own dwellings, without
any respect of persons. All under his discipline became either blockheads or good scholars. I, who was then only seven years old, was
sent to another schoolmaster. . . .

I must now say something of the condition of the Jewish schools
in general. The school is commonly a small smoky hut, and the
children are scattered, some on benches, some on the bare earth. The

343

master, in a dirty blouse, sitting on the table, holds between his knees a bowl, in which he grinds tobacco into snuff with a huge pestle like the club of Hercules, while at the same time he wields his authority. The assistant-teachers give lessons, each in his own corner, and rule those under their charge quite as despotically as the master himself. Of the breakfast, lunch, and other food sent to the school for the children, these gentlemen keep the largest share for themselves. Sometimes even the poor youngsters get nothing at all; and yet they dare not make any complaint on the subject, if they will not expose themselves to the vengeance of these tyrants. Here the children are imprisoned from morning to night, and have not an hour to themselves, except on Friday and a half-holiday at the New Moon. [The New Moon marks the beginning of a Jewish month.]

II. *The Married Life of Young Maimon*

❡I stood, however, not only under the slipper of my wife, but—what was very much worse—under the lash of my mother-in-law [Rissia]. Nothing of all that she had promised was fulfilled. Her house, which she had settled on her daughter as a dowry, was burdened with debt. Of the six years' board which she had promised me I enjoyed scarcely half a year's, and this amid constant brawls and squabbles. She even, trusting to my youth and want of spirit, ventured now and then to lay hands on me, but this I repaid not infrequently with compound interest. [He was now in his eleventh year.] Scarcely a meal passed during which we did not fling at each other's head, bowls, plates, spoons, and similar articles. . . .

Scenes like this occurred very often. At such skirmishes of course my wife had to remain neutral, and whichever party gained the upper hand, it came home to her very closely. "Oh!" she often complained, "if only the one or the other of you had a little more patience!"

Tired of a ceaseless open war I once hit upon a stratagem which had a good effect, for a short time at least. I rose about midnight, took a large vessel of earthenware, crept with it under my mother-in-law's bed, and began to speak aloud into the vessel after the following fashion: "O Rissia, Rissia, you ungodly woman, why do you treat my beloved son so ill? If you do not mend your ways, your end is near, and you will be damned to all eternity." Then I crept out again, and began to pinch her cruelly; and after a while I slipped silently back to bed.

The following morning she got up in consternation and told my wife that my mother had appeared to her in a dream, and had threatened and pinched her on my account. In confirmation she showed the blue marks on her arm. When I came from the synagogue, I did not find my mother-in-law at home, but found my wife in tears. I asked the reason, but she would tell me nothing. My mother-in-law returned with a dejected look, and eyes red with weeping. She had gone, as I afterwards learned, to the Jewish place of burial, thrown herself on my mother's grave, and begged for forgiveness of her fault. She then had the burial place measured, and ordered a wax-light, as long as its circumference, for burning in the synagogue. [Such customs were common among the Jewish and Christian masses.] She also fasted the whole day, and towards me showed herself extremely amiable.

III. *Prince Radziwill and His Jews*

⟨Prince Radziwill [1734–1790] was, as Hettman [a general] in Poland and Voivode [a high official] in Lithuania, one of the greatest magnates, and as occupant of three inheritances in his family owned immense estates. He was not without a certain kindness of heart and good sense; but, through neglected training and a want of instruction, he became one of the most extravagant princes that ever lived. . . .

Who can describe all the excesses he perpetrated? A few examples will, I believe, be sufficient to give the reader some idea of them. A certain respect for my former prince does not allow me to consider his faults as anything but faults of temperament and education, which deserve rather our pity than our hatred and contempt.

When he passed through a street, which he commonly did with the whole pomp of his court, his bands of music, and soldiers, no man, at the peril of his life, durst show himself in the street; and even in the houses people were by no means safe. The poorest, dirtiest peasant-woman, who came in his way, he would order up into his carriage beside himself.

Once he sent for a respectable Jewish barber, who, suspecting nothing but that he was wanted for some surgical operation, brought his instruments with him, and appeared before the prince. [Barbers used to perform minor surgical operations.]

"Have you brought your instruments with you?" he was asked.

"Yes, Serene Highness," he replied.

"Then," said the prince, "give me a lancet, and I will open one of your veins."

The poor barber had to submit. The prince seized the lancet; and as he did not know how to go about the operation, and besides his hand trembled as a result of his hard drinking, of course he wounded the barber in a pitiable manner. But his courtiers smiled their applause, and praised his great skill in surgery.

He went one day into a church, and being so drunk that he did not know where he was, he stood against the altar, and commenced to pollute it. All who were present became horrified. Next morning when he was sober, the clergy brought to his mind the misdeed he had committed the day before. "Eh!" said the prince, "we will soon make that good." Thereupon he issued a command to the Jews of the place, to provide at their own expense, fifty stone of wax for burning in the church. [A stone was about twenty-two pounds.] The poor Jews were therefore obliged to bring a sin-offering for the desecration of a Christian Church by an orthodox Catholic Christian. . . .

Once he drove with the whole pomp of his court to a Jewish synagogue, and, without any one to this day knowing the reason, committed the greatest havoc, smashed windows and stoves, broke all the vessels, threw on the ground the copies of the Holy Scriptures kept in the ark, and so forth. A learned, pious Jew, who was present, ventured to lift one of these copies from the ground, and had the honor of being struck with a musket-ball by His Serene Highness' own hand. From here the train went to a second synagogue, where the same conduct was repeated, and from there they proceeded to the Jewish burial-place, where the buildings were demolished, and the monuments cast into the fire. [The desecration of synagogues and cemeteries is still common in Central and Eastern Europe.]

BIBLIOGRAPHY

READINGS FOR ADVANCED STUDENTS

Graetz, V, pp. 405–409.
Dubnow, S. M., *History of the Jews in Russia and Poland*, I, pp. 239–241.
JE, "Maimon, Solomon ben Joshua."

ADDITIONAL SOURCE MATERIALS IN ENGLISH

Solomon Maimon: an Autobiography. The autobiography of an eighteenth century Polish Jew, rich in details of Polish life. The life story of a contemporary of his is portrayed in *The Memoirs of Ber of Bolechow (1723-1805)*, translated and edited by M. Vishnitzer.

Jewry and the Individual Jew

D. THE INNER LIFE
OF THE JEW

71.

A Jewish Skipper and His Crew
North Africa, January, 404

EARLY in the year 404, Synesius, a cultured pagan, was returning to his native land Cyrene from a political mission at Constantinople. He spent some time at Alexandria where he saw his brother Euoptius, and set sail from Alexandria for Cyrene hugging the North African coast.

Synesius describes the storm he ran into and how finally he was compelled to land at the town of Azarion, Libya, from which spot he wrote this Greek letter to his brother. The captain and most of the crew on this eventful trip were Jews, and the description of them is an interesting contribution to our knowledge of Jewry in the early Byzantine period.

Synesius, who was a famous writer, later became a Christian and a bishop. He died about 415.

⟪Although we started from Bendideum at early dawn, we had scarcely passed Pharius Myrmex by noonday, for our ship went aground two or three times in the bed of the harbor. [Bendideum and Pharius Myrmex are parts of the harbor of Alexandria.] This mishap at the very outset seemed a bad omen, and it might have been wiser to desert a vessel which had been unlucky from the very start. . . .

Hear my story then, that you may have no further leisure for your mocking wit, and I will tell you first of all how our crew was made up. Our skipper [Amarantus] was desirous of death owing to his bankrupt condition; then besides him we had twelve sailors, thirteen in all! More than half of them, including the skipper, were Jews—a graceless race and fully convinced of the piety of sending to Hades as many Greeks as possible. [Greek writers, particularly Apion, often accused Jews of hating non-Jews.] The remainder were a collection of peasants who even as late as last year had never gripped an oar, but the one batch and the other were alike in this, that every man of them had some personal defect. Accordingly, so long as we were in safety they passed their time in jesting one with another, accosting their comrades not by their real names, but by the dis-

tinguishing marks of their misfortunes, as to call out "the Lame,"
the "Ruptured," the "Lefthanded," the "Goggle-eyed." Each one
had his distinguishing mark, and to us this sort of thing was no small
source of amusement.

The moment we were in danger, however, it was no laughing
matter, but rather did we bewail these very defects. We had embarked to the number of more than fifty, about a third of us being
women, most of them young and comely. Do not, however, be too
quick to envy us, for a screen separated us from them and a stout
one at that, the suspended fragment of a recently torn sail, to virtuous
men the very wall of Semiramis. Nay, Priapus himself [the god of
sensuality] might well have been temperate had he taken passage
with Amarantus, for there was never a moment when this fellow
allowed us to be free from fear of the uttermost danger.

As soon as he had doubled the temple of Poseidon [in Alexandria]
near you, he made straight for Taphosiris [a small town on the
rocky coast west of Alexandria], with all sails spread, to all seeming
bent upon confronting Scylla [the reefs], over whom we were all
wont to shudder in our boyhood when doing our school exercises.
This manoeuvre we detected only just as the vessel was nearing the
reefs, and we all raised so mighty a cry that perforce he gave up his
attempt to battle with the rocks. All at once he veered about as
though some new idea had possessed him, and turned his vessel's
head to the open, struggling as best he might against a contrary sea.

Presently a fresh south wind springs up and carries us along, and
soon we are out of sight of land . . . a gale commenced to blow
from the north, and the violent wind soon raised seas mountains high.
This gust, falling suddenly on us, drove our sail back, and made it
concave in place of its convex form, and the ship was all but capsized
by the stern. With great difficulty, however, we headed her in.

Then Amarantus thunders out: "See what it is to be master of the
art of navigation. I had long foreseen this storm, and that is why I
sought the open. I can tack in now, since our sea room allows us
to add to the length of our tack. But such a course as the one I have
taken would not have been possible had we hugged the shore, for in
that case the ship would have been dashed on the coast." Well, we
were perforce satisfied with his explanation so long as daylight lasted
and dangers were not imminent, but these failed not to return with
the approach of night, for as the hours passed the seas increased continually in volume.

Now it so happened that this was the day on which the Jews make
what they term the "Preparation" [Friday night, *ereb Shabbat*],

and they reckon the night, together with the day following this, as a time during which it is not lawful to work with one's hands. They keep this day holy and apart from the others, and they pass it in rest from labor of all kinds. Our skipper accordingly let go the rudder from his hands the moment he guessed that the sun's rays had left the earth, and throwing himself prostrate "allowed to trample on him what sailor so desired" [Sophocles, *Ajax*, 1146].

We, who at first could not understand why he was thus lying down, imagined that despair was the cause of it all. We rushed to his assistance and implored him not to give up the last hope yet. Indeed the hugest waves were actually menacing the vessel, and the very deep was at war with itself. Now it frequently happens that when the wind has suddenly relaxed its violence, the billows already set in motion do not immediately subside; they are still under the influence of the wind's force, to which they yield and with which they battle at the same time, and the oncoming waves fight against those subsiding.

I have every need of my store of flaming language, so that in recounting such immense dangers I may not fall into the trivial. To people who are at sea in such a crisis, life may be said to hang by a thread only, for if our skipper proved at such a moment to be an orthodox observer of the Mosaic law, what was life worth in the future? Indeed we soon understood why he had abandoned the helm, for when we begged him to do his best to save the ship, he stolidly continued reading his roll. [The captain no doubt was reading the Torah, the Pentateuch.]

Despairing of persuasion, we finally attempted force, and one staunch soldier—for many Arabs of the cavalry were of our company—one staunch soldier, I say, drew his sword and threatened to behead the fellow on the spot if he did not resume control of the vessel. But the Maccabean in very deed was determined to persist in his observances. However, in the middle of the night he voluntarily returned to the helm. "For now," he said, "we are clearly in danger of death, and the law commands" [that the Sabbath be violated where life is at stake, Yoma 8:6]. On this the tumult sprang up afresh, groaning of men and shrieking of women. All called upon the gods, and cried aloud; all called to mind those they loved. Amarantus alone was in good spirits, for he thought to himself that now at last he would foil his creditors. . . .

But day broke . . . and never, I know, did we behold the sun with greater joy. The wind grew more moderate as the temperature became milder, and thus, as the moisture evaporated, we were able to work the rigging and handle the sails. We were unable, it is true, to replace our sail by a new one, for this was already in the hands of the pawnbroker, but we took it in like the swelling folds of a garment, and lo, in four hours' time we who had imagined ourselves already in the jaws of death, were disembarking in a remote desert place, possessing neither town nor farm near it, only an expanse of open country of one hundred and thirty stadia. Our ship was riding in the open sea, for the spot was not a harbor, and it was riding on a single anchor. The second anchor had been sold, and a third Amarantus did not possess. When now we touched the dearly beloved land, we embraced the earth as a real living mother. . . .

So much for my story. The divinity has shaped it for you in mingling the comic with the tragic element. I have done likewise in the account I have given you. I know this letter is too long, but as when with you face to face, so in writing to you I am insatiable, and as it is by no means certain that I shall be able to talk with you again, I take all possible pleasure in writing to you now. Moreover by fitting the letter into my diary, about which I take great pains, I shall have the reminiscences of many days. Farewell. . . .

BIBLIOGRAPHY

READINGS FOR ADVANCED STUDENTS

Kingsley, C., *Hypatia*. This fine historical novel deals with the Mediterranean world of this day. Synesius appears in Chapter XXI as "the squire-bishop."

ADDITIONAL SOURCE MATERIALS IN ENGLISH

Fitzgerald, A., *The Letters of Synesius of Cyrene*, letter No. 4, pp. 80–91. This is the complete letter of which a part has been quoted above.
Socrates Scholasticus in his *Ecclesiastical History*, Book VII, chapters XIII–XVII, in *A Select Library of Nicene and Post-Nicene Fathers of the Christian Church*, Second Series, Vol. II, discusses the conflicts between the Jews and Christians in Alexandria.

72.

Bodo and the Jews
838–847

THIS is a Christian account of the conversion of a prominent Frankish churchman to Judaism. This event, which was something of a sensation in its day, took place during the reign of Louis, the Pious (814–840), the son of Charlemagne.

Bodo, a chaplain at the imperial court, was influenced to desert Christianity because of theological scruples and the moral laxity of the Frankish court. In Moslem Spain, where he sought refuge, Bodo, with all the enthusiasm of a recent convert, became a zealous missionary for his new faith and an implacable opponent of Christianity. The year following his flight (840) he entered into a polemical correspondence with Pablo Alvaro, a Cordovan Christian worthy, who had been born a Jew. Each one, through argument and abuse, tried to lead the other back to the very faith to which the other had originally belonged. Both were unsuccessful. In 847, Bodo, as fanatical on his side as Alvaro, Eulogius and the Christian "Zealots" of Cordova on their side, attempted to secure the forcible conversion of the Spanish Christians to Islam or Judaism.

The following selections are taken from the *Annals of the Cloister of St. Bertin*, an official Latin history of the Western Frankish Empire. The second part of the *Annals* (835–861), which includes the succeeding extracts, is ascribed to Prudentius, Bishop of Troyes.

⟪ANNO. 839. In the meantime the report of an exceedingly mournful event, one that was lamentable to all followers of the Catholic Church, became known. Bodo, a deacon, born of an Alemannic [South Germanic] family, had been inducted, to some extent almost from the cradle, into the Christian religion by means of the palace-school teachings in the religious and secular sciences.

The preceding year [838] he had begged and secured permission from the imperial couple [Louis the Pious and Judith] to hasten to Rome in order that he might pray there, and had also been presented with many gifts. Allured by [Satan] the enemy of mankind, he now abandoned Christianity and declared himself a Jew.

Indeed, as soon as he entered into his plan of treachery and depravity with the Jews, he was not even afraid to plot slyly to sell to the heathen those whom he had taken with him. [He sold his Christian slaves to the pagans.] After these had been sold one by one he kept with him but one person who was reputed to be his nephew, and then—we must tearfully relate—he denied the Christian faith and became a professing Jew. He had himself circumcised [839], allowed his hair and beard to grow long, changed his name, and boldly assumed the name of Eleazar instead. He girded himself moreover with a soldier's belt and joined himself in marriage with the daughter of a certain Jew. His nephew, who has been mentioned, also went over to Judaism after pressure had been brought to bear on him. Finally, overcome by wretched lust, Bodo went with some Jews to Saragossa, a Spanish city, in the middle of the month of August. [Saragossa was now in Moslem hands.]

The great difficulty experienced in persuading the Emperor that this thing was true shows clearly to every one how much sorrow this affair caused the imperial couple and all those redeemed by the grace of the Christian faith. . . .

Anno. 847.   Bodo, who a few years before this had deserted the Christian truth and had succumbed to the Jewish perfidy, had progressed so far in his villainy that he zealously tried to incite the minds of the Saracens, of the king as well as the people, against all Christians dwelling in Spain. [Under Abd-al-Rahman II (822–852) religious conflicts between Christians and Moslems were frequent.] They, the Christians, must either desert their religion and convert themselves to the Jewish madness or to the Saracen folly, or otherwise all be killed without question! Because of this a petition of all the Christians of that kingdom was tearfully sent to King Charles [d. 877] and to the bishops and other estates of our faith in his kingdom [of France] that the above mentioned apostate be extradited in order that he should no longer be a hindrance or a mortal danger to the Christians who live in Spain. [There is no record that the Moslems surrendered Bodo to Charles after this protest.]

BIBLIOGRAPHY

READINGS FOR ADVANCED STUDENTS

Katz, S., *The Jews in the Visigothic and Frankish Kingdoms of Spain and Gaul*, pp. 27, 40–41, 45–46, 69.
Williams, A. L., *Adversus Judaeos: a Bird's-Eye View of Christian Apologiae until the Renaissance*. Chap. xxii, "Alvaro and Bodo."

73.

A Jewish Merchant in Arabia and Thibet
about 913

Jewel story

IN THE Middle Ages Jewish merchants from the Near and Middle East frequently went as far east as China. In all probability it was a group of Persian Jewish merchants who settled in K'ai-Fung-Foo between the tenth and the twelfth centuries and there founded the Chinese Jewish settlement which died out only recently.

Jewish merchants penetrated China to sell Indian cotton goods and to bring back luxury-wares such as porcelain, silks, jewels, and musk. Jews went east to make their fortunes all through the medieval period. As late as the eighteenth century, Mordecai Hamburger, a son-in-law of the famous Glückel of Hameln, left London a poor man and returned from India about ten years later with a fortune in precious stones.

The following account is taken from the Arabic *The Wonders of India* (*Adjaib al-Hind*) of Buzurg ibn Shahriyar of Ramhurmuz. In this work, written about 953, the author recounts for us many tales of India, the Indian Archipelago, China, and Thibet. Some of his stories are apparently exaggerations; others are obviously authentic. The one given below tells the story of Ishaq (Isaac), a Jewish merchant prince. The arbitrary treatment which he met at the hands of the Calif and his officers was quite typical of the times. It is curious that Ibn al-Furat, the contemporary Vizier, who was noted for his greed, made no attempt to lay hands on the fortune of Ishaq. Ibn al-Furat at this time "banked" with the Bagdad Jewish financiers, Joseph and Aaron. From other Arabic sources for this period we know that wealthy Jews often came to a sorry end at the hands of rapacious Moslem officials.

greedy

I.

❝Among the curious stories of merchants, travelers, and persons who have made their fortunes at sea is that of Ishaq, the son of a Jew.

He was a man who gained his livelihood through the business brokers at Oman [now Suhar in south-eastern Arabia]. In conse-

355

quence of a quarrel with a Jew, he left Oman and went to India. In all he possessed only about 200 dinars. After being away thirty years, during which nobody heard anything of him, he returned to Oman in the year 300 [912–913 C.E.]. I learned from several sailors of my acquaintance that he had arrived from China on his own ship, and that the whole of its cargo belonged to him.

In order to avoid examination of his goods and payment of customs, he compromised the matter with the Governor of Oman, Ahmed ibn Helal, for a sum of more than 1,000,000 dirhems. On one single occasion, he sold to Ahmed ibn Merwan 100,000 mithcals [a weight, of over four grams, for precious metals and drugs] of musk of first quality, and the purchaser thought that it was all he had. He did a business with the same man for 40,000 dinars worth of textiles, and then another business of 20,000 dinars with another person. At the request of Ahmed ibn Merwan, Ishaq consented to a reduction of one silver dirhem per mithcal, and this discount amounted to 100,000 dirhems.

His prodigious good fortune made a stir in the country and excited the envious. A ruffian, who could not get from Ishaq what he wanted, left for Bagdad, went to see the Vizier, Ali ibn Muhammed ibn al-Furat [Vizier in Bagdad 908–924], and made calumnious reports about the Jew. The Vizier did not listen to him. Then this man insinuated himself into the company of a wicked person of the court of the Calif Muktadir Billah [908–932], pretended to be a bearer of good tidings, and in his own way told the story of the Jew.

"A man," said he, "left Oman without owning anything. He returned with a ship laden with musk worth a million dinars, silken stuffs, and porcelain of an equal value, jewels and precious stones for at least as much, to say nothing of a heap of wonderful things from China. This man," he added, "is a childless old man. Ahmed ibn Helal has received half a million dinars' worth of goods from him." All this was told the Calif, who found the matter very surprising, and immediately sent one of his black eunuchs, called Foulfoul, with thirty slaves, charged with a message for the Governor of Oman, ordering him to deliver this Jew up to the eunuch and to send a messenger to the Calif himself.

When the eunuch arrived at Oman and Ahmed ibn Helal came to know of the orders of the Calif, he ordered that the Jew should be kept in sight, but promised him, however, to extricate him for a large sum which he demanded for himself. Then he had the merchants told of this secretly, pointing out to them the danger that lay for them in the Jew's arrest, and for foreigners and for inhabitants occupied in business, all thus delivered up to arbitrary power and the envy of wretched and base men.

Thereupon, the markets were closed. Papers were signed by the citizens and the foreigners, certifying that after the Jew's arrest no ships landed any more at Oman, and that the merchants left, and that they gave each other advice never to approach the borders of Iraq, where there was no longer any safety for one's property. They added that Oman was a city where there were many great and rich merchants from all countries, but that there was no other guarantee of safety than the duration of the justice of the Calif and his Emir, his consideration for merchants, and his protection against the envious and base.

The merchants raised a tumult in the city, cried out against Ahmed ibn Helal, and grew very angry, so much so that the eunuch Foulfoul and his followers had to leave the city, take leave of the Governor, and go away. Ahmed wrote to the Calif, giving an account of the events as to how merchants who had brought their ships to the quay had reloaded their goods and carried them away, so that the merchants residing in the city were in the greatest distress, and said: "We are going to be deprived of every means of existence when ships no longer call here, for Oman is a city the inhabitants of which get everything from the sea. If the small amongst us are thus treated, it will be worse still for the great. Sultans are a fire that devours everything it touches. We cannot resist and it is better for us to go away from before them."

The eunuch and his men had extracted 20,000 dinars from the Jew and had gone back. The indignant Jew hastened to collect all he possessed, freighted a ship, and left again for China without leaving a dirhem in Oman.

At Serboza [in Sumatra] the Governor asked from him a levy of 20,000 dinars as passage-toll to enable him to carry on his journey to China. The Jew would not give anything. The Governor secretly dispatched some of his followers and they killed him. Then he took possession of the Jew's ship and goods.

Ishaq had lived three years at Oman. Persons who saw him told me that on the *Mihrgan* [an old Persian autumnal equinox festival] he made a present to Ahmed ibn Helal of a black china vase, closed by a brilliant golden cover. "What is there in this vase?" asked Ahmed. "A dish of *Sikbaj* [a dish made of meat, flour, and vinegar] which I have prepared for you in China," said the Jew. "*Sikbaj* cooked in China two years ago! It must be in fine condition."

Ahmed lifted the cover and opened the vase and he found in it golden fishes with eyes of rubies surrounded by musk of first quality. The contents of the vase were worth 50,000 dinars.

II.

⁕Among the particulars which the Jew told of China, I will relate the following:

"I went," he said, "to a city called Lubin [Lhó or Bhutan in the Himalayas]. In order to reach it, you have to cross steep mountains. Merchandise is carried on the back of goats, for the road over these precipitous heights is like a series of steps which only those animals can climb. The King of this city was a powerful and respected prince. When I presented myself before him, he was seated on a golden throne encrusted with rubies, he himself being covered with jewels like a woman. The Queen was at his side still more richly apparelled. He had on his neck necklaces of gold and emeralds of inestimable value such as no kings of East or West possessed. Near him there were about 500 young girls of all colors attired in silk robes and jewels. I saluted him.

" 'Oh Arab,' he said, 'have you ever seen anything more beautiful than this?' He showed me a necklace adorned with enamels. 'Yes,' I replied. 'Where?' 'I have,' I replied, 'a unique pearl which I bought at great price to do you homage.' The Queen then said: 'You owe me something. You have a unique pearl. Give it up to me.' And both cried out: 'Run quickly to fetch it.' 'I have come to this city only for that,' I replied, 'and this evening I will bring it to you.' 'No, no,' he said, in a joyous and satisfied tone, 'immediately, immediately.'

"Well, I had ten of them. I went to my lodging; I took nine which I smashed with a stone until they were reduced to powder like flour, and I spread this powder on the ground. I wrapped up the last one in a silk handkerchief which I folded several times round and, having placed it in a box which I carefully closed, I returned to the King.

"Then I started to untie and unfold the handkerchief very slowly. The King had come very near, and the Queen, standing beside me, urged me to hurry. At last, I put the object of their desire before their eyes. The King knelt before the pearl, and so did the Queen, and for it they paid me a very big sum." [Later the Court-Jews achieved wealth by supplying the nobility with precious stones. Cutting of jewels also became a characteristic Jewish trade.]

BIBLIOGRAPHY

REFERENCES TO TEXTBOOKS

Golub, J. S., *Medieval Jewish History*, Sec. IV, "Trade," etc.

READINGS FOR ADVANCED STUDENTS

Fischel, W., "The Origin of Banking in Mediaeval Islam," *Journal of the Royal Asiatic Society*, 1933, pp. 339ff.

Jacobs, J., "Jews and Commerce," *Jewish Contributions to Civilization*, pp. 190ff.

Laufer, B., "A Chinese-Hebrew Manuscript, a New Source for the History of the Chinese Jews." *The American Journal of Semitic Languages and Literatures*, XLVI (1929–1930), pp. 189–197.

JE, "China"; "Commerce."

ADDITIONAL SOURCE MATERIALS IN ENGLISH

Ibn Khordadhbeh, "The Book of Ways and Kingdoms," in E. N. Adler, *Jewish Travellers*, pp. 2–3. This is a brief description of the roads used by Jewish merchants in the ninth century as they travelled from France to China and back.

74.

How the Medieval Jew Understood the Bible
1105

THE first printed Hebrew book that is dated (Reggio, Italy, 1475) is a commentary to the Five Books of Moses by Rabbi Solomon bar Isaac (RaSHI) of Troyes, France, 1040–1105. This commentary, written in a simple, terse Hebrew style, leans heavily on the older rabbinic and Talmudic literature and emphasizes the ethical and the homiletical although it by no means neglects the simple literal meaning (*peshat*). It is this very emphasis on the ethical and the legendary (*derash*), however, that endeared this writer to the average reader. Any Jew who studied the Hebrew Bible, and practically all dipped into it at some time in their lives, began with Rashi, whose comments covered practically all the books of the Bible. He is certainly the most popular Jewish Bible commentator of all times and was known even to Christian scholars. Nicolas de Lyra (d. 1340), one of the most famous of medieval Christian exegetes, took many comments bodily from Rashi, and Luther, as we know, borrowed liberally from de Lyra. This dependance of Luther on de Lyra is reflected in the couplet: "If Lyra had not played, Luther would not have danced."

The following selections will give the reader some concept of how the average medieval Jew saw the Bible through the eyes of Rashi.

EXODUS 33:21: And the Lord said: "*Behold there is a place by Me, and thou shalt stand upon the rock.*"

❲*Behold there is a place by Me:* This phrase means that in the mountain where I am speaking with you I have a place always ready for your needs where I can hide you so that you will not be injured, and from that place you will see what you will see. This which I have just explained is the literal meaning of the verse. But there is a Midrashic interpretation which says that this refers to the place where God speaks. God says: "There is a place *by* me," but God does not say: "I, God, am *in* the place," which shows that God contains the world, but the world does not encompass God.

LEVITICUS 19:18: *Thou shalt not take vengeance*, nor bear any grudge against the children of thy people, but *thou shalt love thy neighbor as thyself:* I am the Lord.

❈*Thou shalt not take vengeance:* A person says: "Lend me your sickle," and the other fellow answers, "No." On the following day the other fellow says: "Lend me your axe," and the person answers: "I won't lend you, just as you didn't lend me." This is vengeance. But how then would you define a grudge? A person says: "Lend me your axe." The other fellow answers, "No." But the very next day the other fellow says: "Lend me your sickle" and the man answers: "Surely, here it is. I'm not like you who wouldn't lend me your axe." Now this is a grudge, because this man was treasuring up hatred in his heart, even though he didn't take vengeance.

Thou shalt love thy neighbor as thyself: Rabbi Akiba [d. about 135] said this is a basic principle in the Torah.

LEVITICUS 24:20: And if a man maim his neighbor, as he hath done so shall it be done to him; fracture for fracture, eye for eye; tooth for tooth; as he hath put a blemish in a man, *so shall it be put in him.*

❈*So shall it be put in him:* Our rabbis have explained that this does not mean putting a real blemish in him, but that he should make good the injury with money. This is done by estimating the injury as one would with a slave who has been injured. The proof for all this is seen in the phrase *putting* [which means that something, money, is *put* from one hand into the other].

DEUTERONOMY 2:12: And in Seir dwelt the Horites aforetime, but the children of Esau *succeeded them;* and they destroyed them from before them, and dwelt in their stead.

❈*Succeeded them:* This phrase expresses present, continued action. It means that I, God, have given the children of Esau sufficient strength to keep on gradually driving out the Horites.

DEUTERONOMY 5:7: Thou shalt have no other Gods *before Me.*

❈*Before Me:* This phrase means in every place where I am, and that, of course, means the whole world. Another interpretation of "before me" is the following: All the time that I exist [that is, forever].

DEUTERONOMY 6:12: Beware lest thou forget the Lord, who brought thee out of the land of Egypt, out of the house of *slaves*.

❊*Slaves:* The Aramaic translation which has "from the house of bondage" is correct. This phrase means God brought you out of a place where you were slaves [not from a house that belonged to slaves].

DEUTERONOMY 8:4: *Thy raiment waxed not old* upon thee, neither did thy foot swell these forty years.

❊*Thy raiment waxed not old:* Because clouds of glory were scouring and cleaning their clothes so that they looked like spick-and-span garments. Also, as their children grew their clothes would grow along with them, just like the shell of a snail that grows with it.

DEUTERONOMY 11:13–14: And it shall come to pass, if ye shall hearken diligently unto My commandments which I command you this day, *to love the Lord* your God, *and to serve Him with all your heart* and with all your soul, that I will give the rain of your land in its season, the former rain and the latter rain, that thou mayest gather in thy corn. . . .

❊*To love the Lord:* Do not say: "I am going to study the Torah in order to become a rich man," or "in order that I may be called Rabbi," or "that I may get paid," but whatever you do, do out of love, and the result will be that honor will come of itself.

And to serve him with all your heart: This means service which is in the heart and this, of course, means prayer.

DEUTERONOMY 32:11–12:   *As an eagle that stirreth up her nest,*
                         Hovereth over her young,
                         Spreadeth abroad her wings, taketh them,
                         Beareth them on her pinions—
                         The Lord alone did lead him.

❊*As an eagle that stirreth up her nest:* God led the Israelites [through the wilderness] with mercy and kindness just like the eagle which is merciful to her young. She does not enter into her nest suddenly, but beats and makes a noise near her fledglings with her wings, as she goes from tree to tree and from bough to bough, in order to awaken the eaglets so that they should be prepared to receive her. . . .

Hovereth over her young: It does not put its full weight on them, but covers them without really touching them. . . .

Spreadeth abroad her wings, taketh them: When the eagle comes to take its young from place to place she does not carry them with her claws like the rest of the birds, because the other birds are afraid of the eagle, which flies higher and may come down upon them. Therefore the other birds, for fear of the eagle, carry their young with their claws. But the eagle fears only the arrow; therefore she carries them on her pinions, saying: "It is better that the arrow enter into me and not into my young." Similarly God said [Exodus 19:4]: "I bore you on eagles' wings." Thus, when the Egyptians pursued and overtook the Israelites by the sea, the Egyptians began to shoot arrows and hurl rocks at them. Immediately [Exodus 14:19–20] "the angel of God who went before the camp of Israel removed and went behind them . . . and came between the camp of Egypt and the camp of Israel [that the angel might receive the arrows and stones]."

BIBLIOGRAPHY

REFERENCES TO TEXTBOOKS

Elbogen, pp. 112–114; Roth, pp. 174–175; Sachar, pp. 185–186.

ADDITIONAL SOURCE MATERIALS IN ENGLISH

The commentaries of Rashi to the Pentateuch are now available in an adequate English translation: *Pentateuch with . . . Rashi's Commentary Translated into English and Annotated*, by M. Rosenbaum and A. M. Silbermann, etc., 5 Vols., London, 1929–1934.

75.

Maimonides on Art and Charity
1180

THE following recommendations and prohibitions are taken from the *Mishneh Torah*, the famous law code published in Hebrew about 1180 by the great Maimonides.

The first selection deals with charity. The point of view expressed here is that of Maimonides, although it is based in large part on Talmudic precedents.

The second selection deals with the medieval attitude to the plastic arts. The second commandment states specifically (Exodus 20:4): "Thou shalt not make unto thee a graven image, nor any manner of likeness, of anything that is in heaven above, or that is in the earth beneath, or that is in the water under the earth." It seems to have been this injunction which prejudiced the medieval Jew against the plastic arts. Statues and figures in earlier times had been associated with Greek and Roman idolatry, and during the Middle Ages sculpture was linked in the mind of the average Jew with Christian worship. However, it should be borne in mind that Maimonides' pronouncements were not accepted unconditionally by all Jews. Some rabbis were more strict, others more lenient in their views.

I. GIFTS TO THE POOR

℄There are eight degrees in the giving of charity, one higher than the other. The highest degree, than which there is nothing higher, is to take hold of a Jew who has been crushed and to give him a gift or a loan, or to enter into partnership with him, or to find work for him, and thus to put him on his feet so that he will not be dependent on his fellow-men. Concerning this it is said [Leviticus 25:35]: "Then shalt thou *uphold* him." *Uphold* him, so that he should not fall and become a dependant.

Lower in degree to this is the one who gives charity [in Hebrew, "righteousness"] to the poor, but does not know to whom he gives it, nor does the poor man know from whom he receives it. This is an unselfish meritorious act comparable to what was done in the

Chamber of the Secret in the Temple where the charitable would deposit [alms] secretly and the poor of better family would help themselves secretly. Related to this degree is the giving to the [public] alms-chest. One should not give to the alms-chest unless he knows that the officer in charge is reliable, wise, and a capable administrator, like Hananiah ben Teradion, for example. [This martyr, (d. about 135), was very scrupulous with charity funds.]

Lower in degree to this is when the giver knows to whom he gives, but the poor does not know from whom he receives. An example of this are the great scholars [of Talmudic times] who used to go about in secret and leave their money at the door of the poor. This is proper practice, particularly meritorious when the officers in charge of charity are not administering properly.

Lower in degree to this is when the poor knows from whom he receives but the giver does not know to whom he gives. An example of this are the great scholars who used to tie up their money in [the corner of] their cloaks and throw them back over their shoulders. The poor would then come and take it without being put to shame.

Lower in degree to this is when one gives even before he is asked.

Lower in degree to this is when one gives after he has been asked.

Lower in degree to this is when one gives less than he should, but graciously.

Lower in degree to this is when one gives grudgingly.

The great scholars used to give a coin to the poor before every prayer and then they would pray, for it is said in the Bible [Psalm 17:15]: "As for me, I shall behold Thy face in 'righteousness' [that is, through 'charity']."

II. *Art and Idolatry*

It is forbidden to make images to serve as ornaments even though they are not to be used for idolatry, because it is said in the Bible [Exodus 20:20]: "Ye shall not make with Me—gods of silver, or gods of gold, ye shall not make unto you." This includes even images of silver and gold which are only made for ornament, lest fools be misled by them and think they are for purposes of idolatry. However, this prohibition against fashioning ornaments applies only to the form of the human being, and hence one is not allowed to fashion any human form either in wood or plaster or in stone. This holds when the form is raised like a design or a mural relief found in a reception hall and the like. When one fashions these he is to be punished. However, if the form were to be engraved or painted like sketches on panels or boards, or be like the figures that are woven into a rug, behold these are permitted. [There is no objection to paintings.]

It is forbidden to wear a ring that has a seal on it in the form of a human being, if the form projects, but one may use it for sealing. If, however, the form is engraved it is permitted to wear it, but it is forbidden to seal with it, inasmuch as the impression made from it would consist of a raised form. Similarly it is forbidden to form, even on a panel, the likeness of the sun and moon, stars, planets, and angels, for it is written in the Bible: "Ye shall not make with Me," that is to say, you shall not make the likenesses of My servants who minister before Me on high. [The painting of the heavenly bodies is forbidden.] One may fashion images of cattle and all other living beings with the exception of man; likewise the forms of trees, plants, and similar things even though the image protrudes.

BIBLIOGRAPHY

READINGS FOR ADVANCED STUDENTS

Abrahams, I., *Jewish Life in the Middle Ages*, 1932, Chap. xvii, "Private and Communal Charities. The Relief of the Poor"; Chap. xviii, "Private and Communal Charity (Continued); The Sick and the Captive."

Frisch, E., *An Historical Survey of Jewish Philanthropy*. Part II, "From the Fall of the State to the Beginnings of Emancipation."

Lowenthal, M., *A World Passed by: Scenes and Memories of Jewish Civilization in Europe and North Africa*. This delightfully written book is the nearest approach in English to a guide-book to extant Jewish antiquities and art materials.

JE, "Alms"; "Art, Attitude of Judaism toward"; "Charity and Charitable Institutions."

ADDITIONAL SOURCE MATERIALS IN ENGLISH

Abrahams, I., *Hebrew Ethical Wills*, 2 vols. These volumes contain a great deal of material throwing light on the medieval Jewish concept of philanthropy.

76.

The Shylock Legend
1200–1587

THE unusual interest in Shylock, the villain of Shakespeare's *Merchant of Venice* (about 1596), has stimulated historians to determine the historic basis, if any, underlying this noteworthy comedy. It is generally accepted today that the "pound of flesh" or "bond" theme utilized by the great dramatist was not a historical reminiscence but an old folk-tale.

The oldest known European version of the tale appeared in Latin, in Lorraine, sometime before 1200. In this work, *Dolopathos*, the villain is not a Jew, but a revengeful slave. The Jew, as villain, appears for the first time in the English *Cursor Mundi*, about 1290.

The source of the Shylock tale in Shakespeare's *Merchant of Venice* goes back, it is believed, not to the *Cursor Mundi* but to an Italian version of the story of the revengeful Jew as portrayed in Giovanni Fiorentino's *Il Pecorone* (about 1378). It is not improbable, also, that Shakespeare was inspired to write on the theme of a villainous Jew because of the public interest in the trial and execution, 1594, of the Marrano physician, Dr. Rodrigo Lopez, who had been accused of attempting to poison Queen Elizabeth.

Another interesting version of the "pound of flesh" theme is found in the 1693 edition of Gregorio Leti's *Vita di Sisto V* ("Life of Sixtus V," 1585–1590) which appeared almost a century after the publication of the *Merchant of Venice*. In this story the villain is a Christian merchant; the victim, a Jew. Most scholars are agreed that the incident in Leti—supposed to have taken place in 1587—is not authentic, but merely another version of an age old tale which still persisted in Italy in the seventeenth century.

The significance for Jewish history of the Shylock story is that it reflects the medieval attitude that the Jew is the "stage villain" and the typical usurer, a concept that is not altogether antiquated even today. Though there were no openly observant Jews in Shakespearean England, the term "Jew" was a synonym there for scoundrel and money-lender.

The first account which follows, taken from *Dolopathos, or the King and the Seven Sages*, treats of a villain who is neither Jew nor

Christian; the second account, the Leti story, portrays the Christian as a villain; the *Merchant of Venice*, not reprinted here, treats of the Jew as the heartless creditor.

I. THE HARD CREDITOR—*about 1200*

❡There was once a nobleman who had a strongly fortified castle and many other possessions. His wife died, leaving him an only daughter, whom he caused to be instructed in all the liberal arts, so far as wisdom could be acquired from the discipline and books of the philosophers, in order that she might thus know how to secure her inheritance. In this hope he was not deceived. She became skilled in all the liberal arts, and also acquired a perfect knowledge of magic. After this it came to pass that the nobleman was seized with an acute fever, took to his bed, and died, bequeathing all his goods to his daughter.

Possessed of her father's wealth, she resolved she would marry no man unless his wisdom was equal to her own. She had many noble suitors, but, denying none, she offered to share her couch with any one who should give her a hundred marks of silver, and when the morrow came, if they were mutually agreeable, their nuptials should be duly celebrated. Many youths came to her on this condition, and paid the stipulated sum of money, but she enchanted them by her magical arts, placing an owl's feather beneath the pillow of him who was beside her, when he at once fell into a profound sleep, and so remained until at daybreak she took away the feather. In this way she spoiled many of their money, and acquired much treasure.

It happened that a certain young man of good family, having been thus deluded, resolved to circumvent the damsel. So, proceeding to a rich slave whose foot he had formerly cut off in a passion, he asked him for a loan of one hundred marks, which the lame one readily gave, but on this condition, that if the money was not paid within a year, he might take the weight of one hundred marks from the flesh and bones of the young man. To this the youth lightly agreed, and signed the bond with his seal. With the hundred marks he went a second time to the damsel, and removing by accident the owl's feather from under his pillow, thus did away the spell, and, having accomplished his purpose, he was next day married to her in presence of their friends.

Forthwith prosperous times came to the young man; he forgot his creditor, and did not pay the money within the appointed time; whereupon the lame one rejoiced that he had found an opportunity of revenge. He appeared before the king, who was then on the throne, raised an action against the youth, exhibited the bond as evidence, and demanded justice to be executed. The king, though horrified at the bargain, had no alternative but to order the youth to come before him to answer the action of the accuser. Then the youth, at length mindful of the debt, and afraid of the king's authority, went to court, with a very great crowd of his friends, and plenty of gold and silver. The accuser exhibited the bond, which the youth acknowledged, and, by order of the king, the chiefs pronounced sentence, namely, that it should be lawful for the lame one to act as specified in the bond, or to demand as much money as he pleased for the redemption of the youth.

The king therefore asked the lame one if he would spare the youth on receiving double money. He refused, and the king was attempting for many days to prevail upon him to agree, when, lo, the youth's wife, having put on man's attire, and with her countenance and voice altered by magical arts, dismounted from a horse before the king's palace, and approached and saluted the king. Being asked who she was, and whence she came, she replied that she was a soldier, born in the most distant part of the world, that she was skilled in law and equity, and was a keen critic of judgments. [Here we have the original "Portia."] The king, being glad at this, ordered the supposed soldier to be seated beside him, and committed to her for final decision the lawsuit between the lame one and the youth.

Both parties being summoned, she said: "For thee, O lame one, according to the judgment of the king and the princes, it is lawful to take away the weight of one hundred marks of flesh. But what will you gain, unless indeed death, if you slay the youth? It is better that you accept for him seven or ten times the money." But he said he would not accept ten times, or even one thousand times, the sum.

Then she ordered a very white linen cloth to be brought, and the youth to be stripped of his clothing, bound hand and foot, and stretched thereon. Which done, "Cut," said she to the lame one, "with your iron, where ever you wish your weight of marks. But if you take away more or less than the exact weight by even the amount of a needle's point, or if one drop of blood stains the linen, know that forthwith thou shalt perish by a thousand deaths, and, cut into a thousand pieces, thou shalt become the food of the beasts and the birds, and all thy kin shall suffer the same penalty, and thy goods shall become state property." He grew pale at this dreadful sentence, and said: "Since there is no one, God alone excepted, who can be so deft of hand, but would take away too much or too little, I am unwilling to attempt what is so uncertain. Therefore I set the youth free, remit the debt, and give him one thousand marks for reconciliation." Thus, then the youth was set free by the prudence of his wife, and returned in joy to his own house.

II. *The Christian Shylock, Rome, 1587*

⟨It was currently reported in Rome that Drake [1586] had taken and plundered St. Domingo, in Hispaniola, and carried off an immense booty. This account came in a private letter to Paul Secchi, a very considerable merchant in the city, who had large concerns in those parts, which he had insured. Upon receiving this news, he sent for the insurer, Sampson Ceneda, a Jew, and acquainted him with it. The Jew, whose interest it was to have such a report thought false, gave many reasons why it could not possibly be true; and, at last, worked himself up into such a passion, that he said: "I'll lay you a pound of my flesh it is a lie." Such sort of wagers, it is well known, are often proposed by people of strong passions to convince others that are incredulous or obstinate. Nothing is more common than to say: "I'll lay my life on it; I'll forfeit my right if it is not true, etc."

Secchi, who was of a fiery hot temper, replied: "If you like it, I'll lay you 1000 crowns against a pound of your flesh, that it's true." The Jew accepted the wager, and articles were immediately executed betwixt them, the substance of which was that if Secchi won he should himself cut the flesh with a sharp knife from whatever part of the Jew's body he pleased. Unfortunately for the Jew, the truth of the account was soon after confirmed by other advices from the West Indies, which threw him almost into distraction; especially, when he was informed that Secchi had solemnly sworn he would compel him to the exact literal performance of his contract, and was determined to cut a pound of flesh from that part of his body which it is not necessary to mention.

Upon this, he went to the Governor of Rome, and begged he would interpose in the affair and use his authority to prevail with Secchi to accept of 1000 pistoles as an equivalent for the pound of flesh. But the Governor, not daring to take upon him to determine a case of so uncommon a nature, made a report of it to the Pope, who sent for them both, and having heard the articles read, and informed himself perfectly of the whole affair from their own mouths, said: "When contracts are made, it is just they should be fulfilled, as we intend this shall. Take a knife therefore, Secchi, and cut a pound of flesh from any part you please of the Jew's body. We would advise you, however, to be very careful; for if you cut but a scruple or a grain more or less than your due, you shall certainly be hanged. Go, and bring hither a knife and a pair of scales, and let it be done in our presence."

The merchant at these words began to tremble like an aspen leaf, and throwing himself at his Holiness's feet, with tears in his eyes, protested it was far from his thoughts to insist upon the performance of the contract. And being asked by the Pope what he demanded, answered: "Nothing, Holy Father, but your benediction, and that the articles may be torn in pieces." Then, turning to the Jew, he asked him, what he had to say, and whether he was content. The Jew answered he thought himself extremely happy to come off at so easy a rate, and that he was perfectly content. "But we are not content," replied Sixtus, "nor is there sufficient satisfaction made to our laws. We desire to know what authority you have to lay such wagers. The subjects of princes are the property of the state, and have no right to dispose of their bodies, nor any part of them, without the express consent of their sovereigns."

They were both immediately sent to prison, and the Governor ordered to proceed against them with the utmost severity of the law, that others might be deterred, by their example, from laying any more such wagers. The Governor, thinking to please Sixtus and willing to know what sort of punishment he had a mind should be inflicted upon them, said, without doubt, they had been guilty of a very great crime, and he thought they deserved to be fined, each of them, 1000 crowns.

"To be fined, each of them, 1000 crowns!" answered Sixtus. "Do you think that sufficient? What! Shall any of our subjects presume to dispose of his life without our permission? Is it not evident that the Jew has actually sold his life by consenting to have a pound of flesh cut from his body? Is not this a direct suicide? And is it not likewise true that the merchant is guilty of downright premeditated murder in making a contract with the other, that he knew must be the occasion of his death, if he insisted upon its being performed, as it is said he did? Shall two such villains be excused for a simple fine?"

The Governor alleging that Secchi protested he had not the least design of insisting upon the performance of the contract, and that the Jew did not at all imagine he would when he laid the wager, Sixtus replied: "These protestations were only made out of fear of punishment, and because they were in our presence, and therefore no regard ought to be had to them. Let them both be hanged; do you pass that sentence upon them, and we shall take care of the rest." In a word, they were both condemned to suffer death, to the great terror and amazement of everybody, though no one durst open his mouth or call it an unjust sentence.

As Secchi was of a very good family, having many great friends and relations, and the Jew one of the most leading men in the synagogue, they both had recourse to petitions; strong application was made to Cardinal Montalto [the grandnephew of the Pope] to intercede with his Holiness, at least to spare their lives. Sixtus, who did not really design to put them to death, but to deter others from such practices, at last consented to change the sentence into that of the galleys, with liberty to buy off that too, by paying each of them 2000 crowns, to be applied to the use of the hospital (which he had lately founded) before they were released.

BIBLIOGRAPHY

READINGS FOR ADVANCED STUDENTS

Friedlander, G., *Shakespeare and the Jew*. A useful introduction to the sources of Shakespeare's Shylock.

Furness, H. H., *Merchant of Venice*, (A new variorum edition), 1895, pp. 287–331; 395–399.

Michelson, H., *The Jew in Early English Literature*, pp. 46ff., 82ff.

JE, "Lopez, Rodrigo"; "Shylock."

ADDITIONAL SOURCE MATERIALS IN ENGLISH

Child, F. J., *English and Scottish Ballads*, 1886, IV (VIII), pp. 45–54, 277–285. Here we have two ballads dealing with the same theme of the "pound of flesh."

Lewisohn, L., in *The Last Days of Shylock*, takes up the story where Shakespeare leaves off.

Shakespeare, W., *Merchant of Venice*.

77.

Jewish Education
about 1180-1680

[handwritten: schoolier - teacher - like]

THE desire for education for both old and young has always characterized the Jewish people.

In medieval Europe, Jewish education, from the point of view of order, content, and all-inclusiveness, reached its height in Arabic Spain from 1000 to 1200. The first selection given below describes what the person who wishes to secure a Jewish and a general education ought to study. This plan of study was to be followed until completed. A brilliant student could cover the ground before he was twenty; others might labor all their lives in vain. This program in its entirety included not only a graded course of studies from the abc's to pure philosophy, but also the necessary bibliographies, to say nothing of pedagogical principles for teachers and students. The author is not original in his plan; he had taken much of his material from the Moslem scholars, particularly al-Farabi (d. 950); and the Arabs, in turn, leaned heavily on the Greeks, particularly Aristotle. This selection forms part of an ethical work, the *Cure of Sick Souls*, written originally in Arabic by a Joseph ben Judah ibn Aknin. Whether or not the author of the *Cure of Sick Souls* is identical with Ibn Aknin (about 1160-1226), the disciple of Maimonides and a famous scholar, is still a moot question.

The second selection includes a number of pedagogical reflections from the ethical and mystical *Sefer Hasidim* ("Book of the Pious") by the famous German mystic Judah He-Hasid of Regensburg (d. 1217). These notes reflect the attitude of the Jews of Germany toward books and learning during the thirteenth century.

The third selection is a brief survey of the curriculum of the Jewish school in Amsterdam in 1680. Jewish education in Holland—and this is true, too, of Italy—had been strongly influenced by its many cultured Spanish and Portuguese settlers. In addition, in both Italy and Holland, the non-Jewish cultural background was on a relatively high plane and the Jews, of course, assimilated much. The result is that in these lands the Jews pursued both general and Jewish studies along approved pedagogic lines. Over to the east, in the Germanic lands and in Poland, Jewish lore was pursued intensively, but without much order and with little attention to sound principles of instruction. This selection is by Shabbethai Bass (1641–1718), a Polish Jewish cantor, educator, and printer, who marvelled so much at the curriculum of the Amsterdam Sephardic community that he prefaced his bibliographical work, *Sifte Yeshenim* ("Lips of the Sleepers"), with an account of it. A generation before Bass's time Spinoza had attended this school; and in Shabbethai's time the rabbi of whom he speaks so respectfully was probably Isaac Aboab de Fonseca (1605–1693), who had once been rabbi in Brazil and was one of the first rabbis and Jewish authors of the western hemisphere.

1. *A Course of Study, Moslem Lands, about 1180*

⟨READING AND WRITING: The method of instruction must be so arranged that the teacher will begin first with the script, in order that the children may learn their letters, and this is to be kept up until there is no longer any uncertainty among them. This script is, of course, the "Assyrian," the use of which has been agreed upon by our ancestors. [The "Assyrian" is the standard Hebrew script, used today.] Then he is to teach them to write until their script is clear and can be read easily. He should not however keep them too long at work striving for beauty, decorativeness, and special elegance of penmanship. On the contrary, that which we have already mentioned will be sufficient.

TORAH, MISHNAH, AND HEBREW GRAMMAR: Then he is to teach them the Pentateuch, Prophets, and Hagiographa, that is the Bible, with an eye to the vocalization and the modulation in order that they may be able to pronounce the accents correctly. . . . Then he is to have them learn the Mishnah [the code of rabbinic law compiled about 200 C.E., and found in the Talmud] until they have acquired a fluency in it. [Deuteronomy 31:19:] "Teach thou it to the children of Israel; put it in their mouths." The teacher is to continue this until they are ten years of age, for the sages said [Abot 5:21]: "At five years the age is reached for the study of the Scriptures, at ten for the study of the Mishnah." The children are then to be taught the inflections, declensions, and conjugations, the regular verbs . . . and other rules of grammar. . . .

POETRY: Then the teacher is to instruct his pupils in poetry. He should, for the most part, have them recite religious poems and whatever else of beauty is found in the different types of poetry, and is fit to develop in them all good qualities. . . .

TALMUD: Then say the wise [Abot 5:21]: "At fifteen the age is reached for the study of the Talmud." [This basic work in rabbinic Judaism comprising both law and legend was compiled about 500 C.E.] Accordingly when the pupils are fifteen years of age the teacher should give them much practice in Talmud-reading until they have acquired fluency in it. Later, when they are eighteen years of age, he should give them that type of instruction in it which lays emphasis on deeper understanding, independent thinking, and investigation. . . .

PHILOSOPHIC OBSERVATIONS ON RELIGION: When the students have spent considerable time in study which is directed toward deeper comprehension and thoroughness, so that their mental powers have been strengthened; when the Talmud has become so much a part of them that there is hardly any chance of its being lost, and they are firmly entrenched in the Torah and the practice of its commands; then the teacher is to impart to them the third necessary subject. This is the refutation of the errors of apostates and heretics and the justification of those views and practices which the religion prescribes. . . .

PHILOSOPHIC STUDIES: . . . . These studies are divided into three groups. The first group is normally dependent on matter, but can, however, be separated from matter through concept and imagination. This class comprises the mathematical sciences. In the second group speculation cannot be conceived of apart from the material, either through imagination or conception. To this section belong the natural sciences. The third group has nothing to do with matter and has no material attributes; this group includes in itself metaphysics as such. [This division of the sciences goes back to Aristotle.]

LOGIC: But these sciences are preceded by logic which serves as a help and instrument. It is through logic that the speculative activities, which the three groups above mentioned include, are made clear. Logic presents the rules which keep the mental powers in order, and lead man on the path of clarity and truth in all things wherein he may err. . . .

MATHEMATICS, ARITHMETIC: The teacher will then lecture to his students on mathematics, beginning with arithmetic or geometry, or instruct them in both sciences at the same time. . . .

GEOMETRY: With respect to geometry two things are included in this term, practical and theoretical geometry. . . .

OPTICS: Then the students are introduced into the third of the mathematical sciences, namely optics. . . . [The measurement of terrestial and heavenly bodies.]

ASTRONOMY: Then they pass on to astronomy. This includes two sciences. First, astrology, that is, the science wherein the stars point to future events as well as to many things that once were or now are existent. Astrology is no longer numbered among the real sciences. It belongs only to the forces and secret arts by means of which man can prophesy what will come to pass, like the interpretation of dreams, fortune-telling, auguries, and similar arts. This science, however, is forbidden by God. . . . The second field of astronomy is mathematical. This field is to be included among mathematics and the real sciences. This science concerns itself with the heavenly bodies and the earth. . . . *prophecy divinations omens*

MUSIC: After studying the science of astronomy the teacher will lecture on music to his students. Music embraces instruction in the elements of the melodies and that which is connected with them, how melodies are linked together, and what condition is required to make the influence of music most pervasive and effective. . . .

MECHANICS: . . . . This includes two different things. For one thing it aims at the consideration of heavy bodies insofar as they are used for measurements. . . . The second part includes the consideration of heavy bodies insofar as they may be moved or insofar as they are used for moving. It treats, therefore, of the principles concerning instruments whereby heavy objects are raised and whereby they are moved from one place to another. . . .

NATURAL SCIENCES, MEDICINE: Let us now speak of the second section of the philosophic disciplines, that is, the natural sciences. After the students have assimilated the sciences already mentioned the teachers should instruct them in the natural sciences. The first of this group that one ought to learn is medicine, that is, the art which keeps the human constitution in its normal condition, and which brings back to its proper condition the constitution which has departed from the normal. This latter type of activity is called the healing and cure of sickness, while the former is called the care of the healthy. This art falls into two parts, science and practice. . . .

After the students have learned this art the teacher should lecture to them on the natural sciences as such. This discipline investigates natural bodies and all things whose existence is incidentally dependent on these bodies. This science also makes known those things out of which, by which, and because of which these bodies and their attendant phenomena come into being. . . .

METAPHYSICS: After this one should concern himself with the study of metaphysics, that which Aristotle has laid down in his work, *Metaphysics*. This science is divided into three parts. The first part investigates "being" and whatever happens to it insofar as it is "being." The second part investigates the principles with respect to proofs which are applied to the special speculative sciences. These are those sciences, each one of which elucidates, along speculative lines, a definite discipline, as for instance, logic, geometry, arithmetic, and the other special sciences which are similar to those just mentioned.

Furthermore, this part investigates the principles of logic, of the mathematical sciences, and of natural science, and seeks to make them clear, to state their peculiarities, and to enumerate the false views which have existed with respect to the principles of these sciences. In the third part there is an investigation of those entities which are not bodies nor a force in bodies. . . .

This is the first among sciences. All the other sciences, which are but the groundwork of philosophy, have this discipline in mind. . . .

11. *Books and Schools, Germany, about 1200*

❰If a man has a book in his hand he must not display his anger by pounding on it or by striking others with it. The teacher who is angry with his student must not hit him with it, nor should the student ward off blows with a book unless the blows are very dangerous.

There was once a student who stuttered and it took him quite a while before he managed to get a word out of his mouth, and when the others laughed at him he would become angry. His teacher, therefore, said to him: "Don't ask questions in their presence. Wait until they leave, or write down your difficulties on paper, and I'll answer you."

A man should not rear an orphan who carries tales for he will get no thanks for it, nor should a person tolerate a talebearer among his pupils, for there will never be any peace among them because of his tattling. Nor should one tolerate a male or female servant who tells tales.

It is written in the Bible [Job 22:23 and 11:14]: "If thou return to the Almighty, thou shalt be built up, if thou *put away unrighteousness far from thy tents.*" If this is true, why then is it necessary to repeat: "If iniquity be in thy hand put it far away, and *let not unrighteousness dwell in thy tents.*" It is merely that the Bible wishes to teach us that the teacher shall not say: "I'll let this mean student remain in order that I may make a better person of him, for he can learn from my good example." It will be of no avail! It is more probable that he will teach the other children in the house to do wrong.

When a person teaches children—some of whom are more brilliant than the others—and sees that it is disadvantageous for all of them to study together inasmuch as the brilliant children need a teacher for themselves alone, he should not keep quiet. He ought to say to the parents, even if he loses by making the division: "These children need a separate teacher; and these, a separate teacher."

[Proverbs 22:6]: "Train up a child in the way he should go." If you see a child making progress in Bible, but not in Talmud, do not push him by teaching him Talmud, and if he understands Talmud, do not push him by teaching him Bible. Train him in the things which he knows.

III. ORDER OF INSTRUCTION OF THE HOLY CONGREGATION OF THE SEPHAR-
DIM, *Amsterdam, before 1680*

℄ Some time ago I came here to the holy congregation of Amsterdam and I visited the schools of the Sephardim a number of times. There I saw "giants [in scholarship]: tender children as small as grasshoppers," "kids who have become he-goats." [These Talmudic phrases mean the young students were growing into scholars.] In my eyes they were like prodigies because of their unusual familiarity with the entire Bible and with the science of grammar. They possessed the ability to compose verses and poems in meter and to speak a pure Hebrew. Happy the eye that has seen all these things. . . .

Now this is the form of organization in the holy congregation of the Sephardim—may their Rock and their Redeemer guard them. They built a house of God, a temple in miniature, a magnificent synagogue. He who has not seen this building has never in his life seen a beautiful place among the Jews! [This synagogue, then the most beautiful in Europe, was consecrated in 1675.] Close by it they built a six room schoolhouse, and its chambers are full of knowledge!

There is a teacher in every room even when there are pupils by the hundreds (and may they keep on increasing!). In the first class the younger children study until they are able to read the prayer book; then they are promoted to the second class. There they study the Pentateuch with the melody of the cantillation marks until they are well versed in the Five Books of Moses down to the last verse. [The emphasis, the second year, is on the chant.]

Then they enter the third class where they study the Pentateuch until they can translate it fluently into their mother tongue [Spanish]. Every week they study carefully the commentary of Rashi to the entire *parashah*. [Every week a different section or *parashah* of the Pentateuch is read in the synagogue.]

Then they go on to the fourth class. There they study the Prophets and the Hagiographa in order, with the melody of the cantillation marks. One boy reads the verse in Hebrew and then he explains it in Spanish and all the other lads listen to him. Then another boy does the same and so on.

Then he goes on to the fifth class where the lads are trained to study the Mishnaic law by themselves until they acquire understanding and intelligence and reach the category of *bahur*. [A *bahur* is a student of the Talmud.] In that class they speak in no other tongue but Hebrew except to explain the law in Spanish. They also study the science of grammar thoroughly. Every day they also learn one Mishnaic law with its Gemara [Talmudic] comment. When a holiday or festival draws nigh all the students then study the relevant chapters in the *Shulhan Aruk* [the standard Jewish law book]; the laws of Passover for the Passover, and the laws of Sukkot for Sukkot. This is kept up until all the boys are familiar with the holiday regulations.

They then move on to the sixth class, to the Talmudic college, to the academy of the rabbi and chief judge—may his Rock and Redeemer guard him. There they sit in class and every day study one law thoroughly with *Rashi* and *Tosafot*. They also discuss the matter by further consulting the legal comments of Maimonides, the *Tur*, the *Bet Yosef*, and the other authorities on law. [These are the great commentators and codifiers of rabbinic law.] In that Talmudic academy they have a special library with a great many books, and as long as the students are in school that library room is also open. Whatever books a person desires are lent to him, if he wishes to study, but he cannot take them out of the building even if he is willing to deposit a valuable pledge.

The hours of instruction are the same for the rabbis and teachers. That is, in the morning when the bell strikes eight all of the teachers and pupils enter into their respective rooms and they study for three hours until it strikes eleven. Then they all go out and when the bell strikes two in the afternoon everyone, as above described, enters again and studies until it strikes five, but in the winter they remain only till they have to go to the synagogue for the evening service. [But in Germany and Poland they studied from dawn till bedtime.]

During those hours when the lads are at home every householder has a tutor who teaches his child to write the vernacular and Hebrew and who reviews the class work with him at the house. He also instructs him in the writing of poems and verse, leads him on the right path, and teaches whatever one may desire.

The above mentioned rabbis and teachers are chosen and appointed by the community and paid out of the treasury of the Holy Brotherhood which is known as the *Talmud Torah* Association. [This "Study of the Torah" Association was established in 1616.] Each one is paid according to his worth, his needs, and his instruction, so much a year. The teacher does not have to fawn on any one and teaches all his pupils alike, whether rich or poor. . . .

BIBLIOGRAPHY

READINGS FOR ADVANCED STUDENTS

Abrahams, I., *Jewish Life in the Middle Ages*, 1932, Chap. xix, "The Medieval Schools"; Chap. xx, "The Scope of Education."

Bevan, E. R., and C. Singer, *The Legacy of Israel*. This is probably the soundest work on the Jewish factors in medieval thought.

Gamoran, E., *Changing Conceptions in Jewish Education*, Chap. i, "The Changing Jewish Curriculum"; Chap. v, "Higher Education—the Yeshibah." An interesting study by a well-known Jewish educator.

Ginzberg, L., *Students, Scholars and Saints*, Chap. i, "The Jewish Primary School"; Chap. iii, "The Rabbinical Student." Essays by an eminent rabbinic scholar.

Jacobs, J., *Jewish Contributions to Civilization*, Chap. iv, "Mediaeval Jews as Intellectual Intermediaries"; Chap. v, "Influence of Jewish Thought in the Middle Ages." Jacobs' essays are usually characterized by a mass of information and a fine style.

Sarton, G., *Introduction to the History of Science*. The massive tomes of Sarton are useful for brief reference to the various Jewish scholars of the Middle Ages who are of importance in the various fields of science and letters.

Schleiden, M. I. [J.], *The Importance of the Jews for the Preservation and Revival of Learning during the Middle Ages*. A eulogistic essay by the famous botanist.

JE, "Education."

ADDITIONAL SOURCE MATERIALS IN ENGLISH

Jacobs, J., *The Jews of Angevin England*, pp. 243-251, 342-344. A medieval Jewish code of education.

78.

A Proposed Jewish College
Mantua, Italy, March 22, 1564

IN 1564 a rather pompous Hebrew broadside was published by David Provenzalo of Mantua and his son, Abraham, asking the Jewish notables of northern Italy to create a Jewish college. The project was not new. Almost a hundred years before this, in 1466, King John of Sicily had authorized the Jews of his kingdom to establish a Jewish university. It is not improbable that the purpose of this proposed Sicilian Jewish institution was to give Jews an opportunity to secure training in the professions of medicine and civil law.

In Mantua, however, the purpose of the proposed college was not, as one might think, to introduce among Jews the humanistic learning of the Renaissance, but to retain in the Jewish fold those students who might wish to get a general education. In other words, if it is necessary that Jews learn the new sciences and languages, they should at least be given a Jewish religious training at the same time, to counteract the non-religious influence of a general education.

David (died after 1572) was not only a great preacher and scholar in Jewish lore, but, as his friendship for the cultured Azariah dei Rossi would indicate, also at home in the humanistic studies which in this century distinguished Italy. He was versed in Italian, Latin, and Greek. His son, Abraham (died 1602), a doctor of philosophy and medicine, was, like his father, at home both in Jewish and general lore.

The Provenzalos, father and son, were part of a group of north Italian scholars, who, without in any sense relinquishing their orthodoxy, attempted to bring into Jewish learning much that they had learned from the Christian world. The Provenzalo family did succeed in establishing a Talmudic academy, but their college project failed, no doubt due to the growing spirit of intolerance. This was the Restoration period when the Church looked askance at all "infidels" and accordingly embittered the life of Italian Jewry.

℀The following are the statutes, laws, and regulations which, with God's help, are ultimately to be established in the institution dedicated to Torah [the whole body of Jewish lore] and to the sciences which our master, the sage, Rabbi David Provenzalo—may his Rock and Redeemer guard him—son of the honored teacher Abraham, of blessed memory, seeks to establish in the confines of his own home here in Mantua, may God protect the city! It is he who is addressing you personally, you holy men, you assembly of the congregation of Israel. Peace, peace be unto you who are far and near.

I, David, have seen the distressing sight and the disturbing spectacle: how, because of our manifold failings, the intelligent Jews are diminishing; how the learned are disappearing from among us without there being any one able to take their place. This is particularly true since the ark of God, the delight of our eyes, has been captured, and there is no one to say, Restore! For the hand of God has been against us to reprove and admonish us for our sins. God has not done a thing like this to any other nation. For the peoples among whom we live are ever increasing in wisdom, understanding, and knowledge, and in all arts, but Israel alone is isolated, desolate, poor, most unsightly, like a lost sheep, like a flock without a shepherd; and this generation, the children who are now being born and are growing up after the setting of our sun, act just like those who have never seen the light. [This paragraph here may refer to the death of some Jewish scholar in Mantua, or to the confiscation of the Talmud, 1553.]

Because of these conditions I am sick at heart and indeed am ready to weep because of all this beauty that is fading in this country. And though I am an old man I am roused by my zeal for the Lord of Hosts because of the schools and the academies which have ceased in our lands as if they had never been, and I fear, God forbid, that Jewish studies may be forgotten. [The confiscation of rabbinic books and the growing intolerance of the Church made study difficult.]

I have also noticed something terrible. People are unconcerned with the eternal life and busy themselves only with this temporal life, or with the secular sciences in the Christian universities—where they also learn their ways. [Many Italian universities were still open to Jews.] And as a result Jewish learning is ready to mourn because Jews praise the unimportant and dismiss the essentials. Therefore I have made up my mind and have definitely resolved and decreed, if God be with me, to turn my house into a college for any man, for any fine young Jew whose heart prompts him to come under the shelter of my roof. Thus every one who seeks Jewish learning and lore may turn here to our great wine cellars of Torah and science; let him drink and forget his intellectual poverty.

Why should we be inferior to all other peoples who have scholarly institutions and places fit for instruction in law and the sciences where students may flock and slake their thirst? Has not the word of God been given to us also? It is befitting for us to follow in the footsteps of those distinguished Jews, our brothers and our teachers, who are establishing numerous academies in Palestine. To be sure, due to the help of the mystical Presence—which has never ceased to operate and never will—the very air of Palestine makes one wise. [Palestine had been having an intellectual revival since the immigration of the Spanish exiles after 1492.] Perhaps God may bethink himself of us, too, so that we may again become a united people. It is therefore also our first obligation in these lands, where we now are, to further and to glorify the Torah until a spirit from on high shall be poured out upon us to restore us as of old and to reestablish our Temple.

Associated with me in this enterprise will be my oldest son [Abraham Provenzalo]—may his Rock and Redeemer guard him— who is a doctor of philosophy and of medicine. He has attained distinction in these sciences after having already gotten a basic Jewish education. He will be a stimulating helper. Through our joint efforts the matter will be furthered and accomplished. We will be able to take advantage of that which is good without relinquishing our hold on that which we already have, that is, we will busy ourselves not only with Torah but also with the sciences.

Now these are the rules that we intend to observe with the aid of God who will help us as He helps anyone whose purpose is lofty. The following requirements, though they be many, will be fulfilled in every sense of the word, without fail. Man has a will whereby he can accomplish anything he wishes if he but have God's help, and so with His aid do we intend to proceed at all times.

I.   First, I will pay particular attention to every one of the students —may their Rock and their Redeemer guard them—so as to pluck out of their hearts every root that brings forth false ideas—if there be any such, God forbid—and to plant in their souls proper beliefs and the right kind of ideas, those in agreement with the Bible and the rabbinic teachings. This is to be done so that their expressions and their intentions in all their actions shall alike be directed toward God, as is proper for every good Jew; that they be zealous in both the rational and the ceremonial commandments; that they go morning and evening to the synagogue; that they acquire good manners and commendable virtues; that they keep themselves from improprieties

—with the result that through my efforts the fruit that will be produced will be good seed, dedicated to God and [Exodus 19:6] "they shall be unto me a kingdom of priests and a holy nation."

II.   Young students who come from out of town to board in my house will be provided with a bed, table, chair, and lamp, and will be completely free from providing for their bodily needs. At the table they will always speak of both religious and secular matters so that there will be imparted to them intellectual and social qualities to be employed in all their conduct, and thus [Exodus 24:11] "they will behold God while eating and drinking." Those who come to register in my home shall not be transients but shall come for a period of five years until they show good progress in their studies, or they must at least stay three years, for one must labor at least that length of time to maintain his grasp on knowledge. [University courses then lasted from four to seven years.]

III.   Our chief study will be that which is the basis of everything: the Biblical and the rabbinic law. . . . [Talmudic law was to be studied from those books which had not yet been confiscated.]

IV.   In studying the Bible we will read the best of the old and the new commentators both for the purpose of explaining the basis for the commandments, judgments, and laws, and for the purpose of understanding the science of the Torah which many call divine philosophy [theology]. We will also add new interpretations which have not yet been published, in accordance with the point of view that investigation is always worth while, for there is no study that does not result in something new. With God's help we will pursue the same method a part of the time with the other Holy Writings such as the Prophets and the Hagiographa as well as with those *Midrashim* that are useful and valuable for furthering knowledge. [*Midrashim* are commentaries to the Bible. They are replete with laws and fables.]

V.   We will read occasionally chapters of the best Jewish philosophers whose writings agree with the teachings of the Bible and the rabbinic authorities, of blessed memory, in order to establish right beliefs, to remove errors, false notions, and a perverted point of view, and to spread among the students the limpid teachings of those believing scholars who follow the true and the right.

VI.   We will fix periods for the study of Hebrew grammar in order to get into its spirit and to know its rules. For many fundamental questions are dependent upon this: both the true meaning of the Biblical verses as well as the understanding of the secrets hidden in them like apples of gold in frames of silver. We will also study the *Masorah* ["Tradition": the science of the correct form of the Hebrew text of the Bible].

VII.   While studying grammar they can also learn to speak idiomatically and write correctly—whether they say little or much—as for instance when dealing with a matter of law. [David himself composed a grammar, *The Tower of David*.] When studying poetry they will be taught the methods of the best of the poets.

VIII.   The students will also be trained to write the "Assyrian" letters [the standard Hebrew script] properly as well as other Hebrew scripts in order that there shall be many scribes among the Jews.

IX.   At special hours the students will learn Latin, which is almost indispensable now in our country, for no day passes by that we do not require this knowledge in our relations with the officials. We have a precedent for this since even the members of the household of Judah the Prince [135–217] were allowed to trim their hair like the pagans because they had frequent contacts with the Roman government. The students shall also write themes in Hebrew and in good Italian and Latin with the niceties and elegances of style that are characteristic of each language and the knowledge of which redounds to one's fame and reputation.

X.   Those who are versed in Latin can read the scientific books dealing with logic, philosophy, and medicine and thus get acquainted with them step by step, so that any one who wishes to become a physician need not waste his days and years in a university among Christians in sinful neglect of Jewish studies. On the contrary, through his own reading he should inform himself gradually of all that he need know, and then if he should study in a university for a brief period he can, with God's help, get his degree. [However this very year, November 13, 1564, a papal bull made it difficult for Jews to get degrees.] After this he may enter practice with competent Jewish and Christian physicians. But even those who do not as yet know any Latin may read those scientific books which have already been translated into Hebrew, and thus save time, for the basic thing in knowledge is not language but content, for everything depends on what the mind really grasps. [Many Arabic and Latin works on science had already been translated into Hebrew.]

XI.   Furthermore, by the aid of competent men the students will be made proficient in the different types of Christian scripts. And likewise in the science of arithmetic and calculation they will do many problems. And they will get many-sided instruction in the various forms of arithmetic, geometry, and fractions. They will also be taught and made familiar with the usual studies such as arithmetic and geometry, which have already been mentioned, as well as with geography and astrology. [Some famous geographers and map-makers were Jews.] All these disciplines will be taught by us to the limits of our capacity, and no student will have to go anywhere else to study, for we will carry them as far as we can. For more advanced instruction we will find a competent scholar to work with us.

XII.   At fixed periods the students will engage in debates in our presence both in matters of Jewish law and in the sciences, in order to sharpen their minds. Each young man will learn more or less in accordance with his individual capacity—the main thing is that they be religious in spirit. Also they will gradually be taught to speak in public and to preach before congregations. [The graduates would also be prepared to serve as rabbis.]

If God will grant us the merit of having a great many pupils, we will secure more instructors who will look after them properly, to give each student his just due. May the pleasantness of the Lord our God be upon us and mayest Thou establish the work of our hand. Amen. May it be Thy will.

Now this is part of the curriculum which we lay before all learned Jews in order that those who read this may realize that God constantly rules the world, in the interest of both townspeople and villagers. Let not these Jews who live in the outlying hamlets say that no one is providing for them and furnishing them with the blessings of religion, for unto them has the verse [Abot 4:14] "Go to a place of Torah" been said. I pray and beseech God that He will bring it about through me that many people will have the merit of honoring the Torah and tradition in my home and within my walls, and thus I, too, will find peace and happiness.

Consider this appeal, you leaders of the people, the people of the God of Abraham. Let him who is for his people respond. These are the words of your servant who seeks the welfare of his people and greets you: David Provenzalo of Mantua, the son of our honored teacher Abraham, of blessed memory.

[Abraham Provenzalo adds a postscript:]

And I, Abraham, David's son, a mere physician, who am but dust and ashes, hope for salvation through the plan described above, expecting it to redound forever to your welfare and to ours, and I have no wish to concern myself further with medicine if God will but grant me the merit of being a sharer in this great work. Peace.

THIS IS NO ADDITION BUT BASIC

All this, I, the humble David, have thoughtfully worked out in order to rouse the leaders of the Jewish communities that they might agree to magnify the crown of the Torah and the sciences in a specific spot, according to the program I have already prescribed, and in addition establish a large college of scholars and scribes in a sacred spot where dwells the president who is to be appointed. [David expected to become the president.] The various provinces and cities ought to support it for there is no greater good than this. Education is as important as all other commandments put together, and I do hope that this institution will achieve great glory in the service of the public.

In truth it is fitting for all Jews in our part of the country to further this religious work mightily by opening their hands in order to do this thing adequately. [David appeals to the leaders for monetary support.] Then it will be possible to secure the aid of many learned and skilled instructors, every one of whom will work in his own field—for it is manifestly impossible for one or two men to give adequately all the lectures we have suggested above except with great difficulty or by effort that is all too strenuous. Especially will this be true if the students—may their Rock and Redeemer guard them—are divided into separate classes which would have to recite their lessons before their teachers.

With the help of the Jewish communities it would be possible to hire a number of learned men, part of whom would be engaged in teaching Talmudic law, and the other part, the respective sciences. Thus everything would work out well even with respect to the things that we have not presented. [The school with its four colleges of arts, medicine, Jewish theology, and law is to be a complete university.]

Since among the poor Jews there are some who would like to study but have not the means, the leaders of the communities would also be able to help every intelligent and brilliant student who cannot afford a large expense. And although there may be many students, I am willing, for God's sake, to bend my shoulder and to bear the yoke of preparing for their needs, and for a reasonable price provide them with a good home which I will rent for this purpose and where they will be more than welcome.

I pray that God be with me and that the Jewish leaders support me by making the choice that will benefit them and their children after them. That which has inspired me to undertake this fine work was the realization that to begin a task is more than to half-finish it, and just as splinters may kindle large logs even so do I wish to arouse those, who are more important than I, to finish the work properly. It is for these reasons that I have decided to publish these plans and to send them to the various Jewish communities in our neighborhood, in order that the humble may see and rejoice and run to accomplish a good deed whereby the merit of their fathers will stand them in good stead. May God stand by us and help us and dispense blessing on the work of our hands and may His covenant of life and peace abide with us.

Rise, ye sons of the living God and be mindful to give glory and honor to the law of the Lord.

Haste, seek wisdom, acquire understanding, increase scholars in Israel.

Send your sons to a place of Torah and let it be established where every one can attain that which he seeks.

Through the merit of this great deed the redeemer of Israel shall awake, haste, and come!

BIBLIOGRAPHY

READINGS FOR ADVANCED STUDENTS

Baron, S., "Azariah de Rossi's Attitude to Life *(Weltanschauung),*" *Jewish Studies in Memory of Israel Abrahams,* pp. 12–52. De Rossi, the famous scholar, was an intimate of the Provenzalos who, no doubt, shared many of his views.

Bettan, I., "The Sermons of Judah Moscato," *Hebrew Union College Annual,* VI (1929), pp. 297–326. Moscato, like de Rossi, was also a friend of the Provenzalos and shared their interest in secular studies.

Roth, C., "The Medieval University and the Jew," *The Menorah Journal,* XIX (1930–1931), pp. 128–141.

JE, "Abraham ben David Provençal"; "David ben Abraham Provençal"; "Mantua."

79.

The Woman Who Refused to Remain
the Wife of an Innkeeper
Pavia, Italy, 1470

ABOUT February, 1470, Hakkym ben Jehiel Cohen Falcon had trouble with his wife. She detested his business, innkeeping, and finally deserted him. The following Hebrew account as told by the husband relates the history of her grievance and her return to him.

The story is in the form of a request by Hakkym for a legal opinion from Joseph Colon (about 1420–1480), then the leading rabbinical authority in Italy. When the wife deserted her husband she spent a day and a night away from home among strangers. Now the Jewish law is particularly rigorous with respect to the wives of descendants of the priestly line, and Cohen, as his name indicates, was of priestly origin. The question, then, is, whether or not this woman, while away from home, was guilty of any indiscretion. Colon in a lengthy "answer" decided that there was no reason to assume that anything wrong happened to the woman and permitted her to remain with her husband.

This notable rabbi, who with the aid of two other authorities rendered this decision, was distinguished for his scholarship and sterling character. He is responsible for the well known decision that if one Jewish community is in distress another may be taxed to contribute to its support. His family was of French origin and claimed descent from the famous Rashi. Colon was a name common among Jews; therefore some scholars have made the suggestion that Cristobal Colón (Christopher Columbus) himself may have been of Jewish origin.

❰[Hakkym writes his story to Rabbi Joseph Colon:]
In order to relate everything that has happened to me I shall tell you in detail what my business is and I shan't hide a thing from you, sir. Now this is the matter concerning which I make inquiry of my master:

For the last several years I have made my living as an innkeeper in Pavia, and this was my business up to the year 230 [1469] when my wife began to trouble me saying: "You've got to leave this business," and she gave me some good reasons for it. After she had kept hammering away at me every day for about six months and I had paid no attention to her—I kept pushing her off—the quarrel between us regarding this affair reached its climax about the beginning of Adar 230 [February, 1470]. While I was in the house teaching my daughter, my wife picked herself up right at noon, took all the silver vessels and her jewelry, and repaired to the house of a Gentile woman, a neighbor, to whom my wife went frequently. This woman used to sew linen clothes for me, for my household, and for the guests who used to come to my place. She was also my laundress.

My wife was in the house of this Gentile woman about a half an hour before I inquired of my daughters where she had gone—for I was intent on teaching my daughter. Suddenly, however, my thoughts rose up and stirred me to ask my daughters: "Girls, where is your mother?" They told me that she had gone outside and that my four year old little girl, holding her right hand, had gone with her. I thereupon went after her, seeking her in Jewish homes unsuccessfully, till my heart told me: "Go to the house of the Gentile; perhaps she's staying there." So I turned in her direction and came to the house of the Gentile woman but found the door locked. I knocked and the husband of the woman opened the door at once, but when he saw that it was I, the husband of the woman who just come into his home, he was distressed and tried to close the door, but he couldn't, for I entered by force. When the auxiliary bishop, who was there, heard my voice, he said to me: "Come on in and don't be afraid."

There were present there, in addition to the auxiliary bishop, two citizens, the bishop's chaplain, and two Gentile women seated beside my wife, who was on a bench with her daughter in her arms. As I came into the house the auxiliary bishop said to me: "Is this your wife?" and I answered: "Yes, my lord."

"According to what we now observe," he said again, "another spirit has clothed your wife, who wishes to change her religion; therefore are we come to encourage her to turn to the Christian religion if she has really set her heart on it. If not, we advise her to return to her people and to her God." [This fair attitude did not always characterize the actions of the Church.]

I then asked his permission to have an earnest talk with her in German, and he gave me permission to speak with her in any kindly way as long as I did not scold her. [The Christians about her evidently knew no German or Yiddish.] Now this is what I said to her: "Why have you come here and why don't you return home?" To which she answered: "I'm going to stay here and I don't care to return, for I don't want to be the mistress of a tavern." "Come on, come on back," I said to her, "I have already promised you, you can do whatever your heart desires in this matter."

"You can't fool me again," she responded. "You've lied to me ten times and I don't trust you." And as she was speaking to me after this fashion I said to her: "Why have you your little daughter in your arms?" "Take your daughter and go," she answered, and I took her in my arms. Then as I turned to go my way the auxiliary bishop said to me: "Look here, Falcon, don't be disturbed about your wife. No pressure will be brought to bear on her. Nothing will be done in haste, but quietly, calmly, and with her consent. Before we make a decision in this matter we will place her in a cloistered spot, among virtuous nuns, where no man may enter. She'll have to stay there forty days until she completes the period of her isolation and reflection—for this practice has been established by the founder of Christianity that one may determine what is in the heart of those who come to change their religion, and also in order to prevent confusion to Christianity." [The woman, as a catechumen, one about to be baptized, was allowed forty days to make up her mind; it was, however, Pope Gregory I (590–604) and not Jesus who established this forty-day period of preparation.]

When I heard this I turned homeward weeping as I went. My oldest daughter came out to meet me, and I told her all about the unseemly affair that had happened to me. She ran to her mother to find out what she had in mind. "Go on back to the house and don't be concerned, and don't bother about me," her mother said to her. Whereupon the girl ran to a prominent Jewess. Then the both of them came to the girl's mother, and the Jewess spoke to her. Behold, the entire conversation of this Jewess is recorded in a deposition that has been forwarded to you.

Within about a half an hour after this had happened the bishop himself ordered the woman to be taken to a convent in which a very rigorous Christian discipline prevailed and which, of all the convents, was the most isolated from man. Such convents are shut off so completely that no man can enter there except on rare occasions or in case of an emergency. For instance, the bishop would go there when there was an absolute need, or the physician, who was assigned to them, would come there with the permission of the bishop if one of the nuns took sick. When my wife went to the convent she was accompanied by seven Gentile women and two citizens, and she remained there all that day and all that night.

However, her spirit was moved for good, and when the morning came she sent word to the bishop that she earnestly desired to return to her home saying: "I am the wife of a *cohen* [a "priest"], and if I stay here a day or two I can no more return to the shelter of his home, for he must divorce me." [The wife of a *cohen*, a descendant of the Jewish priestly caste, was expected to be above suspicion.] The Jews, too, knew of her intention to return through the bishop himself, for in the morning a certain Jew by the name of Zalman went to him to see in what honorable way they could recover the valuables which she had taken with her from her husband's home. Then the bishop said: "Hasn't she just told me that she is returning home? Why do you ask about the valuables when she's coming back and will bring with her all that she has?"

When Zalman heard this he was scared to death, thinking—God forbid—that this was a pretext for making a false accusation against the prominent Jewess, for such things had happened. [Zalman probably was afraid that the prominent Jewess might be accused of preventing the innkeeper's wife from becoming a Christian. It was a capital offense to dissuade Jews who wished to convert to Christianity.]

Therefore Zalman said to the bishop: "Let her stay between three and ten days until she really knows what she wants to do." To which the bishop responded: "How can you say such a thing, for the woman has said that her husband would not be permitted to take her back if she should stay there another night, for she is a priest's wife." When Zalman saw that this was not a trick, he said to the bishop: "Act in accordance with your authority, and do that which is good and right in the eyes of God and man."

The bishop then sent for me and came to meet me—for he had gone to the convent—and he repeated to me all the things that had been said and done, and said further: "Look here, your wife wants to return to your home, but I fear that you may vex her with words and reproaches. Don't do it. For wherein has she sinned against you? And although she says that she has no cause to fear, nevertheless I beg of you, please do not reprove her or oppress her. Return to her as of old and I'll do this for you: I'll cross-question her in the presence of witnesses, as is meet to be done in such a case," and so he did. [The purpose of the bishop's questioning was to determine if she had been with any man since she left her husband the day before.] Toward evening God's light shone on that bishop, for he restored my wife to her home, and she is there now, weeping for her sin, imploring forgiveness and pardon and condonation, and afflicting her soul, and may God forgive her.

Therefore your humble servant, here undersigned, requests my lord to be so kind as to inform me—if I have found favor in your learned sight—whether my wife is permitted to live with me or not. And this is the inquiry which I make of you, even as I might bring my case before a divine oracle, and I shall adhere closely to whatever you command me. It will be ascribed to you as an act of righteousness if you clarify this distressing situation, and may God be kind and gracious unto you and give you opportunities greater even than your ancestors' to spread Torah and to impart knowledge to the people, for your ways are ways of pleasantness.

BIBLIOGRAPHY

READINGS FOR ADVANCED STUDENTS

Graetz, IV, pp. 294–295.

Abrahams, I., *Jewish Life in the Middle Ages,* 1932, Chap. v, "Social Morality"; Chap. vii, "Monogamy and the Home"; Chap. viii, "Home Life (Continued)."

JE, "Catechumens, house of"; "Colon, Joseph b. Solomon"; "Conversion to Christianity"; "Domus conversorum."

80.

Palermo and Alexandria
1488

O BADIAH BERTINORO, an Italian rabbi of the fifteenth century, was a very distinguished rabbinic scholar. His fame rests on his simple but admirable Mishnah-commentary which is used by every student of rabbinics. Obadiah left his home in Italy and set out for the Holy Land where he ultimately became its outstanding spiritual leader and contributed much toward raising the level of the declining Jewish community. He died sometime after 1500.

From Jerusalem he sent back home to Italy three Hebrew letters describing his experiences on the trip from Sicily, through Rhodes, to Egypt and Palestine. The first letter is the most interesting; it was sent August 15, 1488 to his aged father.

From this letter have been taken the following brief descriptions of the Jewish communities of Palermo in Sicily and Alexandria in Egypt. Palermo at this time presents a picture of the Jewish community crushed by its Spanish-Aragonian rulers who finally expelled them four years later when all Spanish Jews were exiled, 1492. The picture of Alexandrinian Jewry is typical of a Levantine Jewish community in a Moslem setting.

❲Palermo is the largest city and the capital of Sicily, and contains about 850 Jewish families, all living in one street which is situated in the best part of the town. They are poverty-stricken artisans, such as coppersmiths and ironsmiths, porters and peasants, and are despised by the Christians because they are all tattered and dirty. They are obliged to wear a piece of red cloth, about the size of a gold coin, fastened to the breast, as a [Jew-] badge. The labor imposed upon them by the government weighs heavily on them, for they are compelled to go into the service of the king whenever any new labor project arises; they have to drag ships to the shore, to construct dykes, and so on. They are also employed in administering corporal punishment and in carrying out the sentence of death. [Jews in Crete, too, were compelled to act as executioners.]

Among the Jews there are many informers who have no sense of right or wrong and who continually betray one another shamelessly. If one Jew hates another, he conjures up some false accusation against him that is absolutely without foundation. And if the matter is investigated and found to be false, one does not hold it against the informer, for according to the law and custom of the country the man who defames his fellow man is not punished, even though he has not substantiated his accusation. The people here are also very careless in matters of sexual hygiene, and most of the fiancées are already pregnant by the time they are married. . . .

The synagogue is surrounded by numerous buildings, such as the hospital, where beds are provided for sick people and for strangers who come there from a distant land and have no place to spend the night. There is a ritual bath there, and also a large and magnificent chamber where the representatives sit in judgment and regulate the affairs of the community. There are twelve of these, and they are chosen every year; they are empowered by the king to fix the taxes and duties, to levy fines, and to punish with imprisonment.

This institution has become a source of great trouble to the people, for men of no name and of bad character frequently prevail upon the viceroy, by means of gifts, to appoint them representatives. After they have given these bribes they take the income of the synagogue and of the community which is now under their control, and turn it over to the viceroy and his officers in order to insure their support. Then because they are able to do whatever they want, they crush the people under a heavy burden. The evil of these representatives is exceedingly great and the poor cry aloud at the oppression under which they continually suffer. Indeed, the protest of this city has mounted to the very heavens. . . .

*   *   *

We went ashore in the bark and then travelled to Alexandria on foot, a trip of eighteen miles, for we could not find any donkeys to ride. We reached Alexandria, faint and weary, on the eve of the 14th day of Shebat [January 12, 1488], and God roused up one of the princely Jews there, Moses Grosso by name, who was the interpreter for the Venetians. He was rich and very much liked in that country, even by the Moslems. He went to meet us outside the city gates and saved us from the Moslems who were at the gates, for they rob and plunder at their pleasure the foreign Jews who come in. He brought me to his home and I was not able to leave his house all the time I was there. I used to read with him a cabalistic book which he had, for he was attached to that lore. Through this I made a good impression on him and he became very attached to me. On the Sabbath which I spent with him, he brought me to his dining room and made a feast to which he also invited my companions, the Sephardic Jew and his two sons.

Now this is how the Jews in all Moslem lands are accustomed to make a feast on the Sabbath. They sit in a circle on a rug and the butler stands beside them. There is no table; only a small cloth is spread out on this rug and all kinds of fruits which are in season are then brought out and laid on it. The host now takes a glass of wine, pronounces the blessing of sanctification [for the Sabbath Eve, Kiddush], and empties the cup completely. The butler then takes it from the host, and hands it around successively to the whole company, and every one drinks a cup of wine. Then the host takes two or three pieces of fruit, eats some, empties a second cup which the butler has handed him, and all who are seated about say: "Health and life." The one who sits next to him then takes some fruit, and after the butler has given him, too, a cup of wine, he says [to his host]: "To your happiness," and the company responds: "Health and life," and so it goes around.

After this they partake of a different kind of fruit, another glass is filled; and this is continued until they have emptied at least six or seven. Sometimes they drink to a fragrance for they bring in dudaim flowers which, so Rashi tells us, are called jasmin in Arabic. It is a plant bearing only flowers which are very fragrant and invigorating. They smell these dudaim and then drink a cup of wine. The wine in these parts is very strong—this is especially the case in Jerusalem—and they drink it undiluted. After they have finished drinking as many glasses as they wish, a large platter full of food and meat is brought in, and every one puts his hand into it and takes whatever he wants. They eat in a great hurry, but not much.

At that Sabbath feast, the above mentioned Moses brought us preserved plums, fresh ginger, dates, raisins, almonds, and coriander-seed candy. With every course there was a cup of wine: sometimes it was raisin wine (and it was very good); once a Malmsey from Crete, and once a native wine. And I drank plenty with him. . . .

In these parts the Sabbath is more strictly kept than in any other, for no one goes outside the door of his house on the Sabbath either for a walk or for any other matter except, of course, to fulfill a religious commandment: either to go to the synagogue, or to the house of study. It is not even necessary to add that there is not a single person who makes a fire in his home on the Sabbath or re-kindles a lamp that has gone out. They do not even allow a Gentile or a slave or a maid to light it. [This rigid observance shows Karaite influence.] All who know how to read the Holy Scriptures read all day after having slept off the effect of their wine.

In Alexandria there are about twenty-five Jewish families now, and two ancient synagogues. The one is large and somewhat dilapidated; the other, smaller. Most of the community pray in the smaller synagogue for it is associated with Elijah the prophet, of blessed memory. They say he revealed himself in it, in one of its corners, to the pious among them. That corner is the south-eastern one, and they keep a perpetual lamp burning there. They say that not long past—less than twenty years ago—Elijah revealed himself there in the guise of an old man, but blessed is he who knows the truth. [The legendary Elijah constantly reveals himself to the pious and aids them.]

In all Moslem countries no man enters a synagogue with his shoes on, but barefooted. Even when one comes into another man's courtyard he leaves his shoes in the court at the door as he enters into the house, and everybody sits on the ground on mats or on a carpet.

Alexandria is a very large city, surrounded by a wall and encircled by the sea. Now, although two-thirds of it is a desolate wilderness and there are fine, large houses without inhabitants, its appearance indicates it was once unusually beautiful, as do the inhabited courtyards in which there are mosaic-like stone pavements with peach and date trees in their midst. All the houses are, as a rule, beautiful and large but there are few people in them because of the bad climate which has prevailed there for several years. It is said that those who are not accustomed to the air and who remain here long die or certainly fall sick. Most of the inhabitants are stricken with eye trouble [probably trachoma].

People come to this city from the corners of the earth for wares. There are four consuls there now from Christian lands: a Venetian, a Genoese, a Catalonian, and an Anconanite [Papal States]. All the merchants who hail from all the different Christian nations can carry on their business only in accordance with their instructions. Every night the Christians who are in the city have to shut themselves in their houses and the Moslems lock them in from the outside, and every morning they open them again. Likewise every Friday, from noon until evening, when the Moslems are in their mosques, the Christians in town must go to their homes, and their gates are locked on the outside. Whatever Christian may be found outside at that time, well, his blood is on his own head!

There is no end to the money which comes to the King from the customs on goods which enter and leave through Alexandria, for all wares have to pay a very large duty there. One must also pay six per cent on drafts. But as for me, God saved me, and I did not have to pay duty for the moneys that I had with me. There is no fine or punishment for defrauding or evading the customs throughout all Egypt.

BIBLIOGRAPHY

READINGS FOR ADVANCED STUDENTS

Graetz, IV, pp. 396–399; Margolis and Marx, pp. 518–519.
Waxman, M., *A History of Jewish Literature*, II, pp. 113–114, 492–495.
JE, "Alexandria"; "Bertinoro, Obadiah b. Abraham"; "Palermo."

ADDITIONAL SOURCE MATERIALS IN ENGLISH

Adler, E. N., *Jewish Travellers*, pp. 209–250, "The Letters of Obadiah Jaré da Bertinoro (1487–90)." Adler also includes translations of the itineraries of a number of other notable Jewish travellers.
Miscellany of Hebrew Literature, I, pp. 113ff., "Selections from Two Letters Written by Obadja da Bertinoro in the Years 1488 and 1489."

81.

A Jewish "Beautician"
Rome, 1508

JEWISH women, like their men, were engaged in all sorts of trades. The following Italian letter, written by the Jewess Anna of Rome to Catherine Sforza (1463–1509), who was then probably at Florence, expatiates on the virtues of certain facial creams and lotions and describes their application.

We know nothing of Anna; of Catherine, one of the most striking figures in Italian history of the fifteenth century, we know a great deal. As Lady of Forli she had pointed out to her anti-Jewish officials in 1490 the economic value of bankers, and it was at her suggestion that the magistrates invited a rich Jew of Bologna to Forli on condition that he provide credit for the local citizens. The magistrates, in turn, guaranteed the security of his capital.

When Anna's letter was written Catherine was already forty-five years of age, tired after a lifetime of plotting, fighting, and murdering. She had been married at fourteen, had borne eight children, and had buried three husbands. Once she had been considered a very beautiful woman and she was desirous of maintaining her "fair and fine complexion." Let us hope she succeeded.

⊄To the most illustrious Madonna, Caterina de Reariis, Sfortia Vicecomitissa, Countess de Imola, my most honored patroness. Wherever she may be.

Permit me, most illustrious Madonna, to commend myself to you and to send you greetings. Messer Antonio Melozo, Esquire, has been here on behalf of your Highness to inquire of me if I will not give him as many kinds of facial cream as I have.

To begin with, I gave him a black salve which removes roughness of the face, and makes the flesh supple and smooth. Put this salve on at night, and allow it to remain on till the morning. Then wash yourself with pure river water; next bathe your face in the lotion that is called *Acqua da Canicare;* then put on a dab of this white cream; and then take less than a chickpea grain of this powder, dissolve it in the lotion called *Acqua Dolce* and put it on your face, the thinner the better.

399

The black salve costs four *carlini* an ounce; the *Acqua da Canicare*, four *carlini* a small bottle. The salve, that is the white cream, costs eight *carlini* an ounce; the powder, one gold ducat an ounce, and the *Acqua Dolce* will cost you a gold ducat for a small bottle.

Now if your illustrious Highness will apply these things, I am quite sure that you will order from us continually.

I commend myself to your Highness always.

Rome, the 15th of March, 1508.

Your Highness' servant
ANNA THE HEBREW.

[P.S.] The black salve is bitter. If it should happen to go into the mouth, you may be assured that it is nothing dangerous; the bitterness comes from the aloes in it. [To poison one's enemies was not uncommon then!]

BIBLIOGRAPHY

ADDITIONAL SOURCE MATERIALS IN ENGLISH

Ellis, H., *Original Letters, Illustrative of English History, etc.*, III, pp. 52–55. This is a letter of Esperanza Malchi, a Jewess, to Queen Elizabeth, accompanying a present of certain articles of dress from the Sultana Mother at Constantinople. In return the Sultana Mother requests face and hand lotions.

82.

Jewish Books and Their Printers
1531-1719

THE introduction of printed books was of profound importance for Jews as it was for all groups. It meant that books could now be manufactured in large numbers and distributed at a relatively low cost. It made learning easier and cheaper and thus helped democratize learning among the Jews.

The following five selections touch upon various aspects of the printed book. The first selection is a title page of the Hebrew grammar *Miklol* ("Perfection") of the famous French grammarian and exegete David Kimhi (d. 1235). The work was published in Constantinople about 1532 by the great Hebrew printer, Gershon Soncino, who published many important Hebrew, Italian, Latin, and Greek books in Italy and Turkey from 1488 to his death in 1534.

This title page offers a brief summary of his notable career. His statement that his ancestor Moses drove the monk Capistrano out of Fürth is probably legendary. There is no record of Jews in Fürth in those days; Graetz suggests Soncino might have meant, instead, Firet in Hungary. Another family legend says that a Soncino killed Capistrano in battle in Transylvania in 1479. The fact is that Capistrano, who incited the German masses against the Jews, 1451–1453, died peacefully in bed in 1456.

1. *Gershon Soncino Writes a Title Page, Constantinople, 1531-1532*

℃The Book *Miklol:* all divisions of grammar are explained in the first part; after that comes the dictionary. Written by Rabbi David ben Joseph ben Kimhi the Spaniard.

[Printed] By me, Gershon Soncino, son of the sage, Rabbi Moses, son of the scholarly sage, Rabbi Israel Nathan, son of Samuel, son of Rabbi Moses of blessed memory who fought against that scoundrel Fra Juan di Capistrano in the city of Fürth and drove him out with all his cohorts. This Moses was the fifth generation after Rabbi Moses of Speyers who is mentioned in the *Tosafot* of Touques [in France. *Tosafot* are notes to the Talmud]. In the twelfth year of the mighty king, our lord the king Sultan Sulaiman [1531-1532], may his Majesty be exalted, in Constantinople the city. Printed with the verses vocalized and with references. . . .

May He, the blessed One, allow His splendor to radiate on him who waits and hopes for His love, and may He guide me in His truth and teach me, even as He has led me from strength to strength since my youth. I labored and discovered some books that had been stored and hidden away for a long time, and I brought them forth to the light of the sun, and they shine like the radiance of the firmament: namely, the *Tosafot* of Touques of Rabbi Isaac and Rabbenu Tam [both twelfth century descendants of Rashi]. I went as far as France and Chambéry and Geneva, to the very places where these writings were conceived, in order to give the public the benefit of them, for in Spain, Italy, and in all lands we heard only of the *Tosafot* of Sens: by Rabbi Perez, Rabbi Samson, and their associates [noted French Talmudists of the 13th century].

I published innumerable books dealing with our holy Torah, besides twenty-three Talmudic tractates, which are commonly studied in the rabbinic academies, with the Rashi commentary and the *Tosafot*. The Venetian printers copied my books and published, in addition, whatever they could lay their hands on. They tried hard to ruin me, but thus far God has helped me. And, although time the deceiver has played havoc with me, while there is yet a breath in my body I shall not cease to issue good editions in order to lighten the burdens of those who read them and to illumine their darkness, if only God will be with me.

[Gershon came to Turkey from Italy about 1529.] And although my life is spent and I have come to a strange land—like a beast about to perish—God, may He be exalted, will still be my help and my support in my old age! He will remember me kindly for having helped the Marranos of Spain, and particularly those of Portugal, for I bestirred myself with all my power and at the risk of my life, in order to save them from those who would despoil them. I led them back to seek refuge in the shadow of the Almighty that they might lodge under His pinions even as at this day.

He, the Blessed One, is my constant hope.

Blessed be the name of Him who is ever to be praised.

*   *   *

Two of the best known Jewish printers of sixteenth century Venice are Cornelio Adelkind and Meir Parenzo. Adelkind—who became a convert to Christianity—was for many years employed by Daniel Bomberg (d. about 1549), a Gentile who was the first important publisher of Hebrew books in Venice. Bomberg brought out the first complete editions of the Babylonian and Palestinian Talmuds.

Meir Parenzo, who at first had worked with Adelkind at the Bomberg presses, later joined with Bragadini, another Gentile firm that finally dominated the Hebrew press in Venice.

Adelkind and Parenzo in 1545 published the Psalms in a Yiddish translation made expressly for them by the noted Jewish scholar Elijah Levita (d. 1549). In the following epilogue to this edition the two Jewish printers appeal to their readers for a liberal patronage.

11. *A Printer's Appeal for Customers, Venice, 1545*

⫷Cornelio Adelkind writes this to the pious young women and to men who have not had time to study:

During my youth I devoted all my energies to helping to print many great and precious books, as may be seen in all books printed at Daniel Bomberg's press, in which my name is inscribed in front and in back. When I grew old I considered that I had done nothing for pious young women and for men that had not time to study in their youth, but who would like to spend their time on Sabbath or Festivals reading religious literature and not *Dietrich of Bern* [German medieval folk-epic] or *Schoene Glueck*.

And for the sake of those that want to read God's word, for there are few [Jewish] books written in German that are well and correctly translated, I went to Rabbi Elijah Levita and entered into agreement with him to translate several books for me, and first of all the Psalms, according to rules of grammar. And soon, God willing, I shall print Proverbs and Job and Daniel well translated. And if God lets me live yet a while, I shall make it easily possible for young and old to know what is written in the Bible, which is now, alas for our sins!, better known to others than to ourselves. Therefore I beg you, dear pious young women and men, buy the Psalms cheerfully and kindly and give us money that we may soon begin to print Proverbs. Amen.

This we beg of you, your servants

CORNELIO AND MEIR PARENZO.

*   *   *

A great many Hebrew and Yiddish books have been prefaced by a *haskamah* or "approbation" of the rabbis and communal leaders. Originally this "approbation" was a simple recommendation by some notable or competent person. Later, in the sixteenth century, when the Church extended its censorship, the Jews, in fear of the Inquisition, themselves censored not only old Jewish books, but new ones, too. The *haskamah* now gradually widened its scope: it became a license to publish, a book review, a "blurb," a guarantee of absence of any reference objectionable to Christians, an assurance of Jewish orthodoxy, and a copyright. The last was a natural outcome: the licensing board of rabbis and laymen attempted to protect the author and publisher by forbidding others to pirate the edition. The copyright scheme had the tendency, however, to prevent the publication of cheaper editions which might have benefited the reading masses.

Haskamot have their value as sources for history: they tell us about the author, his work, his aspirations, and at the same time give us some information about the undersigned rabbis and communal officials.

The following approbation was written for *Bedek Ha-Bayit* ("Repairing of the House") which contains supplements and corrections to the *Bet Yosef* ("House of Joseph"), a capacious commentary on rabbinic law; both books are by the noted scholar, Joseph Caro. This approbation is dated 1600, but the book was not published till 1606.

III. *An Approbation, Venice, 1600*—PERMIT OF THE RABBIS

℟Whereas, there have appeared before us the wise, the perfect one, etc., Isaac Gershon [noted corrector of Hebrew books], and his worthy associate, Menahem Jacob Ashkenazi, and have testified that they have gone to much labor and trouble, have expended great sums, and have spared no expense, all in order that they may bring to light, in as beautiful and excellent an edition as possible, the secrets of a work of great worth, through which the public good will be advanced, viz., the book called *Sefer Bedek Ha-Bayit*, by the sage, the wonder of the generation, our master and teacher, Joseph Caro of blessed memory;

And whereas the work is to be completed, as a service to God, with the utmost beauty and perfection;

And whereas they fear "lest they sow and another reap," doing all their work in vain [lest some one pirate their edition], and lest they make all their expenditures only "to leave to others their wealth";

Therefore they have sought and have asked us, the undersigned, to aid them through the uttering of a ban, and the publishing of a rabbinic notice to the effect that no injury or harm shall come to them through any man.

And whereas permission has likewise been granted them by the nobles, the Cattaveri (may their majesties be exalted!), that their desire and wish should be fulfilled [the Cattaveri were a board who, among other things, licensed books],

Now therefore we, the undersigned, decree, under threat of excommunication, ban, and anathema through all the curses written in the Bible, that no Israelite who calls himself a Jew, man or woman, great or small, be he who he may, shall purpose to publish this work, or to aid any one else in publishing it, in this or any other city within ten years, except it be by the will and permission of the associates above mentioned;

And let it be likewise understood that by this decree of excommunication, ban, and anathema, no Israelite is allowed to buy a copy of the book mentioned from any man, Jew or Christian, be he who he may, through any manner of deceit, trickery, or deception, but only from the above mentioned Menahem Jacob Ashkenazi. For thus it is desired by the scholar mentioned above [Isaac Gershon], that all copies of the above mentioned book shall be published and sold by Menahem Jacob.

Upon any one who may transgress against this our decree of excommunication, ban, and anathema—may there come against him "serpents for whose bite there is no charm," and may he be infected "with the bitter venom of asps"; may God not grant peace to him, etc.

But he that obeys—may he dwell in safety and peace like the green olive tree and rest at night under the shadow of the Almighty; may all that he attempts prosper; may the early rain shower with blessings his people and the sheep of his pasture.

"And ye who have clung to the Lord your God are all of you alive this day." Amen. May it be His will.

Thus sayeth Benzion Zarfati, and thus sayeth Loeb Saraval, [and thus sayeth] Baruch ben Samuel.

On Thursday, the 13th [15th] day of Nisan, 5360 [March 30, 1600], I published this ban, by command of the authorities mentioned above, in every synagogue in the community of Venice.

Eliezer Levi,
Beadle of the Community.

* * *

The Counter Reformation, which began with the intolerant Pope Paul IV in 1555, brought with it the systematic censorship of Hebrew books and manuscripts in Italy and other lands. Any Hebrew book containing a statement objectionable to the Church could be seized and either destroyed, or expurgated and then restored to its original owner.

The Christian states—with certain exceptions—did not appoint censors to examine in advance new Jewish books for heretical content. The burden of advance expurgation was put upon the Jews themselves. After publication the Inquisition authorities had the right and duty to examine the published works and, if necessary, punish the authors for any real or alleged anti-Christian statement.

This fear of the Inquisition explains the terror of the Venetian Rabbi, Leon of Modena, who discovered in 1637 that his Italian *Historia de gli riti hebraici* ("History of Hebrew Customs"), first written for a Protestant king, had been published in Paris without being corrected by him and was being circulated in Catholic Italy.

In the following selection from his autobiography, *Hayye Yehudah* ("The Life of Judah"), Leon (Judah) of Modena tells how he succeeded in escaping punishment.

iv. *The Censorship of Hebrew Books in Italy, 1637*

ⒸI was worried, terrified, and very greatly distressed. Among my many troubles and griefs I never experienced anything like this since I saw the light of day, in spite of the fact that almost daily I have had much to cope with. This is due to the fact that about two years before [in 1635] I gave a book to read to a certain Frenchman by the name of Monsieur Giacomo Gaffarel who knew Hebrew. More than twenty years ago [really in 1616] I had written this book at the request of an English nobleman [probably Sir Henry Wotton, English Ambassador at Venice,] who wanted to give it to the King of England [the Protestant James I, d. 1625]. In this work I recount and discuss all the laws, statutes, and customs of the Jews nowadays in the Diaspora. I didn't take any precautions at that time against writing things in it of which the Inquisition might disapprove, for it was only a manuscript to be read by men who did not even belong to the Catholic Church.

After the Frenchman, whom I have just mentioned, read the book, he asked me to let him have it so that he might print it in France. I agreed and I never thought of correcting those things which in print might be unacceptable to the Italian Inquisition.

After two years, after I had given up hope that the Frenchman would print it, a man brought me a letter from Gaffarel on the second day of Passover, 5397 [April 10, 1637] informing me that he had published the above described book in Paris. In no wise did he mention to whom he had dedicated it, or whether he had changed anything in it, or the like.

I was startled and went to examine the copy which I had retained after I had written the book. I found four or five specific things of which one was forbidden to speak, much less write, to say nothing of printing, without permission of the Inquisition. Then I cried out in anguish and tore out my beard. I was aghast for I reasoned that when this book would come to Rome and be opened and examined there it would get all the Jews into trouble. The Gentiles would say: "What impudence! To print something in the vernacular, telling the Christians not only what the Jewish laws are, but even things that are anti-Christian, and that without our consent." And as for myself, where could I go? I couldn't find refuge in Ferrara or in any other Italian city.

I was really painting my danger worse than it was, for in the last analysis the words were not so objectionable. I groaned a great deal and was sick at heart and almost lost my mind. None of my friends could comfort me. But the Lord our God who is gracious and merciful prompted me to listen to the advice of the Inquisitor, may he be blessed and praised, for in his relations to me he acted like a righteous Gentile. I thereupon made a voluntary declaration at the Inquisition [April 28, 1637]. This declaration protected me from everything; I placed my reliance upon it, and calmed down after a month of indescribable suffering and distress.

After some time this Frenchman of whom we have been speaking came to Rome, and from that city sent me a copy of the book that had been published in Paris. I saw that he had acted wisely and considerately by removing four or five of those statements which I feared. He also prefaced the book with a letter praising me and the work most generously.

He dedicated the book to the royal French Ambassador [at Venice, Claude Mallier] who had come here to reside at the seat of government—may its glory be exalted. The Ambassador wrote me a letter in which he assured me of his favor and that of the King. Then I had a real rest from my fear and terror.

In spite of the fact that that edition had many errors in nicety of expression, and in spite of the fact that there were some things left in it which I feared might still not be acceptable to the Gentiles, nevertheless I agreed to republish it here in Venice [1638]. For the reasons suggested above, I thereupon removed some things and added others, as I saw fit, and this book today is for sale at Gentile booksellers. Till now, almost six months later, I have heard nothing but praise for it. In this second edition, too, as in the first, I made my dedication to the Ambassador himself, and he gave me a gift of thirty-four ducats, which paid the expenses of publication.

* * *

A colophon is an inscription put at the end of a book for the purpose of imparting information about the author or the publisher. Therefore, colophons are frequently good sources for Jewish history and throw light on various aspects of the political and cultural life of the Jew.

The following Hebrew colophon comes from *Zinzenet Menahem*, ("Menahem's Jar"), a legal work by a rather obscure rabbi, Menahem Zebi (1646–1724), who had served in Wengrow in Poland and in Holleschau in Moravia. The author admits naively in his title page that his book is veritable "hot manna" whose taste is "like wafers made with honey." As a part of this title page he reprints a letter of introduction from the Council of Four Lands, dated 1691, urging some printer to print this book and to make haste because, back home, Menahem's disciples "who drink in his words with thirst are now like sheep without a shepherd."

v. *The Revelations of a Colophon, 1719*—APOLOGY

❡The statement of Menahem, the son of the late worthy and notable, Rabbi Zebi Hirsch, of blessed memory, who was the son of the late worthy and notable Rabbi Menahem Mendel of the holy community of Posen:

I wish to express my thanks to God, in accordance with His righteousness, for all the good which he has bestowed upon me since I left the womb of my mother, that valiant, modest woman, Dame Breindel, the daughter of the scholar, Rabbi Abraham Katz Shrenzels Rapoport [1584–1651] of the holy community of Lemberg.

This page is too small to contain all the evil experiences which have happened to me up to this day, Tuesday, the 13th of Tishri, 480, according to the shorter reckoning [September 26, 1719].

It was the year of the war with Sweden, 415 [1655]—I was then nine years old and an advanced student—that they took a great deal of money from my father's home and destroyed all our houses. They were well-built, too. They razed everything to the very foundation, as it is now. The war lasted three years and I forgot everything that I had learned.

By God's mercy, however, we returned to the above mentioned holy community [Posen], during the week of *Ekeb*, 416. [*Ekeb*, taken from Deuteronomy 7:12–11:25, was read in the synagogue August 12, 1656.] It seems to me that it was on the 18th [of Ab that we returned]. I studied with that brilliant scholar, the late Rabbi Zelki, and he brought my knowledge back to me. My father-in-law, too, the late chief and leader, Rabbi Judah Loeb, who was a communal leader in Pinczow, kept his eyes on me and encouraged me to study.

I succeeded in attaining the rabbinic degree, was accepted as Rabbi on the first of the month of Ellul 433 [August 13, 1673], and had a great many students.

I decided to write down my notes on the law, my *responsa*, and my new views on Talmudic materials. [*Responsa* are "answers" to religious and legal questions.] People said to me: "What are you waiting for? You ought to have your studies preserved in a permanent form, in a book." When I came to my teachers and propounded some of my views to them they also encouraged me and urged that my words be written down with an iron pen [printed] without delay.

But fate hindered me till now that I have come to the holy community of Berlin. May the Lord be good to them as they were good to me. Blessed is the Lord who has helped me thus far to print half of one of my books which is called *Zinzenet Menahem* ["Menahem's Jar"]. May God also find me worthy to publish the book *Lehem Menahem* ["Menahem's Food"], a Talmudic and *responsa* work, and also to finish the second half of the *Zinzenet Menahem*, and to publish the *Taame Menahem* ["Menahem's Reasons"], a work on Rashi. [Rashi of Troyes, 1040–1105, was the greatest rabbinic commentator.]

It is my wish that all scholars and every reader of this book who may find any errors in it, shall not hold me responsible for there was a great deal of work involved. It is impossible to get along without mistakes. This is particularly true of a work that has never been published before. And may God in return deal kindly with you.

BIBLIOGRAPHY

READINGS FOR ADVANCED STUDENTS

Margolis and Marx, pp. 480–481.

Amram, D. W., *The Makers of Hebrew Books in Italy*. Thus far the most extensive study in English on the subject.

Bloch, J., "Venetian Printers of Hebrew Books," *Bulletin of the New York Public Library*, February, 1932.

Marx, M., "Gershom (Hieronymus) Soncino's Wander-Years in Italy, 1498–1527. Exemplar Judaicae Vitae," *Hebrew Union College Annual,* XI (1936), pp. 427–501. A scholarly study.

Popper, W., *The Censorship of Hebrew Books.* This work contains a great deal of material dealing with printing, censorship, and the like.

Roth, C., *Venice* (Jewish Communities Series), Chap. vii, "Hebrew Printing at Venice."

Schechter, S., *Studies in Judaism,* First Series, 1896, Chap. xi, "Titles of Jewish Books."

JE, "Adelkind"; "Approbation"; "Bomberg, Daniel"; "Censorship of Hebrew Books"; "Colophon"; "Levita, Elijah"; "Soncino"; "Title-page"; "Titles of Hebrew Books"; "Typography."

ADDITIONAL SOURCE MATERIALS IN ENGLISH

Coryat, T., *Coryat's Crudities,* 1905, I, pp. 370–376. In 1608 Thomas Coryat, the English traveller, argues with a rabbi in the Venice ghetto who might have been Leon of Modena. This selection from Coryat is also reprinted in *Transactions of the Jewish Historical Society of England,* XI (1924–1927), pp. 217–221.

The Ferrara ordinances in which the Jews lay down regulations for self-censorship of their works may be found in L. Finkelstein, *Jewish Self-Government in the Middle Ages,* pp. 304ff., and I. Abrahams, *Jewish Life in the Middle Ages,* 1932, pp. 85ff.

83.

Turkish Jewry
1553–1555

URKEY in the sixteenth century was probably the most powerful empire in the world and sheltered a large and growing Jewish
population which had fled from the various Christian lands of central
and western Europe.

Among the exiles from the Spanish Peninsula who sought refuge
in Constantinople was a family of Portuguese Marranos, the Mendes—
known among Jews by the name of Nasi—a group of international
bankers who had fled from Lisbon to Antwerp, then on to Venice,
and finally to Turkey by way of Ferrara. In Venice, Gracia Mendesia
Nasi, now the head of the house, was betrayed to the authorities
(about 1549) by her sister who was anxious to wrest her own
husband's estate from Gracia, into whose care it had been entrusted.
Fortunately for Gracia, her nephew and business agent, Joseph Nasi,
succeeded in inducing the Turkish Sultan Sulaiman II (1520–1566)
to intervene on her behalf to recover the confiscated moneys taken
from her as a Christian heretic. Sulaiman tolerated the immigration
of Spanish Jewish artisans because he found them useful in the
manufacture of munitions; he encouraged the immigration of the
wealthy and cultured Spanish and Portuguese Marranos because of
their commercial connections, their knowledge of European political
conditions, and their unquestioned loyalty to the Moslem state which
offered them a safe refuge from the arms of the dreaded Spanish
and Portuguese Inquisitions.

The following description of Turkish Jewry and of the Mendes
is taken from the German diary of Hans Dernschwam. Dernschwam,
who was born in Bohemia in 1494 and died there about 1568, was a
trusted employee of the Fuggers, the richest international business
concern in sixteenth century Europe. He was a highly educated man,
had books of Jewish interest in his fine library, and was a friend of
the Hebraist, Sebastian Münster. He travelled in 1553–1555 at his
own expense through the Balkans, European Turkey, and Asia Minor,
making notes of the things that interested him. He has considerable
material on the Jews, although like other intellectuals of his day he
disliked them.

《Furthermore, the Jews and foreign merchants from Poland, Reussen [White Russia], Wallachia, and Hungary, as is their wont, know how to travel about in Turkey. No limitations are anywhere placed on their importing goods as long as they pay the custom duties to the sultan. [In most Christian lands limitations in importing goods were placed on Jews.] They march into a caravansary, wherever they want, run about in their own garb, and some of them have barely twenty or fifty florins worth of goods such as Hungarian knives, caps, Prussian russet-leather, brandy made of beer, linen, etc. Unquestionably all the Jews are spies for both sides [Christians and Turks] and he who has the courage can travel with these fellows anywhere, deep into the interior of Egypt or Asia. They travel in large bands, for the Arabs are desperate robbers. . . .

In Turkey you will find in every town innumerable Jews of all countries and languages. And every Jewish group sticks together in accordance with its language. And wherever Jews have been expelled in any land they all come together in Turkey as thick as vermin; speak German, Italian, Spanish, Portuguese, French, Czechish, Polish, Greek, Turkish, Syriac, Chaldean, and other languages besides these.

As is their custom every one of them wears clothes in accordance with the language he speaks. Usually the garments are long, just like those of the Wallachians, the Turks, and the Greeks, too, that is, a kaftan. This is a long tunic, tied about at the waist, over which is a sort of skirt made of cloth of good quality and silk.

Just as the Turks wear white turbans, the Jews wear yellow. Some foreign Jews still wear the black Italian birettas [square caps]. Some who pretend to be physicians or surgeons wear the red, pointed, elongated birettas.

In Constantinople, the Jews are as thick as ants. The Jews themselves say they are very numerous. However, in the tax list of the past year of 1553 there are supposed to have been 15,035 Jews, not counting women and children, and 6,785 Christians, such as Greeks, Armenians, Caramanians, all of whom pay the sultan the tax called the *Kharadj* [tribute. Stephan Gerlach in 1574 estimated there were 30,000 Jews there]. The Jews are despised in Turkey as they are anywhere else; possess no estates although many own their own homes.

In those places where they can find shelter and have their own quarters or a place to make a living, they prefer to live in the houses of others and pay rent. Most of these houses belong to the mosques, to the priests. When the houses burn down the Moslem priests have to build them again. These houses are miserable, stinking affairs;

the people live one on top of the other so that it is only natural that they have an epidemic every year. They live in the lower part of the city near the sea.

Not far from Adrianople is a city on the Aegean called Salonica. It is believed that more Jews live there than in Constantinople; they say about 20,000. [Up to the end of the World War Salonica had more Jews than non-Jews.] Many are cloth-weavers whose products are sold throughout Turkey. . . .

In Alexandria, in Missr (that is to say, Cairo), in Aleppo, in Antioch in Syria, and in Jerusalem and everywhere else there are many Jews. Those Jews that are old, who have a little money, travel to the Holy Land, to Jerusalem, and still hope that they will some day all come together, from all countries, into their own native land and there secure hold of the government. [Jewish nationalism was very strong in the 16th century.] The well-to-do Jews send money to Jerusalem to support them, for one cannot make any money there, nor is there any money there. . . .

There are forty-two or more synagogues in Constantinople. Every Jewish nationality goes to its own synagogue.

The Jews lend nothing to the Turks. The latter are not to be trusted.

The Jews are allowed to travel and to do business anywhere they wish in Turkey, Egypt, Missr (that is, Cairo), Alexandria, Aleppo, Armenia, Tataria, Babylonia as far as Persia, Reussen, Poland, and Hungary. There is no spot in the world which hasn't some of its Jews in Constantinople, and there are no wares which the Jews do not carry about and trade in. Just as soon as a foreign ship comes in from Alexandria, Kaffa [now Feodosia in the Crimea], Venice, and other places, the Jews are the first to clamber over the side.

They import all the jewels that come to Constantinople from India by way of Persia. They can ask 200 florin for a stone that isn't worth a penny. . . .

Many Marranos—that is Jews who turned Christian, as in Spain, or voluntarily became Christians in other places—when they can't make an honest living abroad, go crooked, and in order to escape the gallows all come to Turkey and become Jews again. They endure contempt, poverty, hunger, and thirst in order to be able to have time for themselves and not be kept captive by the Turks like the Christians. They tolerate all sorts of knavery and roguery. They are not ashamed to commit any villainy.

Those Jews, too, who wander from country to country and allow themselves to be converted two or three times in order to make some money and at the same time learn a trade, are all to be found in Constantinople and Turkey. Their trade supports them to some extent as, for instance, a bookbinder who was long settled in Breslau and who came here with two sons. His daughter came approximately the following year, in 1552. [This bookbinder probably pretended to be a Christian in Germany.] . . .

About the year 1552, before we entered Turkey, a scholarly German died at Constantinople. He knew both Greek and Arabic; got in among the Jews and accepted their faith. He also learned Hebrew. Must have committed a crime somewhere abroad or been an Anabaptist. Said to have studied at Wittenberg. [Anabaptist was the sixteenth century term for any radical. Today we use the term "Communist."] . . .

The Jews boast that many Christians come into the country every year and become Jews. Also, while we were still in the city, a number of Jews became Turks. . . .

There are all sorts of artisans among the Jews who make a living selling their products publicly, for in Turkey every man is free to carry on his trade at home, in a shop, or on the streets. Whether he is skilled or not, knows little or much, no one has a word to say if he only pays his tax to the sultan and his rent for his shop. [Unlike the Christian lands, there were no limitations on Jews in Turkey in the practice of the crafts and commerce.] . . .

There are two cloth-shearers among the Jews and some among the Greeks, too. The Jews of Constantinople also have a printing press and print many rare books. They have goldsmiths, lapidaries, painters, tailors, butchers, druggists, physicians, surgeons, cloth-weavers, wound-surgeons, barbers, mirror-makers, dyers . . . silk-workers, goldwashers, refiners of ores, assayers, engravers. . . .

Their medical doctors cannot be learned in medicine and surgery for many of them know no Greek or Latin and are not students of philosophy. Those of whom I have heard know nothing beyond Hebrew and Arabic. They have stolen everything from Galen [a famous Greek medical authority, d. about 200 C.E.], and have a few prescriptions which they have gotten from Italian druggists in Italy and from their parents who were druggists' clerks. There are no other learned doctors in Turkey. There is one, however, by the name of [Solomon Ashkenazi, a famous physician and diplomat, d. before 1605] who used to frequent the embassies. He knows Latin, philosophy, and Italian well. He has brought speedy relief to some people.

The sultan has never used any but a certain Jewish physician [Moses Hamon, d. about 1554] who probably rendered good service to him and the court. He was allowed to build a large stone house of three or four stories in the Jewish quarter. He died while we were at Constantinople. His son [Joseph] is also said to be a physician. He now has his father's position; is said to have a prescription to cure a bellyache. . . .

The Jews also have a few druggists, and as is usual in Turkey, they have dirty shops; not as among the Christians, stores, fine places. . . .

In 1553 an old Portuguese woman [Gracia Mendesia Nasi] came to Constantinople from Venice with her daughter and servants. The Jews are not in agreement as to who her husband was and what his name was. Some say he was called Diego Medes and his brother was named Francisco of Antwerp. [Dernschwam was confused. Her husband was Francisco Mendes and his younger brother was Diogo.]

She is reported to have escaped with great wealth from Portugal to Venice [about 1543] after her husband's death; is said to have a sister there who was supposed to come here, but has somehow been detained.

The Jews are very proud of her; call her a *seniora*. She lives also in luxury and extravagance; has many servants, maids also, among them two from the Netherlands.

She is said to have been formerly a Marrano and here to have become a Jewess again. She does not live at Constantinople among the Jews, but at Galata in a country home and garden for which she is said to pay a ducat a day rent.

The Venetians are reported to have arrested her and to have refused to let her go on. She is then said to have intrigued with the sultan's physician [Moses Hamon] who had a son and hoped she would give him her daughter. The sultan is then supposed to have taken the part of the *seniora* and they had to let her go from Venice.

Her husband [Francisco Mendes] is said to have been a Marrano, and when he died had begged of her that his remains be carried from the Christian land and sent to Jerusalem and there be buried. This she did in 1554. Accompanied by a large contribution the bones were sent there and were buried by the Jews.

She is a dangerous woman, like Barbara of Cologne [Cilli(?), the notorious German Empress, d. 1451]. Carries on a large overseas business in wool, pepper, and grain with Venice and Italy.

She had promised to give her daughter to a Portuguese or Spaniard. He has been at the court of the Emperor of the Holy Roman Empire. Christian prisoners know him by sight. Is said to be her sister's son. [He was really a son of one of her husband's brothers.] The Jews who are around him daily do not agree as to his name, in order that people should not learn to know such rogues. He is said to have been named Zuan Mykas [Juan Miguez] or Sixs; his father is said to have been a physician by the name of Samuel. [Juan Miguez was Joseph Nasi, later Duke of Naxos, husband of Reyna, daughter of Gracia.]

This rogue whom I have just mentioned came to Constantinople in 1554 with over twenty well-dressed Spanish servants. They attend him as if he were a prince. He himself wore silk clothes lined with sable. Before him went two janizaries with staves, as mounted-lackeys, as is the Turkish custom, in order that nothing should happen to him. He had himself circumcised in the month of April, 1554.

Right after this the aunt married off the daughter [Reyna] to him and before and after the wedding, for months, she entertained lavishly. The French ambassador [Condignac] also came over from Constantinople to Galata on St. Bartholomew's Day [August 24], and they were very ceremonious to one another. So the Jews tell me who were with them daily. Even as birds of a feather flock together, so do other scoundrels and betrayers of Christendom.

He is a large person with a black trimmed beard.

The servants who came with him and with the women have also all been circumcised and have become Jews; must have been thieves and Marranos who were whipped out of town in some other place. Since they now see how Jews are despised here and what a poor country Turkey is they are now said to regret their step very much, although before they came here they were bold enough. Such scoundrels will turn up again in the course of time among the Christians and commit villainy.

The *seniora*, whom I have mentioned, and her son-in-law live in such state that it would amply befit a prince. They feed about eighty people a day; must have cheated people somewhere. Something must be wrong with them. They allege that they have left a lot of wealth behind them; also that some is following them on the sea. And considering the cost of living in Turkey, their wealth will soon shrink here. They gave the pashas a lot, and distributed several thousand ducats to the poor Jews or their hospital.

The above mentioned Portuguese, like other Spaniards at the Imperial Court, must have practiced jousting and tilting. He brought in all sorts of equipment such as armor, helmets, guns, long and short lances, also battle axes and large and small muskets. And even at Galata in his garden he retained this mummery of having his servants tilt and joust. . . .

The Jews do not allow any of their own to go about begging. They have collectors who go about from house to house and collect into a common chest for the poor. This is used to support the poor and the hospital.

BIBLIOGRAPHY

REFERENCES TO TEXTBOOKS

Elbogen, pp. 123–124; Roth, pp. 253–258; Sachar, pp. 221–223.

READINGS FOR ADVANCED STUDENTS

Graetz, IV, pp. 400–408, 571–581, 593–630; Graetz-Rhine, IV, pp. 423ff.; Margolis and Marx, pp. 486–487, 512–517.

JE, "Constantinople"; "Mendesia, Gracia"; "Nasi, Joseph, Duke of Naxos"; "Nasi, Reyna"; "Salonica"; "Turkey."

84.

Gambling: an Attack and a Defense
1584

GAMBLING was a vice not uncommon among Jews. Laws of the Jewish community against games of chance are found in almost all lands. In 1584, when only thirteen years of age, Leon of Modena wrote *Sur Me-ra* ("Turn Aside from Evil"), a dialogue on gambling. Eldad, one of the debaters, attacks it as a vice; Medad, the other, defends it as a sport.

Leon of Modena (1571–1648) was a famous rabbi and author of Venice. He was versed not only in Hebrew lore, but also in the sciences and arts of the cultured Italy of his day. Despite his spirited attack on gambling he failed to take his own words to heart: he confesses in his autobiography that he was an inveterate gambler. This clever dialogue which is written in classical Hebrew, is an evidence of his literary skill.

IN WHICH ELDAD ENDEAVORS TO PROVE THAT THE GAMBLER TRESPASSES EACH ONE OF THE TEN COMMANDMENTS, AND MEDAD RETORTS

℃ELDAD: If with all human effort you draw out words and arguments to institute a comparison between gaming and commerce, in order to prove that one is similar to the other, inasmuch as they both equally tend to increase or diminish one's possessions, wealth, and the coveted things of this world; I would still ask, how you could possibly defend this pursuit when it is understood that they who walk in its ways are workers of iniquity? Each commits thereby an act of rebellion towards his Maker, and gradually estranges himself from Him, since he takes money from his fellow-man by wicked and thievish methods, without giving him a *quid pro quo*, and without any labor on his own part.

If you go into the matter thoroughly, you will see that the gambler trespasses all the Ten Commandments, the very foundation of the Law of Moses and of his Prophecy, acknowledged not alone by the people of Israel, holy unto the Lord, but also by those nations among whom we dwell. First, with regard to those Commandments from the words [Exodus 20:2,8] "I am the Lord thy God" unto the fourth, "Remember the Sabbath Day." These all warn against the sin of idolatry; and beyond doubt he trespasses against each one of them. For, as soon as his star is unlucky, and he loses everything, he will be beside himself, will grow full of fury and anger; and it is clear to us that our Rabbis were right when they said that "the man of anger is like the idolator [in forgetting his God, *Zohar*, Genesis 27b]." They have even expressed the same idea more clearly when they remarked: "A gambler is an idolator," basing their dictum on the Scriptural phrases; "And Sarah saw the [idolatrous] son of Hagar . . . playing [gambling]"; "And the people [after they made the golden calf, an idol,] sat down to eat and drink, and they rose up to gambol [gamble]." [*Genesis Rabbah* 53:15.]

As regards the third Commandment [Exodus 20:7]: "Thou shalt not take the name of the Lord thy God in vain," etc., it is self-evident to all, that at every moment during play, at every opportunity for sinning, or differences among players, a man will commit perjury; he will swear thousands of vain and false oaths, dragging his soul down to earth—a dark and dreary outlook.

And how easily the Commandment referring to the Sabbath Day is broken! A man is playing on Sabbath Eve, near dusk; the loser, in the forlorn hope of winning back what he has lost; the winner, whose greed for gain is not satisfied, hoping to make more, suddenly find that the Sabbath has overtaken them, and they have infringed the sanctity of the day. In many other ways, too, this can happen to players.

The honoring of father and mother is equally jeopardized by this pursuit. Properly speaking, it is the duty of father and mother to correct and chastise the son who is addicted to gambling, in the endeavor to bring him back; but the son who is steeped in this sort of thing, which has become to him as second nature, will give them no ear. He answers them harshly, and this is a source of bitterness to their lives, for he has ignored the command [Leviticus 19:3]: "A man shall fear his mother and his father."

Furthermore, when a man realizes that he has lost his money, the fire of envy and hatred will burn within him against his fellow-man; or he will seek a pretext to quarrel with him, remarking, "The game was not so," calling him a wicked scoundrel, anxious to rob him of his own. The other will retort, and the discussion, having become heated—we cannot predict where it will end. It may even be that each will draw his sword, so that one gets killed, and the command of the Lord [Exodus 20:13], "Thou shalt not murder," be transgressed.

A gambler will mix with loose women. In his rage he will utter obscene and filthy expressions, and concerning such a sin our Rabbis have said [Shabbat 33a]: "The one who defiles his mouth with un-hallowed words has no share in the bliss of the world to come."

Words are the index to actions; the mouth makes the first move, and the organs of action do the rest. This is all contained in the pro-hibition [Exodus 20:13]: "Thou shalt not commit adultery."

Now, when he has been left destitute, left entirely without money, it is natural that all his thoughts are misdirected the livelong day. He broods upon how he may steal secretly, or rob his fellow-creatures openly, hoping by this means to make up for his deficiencies, with the result that he will be like the chief baker, Pharaoh's servant, hanging between heaven and earth, for not having observed the warning [Exodus 20:13]: "Thou shalt not steal."

It may happen, too, in the course of a game with his friend, that they may form a compact to share the profits equally, and a mis-understanding arising, a third party is called in to arbitrate; but he, being a friend of one of the players, gives the decision in favor of that friend, to wit, unjustly; what becomes now of the command [Exodus 20:13]: "Thou shalt not bear false witness against thy neighbor"? It is thrown overboard.

And it stands to reason, that if a man is not particular with regard to the law of stealing, he will be less careful as regards the prohibition [Exodus 20:14]: "Thou shalt not covet"; for whatever his eyes see, his heart will desire with a longing which will never satisfy the eye of covetousness.

Consider and answer now, whether the evil of this wicked pastime is not monstrous enough to reach unto Heaven. . . . Surely the one who touches such a diversion cannot go unpunished!

MEDAD: You have employed many words to condemn this sport, but you have nevertheless said nothing effectual to cast a stigma upon it which might not apply equally to every other human pursuit. For [Ecclesiastes 7:9] "anger resteth in the bosom of fools" even in trivial matters, but the sensible man is patient at all times.

This is my experience. I saw a man yesterday losing 400 gold-pieces, and he never uttered a word by way of cursing his luck; only once he exclaimed: "Thou, O Lord, art righteous!" On the other hand, I knew a man who, on receipt of the news that corn had depreciated in value—he was a corn and wine-dealer—went up to the roof, threw himself down, and was killed.

And where will you find the occasion for more wicked and per-plexing oaths than among merchants, which they employ to confirm their statements in the course of buying and selling?

And with regard to your apprehension as to the violation of the Sabbath, this may apply as well to the tailor, shoemaker, and every other workman who is desirous of increasing his profits.

There are, furthermore, many other diversions which might lead to the breaking of the command to honor father and mother, or to the commission of murder and adultery.

And the same is the case with stealing, which a poor fellow in straitened circumstances justifies by saying, it is not for stealing that he is hanged, but owing to his unlucky star and hard times.

As far as concerns false swearing, this may occur in any form of partnership; and covetousness, even outside gaming, is well known to reside naturally in the heart of man.

To sum up the matter: a perfectly righteous person will be as upright in commercial pursuits as in sport or anything else; whilst a wicked person will act wickedly in the one matter as in the other.

And now, finally, I say, go and reflect upon this one point. If, as you insist, this is such robbery and an intolerable sin, why did not our rabbis of old prohibit it to us and our descendants in a clear, decisive, and express manner? Considering, too, as is well known, that their object was ever to keep us aloof, not alone from transgression and wickedness itself, but even from that which in a remote degree might lead to its commission, and they, therefore, in their exalted and perfect wisdom, instituted one fence and safeguard upon another to protect the law—what conclusion can we arrive at from the consideration that they never lifted up their voice against this diversion, but that they found therein nothing of vice or vanity, as you would have us believe? [But in the next chapter, Eldad brings proof that the leading rabbis of the Middle Ages opposed gambling and Medad attempts to refute him.]

BIBLIOGRAPHY

READINGS FOR ADVANCED STUDENTS

Abrahams, I., *Jewish Life in the Middle Ages,* 1932, Chap. xxi, "Medieval Pastimes and Indoor Amusements"; Chap. xxii, "Medieval Pastimes (Continued). Chess and Cards."

JE, "Gambling"; "Games and sports."

ADDITIONAL SOURCE MATERIALS IN ENGLISH

Gollancz, H., *Translations from Hebrew and Aramaic,* pp. 161–219, "On Games of Chance." This is the complete translation of Leon of Modena's little work on gambling.

85.

Anti-Christian Polemics
Lithuania, before 1594

THE medieval world was a world of polemics and religious disputations. There is hardly a century since the rise of Christianity in which Christian works were not written against Judaism and replied to by Jews. Disputations occurred frequently, too frequently for the Jews, who entered with no alacrity into such discussions in which their opponents were also the judges. They could hardly hope to emerge with honor to themselves, nor was intimidation always absent.

The most famous of polemical works is the Hebrew *Hizzuk Emunah* or *Faith Strengthened* by Isaac ben Abraham of Troki (1533–1594), the most distinguished writer among the Karaite Jews of Poland and Lithuania in the sixteenth century. He was obviously a person of some secular training; he certainly knew the New Testament in the Polish. His Hebrew style is almost classical in its plastic simplicity.

Isaac evidently set out to refute all the basic theological principles of Christianity which differ from Judaism, and at the same time to demonstrate the superiority of his own faith. He certainly succeeded in writing the most complete anti-Christian handbook, and that with a minimum of diatribe—no mean accomplishment. It made quite a stir in the theological world and has since been translated into Latin, Yiddish, Spanish, English, and German. Refutations of it have been written in every century; the latest, a two-volume work, *A Manual of Christian Evidences for Jewish People*, by A. Lukyn Williams, appeared in 1911–1919. Voltaire, who probably knew this book in its Latin form, says of it: "The most inveterate unbelievers have cited almost nothing which is not in the *Fortress of Faith (Faith Strengthened)* of Rabbi Isaac." The following five selections are typical of Isaac's approach.

I.   A certain Greek once addressed me in the following words: "Do you know wherefore you have no longer a king of your own people? It is because you have rejected the faith of Jesus Christ and His kingdom, for He was the king of Israel. On this account the empire of Israel has been destroyed."

I replied to him: "It is known and evident from the words of the prophets that, in consequence of our manifold iniquities, our kingdom was destroyed in the time of Nebuchadnezzar, King of Babylon, when this king led Zedekiah, King of Judah, captive to Babylon.

"This event took place more than four [almost six] hundred years before the existence of Jesus. The Jews were then successively subjects of the Babylonians, Medes, and Greeks. Long before the birth of Jesus we had been kept in servitude by the Romans. You may see that proved in your Gospel of Luke 3:1: 'In the fifteenth year of the reign of Tiberius Caesar, Pontius Pilate being governor of Judaea, etc.' See also John 19:15: 'Pilate saith unto them, Shall I crucify your king? The chief priests answered, 'We have no king but Caesar.' Now, as to your ascribing to Jesus the government of Israel, we are at a loss to know who made him king, and where he ruled over Israel, seeing that the authorities sentenced him to death as they would the humblest person. As a matter of fact the Roman kings were responsible for his death and the death of his disciples and apostles, and in spite of this the Roman state still persists.

"But you, the people of Greece, were the first to acknowledge Christianity and you still continue your faith in him; and nevertheless, your government has been destroyed, and you have no longer a king of your own people: for a Mohammedan ruler, the Turkish sultan, who is now in possession of the Holy Land, extends his sway over Greece.

"Similarly, although the kingdom of Hungary holds to the faith of Jesus of Nazareth, nevertheless it has been rent and ruined. It has no native Hungarian sovereign as of old, but is ruled by the king of the Turks. There are many other Christian states which formerly elected their own kings, and now are subjected to the Ottoman power. On the other hand, you see the Mohammedans not only disbelieving the doctrines of Jesus, but even mercilessly persecuting the followers of his faith, and notwithstanding this, the empire of the Turks enjoys undisturbed prosperity."

II.   Matthew 5:43: "Ye have heard that it hath been said, 'Thou shalt love thy neighbor, and hate thine enemy.'" Truly, you may also see in this verse that Matthew has made a false statement, for nowhere in the Pentateuch or in the Prophets have we found the statement that you should hate your enemies. On the contrary, it is written in Exodus 23:4-5: "If thou meet thine enemy's ox or his ass going astray, thou shalt surely bring it back to him again. If thou see the ass of him that hateth thee lying under its burden, thou shalt forbear to pass by him; thou shalt be sure to help him get it up." See also Leviticus 19:17–18: "Thou shalt not hate thy brother in thy heart: thou shalt surely rebuke thy neighbor and not bear sin because of him. Thou shalt not take vengeance, nor bear any grudge against the children of thy people, but thou shalt love thy neighbor as thyself. I am the Lord." Again, in the Book of Proverbs 24:17: "When thine enemy falleth do not rejoice, and when he stumbleth let not thine heart rejoice." And Proverbs 25:21: "If thine enemy be hungry, give him bread to eat, and if he be thirsty, give him water to drink."

III. Matthew 10:34: "Think not that I am come to send peace on earth: I came not to send peace, but a sword. For I came to set a man at variance against his father, and the daughter against her mother, and the daughter-in-law against her mother-in-law." The same matter is treated in Luke 12:51.

Thus you see from his own statement that he could not be the Messiah inasmuch as he had not come to bring peace on earth, but a sword. For, regarding the expected Messiah, Zechariah in 9:10, says: "And he will speak peace unto the nations." Concerning that Messianic period it was prophesied by Isaiah in 2:4; and by Micah in 4:3: "Nation shall not lift up the sword against nation, etc."

From his own statement that he will "set a man at variance against his father, etc.," he evidences even more that he was not the Messiah, for in the age of the expected Messiah there will appear the prophet Elijah, concerning whom it is said, Malachai 3:24: "And he shall turn the heart of the fathers to the children, and the heart of the children unto their fathers."

IV. Matthew 13:55–56; it is related here that the Jews said of Jesus: "Is not this the carpenter's son? And is not his mother called Mary, and his brethren James, and Joseph, and Simon, and Judas? And his sisters, are they not all with us?" See also Mark 6:3.

This verse refutes those who believe that Joseph never had any relations with Mary, before or after the birth of Jesus. If this were true, who then gave birth to his brothers and sisters?

V. Matthew 27:46: "And about the ninth hour, Jesus cried with a loud voice, saying, 'Eli, Eli, lama sabachthani?'—that is to say, 'My God! my God! why hast thou forsaken me?'" See the same passage in Mark 15:34.

By this exclamation, Jesus clearly announced that he was not a

God, but was like other mortals, who invoke God in the day of trouble.

BIBLIOGRAPHY

READINGS FOR ADVANCED STUDENTS

Graetz, IV, pp. 646–649.
Mann, J., *Texts and Studies in Jewish History and Literature*, II. See "Isaac ben Abraham Troki" in Index.
Waxman, M., *A History of Jewish Literature*, II, pp. 449–451.
JE, "Polemics and Polemical Literature"; "Troki: Isaac ben Abraham Troki."

ADDITIONAL SOURCE MATERIALS IN ENGLISH

Mocatta, M., *Hizzuk Emunah or Faith Strengthened*. This is a translation, somewhat free in spots, of the famous polemical work of Isaac of Troki. Much of the *Hizzuk Emunah* is also translated in A. Lukyn Williams, *A Manual of Christian Evidences for Jewish People*, 2 vols.

86.

The Notebook of Asher Ben Eliezer Ha-Levi
1598–1634

SOME time before 1635 Asher ben Eliezer Ha-Levi of the town of Reichshofen in Alsace made his last entry in his Hebrew *Book of Memories*. He wrote this personal chronicle to remind himself of what had befallen him and to thank God for all things, whether good or bad. They could not all have been good for he admits that he finally took an oath to drink only at religious ceremonies and to limit his playing to chess and checkers. Occasionally he writes of events affecting Jewry at large. Asher was still a young man when he stopped making entries in his book—he was born in 1598—but even so his life was rather eventful for he lived during the stormy days of the Thirty Years' War (1618–1648).

Three selections from this interesting chronicle are given below. The first tells of his escape from drowning; the second describes a successful effort of Vienna and Prague Jews to save their religious writings from confiscation; and the third tells of Asher's troubles with the local authorities.

1. *A Narrow Escape, 1625*

❡ "Blessed be He who shows loving kindness to the undeserving, for he requited me with every kindness" in the dead of night, on Monday, in the early morning of the 9th of Kislew, 386. [December 8, 1625. This blessing is recited on escape from peril or recovery from illness.] I was riding alone from Pfaffenhofen to Reichshofen, and I was fording the river here, opposite the leper-house, in order to get on to the meadow. But as I climbed onto the shore, which was a little steep, my horse fell backward. My head and the upper half of my body were thrown into the water and mud, the lower half was left sticking in the air, and the waters covered me. If my horse had fallen on me then, there would have been no remedy for me, but God helped and saved me from such a nasty death, for I seized hold of the willows and thus escaped, by the aid of the Creator, Blessed be He, who performs miracles. [Asher was crossing a branch of the Moder when he fell in. He was probably not altogether sober.]

426

11. *Defamation in the Hapsburg Lands, 1626–1627*

❡A scoundrel who had changed his religion made a false accusation against the Jews in the communities of Vienna and Prague, and, as a result of this, from that time on the foundation of Israel, that which sustains it, began to totter in all those lands. For this apostate made a pact with the priesthood, and an order was issued to gather all the holy books of the Jews to a designated spot. It was indeed a time of distress for Israel.

They appealed to the Emperor, but he did not care to listen, saying that he had no opinion in the matter and would have nothing to do with it. This happened in the first part of the year 387 [autumn of 1626].

The Jews prayed to their Father in heaven, and He prompted the Jewish leaders to travel to the Pope, to the city of Rome, where he gave them the very letters they wished to the Emperor [Ferdinand II, 1619–1637] and to the clergy, in order to defeat the evil designs of the enemy. When the oppressor [the apostate] heard of this he ran away and fled for his life. May the Lord frustrate all the devices of the crafty! I heard the good news in the month of Adar, 387 [February-March, 1627], and according to rumor, if he had not fled he would have been burnt to ashes. But God will execute His vengeance upon him.

111. *Trouble with the Local Officials, 1629*

❡"Surely the Lord's mercies are not consumed, surely his compassions fail not [Lamentations 3:22]." On Wednesday, the 24th of Ellul, 389 [September 12, 1629], that wretch, Jacob von Wangen, our overseer, came here to Reichshofen. He sent for me and said: "What have you done? Who allowed you to move without permission from your house on the other side of the brook to this large house? In the second place, you have deceived me, for you know that it is written in your charters that no Jew may lend a Christian more than twenty florins without authority from the overseer. Now why have you lent the Christian, Wagners Tiebold, thirty-six florins without permission?" [According to the Strasbourg constitution of 1613, the overseer was right: Asher had violated the law.]

None of my excuses helped because he was looking for a pretext to hurt me. The upshot of the matter was that he ordered me to clear out of the house within two days, and the amount of the debt itself was to go to the rulers. In addition I was to pay a fine of ten florins. I begged for mercy a number of times, but it was no use, and I went home with a broken heart. I didn't have any more strength and I wept bitterly, for the loss of my livelihood—God forbid—was involved. However, after this, though my heart was faint, I gave thanks to the Cause of all causes, and I ascribed the fault to my great sins, and not to my bad luck, for the Jewish people are not dependent on luck [Shabbat 156a].

My father-in-law—long may he live—exerted himself on my behalf with the result that on Friday, close to Sabbath eve, the matter was settled and my sorrow was turned to joy and happiness, for the overseer went back on his original decision. Of course, only after having been bribed two thalers!

Blessed be the Lord God who bestoweth loving kindness on the undeserving. "The voice is the voice of Jacob [but the hands are the hands of Esau." Genesis 27:22. A dig at *Jacob*, the overseer, who was placated only after his *hands* had received a bribe].

BIBLIOGRAPHY

READINGS FOR ADVANCED STUDENTS

Graetz, IV, pp. 700–708; Margolis and Marx, pp. 547–550.

Grunwald, M., *Vienna* (Jewish Communities Series). "The Second Community," pp. 75–112, throws light on the economic, cultural, and political life of a typical seventeenth century Jewish community in Central Europe.

JE, "Alsace"; "Disabilities"; "Prague"; "Vienna."

87.

Seventeenth Century Memoirs

JEWISH memoirs of any length appear for the first time in the seventeenth century. They constitute valuable sources for an understanding of the personal life of the ordinary individual, his petty quarrels, his vices, his ideals, his relation to his fellowmen. They thus present a picture of the life of the average Jew.

The first group of extracts given below is taken from the memoirs of Joseph of Sienna in Italy. This Joseph, who was born about the beginning of the seventeenth century, was a trader, dealing in old clothes, remnants, and the like. He also did considerable trading in costumes used at the carnival season. He seems to have been an unusually quarrelsome fellow and probably wrote down these Italian memoirs to keep his grudges fresh in his mind. Not every Jew who lived in the ghetto was of heroic stature.

The second group of extracts is taken from the autobiography of a young Jew born in Meseritsch, Moravia, in 1668. His biography, written in a poor Hebrew, covers the first seventeen years of what must have been a very undistinguished and unhappy life. Our Moravian hero, who incidentally forgets to tell us what his name is, describes in some detail the economic struggles of his parents and his own commendable efforts to attain an education.

1. *The Troubles of Joseph of Sienna, 1625–1632*

❡I record how, in the year 1625, the Grand Duke came to Sienna, and Messer Abraham Pesaro and Messer Buonaventura Gallichi were appointed to collect the levy [in kind for the entertainment of the Grand Duke]. From me, they demanded a pair of sheets, a bed-canopy, a blanket, and a pillow—twice as much as they imposed upon any one else. I gave them everything they asked, but the said Abraham thrice threw what I gave into the middle of the street with great contumely and derision, telling me that it was not enough, and that they desired better stuff. The said articles were however worth more than ten *scudi*.

At the same time, in order to increase my dishonor and harm, they sent the constables and ordered them to distrain upon me, and not to accept the aforementioned goods. In this matter I received more consideration from the court than from them, for they accepted the same articles and did not distrain upon me, though they fined me one *lira*. The aforementioned Abraham boasted many times of this contumely. I have put it all on record, in order to remember both pleasure and displeasure. . . .

I record how, in the month of July, 1632, I purchased from Chichio, the ragman, several pieces of second-hand black damask, in the presence of Moses Galletti and Prospero Arcidosso, who at that period were working for Abraham Pelagrili in the shop beneath my house, which I had let to him. The said Moses and Prospero said that they wanted a share, since I had made the purchase in the doorway. So as not to quarrel, I replied that if they gave me the money which it cost, I would let them have it. They agreed, and told me to wait for the said Abraham Pelagrili, who would either give me the money, or else let me keep it for myself. I was willing, and waited until the said Abraham came. When he arrived and I asked him whether he wanted the said damask, he replied that he wanted to see it first. Although there was no need for me to show him it until he gave me the money it cost, I let him see it in order to content him. He said that he did not want it, and left it to me.

Some days after, I cut the said damask at the bench in my shop. The said Abraham, who was present, robbed me of a piece, and had it cut into a number of caps by a Jew from Rome named Messer Lazaro de Importanza, and had them made up by him. On the day of the Madonna of the Tower, on the . . . . 1632, he showed me one of these caps, already made of this same damask. I immediately recognized my stuff, and asked him where he had got the said damask. He refused, and would not tell me; whereat I replied that I certainly would not give it back to him until he told me from whom he had received it, since at the same time there had been stolen from me a taffeta riband worked with silver, a bonnet, and other articles.

He then told me that he had bought it from Prospero Arcidosso. I thereupon informed him that I wished to show it to the said Prospero, and know from him whether he had sold it to him, and that then I would give him back the cap. So, finding the said Prospero, I asked him whether it was true that he had sold the said damask to the said Abraham. He immediately replied to the same Abraham and said: "Abraham here came to find me, and told me to tell you that I had sold it to him, and I answered him that I would not say such a thing, because it was not true, for I have not sold him anything. But I was present when you were cutting up this damask on your counter, and I saw a piece fall down, and he ran to pick it up, and had three caps made out of it." When I heard this, I said to the said Abraham: "I will not give you the cap back because it is my property, and it is not true that you bought it from Prospero, as you said." He tried to force it out of my hand, and we came to blows, and we were divided, and I kept the cap.

While matters were at this stage, the said Abraham Pelagrili with his father [Solomon] and his brother Joseph accosted me in the evening, at the time of the afternoon service, and laid hands on me, saying: "Give me back my cap, or else I will get it out of you in blood!" To which I replied: "If it were your cap, I would have given it back, but, because it is my stuff, I will never do so." Seeing all three of them on me, I backed into the shop of Messer Samuel Nissim, and took from the man a pair of scissors and struck the said Abraham in the breast with them, saying: "Keep back, and do not come all three of you on to me!"

Feeling the scissors at his breast, he cried out: "I am a dead man," and threw himself to the ground, but it had not done him any harm at all. Fearing that I had wounded him, I turned back towards San Martino. They caught me up six yards from San Martino, and Abraham and his father held me, and Joseph his brother struck me behind with a knife, and wounded me to death.

I stayed in bed for twenty-three days, with a physician and two surgeons. Prospero Arcidosso and Moses Galletti gave evidence unfavorable to me, saying that it was neither Abraham nor Solomon his father, but Moses his brother. They said this because Moses was under age, and could not be punished. But it was in no wise true that it was Moses, and they testified falsely; and that wound cost me upwards of twenty *scudi*.

11. *Boyhood in Moravia, 1663–1681*

❡My grandfather, Jacob Ha-Levi, was then rich and prosperous. My grandmother [Lieble], his wife, was very pious and charitable, and went every morning and evening to the synagogue; and so was my mother Gnendel even in a higher degree; she was, moreover, a very intelligent woman. My father continued to study the Torah. Three or four years after the wedding, in the winter [of 1663], the Mohammedans and Tatars swept over Moravia to destroy it, and all fled in confusion and terror to Bohemia. My grandfather, who was a rich man, lost nearly all his property, so that but very little of their fortune remained in their hands. My grandfather, his wife, two daughters, and my father and mother with the rest of the family remained in Bohemia.

They finally came to Lichtenstadt, where my father secured a post as an elementary Hebrew teacher. He remained there for a few years; then he returned and found his house entirely empty. My mother then showed her ability in supporting the family by her own efforts, and started to manufacture brandy out of oats in a copper alembic, as was the custom in those parts. This was hard labor, but she succeeded. In the meantime, my father pursued his studies.

One day a holy man, Loeb, the Rabbi of Trebitsch, whose authority extended over Meseritsch, where my father lived, came to our town and stayed in our house. [Aryeh Loeb, later chief rabbi of Moravia, died 1684.] When he saw the troubles of my mother, his cousin, he had pity on her, and gave my father some gold and silver merchandise, such as rings, to get him used to trade in an honest and intelligent way. My father was successful and did a good business. Incidentally this brought him the acquaintance of the Count who owned the city. The latter liked him, and turned over to him the distillery in which they were working with eight great kettles, and he gave him servants to do the work and grain to prepare brandy. For this my father paid him at the end of the year a specified amount, in addition to paying a certain percentage of the income in taxes, as was customary. From that time he became prominent. My mother bore him first a daughter who died, then three sons, my rich and prominent brother Kalman, my poor self, and a son Moses, who died during the year after his mother's death.

When my mother was at last able to rest from her hard work, she fell sick in consequence of the heat and the fumes of the brandy, and she died at the age of thirty-four years. May her merit sustain us in all our troubles, for there was no one in our town or outside of it who was like her in wisdom, piety, and charity. She died on a Sabbath, the 24th of Iyyar, 5432 [May 21, 1672]. I was then four years old, and my older brother seven.

In the course of the next year my father married again a great lady, Freidel, the daughter of Meir, the shohet [the ritual-slaughterer] from Vienna. At the same time my father gave his sister Pessel to his brother-in-law, Samuel [son of Meir] for a wife, so that they made an exchange. The wife of my father was herself still a young child who did not know how to bring us up in cleanliness as is necessary with little boys, nor could she properly care for us when we were sick. We have to thank God and the help of our paternal grandmother Lieble, and her good daughters, that we grew up at all. Even so Moses, who was only one year old, died.

After my mother's death my father began to strive for prominence and power, for as long as my mother lived she kept him back and reproved him as a mother does with her son. . . . Now the Count sold his property after three years and went to war against the enemies in foreign lands. He left my father in the hands of another Count who had bought the town; but the latter was not as favorable to my father as the former. My father thought it was the other way, and he relied on a broken reed [the new Count] to combat his enemies, Jews. These, however, were numerous and more cunning and deliberate, for my father at that time was hasty in all his actions, and sometimes transacted his business without taking proper counsel and consideration, and he planned great undertakings to increase his wealth and honor, but it turned out the other way.

His enemies ruined his reputation with the Count. The latter made charges against him in connection with the distillery and other business matters, and put him into prison for two months. Since the first Count was far away, nothing could be done to save my father, and he had to give up half his wealth in order to be released. On this occasion his enemies wreaked their revenge on him, saying [Shabbat 32a]: "when the ox has fallen, sharpen the knife"; and they urged the Count to expel my father, together with his old father Jacob, from his property. The Count did so. He expelled my father in Tammuz, 5435 [July, 1675], while my grandfather fled with my grandmother in secret, for he owed money to many Gentiles and could not pay. I was at that time seven years old.

My father found a temporary shelter in the town of Humpoletz, a town of wool-weavers, and he traded there for a year, while I was cut off from study and good deeds and left to myself. He then went to a village, Wostrow [?], for the Count had in the meantime returned from the military expedition and bought this village, and my father followed him there.

As for myself, I was constantly going back in my studies as well as in manners and conduct. After a while my father decided to send me to Prague, which was a day's journey. My older brother was also there; it was winter then, and I was nine years old. There, too, I did nothing, for my father did not know how to arrange matters properly, and in his endeavor to save money he placed me for a small sum in charge of a teacher, who took little care of me, while I needed great attention if I were to be taught with any success.

At that time my power of comprehension and my memory were weak as a result of illness. I was full of ulcers, and the meals I ate were very unwholesome for me, for it is the custom in Prague to eat at the midday meal peas and millet with a little butter, which proved very injurious to me. But nobody looked out for me to give me medical treatment. Although my father came several times to Prague he did not notice this. I gratefully remember Loeb Fleckeles, who gave me meals in his house and kept me for about six months for a small sum, my father paying him about six gulden a month. He wished me to be a companion for his son Simon, who was then five years old, and I helped him by taking him to school and going over his lessons with him.

At that time I was very humble and ready to be a slave to everybody, and to do anything I was ordered. If my father only had left me in this house, I would have become used to good manners and learned a little more than in the village of Wostrow among the country people. My father, however, wished to save money and took me home; my older brother was there at the time also. He thought that he himself would teach us; and my brother, who was thirteen or fourteen years old, actually learned from him haggadic literature, such as Rashi and *Midrashim*, as well as the laws of *shehitah* [ritual slaughter], but I needed a special teacher. My father started to teach me Gemara Sotah once or twice, though I had never before studied Talmud or even Mishnah.

Thus a long time passed by without my learning anything, until I became a thorn in my own eyes and even more so in the eyes of my father, because I was a boor brought up in dirt without any cleanliness, for the lack of a mother; and I remember that at the age of eleven I ran around barefooted and without trousers, and no one cared. My father then had many little children, for his wife bore him almost every year a son or a daughter. I am sure that if anybody had announced my death to him at that time he would have thought this good news, for he considered me ignorant and good for nothing, so that my existence was a burden to him. My brother was a strong boy who did hard work in the slaughter-house and made himself otherwise useful, while I was oppressed by all the members of the house; everybody ordered me around. . . .

In this winter [1680–1681] my father made great profits, and was successful in all his transactions with various kinds of merchandise. From my own impulse I made up my mind to go to some Jewish community to study Torah, for I was ignorant; and God had shown great kindness to us [by granting prosperity]. My father promised, but did not keep his word; I often saw guests come [with whom my father went away] and he had promised to take me with him to Moravia, but he changed his mind. This happened several times, and the obstacle was that the necessary clothing for me was not ready, as no one looked upon me with kindness. My father's wife [my stepmother] had her hands full with her own little ones.

One night before my father was to leave I was awake the whole night sewing for myself sheepskins which are called *Pelz*, and I made a kind of a long gown for underwear, and something for my feet. I took secretly some shirts so that my father should not notice anything, and before daybreak I went to the place where the sleigh was prepared for my father, and stayed there.

When he came it was still dark before daylight, and when he noticed me he thought the house-dog was there, and he wanted to kick him away. I then said: "Father, this is thy son who is ready to serve thee on the way which I take in order to study." There were many strangers present, business men who had come to buy wool. They saw my good resolve, though I was very young [twelve years old], and urged my father to take me along; they were sure I would become a great scholar and a good man. My father then answered that it was impossible to take me along, for I had no proper clothing and it was very cold. I then showed my cleverness, how I had prepared for myself everything necessary for the journey. He finally agreed and took me along; but the cold was so severe that several times I thought I was going to die; the snow was falling and the wind blew it into our faces, and it caused my father great pain. . . . But [Pesahim 8b] those who are travelling for the fulfillment of a *Mizwah* [meritorious act] suffer no harm, and we reached Herschmanik.

BIBLIOGRAPHY

READINGS FOR ADVANCED STUDENTS

Grunwald, M., *Vienna* (Jewish Communities Series). The social life of the Jew in Hapsburg Vienna of the seventeenth century is described in "The Second Community," pp. 75–112.

Roth, C., *Venice* (Jewish Communities Series). A description of Italian Jewish social life of the seventeenth century may be found on pp. 72–244.

ADDITIONAL SOURCE MATERIALS IN ENGLISH

Lowenthal, M., *The Memoirs of Glückel of Hameln*. This autobiography throws a great deal of light on economic and social conditions in north and central Germany of the second half of the seventeenth century.

Maimon, S., *Solomon Maimon: an Autobiography*. A comparison of the boy-hood days of Maimon in eighteenth century Poland with our Moravian hero of the seventeenth would be most instructive.

Marx, A., "A Seventeenth-Century Autobiography," *JQR*, N. S., VIII (1917–1918), pp. 269–304. An autobiography of a seventeenth century Moravian student of which part has been cited above:

Roth, C., "The Memoirs of a Siennese Jew (1625–1633)," *Hebrew Union College Annual*, V (1928), pp. 353–402. Two incidents of this auto-biography have been reprinted above.

88.

Leon of Modena on Jewish Languages and Money-Lenders
1616

ABOUT 1616 Leon of Modena (1571–1648), the cultured rabbi of Venice, wrote an elementary survey of Jewish life and customs for some of his Christian friends. This was the Italian *Historia de gli riti hebraici* which was first printed in 1637 and proved so popular that it was translated into English, French, Dutch, Latin, and Hebrew. The English translation (1707) by Simon Ockley was called *The History of the Present Jews throughout the World.*

This work was one of the first attempts of a Jew to give non-Jews an uncolored and accurate picture of Jewish custom, ceremonial, and thinking, and it was accepted as such for centuries by Christian scholars and statesmen.

The following selections from this small but interesting work describe the languages of the Jews and their reasons for engaging in money-lending.

I. OF THEIR LANGUAGE, PRONUNCIATION, WRITING, AND PREACHING

❡ There are but few Jews now-a-days that can maintain a continued discourse in Hebrew, or the Holy Language, which they call *leshon ha-kodesh,* in which the twenty-four books of the Old Testament are written; nor yet in the Chaldee [Aramaic], or *Targum,* which was their common language whilst they were a people, because they have learned and are brought up in the language of the country where they are born. So that in Italy they speak Italian, in Germany High-Dutch [German], in the Levant and in Barbary [North Africa] they speak Turkish or Morisco [Berber], etc.

Nay, they have made these exotick languages so much their own, that a great many which have removed out of Germany into Poland, Hungary, and Russia have made the High-Dutch the mother-tongue to all their posterity; and those Jews that go out of Spain into the Levant for the most part speak Spanish. In Italy they speak both the one and the other, according to the place from whence their parents came. [This High-Dutch is now Yiddish; the Spanish is called Ladino.] So that the common people use in their ordinary discourse the language of the nation they dwell in, mixing now and then a few broken Hebrew words among it. The learned men among them have the Scripture more ready, but there are but very few except the Rabbins that can maintain a continued discourse in the Hebrew tongue elegantly and according to its due propriety.

As for the pronunciation of the Hebrew, they differ so much among themselves that the German Jews can scarce be understood by the Italians and Levantines; but there are none of them that speak more clearly and agreeably to the rules of grammar, which they call *dikduk*, than the Italians.

The Hebrew tongue being of so narrow a compass (for there are no ancient books now left except the XXIV of the Scriptures, out of which they must take all), the Rabbins have for greater convenience enlarged it by making use of a greal deal of the Chaldee, and some small matter of the Greek and other languages. And besides, they have coined a great many names for things, which has been imitated since by writers in every age, who have borrowed necessary terms of art, to render themselves intelligible, when they talk of philosophy and other sciences. [Through the rabbinical Hebrew, composed of Hebrew, Aramaic, Greek, etc., the Jews could express themselves in all the arts and sciences.]

This sort of rabbinical Hebrew they use in their books, in their contracts, in their private notes, in their publick business, etc. But in their familiar [personal] letters, either of compliment or business, they write most commonly in the language of the country where they live, only some of them use the Hebrew character [script]. Only the Jews of the Morea [the southern peninsula of Greece] write all in Hebrew.

When they preach, they use the language of the country that all the congregation may understand them. They quote the texts of Scripture and the Rabbins in Hebrew, and then interpret it in the vulgar tongue.

Their manner of preaching is: When all the congregation are silent in the synagogue, he that is to preach (which is easily granted to any one that desires it), either with his *talit* [praying-shawl] or without it, stands against the little wooden table. . . . and begins with a verse taken out of the lesson which is read that week, which they call a *noseh*, a text, which he seconds with a sentence out of the Rabbins, called *maamar*. Then he makes a preamble or preface, and proposes a subject pertinent to the lesson whence he took his text; he discourses upon it, and quotes texts of Scripture and the Rabbins, every man according to his own stile, which is very different among the several countries.

This is done mostly upon Sabbath days and the chief festivals, except there be a funeral-oration for some person of note (which is done upon any day, tho' it be no festival) or some other extraordinary occasion.

II. OF THEIR TRADING AND USURY

⟨They are obliged, not only by the laws of Moses, but by the Oral [rabbinic] Law also, to be exact in their dealings, and not defraud or cheat any one, let him be who he will, either Jew or Gentile, observing at all times and towards all persons those good rules of dealing which are so frequently commanded them in the Scripture, especially in Leviticus 19 from verse eleven to the end. ["Ye shall not steal, etc."]

As for that which some have spread abroad, both in discourse and writing, viz., that the Jews take an oath every day to cheat some Christian, and reckon it a good work: it is a manifest untruth, published to render them more odious than they are. So far is it from that, that many rabbies have written—particularly, one Rabbi Bahya has made a long discourse about it in his book intitled *Kad Ha-Kemah* ["Flour Jar"], letter *gimel*, *gezelah*, where he says—that it is much greater sin to cheat one that is not a Jew, than one that is, both upon the account that the thing is bad in itself, and because the scandal is greater. [Bahya ben Asher, d. 1340, was a Spanish cabalist and Bible-commentator.] And this they call *hillul ha-shem*, that is, prophaning the Name of God, which is one of the greatest sins. Therefore if there are any found among them [those] that cheat or defraud, it ought to be attributed to the ill disposition of that particular person, for no such practice is in any wise allowed, either by their laws or Rabbins.

'Tis very true, that the narrowness of their circumstances which their long captivity has reduced them to; and their being almost everywhere prohibited to purchase lands or to use several sorts of merchandizes, and other creditable and gainful employments, has debased their spirits, and made them degenerate from their ancient Israelitish sincerity.

For the same reason, they have allowed themselves the liberty to take usury [interest], notwithstanding it is said in Deuteronomy 23:20: "Unto a stranger thou may'st lend upon usury, but unto thy brother thou shalt not lend upon usury." In which place, the Jews cannot understand by the word "stranger" any other besides these seven [pagan] nations, the Hittites, Amorites, Jebusites, etc., which God had commanded to be destroyed by the sword. But because they [the Jews] are not suffered to use the same means of getting a living as others which are brethren by nature, they pretend they may do it lawfully. [If the Jews had other ways of making a living they would not lend out money at interest.]

And of these seven [pagan] nations only are all those passages of the Rabbins to be understood, where they give any allowance to use any extortion (because it was so often declared in Scripture), and not of those people among which the Jews are now planted and suffered to dwell, and are used kindly by the princes of the countries, especially amongst the Christians; because this would not only be against the written [Law], but also against the law of nature.

BIBLIOGRAPHY

REFERENCES TO TEXTBOOKS

Elbogen, pp. 99–101; Sachar, pp. 199, 255–258.

READINGS FOR ADVANCED STUDENTS

Graetz, V, pp. 65–74; Margolis and Marx, pp. 510–511; see also "usury" in Index.

Abrahams, I., *Jewish Life in the Middle Ages*, 1932, pp. 256–264 on usury.

Loewe, H., "On Usury," The Jewish Historical Society of England, *Starrs and Jewish Charters Preserved in the British Museum*, II, xcvff. A scholarly excursus on the subject of usury.

Roth, C., *Venice* (Jewish Communities Series). See "Modena, Leone da," in Index.

Waxman, M., *A History of Jewish Literature*, II. See "Judah Leon de Modena" in Index. See pp. 613ff. for Yiddish.

Catholic Encyclopedia, "Usury."

JE, "Banking"; "Judaeo-German"; "Judaeo-Spanish Language and Literature"; "Leon (Judah Aryeh) of Modena"; "Usury."

ADDITIONAL SOURCE MATERIALS IN ENGLISH

Ockley, S., *The History of the Present Jews throughout the World*, 1707. This is a translation of Leon of Modena's famous work on the Jewish people and their customs.

89.

A Letter of Baruch Reiniger, a Butcher,
Prague, November 22, 1619

ON Friday afternoon, November 22, 1619, about a year and a half after the Thirty Years' War had begun in central Europe, the Jews of Prague sent off a batch of letters—most of which had just been written—to the city of Vienna. The mail bag was seized and the letters stored in the archives, and it was not until the twentieth century that they finally saw the light of day. Thus we now have the opportunity of studying Jewish life in its reality and essence, for these letters are truly personal and not written for publication. Practically all were written in Yiddish—German with an admixture of Hebrew—then the mother-tongue of Jews from Alsace east to the Russian border.

The following letter was written by Baruch Reiniger of Prague, who was in the meat business, to his son-in-law, Mr. Falk, in Vienna. As in most Yiddish letters of that time, there is a very liberal sprinkling of pious Hebrew phrases which were repeated mechanically.

℀To be given to my dearly beloved and pleasant son-in-law—who fears sin and all whose deeds are worthy—the respected Mr. Falk.

He who delivers this letter on him be blessing.
From the holy community of Prague.

Because of the approaching Sabbath I will write briefly. May there be only joy and happiness to my dearly beloved and pleasant son-in-law—he who fears sin and all whose deeds are worthy—namely, to the respected Mr. Falk—long may he live; and to my daughter, your wife, the charming, modest Dame Sarel—long may she live—who is like a perfect burnt-offering; and to your sons—long may they live—with whom God has graced you. Let me mention each one by name: the honored Ichel—long may he live—and the honored David—long may he live.

Important things come first. I am glad to announce the good tidings that we are well and I hope that it will so continue for all generations. Further, dear son-in-law and my dear child, I want to tell you that I got your letter through the messenger, and I can now realize that for a long time you did not get my letters, for I have written you several times and never got an answer from you. [It was difficult to get letters through in war time.]

I wrote you that Traune [Sarel's sister] is now engaged—may she have good luck—and is getting a fine young man. He is the son of my brother Abram's wife's brother. His father's name was Leb and his name is Hosea. He owns part of a house, has a stand in the *Tendel* market [the market for old clothes and odds and ends], and a shop in the meat market. I am to give 250 [gulden?] as a dowry. May the good Lord see that I get it!

She has been engaged since after *Shabuot* and, God willing, she is going to be married on *Hanukkah*—may it come auspiciously— together with your auntie's daughter.

May the good Lord help us, I thought surely I could get something from you, for you know my financial condition, and I've gotten in so deep—may the good Lord get me out of it. Furthermore I want you to know that I have just spent a great deal on my children—long may they live. They were all sick, some with the pestilence and others with the smallpox; all sick at the same time, and Traune sickest of all. But the good Lord had compassion so that nothing happened to any of them. Well, now, shall I write you any more news; what's the use, dear child? [Baruch wants to borrow money from his son-in-law to pay the dowry to Hosea.]

Traune is very anxious that you shan't forget her when she has her wedding. However I'll still have to owe Hosea the half of the dowry until the good Lord helps me again. [Sometimes a bridegroom would not marry unless the whole dowry was paid in advance.]

With this I shall stop this time. May the good Lord save you from every distress. This is the supplication of your father-in-law and your father, Baruch, who is known as Baruch Reiniger Btzarn [?], the son of my respected father Juda, of blessed memory. Regards to your father and mother—long may they live—and all your dear ones. My wife and children—long may they live—all send their regards. Dear children, don't hold my bad writing against me. In my haste I have written this in my shop in the meat market.

BIBLIOGRAPHY

READINGS FOR ADVANCED STUDENTS

Abrahams, I., *Jewish Life in the Middle Ages*, 1932, Chap. ix, "Love and Courtship"; Chap. x, "Marriage Customs."

Grunwald, M., *Vienna* (Jewish Communities Series). For a picture of Vienna in the time of Baruch Reiniger, see pp. 75ff.

90.

Ten Commandments for the Married Woman
before 1620

MOST of the Jewish literature of the Middle Ages is written in Hebrew, but inasmuch as many Jews did not understand their ancient tongue, books were written for them in Judaeo-German, that is, Yiddish. Most of these Yiddish books were written for women, although some were also prepared for the average man.

Sometime before 1620, Isaac ben Eliakim of Posen, a Polish Jew who later lived in Prague, wrote a Yiddish ethical work which he called *Leb Tob* ("A good heart"). The purpose of this scholar was to teach the average man and woman the basic laws and moral principles of Judaism and to encourage a more fervent spirit in the heart of the worshipper. He was successful, for his book was very widely read in the Germanic and Slavonic lands; it went through at least nineteen editions in less than a hundred years.

The following selection is taken from the chapter on marriage. It reflects the attitude of his generation toward the duties of a Jewish wife to her husband.

❪This is the story of a queen who gave her daughter in marriage to a young king and then gave her the following instructions, inasmuch as she was about to be married. Since she was sending the daughter away for her marriage she said to her: "My dear child, I am giving you away and am turning you over to a stranger, and I don't know what sort of a person he is, so I am going to instruct you and give you ten rules. If you keep my instruction everything will be well with you, but if you don't heed my advice, things won't go right with you. Therefore take these ten rules to heart and think of them day and night, early and late, and if you do this your husband will love you as he does the heart in his body.

"The first, my dear daughter, is to beware of his anger, lest you enrage him. When he is cross, don't you be jolly; and when he is jolly, don't you be cross; and when he is angry, smile at him and answer him with kind, soft words and speak pleasantly to him. Thus you will still his anger.

"The second, my dear daughter, concerns his eating and drinking.

Search and consider and reflect about his food, about that which he likes to eat, and let these be your words: 'My lord, wouldn't you rather have something else to eat?' Urge him. Try to have his meals ready at the proper time, for hunger does nobody any good. When he comes home and doesn't find his meal ready at the proper time, he'll get angry. Should he have gotten drunk, don't tell him what he did, or what he said in his drunkenness; and if he tells you to drink, you drink, but don't drink yourself drunk, lest he should see you in such a state and learn to hate you.

"The third, my dear daughter. When he sleeps, guard his sleep that he not be awakened, for if he doesn't get a good night's rest he may become very angry.

"The fourth, my dear daughter. Try to be thrifty and careful with your husband's money and make an effort not to bring any loss to him. Don't give anything away without your husband's knowledge, unless it be a small thing which he wouldn't care about.

"The fifth, my dear daughter. Don't be anxious to know his secrets; and if you should know anything of his secrets don't confide them to any one in the whole world; and those things, also, which he boasts about to you, tell to absolutely no one.

"The sixth, my dear daughter. Find out whom he likes and like that person, too, and him whom he dislikes, you dislike, too. Don't like his enemies, and don't hate his friends.

"The seventh, my dear daughter. Don't be contrary with him. Do everything he tells you. If he tells you anything, let his words find favor with you. Don't say to him: 'You haven't said the right thing,' or 'My advice is better than your advice.'

"The eighth, my dear daughter. Don't expect of him anything that he considers difficult. He may take a dislike to you because you expect something of him which he believes is too hard.

"The ninth, my dear daughter. Heed the requests which he may make of you, awaiting in turn that he will love you if you do so, and will be your slave and will serve you with joy.

"The tenth, my dear daughter. Be very careful to guard against jealousy. Don't make him jealous in any way. Don't say anything that might hurt him, and let him have his own way in everything. Make an effort in all things to do what pleases him and don't do what he doesn't like. If you treat him like a king then he, in turn, will treat you like a queen.

"Now, my dear daughter, take these ten rules of instruction with you as your provision and let them be as a reminder to you throughout all your life."

BIBLIOGRAPHY

READINGS FOR ADVANCED STUDENTS

Abrahams, I., *Jewish Life in the Middle Ages*, 1932, Chap. vii, "Monogamy and the Home"; Chap. viii, "Home Life (Continued)."

Freehof, S. B., "Devotional Literature in the Vernacular," *Yearbook: Central Conference of American Rabbis*, XXXIII (1923), pp. 375–415.

The Jewish Library, Third Series, ed. by Leo Jung, 1934. This series of essays concerns itself with the Jewish woman throughout the ages. There is much material here—including a bibliography—for a detailed picture of the medieval Jewess.

Schechter, S., *Studies in Judaism*, First Series, 1896, Chap. xiii, "Women in Temple and Synagogue."

Waxman, M., *A History of Jewish Literature*, II, Chap. xii, "Judaeo-German Literature."

JE, "Husband and Wife"; "Judaeo-German Literature"; "Marriage."

91.

The Barbers' Guild at Cracow
Poland, 1639

THERE are records of Jewish guilds in Alexandria and Asia Minor as far back as the days of the old Roman Empire; and during the Middle Ages, too, Jewish craftsmen banded together into associations in a number of the Mediterranean lands. The older guilds were concerned primarily with charitable and religious activities; the newer ones, beginning with the seventeenth century, especially in Poland, with the attempt to improve their economic status, particularly by controlling competition. Their policy was: "live and let live"—for members. In this as in most other respects the Jewish guilds closely patterned themselves after their Christian models.

Jews formed their own associations through necessity. As Jews they could not participate in the religious life of the Christian guilds. Moreover, the latter made every attempt to limit the practice of their trades to Christians alone, but they were not successful, for Jewish guilds arose and were grudgingly tolerated by the Christian craftsmen, accepted by the state, and recognized by the Jewish community-council. These guilds, however, played no real significant role in the economic life of the Jewish group.

The following account describes the organization of the Jewish master-barbers in Cracow in 1639. Although but seven in number they organized along guild lines. Barbers in those days—unlike their modern successors—did considerable minor surgical work. The striped barber-pole, which still survives, symbolizes the bandaged, bleeding arm, and is reminiscent of the surgical work barbers once performed. In Cracow, as in other towns, there were trained Jewish physicians as well as male nurses. The barbers occupied a place somewhere between the two. Jewish barbers did not as a rule solicit Christian trade, for the Council of Four Lands objected, fearing that blood-letting would lay open the Jews to the charge of ritual-murder.

The following selection, originally in Hebrew, is taken from the archives of the Jewish community-council of Cracow. The Jewish council, by incorporating these laws into its records, made their provisions mandatory for every Jew in the city.

❡Whereas the association of barbers has noticed apprentices breaking away from their masters and considering themselves equal in knowledge to competent physicians, with the result that a great deal of distress has been caused by them, for they have endangered the lives of people through their blood-letting and their healing of bruises and wounds—for these apprentices are inexperienced in this important work since they have not served under good, competent physicians, but have based their work only upon their limited, confused intelligence—and whereas they also hurt competent tax-paying physicians and make it impossible for them to make a living and to support their families [the barbers here call themselves physicians];

Therefore, the following seven law-abiding master-barbers, Sender the barber [who was also the Jewish communal physician for the poor], Shmerl the barber, his brother, Hirsch, Hayyim the barber, Moses the barber—may his Rock and Redeemer guard him—and Jehiel the barber, have agreed—and have actually shaken hands and have made a binding compact—to affirm and to maintain in the most effective way possible everything that is specified below, as if executed in the presence of the highest court, and as if approved by the chief officials and the town-council itself, namely:

1. First, they are obligated to make a weekly collection for charity among their members, receiving as much as the generous instincts of each one prompt him to give. [This money might be used for the widows and orphans of guild members.]

2. No barber may keep in his shop more than one apprentice to teach the trade to. This apprentice must bind himself for three successive years. [In the third year the apprentice became a journeyman and was paid. Before this he probably got his board only.] During the first two years the apprentice shall under no circumstance be permitted to bleed a patient; and even in the third year he shall not be allowed to let blood except when his master is at his side. This is in order that he may practice and accustom himself to the work properly, and not faint or become slip-shod in his profession.

3. Each barber may, as is the custom, engage another apprentice as a partner who is to get one-third of the profits. However, such an apprentice may be employed only on the specific condition that the majority of the members of the above-mentioned association agree to allow him to become a partner; and once the majority of the members of the association have agreed upon him then none of them may, whether by an offer of money or by verbal inducements, coax him away. This same prohibition applies to the apprentice who

has bound himself for three years. Whoever among the barbers violates this prohibition is required to give, as an unquestioned obligation, one old-*thaler* to charity, not to mention other severe penalties which will be imposed upon him. [Money received from fines was usually applied to the expenses of the guild.]

4. They have also agreed that all the apprentices who bind themselves to work in a barber shop—whether as an apprentice for three years or as a partner in the manner stated above—are compelled, first of all, to obligate and record themselves in the minute-books of the Jewish community to the effect that they will not marry a local girl, in order not to cast additional burdens on the people of this community—may their Rock and their Redeemer guard them! [An apprentice was too poor to support a wife.] If any one of these apprentices will not obligate himself in the matter described above, it will then be absolutely forbidden any barber, under threat of the most severe penalties, to keep him in his employ even a single day.

5. The above mentioned barbers have also bound themselves not to raise prices and thus impose a burden upon the people of our community, but will accept the fee that people have been accustomed of old to pay for blood-letting, cupping, hair cutting, and the healing of bruises and wounds, so as not to give rise to any complaint against themselves on the part of the people of our community. On the other hand they will not cheapen or lower—God forbid—their fees by being too liberal, and foregoing that which is their just due by accepting less than one *Groschen* net from every one for cupping. Whoever will transgress by treating the matter of fees lightly will always have to give to charity, as an unquestioned obligation, a half a gulden, not to mention other punishments, and both he and any one he may send will be prevented from doing any more work.

6. The barbers have also agreed that if a member of the community should happen to call in a barber just for a short time and not be satisfied with him, and then take another in his place, the second is not permitted to begin his service until the customer pays the first barber for the work he has done and performed. And under no circumstance is the second barber permitted to cast any aspersions on the first colleague or to vaunt himself at his expense. It goes without saying that one barber should not poach upon the preserves of another, under threat of a fine which the officers and judges of the community will impose upon him. [The wife and children of a barber would sometimes steal customers away from his competitor.]

7. If it should happen that a householder summons two barbers

at the same time, then if both arrive together while the wound is still open, they must share the fee and the expenses equally. If, however, one arrived first and closed the wound, the second barber is expected to leave the home of the patient immediately.

8. The barbers have also agreed that if a competent barber who does not belong to our community should settle in our midst, and even though he be acceptable to the entire community, but if he should not be willing to bind himself by a hard and fast pact to accept all the rules above recorded, then the barbers are bound to uphold one another in opposing that man. [Both Christian and Jewish guilds opposed any one's practicing their trade unless a member of the guild.] They will employ every possible means to prevent him from doing his work until he submit to the observance and performance of all the above mentioned prescriptions without the slightest omission.

9. The barbers' association obligates itself to do likewise to barbers who are residents of our community but who are now out of town. It will take rigorous measures to prevent them from doing any of the above-described work until they first agree to carry out all that has been recorded here.

10. These prescriptions apply particularly to sons-in-law. They are not to interfere with any of these above mentioned provisions, but must carry them out; and the barbers are in duty bound to oppose them and to prevent them from engaging in the work. [Sons-in-law, unless guild members, must not practice the trade.]

11. The seven barbers above mentioned have also agreed that there shall be brotherliness and friendship among themselves, and that during the three festivals they will have a good time, enjoy themselves to the full, and be glad and merry of heart. [In spite of this injunction there was constant bickering.]

Done in a binding form, with all the authority of rabbinic law, and with an actual handshake, this day, Sunday the 18th [22] of Kislew, 400, according to the shorter reckoning [December 18, 1639. In rabbinic law a handshake consummates a deal].

BIBLIOGRAPHY

READINGS FOR ADVANCED STUDENTS

Abrahams, I., *Jewish Life in the Middle Ages*, 1932, Chap. xi, "Trades and Occupations"; Chap. xii, "Trades and Occupations (Continued)."

JE, "Artisans"; "Engraving and Engravers"; "Hawkers and Pedlers"; "Occupations."

92.

The Cossack Revolt and the Fall of Nemirov
June 10, 1648

BEGINNING with the sixteenth century Poland had sheltered the largest and most important settlement of Jews in Europe. Despite the bitter opposition of the zealous Roman Catholic clergy, the Jews were prosperous and fairly content.

Unfortunately for them, in 1648 Poland became the scene of a terrible civil war and peasant uprising led by the Cossacks. The Greek Orthodox Cossacks, semi-military bands who had been settled in the country north of the Black Sea, were mistreated by their Roman Catholic Polish lords. The Ukrainian peasants, also Greek Orthodox, were particularly bitter against the Jewish stewards of the larger estates: the peasants resented the heavy taxation which the Jews demanded to satisfy their spendthrift Polish masters.

The Cossacks, under their leader Chmielnicki, united the Ukrainian peasants and the wild Tatars against the "heretical" Poles and the "unbelieving" Jews. The sufferings that the Jews now underwent are almost too horrible to relate. This was in 1648–1649.

In 1654 neighboring Russia turned against Poland, a year later the Swedes poured in from the north, and all these groups, including the native Poles, ravaged and massacred defenseless Jewish victims throughout the land.

The following account, which deals with the destruction of the Jewish community of Nemirov in Podolia, is taken from the Hebrew chronicle, *Yewen Mezulah* ("The Miry Depth"). It was published in 1653 by Nathan Hannover, a Polish rabbi who wrote in detail of the tragedy which he knew at first hand. His father was martyred in 1648, and he himself was murdered in 1683 by Hungarian-Turkish troops in the synagogue at Ungarisch-Brod in Moravia.

THE PERSECUTION OF THE HOLY CONGREGATION OF NEMIROV

⟨The oppressor Chmielnicki—may his name be blotted out—heard that many Jews had assembled in the holy community of Nemirov, and that they had a greal deal of silver and gold with them. [Because of the Cossacks, many Jews came from the countryside to the fortress of Nemirov.] He knew also that the congregation of

Nemirov itself was distinguished for its riches. It was once a great and very important community, full of justice and the abode of righteousness, a community of scholars and writers, but now they have been murdered!

Accordingly Chmielnicki—may his name be blotted out—sent a certain leader, an enemy of the Jews, and about 600 swordsmen with him against this honored congregation. In addition he wrote to the magistrates of the city that they should help this band; to this the citizens readily responded that they would help them with all their might and main, not so much because of their love of the Cossacks, but because of their hatred of the Jews. [The Greek Catholic townspeople hated the Jewish merchants, their competitors.]

It came to pass on a Wednesday, the 20th of Siwan, that the Cossacks drew near to the city of Nemirov. [On the anniversary of this day, June 10th, elegies are still recited in Poland.] When the Jews saw the troops from afar they were frightened, though as yet they did not know whether they were Polish or Cossack. Nevertheless all the Jews went with their wives and infants, with their silver and gold, into the fortress and locked and barred its doors, ready to fight them. What did those scoundrels, those Cossacks, do? They made flags like the Poles, for there is no other way to distinguish between the Polish and the Cossack forces except through their banners. Now the people of the town although they knew of this trick, nevertheless called to the Jews in the fortress: "Open the gates. This is a Polish army which has come to save you from your enemies, should they appear."

The Jews who were standing on the walls, seeing that the banners were like the flags of the Polish forces and believing that the townspeople were telling them the truth, immediately opened the gates to them. No sooner had the gates been opened than the Cossacks entered with drawn swords, and the townsmen too, with swords, lances, and scythes, and some only with clubs, and they killed the Jews in huge numbers. They raped women and young girls; but some of the women and maidens jumped into the moat near the fortress in order that the Gentiles should not defile them and were drowned in the water. Many of the men who were able to swim also jumped into the water and swam, thinking they could save themselves from slaughter. The Russians swam after them with their swords and their scythes and killed them in the water. Some of the enemy, too, kept on shooting with their guns into the moat, killing them till finally the water was red with the blood of the slain.

The president of the rabbinical college of Nemirov was also there. The name of this scholar was his excellency, our master and teacher, the rabbi, Rabbi Jehiel Michael, the son of his excellency, our teacher, Rabbi Eliezer, of blessed memory. Jehiel knew the whole rabbinical literature by heart and was proficient in all the known sciences. [Jehiel Michael was also a cabalist.] He had preached to the people on the Sabbath before the calamity and had warned them that if the enemy should come—God forbid—they should not change their religion, but rather die as martyrs. And this is just what the holy people did. [But other histories point out that some Jews did become converted to save themselves and then later came back to Judaism.]

Jehiel also jumped into the water to save himself by swimming when a Russian seized him and wanted to murder him; but the scholar besought him not to kill him, for which he would give him a great deal of silver and gold. The Russian agreed and took him to his house, to the place where his silver and gold were hidden, and the Cossack then let him go alive. The scholar then left that place with his mother, and they hid themselves in a certain house there, all that night until the morning dawn.

On the morrow [Jehiel evidently lay hidden all during the 21st.], the twenty-second of Siwan, the Russians also searched the houses, thinking perhaps some Jew might be hidden there. The scholar then fled with his mother to the cemetery so that if they should kill them they would be in the cemetery and would thus receive burial. But it happened as he approached the place that one of the men of that city, a Russian, a shoemaker, ran after the scholar with a club in his hand and wounded him with it. The mother of the rabbi begged the Russian to kill her instead of her son, but he paid no attention to her and killed first the sage and then his mother. May God avenge their blood.

Three days after the massacre the wife of the scholar buried them; for in all the towns where the persecutions took place they allowed most of the women to live, except the old and sickly, whom they killed.

It happened there that a beautiful girl of a fine and rich family was taken captive by a certain Cossack who married her. But before they lived together she told him in guile that through a magic power that she possessed, no weapon could harm her. "If you don't believe me," she said to him, "just test me in this matter. Shoot at me with a gun and it won't hurt me at all." The Cossack, her husband, thought she was telling the truth, and in his simplicity, shot her with his gun and she fell, dying for the glorification of the Name to avoid being defiled by a Gentile. May God avenge her blood!

It also happened that there was a certain beautiful girl who was to be wedded to a Cossack. [According to another version, this very man was one of the group who had killed her parents and captured her.] She asked him to marry her in one of the Christian churches which stood on the other side of the bridge. He fulfilled her request and with timbrels and flutes led her to the marriage in regal dress. As soon as she came to the bridge she jumped into the water and was drowned as a martyr. May God avenge her blood. There were many such cases, too numerous to record.

The number of all those murdered and drowned in the holy community of Nemirov was about 6000; these met all sorts of terrible deaths, as has already been described. May God avenge their blood! Those of the holy congregation of Nemirov who escaped the sword fled to the honored community of Tulchin, for there, outside the city, was a very strong fortress. [But in Tulchin the Jews were betrayed into the hands of the Cossacks by the Polish nobles. The Cossacks then turned and killed the Poles.]

BIBLIOGRAPHY

REFERENCES TO TEXTBOOKS

Elbogen, pp. 136–139; Roth, pp. 305–307; Sachar, 240–241.

READINGS FOR ADVANCED STUDENTS

Graetz, V, pp. 1–17; Graetz-Rhine, V, pp. 82–96; Margolis and Marx, pp. 551–557.

Dubnow, S. M., *History of the Jews in Russia and Poland*, I, Chap. v, "The Autonomous Center in Poland during Its Decline (1648–1772)."

JE, "Chmielnicki, Bogdan Zinovi"; "Cossacks' uprising"; "Hannover, Nathan (Nata) b. Moses"; "Nemirov"; "Russia (Poland)."

93.

The Ransom of Captives
Eastern and Southern Europe
1649–1708

O NE of the most meritorious acts recommended to the observant Jew is the ransoming of captives from slavery (*pidyon she-
buyim*). As early as the first centuries of the common era a whole
body of law and precedent had grown up, determining what constituted a captive, what captives took precedence in the order of their
ransoming and release, and what were to be the limits of a ransom
in order to discourage professional kidnappers.

Originally, probably, the captives ransomed were only those taken
prisoner in war or on pirate-raids. The term "captive," however,
was soon extended to include the unfortunates imprisoned on false
accusations such as ritual murder and the like, and to include also
the victims of arbitrary, despotic lords and rulers who would often
seize a prominent Jew in order to extort a ransom from him or his
friends. An outstanding illustration of this type of extortion is the
imprisonment of the notable Rabbi Meir of Rothenburg by the
Hapsburg Emperor Rudolph (d. 1291). Meir was in flight and had
reached the Lombard hills before he was recognized and seized
by Count Meinhard of Goerz. Meir, it is said, refused to allow his
friends to pay the enormous ransom of 20,000 marks in silver which
they offered and remained in confinement for seven years till his
death in 1293. But the Emperor finally did make a profit on his
stubborn prisoner, for about fourteen years after the death of Meir,
a pious Jew, Alexander Süsskind Wimpfen, ransomed the bones of
the famous rabbi for a goodly sum.

A not uncommon interpretation of the term "captive" included
Jewish criminals imprisoned by the non-Jewish authorities. Many
Jews felt the need of redeeming these prisoners for fear that under
stress they would desert to Christianity in order to escape punishment. Others believed that to ransom criminals served only to
encourage them in their criminal practices and gave them an opportunity to terrorize the community by the constant threat of
becoming Christian and of defaming the Jewish community.

The first selection below, translated from the Hebrew, is a decree of the Lithuanian National Jewish Council of the year 1649 authorizing every community to ransom immediately any Jewish captive taken by the Cossacks and the Tatars in the fearful riots and pogroms of 1648 and 1649 in Poland and in the Ukraine.

Many of the Tatar allies of the Cossacks brought their prisoners to market in Constantinople and in response to a request from the Jewish leaders of that city the chiefs of Lithuanian Jewry, in association with Polish Jewry, forwarded funds to Turkey for their ransom. This action, described in the minutes of the Lithuanian Council for the year 1652, constitutes the second selection translated below.

The third selection is a translation of a Judaeo-Italian letter sent in 1708 by Rabbi Judah Brieli of Mantua (d. 1722) to the Venetian Jewish committee for the ransom of captives, asking for monetary aid for a Jew taken prisoner on the Italian front during the War of the Spanish Succession.

1. *The Lithuanian National Jewish Council Authorizes the Ransom of Polish Jewish Captives, 1649*

℆[The following action is taken] inasmuch as we have seen how so many Jews, unfortunately, have been taken captive, dispersed among the nations, and as a result have been practically lost among them. Now it has already been made clear in the minutes of the *Medinah* [the Lithuanian National Jewish Council] that in this matter [of the redemption of captives] the involved expenses rest upon the whole *Medinah*. However, it is to be feared that before this has been sufficiently made known, in the customary manner, to the leaders of the communities, the opportunity may pass.

Therefore we have written granting permission to every town and place where there are ten Jews, authorizing them to ransom any one, spending as much as ten gold-pieces without need for any specific application or authorization. And the amount expended shall be accepted [as a legitimate charge] against the accounts of the Lithuanian National Jewish Council. If more than ten—and up to sixty—gold-pieces are spent for the ransom of a Jew, it will be necessary to secure permission from the nearest Jewish community that has, or is accustomed to have, a rabbinical authority. If more than sixty gold-pieces are spent for the ransom of an individual, it will be necessary to secure permission from one of the three chief communities (may their Rock and Redeemer guard them!) or from the district-community to which they are subject. [Brest-Litovsk, Grodno, and Pinsk were the chief Jewish towns.] And as they determine, the amounts expended shall be a legitimate charge against the Lithuanian council.

Whoever takes a zealous interest in this matter [of ransoming captives] is to be commended and will receive his full reward from Him who dwells on high.

II. *The Lithuanian Council Raises Money To Ransom Jewish Captives Held in the Turkish Lands, 1652*

(Whereas the manifold troubles, mishaps, persecutions, and visitations, that unfortunately have come upon our Jewish brethren in the times of storm and stress which they have just experienced, are obvious, evident, and known to all; and

Whereas many of the Jews (those people of God!) have had to leave their country, have gone into captivity, and have been brought to other lands where many of them have already been ransomed at a great expense; and

Whereas the rabbis of Constantinople have sent to us and have described at length their heavy outlay, running into the tens of thousands, which they have expended in this fine religious work, and have besought us to strengthen their hands with a substantial grant —for many are still unransomed, subject to suffering and to captivity;

Therefore it was agreed to make provision for their ransom and to help them [the Constantinople authorities] in this matter until the first of Adar 412 [February 10, 1652]—may it come upon us auspiciously! Within this period [December, 1651—February 10, 1652] voluntary donations to help the captives shall be collected twice in every town and village. And all moneys contributed, as described above, shall be sent by every village, town, and district to their highest court, no later than Purim [February 23, 1652]—may it come upon us auspiciously!

This is to be done in order that the moneys may be ready and prepared to be sent to the chief Jewish authorities at Lublin at the time of the coming Candelmas Fair [which begins on February 2, 1652]. From Lublin the funds are to be sent to the city of their destination [Constantinople]. The Lithuanian deputies who will be in Lublin shall take under advisement how much they shall add to the Lithuanian contributions above described. They shall also study the matter carefully in order to determine what to do and how to transmit the moneys.

But under no circumstance shall they send more than a total of one thousand old-dollars which sum shall include both the donations and the contribution added by the Lithuanian National Jewish Council. If any town or hamlet shall not send money at the prescribed time it shall be compelled to send its quota—and an ample one, too!—to say nothing of other punishments and fines which may be imposed on the offending community.

III. *An Appeal To Ransom an Italian Jewish Prisoner of War, Mantua, Italy, May 6, 1708*

❦Two years ago [1706] David Vita Elia Finzi, a man poor but of distinguished family and a respectable inhabitant of Ostiano, a community near ours, was in the district of Brescia [Lombardy] in order to provide hay for the French. He fell into the hands of the Germans and for a long time suffered all those injuries and troubles to which prisoners of war are subject.

Finally, overcome by fear, he felt compelled to make out a note to that general, who had happened to arrest him, that he would give him 500 doubloons as ransom. Then his relatives, with the aid of some prominent citizens, friends of theirs in Brescia, undertook negotiations to free him and agreed to a ransom of 150 sequins which they collected in large part in our town, and when the full sum was collected they obtained his liberty from them.

But due to the imprudence of the one who managed the affair, the note for 500 doubloons remained with the general who had promised to return it but failed to do so. Then the fortunes of war changed, and, as is known, the general who has been mentioned came to that same place of Ostiano and had Finzi arrested again. At the present time he is in Casellara, a place not far from Governolo [near Mantua, Lombardy]. He has been put into irons with threats that if he does not pay the 500 doubloons the general will take him with him to war.

It is a question therefore of saving a person who is in serious danger of losing his life. One who knows the character of this general assures us that he is a man who keeps his word. Moved therefore anew by the entreaties of his relatives and of the inhabitants of Ostiano and having ascertained that with another 150 sequins we could free him and get the note back, and since this is such a sad case, we make bold to beseech the communities that they also contribute to this work of charity. Indeed this community is ready, although the last time it alone contributed a considerable sum.

Therefore the goodness of you gentlemen is besought to send here, for the purpose indicated, whatever contribution will seem right to your sense of charity. We shall always pray to the Lord

God for your protection and exaltation and for your holy communities, and with devout reverence for you we declare ourselves always ready to serve you.

BIBLIOGRAPHY

READINGS FOR ADVANCED STUDENTS

Graetz, IV, pp. 624–626, 634–640.
JE, "Meir of Rothenberg"; "Ransom."

ADDITIONAL SOURCE MATERIALS IN ENGLISH

Halper, B., *Post-Biblical Hebrew Literature*, II, pp. 123–126, "The Four Captives."

94.

A Gentile Seeks to Force a Jewess into Marriage
Poland, before 1690

THE following brief narrative reflects the numerous problems with which medieval Jewry had to cope. It reveals the fear of defamation by a Gentile, the dread of intermarriage and apostasy, the arbitrariness of individual feudal magnates, and the corporate responsibility of the Jewish leaders for the delinquency, assumed or real, of individual Jews. It is interesting to note, too, the large powers which the rabbi exercised in the Jewish community.

This account, in the form of an "answer" (*responsum*) to a "question," comes from the pen of Hillel ben Naphtali Herz (1615–1690), a famous Lithuanian rabbi; it appears in Hillel's Hebrew notes to parts of the *Shulhan Aruk* which were published in 1691 under the title *Bet Hillel* ("House of Hillel"). Together with other eminent scholars he suffered during the Russo-Polish war of 1655. In 1671 he accepted a call to northern Germany where he became rabbi of the triune community of Hamburg, Altona, and Wandsbeck. He returned in 1680 to Poland where he died.

¶I have been asked about a certain girl who lived with her uncle in a certain town. A non-Jew accused her of having promised him that she would give up the Jewish religion and become his wife. When her uncle discovered what this fellow was saying about her, he sent her away to another town which was under the jurisdiction of a different lord.

Later, when the above mentioned non-Jew found that she had been sent away, he went to his lord, who arrested the rabbi and the council of the Jewish community—may their Rock and their Redeemer guard them—in order to force them to bring the girl before him for trial. [The rabbi and the council were to be held as hostages till the girl was brought back.]

The rabbi and the council have sent to me, asking that the girl be returned to their city in order that she may be put on trial before the lord, and in order that they may thus free themselves from arrest. But the girl has protested most vehemently that she had never discussed this subject with the Gentile at all. . . .

[The question before the rabbi is whether or not one Jew, this girl, may be exposed to danger in order to save a number of Jews.]

She is duty bound to appear in court; and in this decision the late Rabbi Isaac, the great and distinguished scholar, who was the chief rabbi and the president of the academy in Tiktin, agreed with me. And thus we ordered.

Her case came up for trial before the ruler of the city to which she had fled, and he let her go absolutely free, inasmuch as she protested most vehemently that the whole affair was an absolute lie.

BIBLIOGRAPHY

READINGS FOR ADVANCED STUDENTS

Shohet, D. M., *The Jewish Court in the Middle Ages*. One of the best studies in English for an appreciation of the powers of the medieval Jewish court.

JE, "Conflict of Laws."

95.

An Attack on Hypocrisy
about 1700

THE *Kab Ha-Yashar* ("Measure of Right") is one of the most popular of Jewish ethical writings. It was published in two parts in 1705–1706 by Zebi Hirsch Koidanover, a Polish scholar, who fled from his native Wilna to Frankfort on the Main, where he died in 1712. Koidanover's book—which borrows heavily from the *Yesod Yosef* ("Joseph's Foundation") of Joseph Dubno—is characterized by a strong belief in the value of self-mortification and asceticism; his piety is of a severe and rigorous type.

Profoundly influenced by the Lurianic cabala, Koidanover lived in a world of demons, evil spirits, and superstition. His personal misfortunes and his strongly religious nature brought him close to suffering humanity, and he scores in sharp terms wealthy Jewish communal leaders who, through their despotic power, ground the poor in the dust. He wrote his book in Hebrew and added a delightful Yiddish paraphrase so that it might be read by all.

The following selection, which reflects his attitude towards sanctimonious hypocrites, is translated from the Yiddish. The anecdote around which he builds his homily is Midrashic and therefore old, and somewhat resembles the "token" theme in many other medieval folk-tales; nevertheless, the framework of this tale faithfully reflects the author's own time and has, for this reason, value as a source for history.

⟨King Solomon, of blessed memory, wrote in Proverbs that one ought not to be too pious and one ought not to do too much evil. [The allusion, however, is to Ecclesiastes 7:16–17.] Accordingly, our sages have also written [Sotah 22b] that one does not have to guard himself against a really bad man who expresses his evil openly, nor against a really pious man whom one knows well to be sincere, but one must be on guard against him who acts as if he were righteous, who kisses the prayerbook, recites psalms and prayers day and night, yet in money matters is a "crook." People think that he is really pious because he worships so earnestly and stands in praying-shawl and phylacteries the whole day long and prays vigorously, but in most cases people like him are not to be trusted. True piety is determined by one's attitude to money, for only he who is reliable in money matters may be considered pious.

Now consider what is stated in the Midrash *Pesikta Rabbati* [Chap. xxii]. This is what happened: There was once a rich man who had a large fortune, and this man, who was also a scholar and saint, moved to Palestine and took his wealth with him. When he arrived at the Turkish border he rested for a few days in a Jewish community, and there he heard that it was unsafe to travel because of Turkish troops. It was there too that the wealthy traveler saw a man [by the name of Alexander] standing every day in the synagogue in praying-shawl and phylacteries, praying earnestly.

To this person who was worshipping so devoutly the rich man said: "My dear man, I have a favor to ask of you for I don't know of a more devout man in this town than you." Now since the wealthy man really believed that the fellow was pious he said to him: "I have a chest full of money and silver and gold, and I am afraid to take my possessions with me because of robbers. I want to take enough along merely for my expenses until I arrange a home for myself in Palestine, and when things are safer I'll come back to you."

When a half a year had passed the rich man returned from the city of Hebron and went to see Mr. Alexander. He met him on the street and asked for his money and silver and gold. That Mr. Alexander, however, said to him: "I don't know you and haven't received any deposit from you," and he denied everything. The wealthy man then began to cry and to weep and begged Alexander not to do this to him for he was in a foreign country and had no one to whom he could turn and no friend to whom he could appeal. But Alexander did not even answer him.

Then the rich man went to the synagogue and cried aloud to the Holy One, blessed be He, with hot tears, and after his prayers he said to God: "O Master of the universe, I have no one about whom I can complain and weep except You, for I thought that since to You Alexander used to pray so industriously and used to stand the whole day in praying-shawl and phylacteries that he was surely a real saint, but now he denies having my money and my silver and gold which I gave him to take care of for me."

Then the Holy One, blessed be He, smiled at the prayer of the rich man and sent Elijah the prophet to him. "Weep not," said Elijah the prophet. "Go now to Alexander's wife and as a token that you came from her husband mention to her that he ate leaven with her on Passover, and as another token tell her that they both ate breakfast on the holy [fast of] *Yom Kippur*. She will then return your deposit."

The rich man did this, and went to her and mentioned the tokens, and she surrendered to him his chest with his silver and gold, and he then traveled back joyfully to Hebron in Palestine. When Alexander returned home she asked him: "How could you have been such a crazy fool as to transmit such tokens through that man in order that I should return his deposit to him? You yourself have in this wise published your own disgrace: that we ate leaven on Passover, and that we did not fast on *Yom Kippur*. And of course I surrendered the deposit." Then Alexander answered his wife: "I gave no such orders to you." And now that people knew what a fine pair they were, they went immediately, the both of them, and converted themselves.

Therefore one should take care not to trust every man, for a man may pretend to be pious, and people may imagine him to be as devout as Phinehas, but in secret he may practice the evil deeds of Zimri ben Salu. [Numbers 25 tells of Phinehas, the zealous priest, who killed Zimri, a dissolute prince.] Piety is not visible to the eye, but consists in honesty in money matters. He who does not lust after robbery and theft but whose deeds are without deceit, such a one is pious.

BIBLIOGRAPHY

READINGS FOR ADVANCED STUDENTS

Waxman, M., *A History of Jewish Literature*, II, pp. 271–300.
JE, "Kaidanover, Zebi Hirsch."

96.

Ber of Bolechow and His Times
Poland, 1728

ONE of the most valuable sources for Jewish history in Poland and in eastern Europe in the eighteenth century is the autobiographical work of Ber of Bolechow (1723–1805). These Hebrew memoirs are particularly interesting and valuable because they throw light on the life of the average Polish Jew of that time, and are completely devoid of the tendency toward exaggeration which seems to characterize the *Autobiography* of Solomon Maimon, a younger contemporary. Ber writes especially of Jewish life on both sides of the Carpathians: of northeastern Hungary and of eastern Galicia, in which lay his home town Bolechow, which was part of the estate of the great Polish magnate, Count Poniatowski.

Ber was a wine merchant who had a penchant for learning. Unlike his contemporaries he not only knew Hebrew but had some knowledge of Polish and other European languages. He was interested in philosophy, theology, polemics, and general history, and also found occasion to busy himself with Jewish communal affairs.

Some time between 1790 and 1800, when he was about seventy years of age or over, he wrote his memoirs from which the following selection is taken. It tells us of the business experiences of Ber's father, Judah, and of his relative, the farmer Saul Wal.

⟨After [Stanislaus] Poniatowski had been appointed Commander-in-Chief [of the Polish forces, 1728], he sent people to Danzig and to the Fairs of Leipzig, which is in Saxony, ordering them to bring thence many articles, namely, clothes, materials, gold and silver watches, snuff boxes, and other valuables, such as gold and jewelled rings. [Probably Jewish merchants imported these goods for him.] On these purchases he spent great sums of money. With all these things he intended to bribe the gentry, that is, the *szlachta*, to win their favor that they might support him in political affairs, which were being discussed in the chief provincial towns. . . .

Of even more importance than all these presents was the desire of Poniatowski to obtain good wine to entertain the distinguished nobles. It happened that when Poniatowski was at Stryi, there lived there a Jew, the late Saul Wal, who was a very exceptional man, possessed of great ability and profound scholarship, devoted to the welfare of his fellow-Jews, and accustomed to plead their cause before the nobles, by whom he was very greatly respected. . . . [This is not the same Saul Wal reputed to have been king of Poland for a day.]

Saul was engaged in leasing estates from the nobles and cultivating these estates with the help of the serfs. This had been his occupation from his youth. The town of Stryi, with all the surrounding villages, was leased by Saul for many years. Count Poniatowski, when appointed to the position of *starosta* [chief officer] of the town of Stryi, became acquainted with Saul, and soon discovered that he was a man of great sagacity, so that he always consulted him.

Once Poniatowski said to Saul: "I should like to send someone to Hungary to buy me a considerable quantity of good wine. If you know of a fellow-Jew, a trustworthy person who understands the business, I will send him." [This Poniatowski, father of King Stanislaus II, was reported to have been the son of a Jewess.] Saul replied: "I know a Jew who understands the wine business as no one else does; he speaks Hungarian perfectly, and he has been versed from his youth in the Hungarian wine trade."

Saul sent at once for my father [Judah, born in 1673] and introduced him to Poniatowski, who was favorably impressed. He accordingly decided to send my father for the wine, and handed him 2,000 ducats, that is, 36,000 gulden. He also sent with my father the tutor of his sons, in the capacity of a clerk, in order to register the purchase of the wines and the daily expenses, so that a proper account might be kept. The clerk was named Kostiushko. My father did as he was requested by Poniatowski. He bought 200 casks of Tokay wine of the variety called *máslás*. When they both returned from Hungary and brought the wines to Stryi, Poniatowski was very pleased with the purchase; he gave my father 100 ducats for his trouble, and for keeping the accounts properly the clerk Kostiushko was promoted to be steward of our native town Bolechow, and he governed our town for many years.

Saul also received a great reward from this business. From his youth he had been, as I have said, a tenant engaged in the leasing of estates, and had been well versed in all kinds of agricultural work and in cattle-breeding. He held for many years leases of the town of Skole [near Bolechow] with its villages, and also of the starostaship of Stryi with the surrounding localities. [The leasing of estates was a common Polish Jewish occupation.] From this occupation he made enough to keep himself and his family in comfort. He had ten fine sons and one daughter. All his children married into families of rabbis and other notable people. [Rabbis were considered the aristocracy.]

But after Poniatowski had become the *starosta* of Stryi he did not wish to sell the town in lease to anyone, but kept it under his own administration through his officials. Thus Saul was deprived of his living in his old age, and was unable to meet his obligations to certain nobles, to whom he was indebted. My father advised him to take up his own business, the Hungarian wine trade; and Saul followed the advice of my father and went with him to Hungary. He bought wines, brought them back, and sold them at a good profit, which put him in a position to satisfy all his creditors.

BIBLIOGRAPHY

ADDITIONAL SOURCE MATERIALS IN ENGLISH

Vishnitzer, M., *The Memoirs of Ber of Bolechow (1723-1805)*. Ber's memoirs, a part of which has been reprinted above, are very important for an understanding of Polish Jewish life in the second half of the eighteenth century and should be read in conjunction with the contemporary work, *Solomon Maimon: an Autobiography*.

Acknowledgments

THE writer and publishers take this opportunity to express their thanks to the following authors, editors, and publishers for permission to reprint excerpts from their works:

The American Bar Association for Samuel Parson Scott, *Las Siete Partidas*.

The American Jewish Historical Society for Samuel Oppenheim, "The Early History of the Jews in New York, 1654–1664."

David W. Amram for *The Makers of Hebrew Books in Italy*.

Cambridge University Press for Dr. Jessopp's translation of Thomas of Monmouth's *The Life and Miracles of St. William of Norwich, etc.*

The Clarendon Press for Augustine Fitzgerald, *Letters of Synesius of Cyrene*.

Columbia University Press for Marcus Salzman, *The Chronicle of Ahimaaz*.

Dropsie College for Solomon Grayzel, *The Church and the Jews in the XIIIth Century*.

E. P. Dutton & Company for Sir Frank Marzials, *Memoirs of the Crusades by Villehardouin and De Joinville* (Everyman's Library).

Editors of the *Abhandlungen zur Erinnerung an Hirsch Perez Chajes* for "A Jewish Merchant in China at the Beginning of the Tenth Century."

Editors of the *Hebrew Union College Annual* for Cecil Roth, "Memoirs of a Siennese Jew."

Editors of the *Jewish Quarterly Review*, New Series, for Alexander Marx, "The Expulsion of the Jews from Spain," and "A Seventeenth-Century Autobiography."

Editors of the *Johns Hopkins Hospital Bulletin* for Dr. Harry Friedenwald, "The Ethics of the Practice of Medicine from the Jewish Point of View."

F. W. Faxon Company for S. P. Scott, *The Visigothic Code.*

Ginn and Company for James Harvey Robinson, *Readings in European History.*

Harcourt Brace and Company for H. von E. Scott and C. C. Swinton Bland, *The Dialogue on Miracles.*

The President and Fellows of Harvard College for the Loeb Classical Library translations: Wilmer Cave Wright, *The Works of the Emperor Julian,* and Eusebius, *The Ecclesiastical History,* edited by Kirsopp Lake.

The Jewish Publication Society for Israel Abrahams, *Hebrew Ethical Wills.*

The Jewish Theological Seminary for Louis Finkelstein, *Jewish Self-Government in the Middle Ages.*

Luzac and Company for Hermann Gollancz, *Translations from Hebrew and Aramaic.*

The Macmillan Company for Henry Charles Lea, *History of the Inquisition in Spain.*

William Popper for *The Censorship of Hebrew Books.*

G. P. Putnam Company for Victor von Klarwill, *The Fugger News-Letters,* and for Joseph Jacobs, *The Jews of Angevin England.*

Charles Scribner's Sons for T. W. Arnold, *The Preaching of Islam,* for Franklin Bowditch Dexter, *The Literary Diary of Ezra Stiles, D.D., LL.D.,* and for *A Select Library of Nicene and Post-Nicene Fathers of the Christian Church.*

M. Vishnitzer for his *Memoirs of Ber of Bolechow.*

Yale University Press for Franklin Bowditch Dexter, *Extracts from the Itineraries and Other Miscellanies of Ezra Stiles, D.D., LL.D., 1755–1794.*

References to Sources

1.

I. *Theodosiani libri XVI, cum constitutionibus Sirmondianis*, XVI, 8, 1, ed. by Th. Mommsen and Paulus M. Meyer, Berlin, 1905, Vol. I, Part II, p. 887.

II. *Ibid.*, XVI, 8, 6, p. 888; XVI, 9, 2, p. 896.

III. *Ibid.*, Vol. II, *Novella III*, pp. 8–9. We have adopted the dating and the explanation for the publication of the *Novella* suggested by François Nau in "Deux épisodes de l'histoire juive sous Théodose II," *REJ*, LXXXIII (1927), pp. 184ff.

IV. *Corpus juris civilis*, II: *Codex Justinianus*, I, 5, 21, ed. by Paulus Krueger, Berlin, 1892, p. 59.

2.

I. WRIGHT, WILMER CAVE, *The Works of the Emperor Julian*, New York, 1923, III, Letter 51, pp. 177–181.

II. SOZOMENUS, *Historia ecclesiastica*, Book V, Chap. xxii, in J. P. Migne, *Patrologiae cursus completus, series Graeca*, Paris, 1864, LXVII, Cols. 1281–1286. The translation is by Chester D. Hartranft, *A Select Library of Nicene and Post-Nicene Fathers of the Christian Church*, Second Series, New York, 1890, II, pp. 343–344.

3.

I. HAMAKER, H. A., *Incerti auctoris liber de expugnatione Memphidis et Alexandriae*, Leyden, 1825, pp. 165–166. The translation is that of T. W. Arnold, *The Preaching of Islam*, 2d ed., London, 1913, pp. 57–59.

II. BELIN, M., "Fetoua relatif à la condition des Zimmis, en particulièrement

des Chrétiens, en pays Musulmans, depuis l'établissement de l'Islamisme, jusqu'au milieu du VIII° siècle de l'hégire, traduit de l'Arabe." *Journal Asiatique*, Fourth Series, XIX (1852), pp. 103ff. I have translated from the French the "question" pp. 103ff., and the "answer" of Hasan, pp. 120ff.

4.

I. *Forum Judicum*, XII, 2, 16, Madrid, 1815(?). In Karl Zeumer's standard edition of the *Leges Visigothorum*, this paragraph is numbered XII, 2, 17, and is dated February 18, 654. The translation is that of S. P. Scott, *The Visigothic Code (Forum Judicum)*, Boston, 1910, pp. 375–376. Mr. Scott does not specify what edition of the code he has used but it is probably the Madrid edition of 1815.

II. *Leges Visigothorum*, XII, 3, 3, ed. by Karolus Zeumer in *Monumenta Germaniae Historica, legum sectio* I, Hannover, 1902, pp. 432–433.

5.

RIGORD, *Gesta Philippi Augusti*, pars. 6, 12, 13, 15, 16, ed. by H. François Delaborde in *Oeuvres de Rigord et de Guillaume le Breton*, Paris, 1882, I, pp. 15–29. The English translation is from James Harvey Robinson, *Readings in European History*, Boston, 1904, I, pp. 426–428.

6.

SCHERER, J. E., *Die Rechtsverhältnisse der Juden in den deutschösterreichischen Ländern*, Leipzig, 1901, pp. 179–184.

7.

Las siete partidas, VII, 24, 1–11, Madrid, 1843–1844. The translation is by

Samuel Parsons Scott, *Las siete partidas*, Chicago, 1931, pp. 1433–1437.

8.

JEAN, SIRE DE JOINVILLE, *Histoire de Saint Louis*, ed. by Natalis de Wailly, Paris, 1874, p. 31. The translation is that of Sir Frank Marzials, *Memoirs of the Crusades by Villehardouin and de Joinville*, Everyman's Library, London, 1921, p. 148.

9.

I. SCHILTER, JOHANN, *Die Alteste Teutsche so wol Allgemeine Als insonderheit Elsassische und Strassburgische Chronicke von Jacob von Königshoven . . . und mit Historischen Anmerckungen . . . von D. Johann Schiltern*, Strassburg, 1698, pp. 1040–1043.

II. HEGEL, C., ed., *Die Chroniken der oberrheinischen Städte. Strassburg*, Leipzig, 1871, II, pp. 759–764.

III. *Abne Zikkaron*, ed. by S. D. Luzzatto, Prague, 1841, No. 50, pp. 51–52.

10.

KRACAUER, I., *Urkundenbuch zur Geschichte der Juden in Frankfurt a.M.*, Frankfurt a.M., 1911, Part I, No. 416, pp. 193–194.

11.

MARX, ALEXANDER, "The Expulsion of the Jews from Spain," *JQR*, O. S., XX (1908), pp. 240ff.; *JQR*, N. S., II (1911–1912), pp. 257–258. The translation, except for certain revisions, is that of Prof. Marx.

12.

OSORIUS, *De rebus Emmanuelis*, Cologne, 1586, IV, pp. 114a–115b. The English translation is by James Gibbs, *The History of the Portuguese during the Reign of Emmanuel*, London, 1752, I, pp. 224–227.

13.

MARGOLIOUTH, G., "Megillath Missraim, or the Scroll of the Egyptian Purim," *JQR*, O. S., VIII (1895–1896) pp. 277–281. The translation is also that of Margoliouth, pp. 281–288. A few slight changes in the translation have been made on the basis of the *Megillah* published by Isaac Ezekiel Judah in *Reshummot* V (1927), pp. 385ff.

14.

WOLF, LUCIEN, *Menasseh ben Israel's Mission to Oliver Cromwell*, London, 1901, pp. lxxxiii–lxxxiv.

15.

I. OPPENHEIM, SAMUEL, "The Early History of the Jews in New York, 1654–1664," *Publications of the American Jewish Historical Society*, XVIII (1909), p. 5; English translation, pp. 4–5.

II. *Ibid.*, pp. 11–13; English translation, pp. 9–11.

III. FERNOW, B., *Documents Relating to the Colonial History of the State of New York*, Albany, 1883, XIV, pp. 315–318. Corrected translation in Oppenheim, p. 8.

IV. KALM, PETER, *Travels into North America etc.*, translated by John Reinhold Forster, Warrington, 1770, I, pp. 245–246.

16.

STERN, SELMA, *Der preussische Staat und die Juden*, Berlin, 1925, Book I, Part II, No. 12, pp. 13–16.

17.

I. DEXTER, FRANKLIN BOWDITCH, *Extracts from the Itineraries and Other Miscellanies of Ezra Stiles, D.D., LL.D., 1755–1794*, New Haven, 1916, p. 52.

II. *Ibid.*, pp. 52–53.

III. DEXTER, FRANKLIN BOWDITCH, *The Literary Diary of Ezra Stiles, D.D., LL.D.*, New York, 1901, III, pp. 24–25.

18.

FREUND, ISMAR, *Die Emanzipation der Juden in Preussen*, Berlin, 1912, II, No. 4, pp. 22–60. The Lippe-Detmold law appended to paragraph XXII may be found in Adolph Kohut, *Geschichte der deutschen Juden*, Berlin, 1898, p. 753.

19.

HEFELE, CHARLES JOSEPH, *Histoire des conciles, etc.*, Paris, 1907, Book I, Part I, pp. 231, 249–250, 262. The translation is that of James Finn, *Sephardim; or, the History of the Jews in Spain and Portugal*, London, 1841, p. 41.

20.

I. EUSEBIUS, *The Ecclesiastical History*, Book V, Chap. xxiii, ed. by Kirsopp Lake, London, 1926, Vol. I, pp. 502, 504. The translation is that of Kirsopp Lake, pp. 503, 505.

II. EUSEBIUS PAMPHILUS, *Vita Constantini, etc.*, Book III, Chaps. xvii–xx, in Fridericus Adolphus Heinichen, *Eusebii Pamphili scripta historica*, Leipzig, 1869, II, pp. 107–110. The translation is that of Ernest Cushing Richardson, *The Life of the Blessed Emperor Constantine*, Book III, Chaps. xvii–xx, in *A Select Library of Nicene and Post-Nicene Fathers of the Christian Church*, Second Series, New York, 1890, Vol. I, pp. 524–525.

III. *Corpus juris civilis*, Vol. II: *Codex Justinianus*, III, 12, 2, ed. by Paulus Krueger, Berlin, 1892, p. 127.

IV. HEFELE, CHARLES JOSEPH, *Histoire des conciles, etc.*, Paris, 1907, Book I, Part II, p. 1015.

21.

Sancti Ambrosii Mediolanensis episcopi epistolae, etc., Letters XL–XLI, in J. P. Migne, *Patrologiae cursus completus, series Latina*, Paris, 1880, XVI, Cols. 1148–1169. The translation is adapted from that of H. de Romestin, E. de Romestin, and H. T. F. Duckworth, *A Select Library of Nicene and Post-Nicene Fathers of the Christian Church*, Second Series, New York, 1896, X, pp. 440–450.

22.

I. *Sancti Gregorii Magni regestri epistolarum*, Book I, Letter XLVII, in J. P. Migne, *Patrologiae cursus completus, series Latina*, Paris, 1896, LXXVII, Cols. 509–511.

II. *Ibid.*, Book IX, Letter LV, Cols. 993–994. These letters may also be found in the *Epistolae* section of the *Monumenta Germaniae Historica* prepared by Paulus Ewald and Ludovicus M. Hartmann, *Gregorii I Papae registrum epistolarum*, Book I, Letter XLV; Book IX, Letter XXXVIII, 2 vols., Berlin, 1891–1899. I, pp. 71–72; II, p. 67. The paragraph added to the second selection is from Book VIII, Letter XXV. The translations have been adapted from James Barmby, *A Select Library of Nicene and Post-Nicene Fathers of the Christian Church*, Second Series, New York, XII(1895), Part II, p. 93; XIII (1898), pp. 14–15.

23.

I. A. NEUBAUER and M. STERN, *Hebräische Berichte über die Judenverfolgungen während der Kreuzzüge*, Berlin, 1892, pp. 6–8. An emendation suggested by M. Brann in the *MGWJ*, XXXVII (1893), 286, Note 3, has been incorporated. The readings of the Hebrew text given by Hans Lichtenstein in the *ZGJD*, N. S., IV (1932), pp. 155–156, have been adopted.

II. *Ibid.*, pp. 9–10.

24.

THOMAS OF MONMOUTH, *The Life and Miracles of St. William of Norwich, etc.*, Book I, Chaps. iii–v; Book II, Chap. xi, Argument V, ed. by Augustus Jessopp and Montague Rhodes James, Cambridge, 1896, pp. 14–23, 93–94. The translation by Dr. Jessopp may be found on the lower half of the above pages.

25.

A. NEUBAUER and M. STERN, *Hebräische Berichte über die Judenverfolgungen während der Kreuzzüge*, Berlin, 1892, pp. 66–68. Du Cange in his *Glossarium*, Niort, 1883, I, p. 342, Col. 3, bottom, also gives an example of the ordeal by cold water somewhat similar to the one in our text. In another Hebrew source, contemporary with our account, the ordeal is more typical in that the witness sinks and is believed to be innocent and does not float, a sign of falsehood (Simon Bernfeld, *Sefer ha-Demaot*, I, p. 226, bottom).

26.

WILLIAM OF NEWBURGH, *Historia rerum Anglicarum*, Book IV, Chaps. vii–xi, ed. by Richard Howlett in the *Chronicles of the Reigns of Stephen, Henry II., and Richard I.*, London, 1884, I, pp. 308–324. The English translation is by Joseph Jacobs, *The Jews of Angevin England*, New York, 1893, pp. 113–133.

27.

STERN, MORITZ, *Urkundliche Beiträge über die Stellung der Päpste zu den Juden*, II, *Heft* 1, Kiel, 1895, pp. 4–11. The translation of the paragraph on "The Expedition To Recover the Holy Land" is taken from James Harvey Robinson, *Readings in European History*, Boston, 1904, I, p. 339.

28.

STRANGE, J., *Dialogus miraculorum*, Cologne, 1851, I, pp. 96–98. The translation is by H. von E. Scott and C. C. Swinton Bland, *The Dialogue on Miracles*, New York, 1929, I, pp. 107–109.

29.

I. GRAYZEL, SOLOMON, *The Church and the Jews in the XIIIth Century*, Philadelphia, 1933, pp. 275–277, 240, 242. The translation by Grayzel is found on pp. 277–278, 241–243.

II. *Ibid.*, pp. 278–279. The translation is on p. 279.

III. THOMAS CANTIPRATENSIS, *Bonum universale de apibus*, Book I, Chap. iii, Douay, 1627, pp. 17–18.

30.

STERN, MORITZ, *Urkundliche Beiträge über die Stellung der Päpste zu den Juden*, Kiel, 1893, pp. 5–7.

31.

"Host, Desecration of," *Jewish Encyclopedia*, VI, opposite p. 482.

32.

FRIEDLAENDER, GOTTLIEB, *Beiträge zur Reformationsgeschichte, etc.*, Berlin, 1837, pp. 93–90.

33.

I. LUTHER, MARTIN, *Das Jesus Christus ein geborner Jude' sei*, in *D. Martin Luthers Werke*, Kritische Gesammtausgabe, Weimar, XI, pp. 314–315, 336.

II. LUTHER, MARTIN, *Von den Juden und ihren Lügen*, *ibid.*, Weimar, 1920, LIII, pp. 522–527.

34.

HA-KOHEN, JOSEPH, *Emek ha-Baka*, ed. by M. Letteris, Cracow, 1895, pp. 128–130.

35.

The original of this account is found in the *Archivo hist. nacional, Inquisicion de Toledo, Leg. 138 (128?)*. The translation here is that of Henry Charles Lea, *A History of the Inquisition of Spain*, New York, 1907, III, pp. 24–26. The details regarding this case may be found on pp. 23–24, 26, 233–234.

36.

SOCHESTOW, GAWRIL, *Mazzebet Kodesh*, Part IV, Lemberg, 1869, p. 13b.

37.

GODECHOT, JACQUES, "Deux procès de sorcellerie et de sacrilège à Nancy au XVIIIe siècle." *REJ*, LXXXIX (1930), pp. 95–96.

38.

ADLER, MARCUS NATHAN, *The Itinerary of Benjamin of Tudela*, London, 1907, pp. 38–42 of the Hebrew section. The English translation on pp. 39–42 has been adopted with certain slight changes.

39.

KAHANA, ABRAHAM, *Sifrut ha-Historiyya ha-Yisreelit*, Warsaw, 1922, I, pp. 252–253. The Kahana edition of the ban is a corrected copy of the original published in the *Responsa of Rashba*, No. 416, Bologna, 1539, I, 74c–d.

40.

I. "Takkanot Kadmoniyyot," ed. by S. J. Halberstam and annotated by M. Güdemann in *Jubelschrift zum siebzigsten Geburtstage des Prof. Dr. H. Graetz*, Breslau, 1887, pp. 58–59 (Hebrew section).

II. FERNÁNDEZ Y GONZÁLEZ, DON FRANCISCO, *Ordenamiento formado por los Procuradores des las aljamas Hebreas, Valladolid, 1432*, Madrid, 1886. The abstract given here is that made by Louis Finkelstein in his *Jewish Self-Government in the Middle Ages*, New York, 1924, p. 374.

III. BALABAN, MAJER, "Die Krakauer Judengemeinde-Ordnung von 1595 und ihre Nachträge," in the *Jahrbuch der jüdischliterarischen Gesellschaft*, Frankfurt a.M., X (1913), p. 360; XI (1916), p. 105.

IV. DUBNOW, SIMON, *Pinkas ha-Medinah*, Berlin, 1925, No. 327, p. 69.

V. CAHEN, ABRAHAM, "Règlements somptuaires de la communauté juive de Metz à la fin du XVIIe siècle," in *Annuaire de la société des études juives*, première année, Paris, 1881, Art. 17, p. 92; p. 100; p. 105; Art. 9, p. 106; Art. 20, p. 117. Inasmuch as the original Yiddish regulations have not been accessible the translation has been made from the French.

VI. ROTH, CECIL, "Sumptuary Laws of the Community of Carpentras," *JQR*, N. S., XVIII (1927–1928), p. 382.

41.

KRACAUER, I., "Rabbi Joselmann de Rosheim," *REJ*, XVI (1888), pp. 92–93.

42.

I. *Shulḥan Aruk, Oraḥ Hayyim*, 694:1–4; 695:2.

II. *Shulḥan Aruk, Yoreh Deah*, 157:2; 268:2.

III. *Shulḥan Aruk, Eben ha-Ezer*, 1:3; 2:1.

IV. *Shulḥan Aruk, Hoshen ha-Mishpat*, 231:2; 356:1.

43.

I. HANNOVER, NATHAN, *Yewen Mezulah*, Venice, 1653, pp. 11a, 12a.

II. LEWIN, L., "Neue Materialien zur Geschichte der Vierländersynode," Part II, *Jahrbuch der jüdisch-literarischen Gesellschaft*, Frankfurt a.M., III (1905), pp. 88–89.

III. *Pinkas ha-Medinah*, ed. by Simon Dubnow, Berlin, 1925, No. 1, p. 3; No. 61, p. 12; Nos. 136–137, p. 34; No. 261, p. 53.

44.

FREUDENTHAL, MAX, "Die Verfassungsurkunde einer reichsritterlichen

Judenschaft. Das Kahlsbuch von Sugenheim," *Zeitschrift für die Geschichte der Juden in Deutschland,* I (1929), pp. 44–68.

45.

SOCRATES SCHOLASTICUS, *Historia ecclesiastica,* VII, p. 38, in J. P. Migne, *Patrologiae cursus completus, series Graeca,* Paris, 1864, LXVII, Cols. 825–828. The translation is by A. C. Zenos, *A Select Library of Nicene and Post-Nicene Fathers of the Christian Church,* Second Series, New York, 1890, II, pp. 174–175.

46.

I. *Kusari,* ed. by A. Zifrinowitsch, Warsaw, 1911, Supplement, p. 25ff. The translation is that of "A.I.K. D.[avidson]" in *Miscellany of Hebrew Literature,* London, 1872, I, pp. 92ff., except for some necessary changes.

II. HARKAVY, A., *Meassef Niddahim* (Supplement to *Ha-Meliz*) No. 8, 1879. Inasmuch as this text is incomplete it has been supplemented from the text in Zifrinowitsch, pp. 33ff. The translation of "A.I.K.D." has been followed where it agrees with the superior Harkavy text.

47.

I. ELIJAH BEN ABRAHAM, *Hilluk ha-Karaim weha-Rabbanim,* in S. Pinsker, *Likkute Kadmoniyyot,* Vienna, 1860, Appendices, p. 103. The *Hilluk* itself is a Karaitic work ascribed to Elijah ben Abraham (Byzantium? twelfth century?). It is probable that the Rabbanite account of Anan, which he incorporates and quotes, is an extract from Saadia's lost Arabic polemic, *Refutation of Anan* (905).

II. IBN DAUD, ABRAHAM, *Sefer Seder ha-Kabbalah,* in Ad. Neubauer, *Mediaeval Jewish Chronicles,* Oxford, 1887, I, pp. 63–64.

III. LUZKI, SIMHAH ISAAC BEN MOSES, *Orah Zaddikim,* Vienna, 1830, p. 19.

IV. SAHL BEN MAZLIAH HA-KOHEN, *Tokahat Megullah,* in S. Pinsker, *Likkute Kadmoniyyot,* Vienna, 1860, Appendices, pp. 33–34.

48.

Sefer Yohasin, ed. by Marcus Salzman, *The Chronicle of Ahimaaz,* New York, 1924, pp. 3–5 of the Hebrew section. The translation, also by Salzman, may be found on pp. 62–66.

49.

I. GASTER, M., *The Sword of Moses,* London, 1896, No. 44, p. xiv and p. ix.

II. *Ibid.,* No. 68, p. xvi and p. x.

III. *Ibid.,* No. 125, p. xix and p. xi.

IV. *Ibid.,* p. xxvi. The translations by Moses Gaster may be found on pp. 37, 39, 43, and 52.

V. GASTER, M., "The Wisdom of the Chaldeans: an Old Hebrew Astrological Text," *Proceedings of the Society of Biblical Archaeology,* XXII (1900), p. 350. The English translation by Gaster may be found on p. 344. Some slight modifications have been made.

50.

IBN ABBAS, SAMUEL ABU NASR, *Ifham al-Yahud etc.* This work, still in manuscript, is in the Khedival Library at Cairo as part of Ms. VI, 123. The portion relating to David Alroy is printed and twice translated from the Arabic into German in M. Wiener's German edition of *Emek ha-Baka,* Leipzig, 1858. I have accepted the translation of Drs. Munk and Derenburg found on pp. 169–171 of Wiener and have in turn translated it into English.

51.

HA-KOHEN, JOSEPH, *Emek ha-Baka,* ed. by Letteris, Cracow, 1895, pp. 113–117.

52.

I. *Kitbe Shebah Yekar u-Gedulat Ha-Ari z'l*, in *Taalumot Hokmah*, Basel, 1629, pp. 37a–38b.

II. *Hemdat Yamim*, Venice (?), 1763, IV, p. 53b–c.

53.

RYCAUT, PAUL, *The History of the Turkish Empire, from the Year 1623, to the Year 1677*, London, 1687, pp. 174–184.

54.

I. *Shibhe ha-Besht*, Berlin, 1922, pp. 13–14, 16, 18–20, 23. This edition, by S. A. Horodezky, is practically a reprint of the original Kopys edition of 1814. The material, through page twenty-one, was compiled by the publisher, Israel Joffe, on the basis of information given him by Shneor Zalman (1748–1812), the leader of the Lithuanian *Hasidim*. The book, from page twenty-one bottom on, is a compilation made by Dob Bär ben Samuel, the son-in-law of Alexander, one of the *Besht's* secretaries.

II. *Shibhe ha-Besht,* p. 94.

III. *Buzina de-Nehora*, Lemberg, 192–?, p. 64.

55.
"Nusah Takkanat ha-Medinah Shklov," ed. by Ephraim Deinard in *Zimrat Am ha-Arez*, as part of *Kittot be-Yisrael*, New York, 1896, pp. 21–22. (This is a reprint from the periodical *Ner ha-Maarabi*, New York, 1896.) This manifesto, issued originally in Hebrew, has been issued in a Russian translation in P. S. Marek's, "The Internal Warfare within Jewry during the Eighteenth Century" (Russian), in the *Evreiskaia Starina*, XII (1928), pp. 126–127. The translation of Marek was evidently made from a better text than that published by Deinard, and I have accordingly not hesitated to supplement my translation of the Deinard text with material from the Marek Russian text which has been made available to me in an English translation through the courtesy of Rabbi George A. Lieberman. Articles 1–4 and the final date are taken from the Marek text.

56.

I. BER OF BOLECHOW, *Dibre Binah*, ed. by Abraham Jacob Brawer in *Ha-Shiloah*, XXXIII (1917), pp. 333–334, 339, 439–440.

II. LEONHARD, KARL CÄSAR VON, *Aus unserer Zeit in meinem Leben*, Stuttgart, 1854, I, 26ff.

57.
Seder Olam Zuta, ed. by Ad. Neubauer, *Mediaeval Jewish Chronicles*, Oxford, 1895, II, pp. 80–82.

58.
Sefer Yohasin, ed. by Marcus Salzman, *The Chronicle of Ahimaaz*, New York, 1924, pp. 16–20 of the Hebrew section. The translation is also that of Salzman and may be found on pp. 88ff.

59.
IBN DAUD, ABRAHAM, *Sefer Seder ha-Kabbalah*, in Ad. Neubauer, *Mediaeval Jewish Chronicles*, Oxford, 1887, I, pp. 71–73.

60.

I. *Zikron Yehudah*, ed. by Judah Rosenberg, Berlin, 1846, p. 52b.

II. MUELLER, JOEL, *Teshubot Hakme Zarefat we-Lotir*, Vienna, 1881, No. 40, p. 24b.

61.
A. NEUBAUER and M. STERN, *Hebräische Berichte über die Judenverfolgungen während der Kreuzzüge*, Berlin, 1892, p. 64.

62.

I. *Kobez Teshubot ha-Rambam we-Iggerotaw*, ed. by Lichtenberg, Leipzig, 1859, Part II, p. 15c–d.

II. *Ibid.*, II, p. 28b, c, d–29a. I have also made use of the text of this letter in Ms. Adler 2013 published by Alexander Marx, "Texts by and about Maimonides," *JQR*, N. S., XXV (1934–1935), pp. 374–381. The translation of the letter to Samuel ibn Tibbon follows, in large part, that of Dr. H. Adler in *Miscellany of Hebrew Literature*, London, 1872, I, pp. 219–228.

63.

I. IBN TIBBON, JUDAH, *Musar Ab*, ed. by Israel Abrahams in *Hebrew Ethical Wills*, Philadelphia, 1926, I, pp. 56–84.

II. *Zawwaat Eliezer [Eleazar] ben Samuel Ha-Levi*, ed. by Israel Abrahams in *Hebrew Ethical Wills*, Philadelphia, 1926, II, pp. 208–218. The English translations of both wills, with the exception of a few minor changes made for the sake of greater simplicity, are those of Israel Abrahams and accompany the Hebrew text.

64.

Curationum medicinalium Amati Lusitani . . . centuriae duae, quinta videlicet ac sexta, Venice, 1560, last three unnumbered pages. The translation is by Dr. Harry Friedenwald, "The Ethics of the Practice of Medicine from the Jewish Point of View," *The Johns Hopkins Hospital Bulletin*, XXVIII (1917), pp. 259–260.

65.

HA-KOHEN, JOSEPH, *Emek ha-Baka*, ed. by Letteris, Cracow, 1895, pp. 145–147. Steinschneider's suggested identification of Joseph ben Adret as Joseph ben Ardut, *Catalogus lib-* *rorum Hebraeorum in bibliotheca Bodleiana*, No. 2269, has been adopted.

66.

I. GANS, DAVID, *Zemah Dawid*, Prague, 1592, p. 65a.

II. KLARWILL, VICTOR, *Fugger-Zeitungen, etc.*, Vienna, 1923, No. 224, pp. 231–232. The English translation is from *The Fugger News-Letters*, ed. by Victor von Klarwill, New York, 1924, pp. 239–240. This reference to Meisel was already published, with slight variations, in Benedikt Foges, *Alterthümer der Prager Josefstadt, etc.*, 3rd ed., Prague, 1870, pp. 36–37.

67.

MEIR OF LUBLIN, *Manhir Ene Hakamim*, No. 43, Venice, 1618, pp. 26a–c.

68.

I. KAUFMANN, DAVID, *Die Memoiren der Glückel von Hameln, 1645–1719*, Frankfurt a.M., 1896, pp. 34–36.

II. *Ibid.*, pp. 134–137.

69.

This translation, except for some changes, is that of the English edition of 1706: *The Life of Benedict de Spinosa*. Written by John Colerus, Minister of the Lutheran Church, at The Hague. Done out of French. London, 1706, pp. 1–45. The changes made are on the basis of the Dutch original and the literal German translation found in J. Freudenthal, *Die Lebensgeschichte Spinoza's in Quellenschriften, Urkunden und nichtamtlichen Nachrichten*, Leipzig, 1899.

70.

Salomon Maimons Lebensgeschichte, ed. by K. P. Moritz, Berlin, 1792–1793, pp. 43–45, 101–104, 108–113. Except for a few minor changes the translation is that of J. Clark Murray as found in his *Solomon Maimon: an Autobiography*, Boston, 1888, pp. 32–34, 75–77, 81–84.

71.

Synesii epistolae, No. 4, in *Epistolographi Graeci*, ed. by Rudolphus Hercher, Paris, 1873, pp. 639ff. The translation is taken from Augustine Fitzgerald, *Letters of Synesius of Cyrene*, London, 1926, pp. 80–91.

72.

Annales Bertiniani, ed. by G. Waitz [*Scriptores rerum Germanicarum in usum scholarum*], Hannover, 1883, pp. 17–18, 34–35.

73.

I–II. BOZORG FILS DE CHAHRIYAR DE RAMHORMOZ, *Livre des merveilles de l'Inde*, ed. by P. A. van der Lith, Leyden, 1883–1886, Chaps. lx–lxi, pp. 107–113. The translation by Elkan N. Adler, "A Jewish Merchant in China at the Beginning of the Tenth Century," in *Abhandlungen zur Erinnerung an Hirsch Perez Chajes*, Vienna, 1933, pp. 1–5, is made from the French translation by L. Marcel Devic in *Livre des merveilles de l'Inde*, pp. 107–113. Minor changes have been made in the translation.

74.

Rashi al ha-Torah, ed. by A. Berliner, 2nd ed., Frankfurt a.M., 1905, pp. 200, 252, 266, •359, 364, 365, 367, 370, 410.

75.

I. *Mishneh Torah*, Sefer Zeraim, Hilkot Mattnot Aniyyim, X, 7–15.

II. *Mishneh Torah*, Sefer ha-Mada, Hilkot Abodat Kokabim, III, 10–11.

76.

I. JOHANNIS DE ALTA SILVA, *Dolopathos; sive de rege et septem sapientibus*, ed. by Hermann Oesterley,

Strassburg, 1873, pp. 57–61. The English translation is by W. A. Clouston, *The Book of Sindibad*, Glasgow, 1884, pp. 364–367.

II. LETI, GREGORIO, *Vita di Sisto V*, Amsterdam, 1693, Part III, Book II, pp. 134–139. The English version is from E. Farneworth's translation, *Life of Pope Sixtus the Fifth*, London, 1754, pp. 293–295.

77.

I. IBN AKNIN, JOSEPH BEN JUDAH. *Tab-ul Nufus* ("Cure of Souls") in Ms. in the Bodleiana. This selection is part of the 27th chapter of the third section of this book. It was published in M. Güdemann, *Das jüdische Unterrichtswesen während der spanisch-arabischen Periode*, Vienna, 1873, pp. 1–57 (source section). There is a German translation, pp. 43–138, from which the above translation into English has been made.

II. *Sefer Hasidim*, ed. by Jehuda Wistinetzki, 2nd ed., Frankfurt a.M., 1924, No. 662, p. 175; No. 785, p. 197; Nos. 802–803, p. 202; Nos. 823–824, p. 209.

III. BASS, SHABBETHAI, *Sifte Yeshenim*, Amsterdam, 1680, pp. 8a–c.

78.

"Iggeret me-Rabbenu David Provenzalo," ed. by S. J. Halberstam in Brill's *Ha-Lebanon* (Le Libanon), V (1868), pp. 418–419, 434–435, 450–451. This letter, originally a Mantua broadside, is dated the 9th of Nisan, 5324 (March 22, 1564). The copy of *Ha-Lebanon* used—now in Jewish Theological Seminary Library—contains some corrections of the printed text by Halberstam himself. These corrections have been incorporated into the translation.

79.

COLON, JOSEPH, *Sheelot u-Teshubot*, No. 160, Venice, 1519, pp. 168b–169a.

80.

"Miktabim me-Rabbenu Obadiah mi-Bertinoro," ed. by A. M. Luncz, *Ha-Meammer*, III (1919), pp. 95–113. Occasionally the phraseology in the English translation is that of "Selections from Two Letters Written by Obadja da Bertinoro in the Years 1488 and 1489," in *Miscellany of Hebrew Literature*, London, 1872, I, pp. 114ff.

81.

PASOLINI, PIER DESIDERIO, *Caterina Sforza*, Rome, 1893, III, pp. 608–609.

82.

I. KIMHI, DAVID, *Sefer Miklol*, Constantinople, 1532–1534, title page.

II. GRÜNBAUM, MAX, *Jüdischdeutsche Chrestomathie*, Leipzig, 1882, pp. 553–554. The English translation is by David Werner Amram, *The Makers of Hebrew Books in Italy*, Philadelphia, 1909, pp. 187–188.

III. CARO, JOSEPH, *Sefer Bedek ha-Bayit*, Venice, 1606, p. 1a. The English translation, except for minor changes, is that of William Popper, *The Censorship of Hebrew Books*, New York, 1899, p. 95.

IV. *Sefer Hayye Yehudah*, ed. by Abraham Kahana, Kiev, 1911, pp. 56–57.

V. MENAHEM ZEBI, *Zinzenet Menahem*, Berlin, 1719, p. 98b.

83.

BABINGER, FRANZ, *Hans Dernschwam's Tagebuch einer Reise nach Konstantinopel und Kleinasien (1553–55)*, Nach der Urschrift im Fugger-Archiv, München, 1923, pp. 68, 106–117.

84.

LEON OF MODENA, *Sur me-Ra*, III, Leipzig, 1683, pp. 39–51. The translation is by Hermann Gollancz, *Translations from Hebrew and Aramaic*, London, 1908, pp. 185–192.

85.

I. ISAAC BAR ABRAHAM, *Sefer Hizzuk Emunah*, I, 3, ed. by David Deutsch, Sohrau, 1865, pp. 40–41. The translations are based in part on Moses Mocatta, *Hizzuk Emunah or Faith Strengthened*, London, 1851, pp. 17–18.

II. *Ibid.*, II, 11, p. 294; Mocatta, pp. 237–238.

III. *Ibid.*, II, 13, p. 295; Mocatta, p. 239.

IV. *Ibid.*, II, 17, p. 297; Mocatta, p. 241.

V. *Ibid.*, II, 26, p. 306; Mocatta, p. 248.

86.

I. ASHER BAR ELIEZER HA-LEVI, *Sefer Zikronot*, ed. by M. Ginsburger, Berlin, 1913, p. 12.

II. *Ibid.*, p. 16.

III. *Ibid.*, pp. 27–28.

87.

I. ROTH, CECIL, "The Memoirs of a Siennese Jew (1625–1633)," *Hebrew Union College Annual* V (1928), pp. 361, 368–370. The translation is by Cecil Roth and may be found on pp. 379, 387–388. A slight emendation has been made.

II. MARX, ALEXANDER, "A Seventeenth-Century Autobiography," *JQR*, N. S., VIII (1917–1918), pp. 276–283. The translation on pp. 288–299, in which minor changes have been made, is that of Marx.

88.

I. LEON MODENA, *Historia de gli riti hebraici*, Paris, 1637, pp. 35–37.

II. *Ibid.*, pp. 43–45. The English translation is by Simon Ockley, *The History of the Present Jews throughout the World, etc.*, London, 1707, pp. 63–69, 81–85, and incorporates materials first found in the slightly modified Venice edition of 1638.

89.

LANDAU, ALFRED, and BERNHARD WACHSTEIN, *Jüdische Privatbriefe aus dem Jahre 1619*, Vienna, 1911, No. 14, p. 21 (Yiddish section).

90.

ISAAC BEN ELIAKIM OF POSEN, *Leb Tob*, Amsterdam, 1723, pp. 96d–97a.

91.

WETSTEIN, F. H., "Kadmoniyyot mi-Pinkesaot Yeshanim: Takkanot ha-Balbirer," Graeber's *Ozar ha-Sifrut*, Cracow, IV(1892), pp. 604–605.

92.

HANNOVER, NATHAN, *Yewen Mezulah*, Venice, 1653, p. 5a.

93.

I. DUBNOW, SIMON, *Pinkas ha-Medinah*, Berlin, 1925, No. 452, p. 98.

II. *Ibid.*, No. 485, p. 111.

III. *Il vessillo israelitico* XXVIII (1880), pp. 211–212. I wish to express my thanks to Mr. A. Marni of the University of Cincinnati for his kindness in rechecking my Italian materials.

94.

HILLEL BEN NAPHTALI HERZ, *Bet Hillel*, Dyhernfurth, 1691, comment on *Yoreh Deah*, Par. 157.

95.

KOIDANOVER, ZEBI HIRSCH, *Kab ha-Yashar*, Chap. lii, Frankfort on the Main, 1705, pp. 100b–101b.

96.

Zikronot R. Dob mi-Bolehob, Berlin, 1922, pp. 38–39. The English translation, by M. Vishnitzer, is found in the *Memoirs of Ber of Bolechow (1723–1805)*, London, 1922, pp. 67–69. Certain necessary minor changes have been made.

Index

481

JACOB R(ADER) MARCUS was born in Connellsville, Pennsylvania, on March 5, 1896. He began to teach at Hebrew Union College in Cincinnati in 1920. In 1946 he became Adolph S. Ochs Professor of American Jewish History and a year later he established the invaluable American Jewish Archives. His early writings deal with the history of German Jewry, but in recent years Professor Marcus has concentrated on aspects of American Jewish history, producing the two-volume *Early American Jewry* and the three-volume *Memoirs of American Jews*.

Atheneum Paperbacks

Atheneum Paperbacks

STUDIES IN AMERICAN NEGRO LIFE